AF263229

BLACK FREEDOM

BLACK FREEDOM

A VISUAL HISTORY OF JUNETEENTH AND EMANCIPATION DAYS

BLAIR LM KELLEY

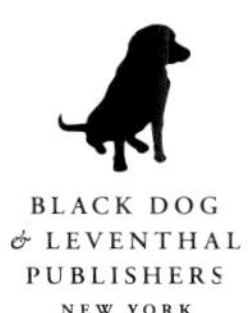

BLACK DOG
& LEVENTHAL
PUBLISHERS
NEW YORK

Black Dog & Leventhal Publishers
Hachette Book Group
1290 Avenue of the Americas, New York, NY 10104

www.blackdogandleventhal.com
BlackDogandLeventhal @BDLev

First Edition: June 2026

Published by Black Dog & Leventhal Publishers, an imprint of Hachette Book Group, Inc. The Black Dog & Leventhal Publishers name and logo are trademarks of Hachette Book Group, Inc.

Black Dog & Leventhal books may be purchased in bulk for business, educational, or promotional use. For more information, please contact your local bookseller or the Hachette Book Group Special Markets Department at Special.Markets@hbgusa.com.

The publisher is not responsible for websites (or their content) that are not owned by the publisher.

Additional copyright/credits information is on page 251

Print book cover and interior design by Katie Benezra

Back cover credits:
Left: Mayra Beltran / Houston Chronicle via Getty Images
Upper right: African American History Research Center, Houston Public Library, MSS0281-PH037, MSS 0281, Reverend Jack Yates Family and Antioch Baptist Church Collection
Lower right: Bob Daemmrich / Alamy Stock Photo

Library of Congress Cataloging-in-Publication Data has been applied for.

ISBNs: 978-0-7624-8693-9 (hardcover), 978-0-7624-8694-6 (ebook)

Printed in China

TLF

10 9 8 7 6 5 4 3 2 1

CONTENTS

INTRO

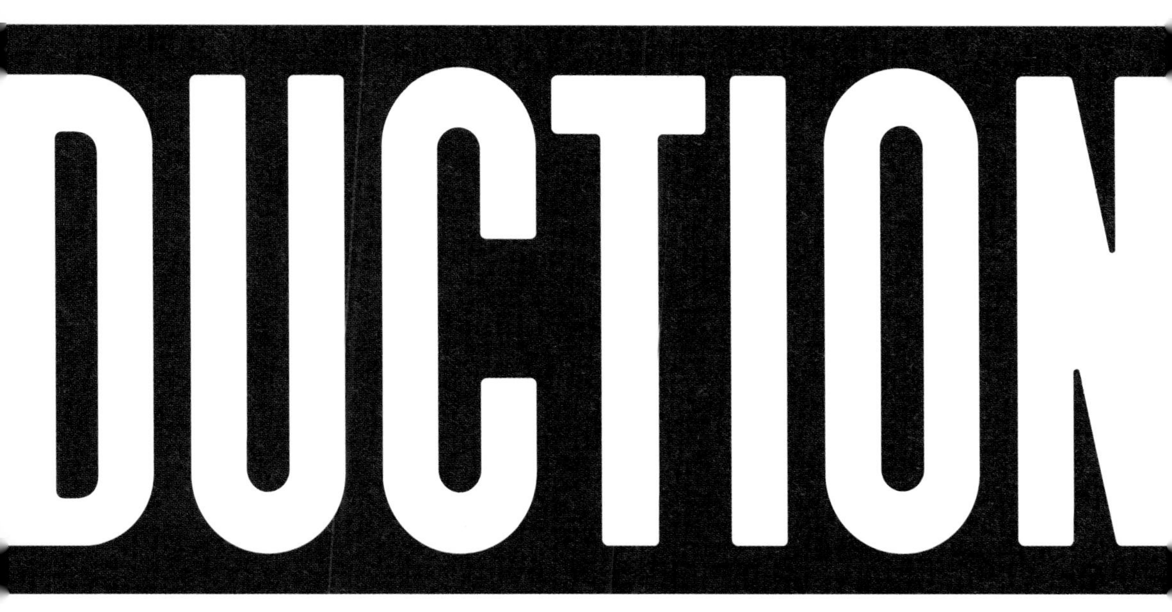
DUCTION

BLACK LIFE IN AMERICA is great art—despite often dire circumstances. Survival grounded in the ability to begin again. To come together to remember the past and imagine a better future. To uplift each other through words and songs. To make beauty. To craft a brilliant turn of phrase. To make delicious food. To smile. To make beautiful music. To take up space. To dance. To march and step high.

The historic celebrations of Black freedom have had many names: Juneteenth, Freedom Day, Emancipation Day, Watch Night, Jubilee. They've been observed on many different days and in different ways. These gatherings stretched across generations and geographies, from the rolling fields of Texas to the bustling streets of Oakland, from the steep hills of Richmond to the historic churches of Savannah. From marching bands and soaring oratory to barbecue and ice cream in the park, Black Americans came together to rekindle old bonds forged while surviving a plantation past. To honor what they had endured and memorialize those who didn't live to see freedom. They were determined to pass down that history to future generations. They would not allow others to define who they were, what they had suffered, or how that history should be remembered. Instead, they insisted, generation after generation, that Black people would tell their own story, protecting their memories of struggle and survival. The moment of victory over the bondage of slavery would be not forgotten but celebrated.

When legal slavery in the United States ended at the close of the Civil War, its shadow remained. New systems of oppression in the form of sharecropping, racial massacres, lynching, and Jim Crow segregation arose to strangle the promise of freedom. The full-flowering promises of emancipation never came to bloom. But Black Americans refused to let these realities silence them. They kept their traditions alive. They kept the history before them, as the old gospel hymn said, to "tell the story of how we've overcome." Wore their Sunday best. Festooned the streets. Gathered with family and play cousins, all their home folks. Ate good food and sipped on red drank. Played their own music loud. Laced wagon wheels with thousands of flowers. Made things beautiful, just for their own pleasure, even if just for a moment.

And so, even as their newfound citizenship rights were stripped away, even as proponents of the Lost Cause sought to rewrite history and cast the Confederacy as noble, Black communities commemorated their freedom with even greater urgency. History was their best weapon, a wedge to make an argument about the patriotism of Black Americans in spite of the injustices of white supremacy. The gatherings were reminders that the history of the fight for Black freedom was something that had to be remembered. Again and again, across the country, they came back together. It was claiming space, a reminder to those who wanted Black people consigned to a second-class citizenship that they belonged. So they took up space in public squares, in parks, along parade routes, in churches, and on Black college campuses. They continued to teach new generations the story of what they had survived as slaves. They continued to reunite with family and home folks. Even in the face of violent repression, Juneteenth and Emancipation Day celebrations were a way to speak the truth, to honor their memories and be inspired once again to continue the fight for full and equal citizenship, that shining moment of jubilee.

The history of these remarkable celebrations is a history of a people who knew what they deserved. Even as the rest of the nation sought to erase the meaning of their freedom, they continued to come together, to march, to speak, to fill the streets, to celebrate in their yards. They insisted: *Freedom matters.*

Bringing together the collection of photographs, etchings, and artifacts for *Black Freedom* has been both a privilege and a challenge. As a historian of the African American experience, I knew from the outset that images chronicling these celebrations would be scarce. Early emancipation celebrations—beginning as far back as 1808, when Massachusetts marked the end of the African slave trade—predated modern journalistic photography. Even after daguerreotypes became available for portraiture, most nineteenth-century newspapers relied on sketches and etchings to depict major events. The massive celebrations that erupted across the country from January 1, 1863, through June 19, 1865, were largely unphotographed, though artists captured glimpses of that joy.

By the turn of the twentieth century, when photography had become more common in newspapers, the biases of white photojournalists shaped the historical record. The era of Jim Crow—the period when segregation laws were cemented, Black voting rights were stripped away, and racial violence was wielded to uphold white supremacy—gave rise to an archival silence. White newspapers had little interest in documenting Black celebrations. White archivists did not preserve Black newspapers, and white institutions refused to collect the papers of prominent Black figures or organizations. The history of Black joy, resistance, and self-determination was deemed unworthy of preservation.

Instead, what we find in mainstream archives from this era are images of racial terror, black-faced caricatures, and portrayals designed to demean and dehumanize. Photographs of Black excellence, Black dignity, and Black public celebration were rare, precisely because they contradicted the racist ideology of the time. That is why the images included in *Black Freedom* are nothing short of extraordinary. Their very existence is an act of defiance. These photographs and sketches offer glimpses of Black communities standing tall, of families reuniting, of children absorbing the history of their ancestors. They show parades winding through city streets, bands playing triumphant marches, elders recounting the sacred story of freedom.

Black photographers, though few in number due to the financial and social barriers of the time, captured what they could. Black journalists chronicled these celebrations in the pages of Black newspapers, ensuring that their communities' histories were not lost. Families preserved memories through oral histories, passing down stories of grand Emancipation Day parades, of the taste of barbecue and pound cake, of sermons that brought entire congregations to their feet.

So, given the history of exclusion, the images included in this book are truly precious artifacts of Black freedom. Capturing and preserving these historic images is a revelation, a reminder of the inherent value of remembering Black life. What remains of these celebrations is a testament to the determination of Black Americans to safeguard their history. Every image in *Black Freedom*—every preserved article, every firsthand account—is evidence of Black resilience. What a joy it is to see Black people facing down the threat of violence to enact their freedom. The very act of being free was resistance. So were the expressions of remembrance. Each of these images is a record of communities coming together to pass down their history to new generations. They would not let the truth of their experiences be whitewashed or erased.

Black people who had been denied resources, autonomy, and public recognition asserted their liberty through these celebrations. They demonstrated, through public gatherings, speeches, music, and performance, the significance of their freedom and their rightful place in American society. Juneteenth and other Black emancipation celebrations were not just moments of joy; they were acts of freedom-making.

White Americans, particularly in the South, used public commemoration to control historical narratives. Through statues, speeches, and regional and national holidays, they preserved a version of history that marginalized or erased Black contributions. In this context, emancipation celebrations were more than commemorative events; they were acts of cultural resistance, historical preservation, and self-affirmation. They countered racist narratives, reclaimed public spaces, and asserted Black belonging in America. Through faith, oratory, memory, performance, and beauty, these celebrations shaped the story of Black freedom—not just as a historical event but as an ongoing process of self-determination. As we continue to observe Juneteenth and other emancipation commemorations today, we honor the legacy of those who understood that celebrating freedom was a means of defending it.

Oh, what a time! Looking at these images, really looking at them closely, is a reminder that being free is an action, an assertion that must be made again and again. These generations gone by understood that freedom had to be celebrated in order to be preserved. *Black Freedom* reveals the history of those celebrations, the Black American reassertion of freedom, the insistence on an independent interpretation of a past, and the desire to commemorate their history accurately. *Black Freedom* builds on those glorious traditions of telling the truth about what we survived and making a guide about how we can survive in the future. Jubilee!

EMANCI

THE LONG

FREE

PATION:

FIGHT FOR

DOM

THE HEADQUARTERS FOR THE PARADE on that brisk New Year's Day in 1898 was the colored YMCA at 214 East Leigh Street, just next to the A. D. Price Funeral Home. Leigh Street was one of the busiest throughfares in Jackson Ward, the vibrant center of the Black community in postwar Richmond, but now it was packed with people coming together to celebrate thirty-five years since the emancipation.

Although the Black militia units that had first been organized during the Civil War were disbanded by Virginia state authorities after Reconstruction ended, threatened as they were by Black men continuing to serve their country in uniform, the Black men who had served remained insistent on donning uniforms. Hundreds of the former soldiers joined Black fraternal lodges and societies whose members wore dress uniforms for their formal ceremonies and parades.

On this day, the Uniform Rank of the Knights of Pythias marched behind the First Battalion Band. The band's drum major, his uniform sashed in bright white satin, led the way, with the blaring trumpets and booming drums marking the tempo for the marchers who followed. The grand marshals of the parade—including anti-lynching newspaperman, banker, and former elected official John Mitchell Jr.—wore "glittering, heavily gold-plated uniforms" that were reported to include a "silk-folding . . . chapeaux, gold cord shoulder-knots, gold-cord aiguilette, gold plated belt and sword, gauntlets and the dark blue regulation suits . . . ornamented with gold-plated buttons." Onlookers could see the glint of the winter sun shining off the enhancements to the uniforms from more than a block away. All the African American lodges in the city and surrounding communities turned out to march in uniform, with the parade stretching the length of several city blocks. It was the largest gathering of Black men in uniform since the Civil War. Women's clubs, their members draped in white, followed the procession of men, and children wearing their Sunday best—boys in suits and overcoats, girls in stockings and lace dresses—followed along. People from throughout the city and several surrounding counties lined the sidewalk, cheering such a spectacle of pride, once unimaginable in the former capital of the Confederacy. They watched from every nook and cranny, some standing in the cold, others on chairs pulled outside, while more onlookers sat on porches or leaned out of windows to get a peek at the Emancipation Day parade. On that day thousands of Black Richmonders gathered, marched, and cheered, an outward expression of the freedom of movement and freedom to gather that they and their forebears had never been legally allowed to exercise as slaves.

The procession led to the historic First African Baptist Church, where congregants packed into the sanctuary. Those who could not fit into the building listened from out on the street. Every Sunday service at the historic Black church was long, but this was one that could not be missed. The program began with prayer and then an impressive solo from young Miss Belle Fitzhugh, whose high soprano reverberated off the walls. The president of the Emancipation Day committee, W. Isaac Johnson, gave a moving opening address welcoming the congregants and marking the historic nature of the occasion. His speech was followed by a formal reading of President Abraham Lincoln's historic Emancipation Proclamation, ensuring that those in attendance who had been too young to remember would hear the historic decree. There was another solo from a Black seminarian from Richmond Theological that was so stirring that the crowd stood and cheered, demanding another song. The ceremony at First Baptist concluded with an address by Reverend Gregory W. Hayes, president of the Virginia Theological Seminary, who spoke stirringly on "true Negro independence"—a fitting subject on what could be considered the celebration of the Black Fourth of July.

The celebration of January 1 wasn't the only Emancipation Day that historically had been celebrated in the city of Richmond. The question of when freedom should be marked had been a matter of spirited debate—was it April 3, the day that the city of Richmond fell to Union troops? Should it have been April 9, the date of Lee's surrender at Appomattox? Or even September 22, the day Lincoln signed the Emancipation Proclamation? The debate among Black city leaders went on for decades, a reminder of their deep investment in freedom's meaning and the joyful urgency with which they claimed and commemorated it.

Emancipation Day celebrations, like the one held in Richmond on January 1, 1898, were deeply connected to a long and arduous struggle for freedom, one that stretched back to the earliest fights against American enslavement and surged forward through the Civil War and Reconstruction. Tracing the long arc of this struggle, from bondage to the Civil War, reveals the intergenerational roots of the fight for Black liberation. Emancipation stood as a powerful reminder that Black people themselves were always the architects of their own freedom. It was their faith and determination that transformed the Civil War from a battle over the Union into a fight for emancipation. It was their activism that pressured the nation to enshrine Black freedom and citizenship into the US Constitution.

IN THE SPIRIT

> Such is the condition of every slave throughout the United States; he owns nothing—he can claim nothing. His wife is not his—his children are not his; they can be taken from him, and sold at any minute, as far as the fleshmonger may see fit to carry them. Slaves are recognised as property by the law and can own nothing except at the consent of their masters. A slave's wife or daughter may be insulted before his eyes with impunity; he himself may be called on to torture them, and dare not refuse. To raise his hand in their defence, is death by law. He must bear all things and resist nothing. If he leaves his master's premises at any time without a written permit, he is liable to be flogged; yet they say we are happy and contented. . . . My father taught me to hate slavery; but forgot to teach me how to conceal my hatred.
>
> —John Swanson Jacobs, *A True Story of Slavery: The United States Governed by Six Hundred Thousand Despots*

Enslaved people lived under a brutal system that denied them even the most basic rights of personhood. They were classified as property, bought and sold at the whims of enslavers, and treated as mere commodities rather than human beings with their own desires. While they may have possessed small personal items—a cloth passed down through generations, a carved keepsake, a secret Bible—nothing they owned was legally recognized as theirs. Even these precious objects had to be hidden away, kept from the grasp of those who claimed dominion over their bodies and their labor.

Marriage, too, was an institution from which the enslaved were excluded. Enslaved couples were forbidden from marrying legally; weddings usually consisted of "jumping the broom," in the tradition of folk customs. Enslaved couples were always at risk of being torn apart, as enslavers had the power to sell husbands away from wives, mothers from children, and siblings from one another. Most devastating was that the enslaved had no right to parent their own children, who were seen merely as another form of wealth for enslavers to exploit.

Slaveholders could control the bodies of the enslaved, but they could never fully control their minds. Those who had been torn from West Africa and brought to America against their will carried with them deeply rooted spiritual traditions. Some worshipped multiple deities, others venerated their ancestors, and still others were practicing Muslims who had memorized long passages of the Quran before being swept up into the trade in slaves. These beliefs held deep meaning for those enduring the unspeakable violence of the transatlantic slave trade. Their beliefs were the groundwork of their resistance in the face of oppression. But over the generations, holding on to their ancestors' faithways was no easy task. The violence of enslavement, the separation from kin, and the forced loss of language made it difficult to preserve the rituals that had once defined their ancestors' spiritual lives.

And yet, amazingly, there is evidence that some practices survived, stripped of their original meaning, but still understood as sacred. One particularly poignant example was the use of an overturned pot during worship, as described by William M. Adams, a formerly enslaved man from Texas: "De slaves didn' have no church den, but dey'd take a big sugar kettle and turn it top down on de groun' and put logs round it to kill de sound. Dey'd pray to be free and sing and dance." In its West African origins, a large communal pot was used to cook a sacred meal of rice after a family member's death. Once the meal had been consumed, the pot was overturned and the community gathered in a ring to sing spiritual songs that they believed would help guide their loved one's spirit to fly free. In America, the violence of dislocation and the loss of language would keep the enslaved from remembering all the details, but they did know that to gather in a circle around an overturned pot was holy, and they believed it had the power to protect them from being caught by overseers, patrollers, and slaveholders. Even as language and memory faded, traces of their African practices remained.

Fearing the power of African spiritual traditions, enslavers sought to impose a narrow form of Christianity on the people they held in bondage. On Sundays—the one day the enslaved were not forced to labor—enslavers would preach to them from their front porches or relegate them to the back pews of white churches, hammering in a singular message: obedience. Again and again, they read from Ephesians 6:5–8: "Servants, be obedient to them that are your masters according to the flesh, with fear and trembling, in singleness of your heart, as unto Christ."

The enslaved, however, noticed that their enslavers never spoke of the Bible's Old Testament. Left to discover its contents on their own, they found the story of Moses, a man born into slavery, separated from his mother, raised by an Egyptian king, and ultimately called by God to lead his people out of slavery, through a wilderness and toward the promised land and freedom. In Leviticus they read about the Year of Jubilee, which declared that every fifty years, all slaves were to be set free, debts erased, and stolen lands returned. They saw, again and again, that the full story of the Bible was not one of submission but of deliverance. The full story of Christianity was grounded in the knowledge of God's favor toward the enslaved. Enslavers never preached the full Bible to Black congregants for fear that the broader message of Christianity was a threat. They believed that they could never adequately control enslaved people if they came to know that they were, in fact, equals in God's eyes. The enslaved shared these hidden truths with one another in secret. In the depths of the woods, far from the prying eyes of their oppressors, they forged a new kind of faith—one that was neither entirely African nor entirely European, but something unique. Their form of Christianity was a radical, independent belief system that blended the wisdom of their ancestors with the liberating power of the broader gospel.

Every aspect of enslaved people's worship had to be clandestine. It was illegal for them to gather without white supervision, so they created hush harbors, hidden spaces deep in the forest where they could worship freely. It was illegal for them to preach, but they did so anyway, crafting sermons of hope and resistance. It was illegal for them to learn to read and write, but those who could read risked everything to share the Word. Some slaveholders were so fearful of literate enslaved people that they punished them by cutting off their fingers or hands. But those who had learned to read the Bible were transformed. They became the meek who would inherit the earth, the captives who would one day be set free.

REBELLIONS

For slaveholders, probably the most frightening thing about Black Christianity was the threat of rebellion. When enslaved men and women drew upon their independent beliefs and fought back to seize their own liberation, they shattered the illusions of control that white enslavers so desperately tried to maintain. The mere possibility of an uprising sent waves of terror through the slaveholding class. News of revolts—whether real, rumored, or in the planning stages—ignited their deepest anxieties, exposing the fundamental contradiction of slavery itself: Those held in bondage would never accept their oppression as natural or just.

Paranoia ran deep in the minds of enslavers. They obsessed over what the enslaved truly thought of their condition, fearing that beneath every quiet act of submission lay seeds of insurrection. From the rice plantations of the Carolinas to the cane fields of Louisiana, from the tobacco farms of Virginia to the emerging cotton empire of Texas, their greatest nightmare was the possibility that the people they held in bondage would one day rise up. Several times, that fear became reality.

Slave revolts erupted in every part of the Americas and the Caribbean between the 1500s and 1800s, leaving an indelible mark on the consciousness of both the enslaved and the enslavers. In the American colonies there was the Stono Rebellion of 1739, in which enslaved Africans in South Carolina killed white colonists and marched carrying banners demanding freedom. Gabriel's Rebellion followed in the wake of the American Revolution, when in 1800 a literate blacksmith hired out to work in Richmond's foundries meticulously organized hundreds of enslaved men, only to be betrayed at the last moment. In the 1803 Igbo Landing in Georgia, seventy-five captured Igbo people murdered the crew of the slave ship where they had been held and then, refusing to accept a life in slavery, drowned themselves in Dunbar Creek. The revolt that began in 1791 on the relatively small Caribbean colony of Saint-Domingue became the most seismic of them all, when enslaved Black people overthrew the French colonizers holding them in bondage and established Haiti as the first free Black republic in the Western Hemisphere. And then there was Nat Turner.

Nat Turner was born in Southampton County, Virginia, in 1800. He was an enslaved carpenter, a deeply religious man, and a preacher. The enslaved community believed he was divinely chosen and thought of him as a prophet "intended for some great purpose." His spiritual visions drove him to lead one of the bloodiest slave revolts in US history.

On the night of August 21, 1831, Turner and more than fifty enslaved and free Black men who joined his rebellion moved from plantation to plantation, slaughtering slaveholders and their families. Armed with axes, knives, and muskets, they stabbed, shot, and bludgeoned fifty-seven white people to death. The uprising lasted for four days, sending waves of panic across Virginia and beyond. Turner's rebellion not only struck fear into the hearts of slaveholders but also sharpened the divide between Black consciousness and white terror. After the rebellion was suppressed by the state militia, Turner evaded capture for over two months, hiding in the woods as white militias scoured the countryside in search of him. When he was finally caught, he was taken to the Southampton County jail, where he dictated his "confession" to Thomas R. Gray, a local attorney. On November 11, 1831, Turner was hanged, but the slaveholders' vengeance extended beyond Turner himself. In the wake of the rebellion, white mobs exacted indiscriminate punishment, killing nearly two hundred enslaved and free Black people, most of whom had no involvement in the uprising.

The Turner Rebellion did more than expose the ever-present fear enslavers harbored—it reshaped the laws governing Black life. In the immediate aftermath, Virginia's state legislature debated the possibility of abolishing slavery altogether. Yet rather than take steps toward emancipation, they chose repression. On March 15, 1832, Virginia passed sweeping new laws designed to suffocate Black autonomy. The new laws made it illegal for Black people—enslaved or free—to "preach, exhort or conduct, or hold any assembly or meeting, for religious or other purposes, either in the day time, or at night." The measure was a direct attack on the independent Black faith practices that had long been a source of radical resistance.

But the restrictions did not stop there. Social gatherings were also heavily policed, as authorities sought to stamp out any space where Black people could gather in numbers. The law transformed free Black people into perpetual suspects, with mere speech becoming a capital crime. Those accused of fighting with a white person, giving "seditious speeches," or even being suspected of theft could be re-enslaved. The message was clear: The fear of Black freedom and citizenship was so great that white lawmakers were willing to criminalize Black life itself. Black congregations, gatherings, and celebrations became sites of terror for enslavers and lawmakers. The very act of coming together was seen as a prelude to rebellion.

Few accurate records exist detailing what enslaved people truly thought about rebellions. Given the extreme danger of expressing even the slightest sympathy for insurrection, both free and enslaved Black people risked their lives by sharing honest opinions on the subject. Any hint of defiance could lead to brutal punishment or death. However, one of the most powerful and direct testimonies we have comes from David Walker, the son of an enslaved father and a free Black mother.

WALKER'S APPEAL

Born in Wilmington, North Carolina, likely just a few years before Nat Turner's birth, David Walker was legally free due to his mother's status. Yet freedom did not shield him from the horrors of slavery. Growing up in the South, he witnessed unspeakable acts of cruelty, including an enslaved man who was compelled to whip his own mother to death. These experiences instilled in Walker a deep and unwavering hatred for the system that dehumanized his people.

As a young man, Walker left the South and moved to Boston, where he became deeply involved in Black antislavery organizations, and where the first communities of emancipated Black people lived. After the American Revolution, revolutionary rhetoric, Black litigation, and protest led most Northern states to move toward ending slavery. The state of Vermont abolished slavery in its state constitution in 1777. Pennsylvania passed a gradual emancipation act in 1780 and was followed by Massachusetts, where enslaved people had been suing for their freedom using the Massachusetts state constitution, which stated that "all men are born free and equal." By 1804 every state north of the Mason-Dixon Line had put a gradual emancipation law in place, but the slow pace of many of the laws left many people in bondage or bonded servitude for decades. Though Northern states were abolishing slavery, Black people were not treated as equals. Racially segregated transportation began in Massachusetts, and some states prevented Black men from voting. But at least the North provided a community for men and women like Walker to advocate for their equal inclusion in society.

In Boston, Walker found his voice as a writer, contributing to *Freedom's Journal*, the first Black-owned newspaper in the United States. He honed his skills as an orator and activist, quickly rising to prominence as one of the most radical antislavery voices of his time. In 1829, Walker made history by publishing his revolutionary pamphlet, *Walker's Appeal, in Four Articles; Together with a Preamble, to the Coloured Citizens of the World, but in Particular, and Very Expressly, to Those of the United States of America*. Knowing that distributing such a document in the Southern states would be nearly impossible,

Walker smuggled copies into the South by sewing them into the lining of sailors' clothing.

The *Appeal* was a searing call to arms. Unlike some abolitionists who advocated for moral persuasion, Walker openly called for the enslaved to take up arms and violently overthrow their oppressors. He saw slavery as an inherently violent institution, one that could be dismantled only through force. "It is no more harm for you to kill a man, who is trying to kill you," he wrote, "than it is for you to take a drink of water when thirsty." Walker rejected the idea, often promoted by pro-slavery Christians, that slavery was a civilizing or Christianizing mission. Instead, he condemned it as a moral abomination.

Beyond its revolutionary call for insurrection, the *Appeal* also articulated a powerful claim to Black citizenship. Walker argued that Black Americans—free and enslaved—were as much a part of the nation as any white person. He fiercely rejected the notion that Black people should be colonized or removed from the country they had built through generations of unpaid labor. "America is more our country," he declared, "than it is the whites—we have enriched it with our blood and tears. . . . Will they drive us from our property and homes, which we have earned with our blood!" These words foreshadowed both the bloody conflict of the Civil War and the post-emancipation struggles of freed people to claim full citizenship and equality.

Walker likely participated in Boston's annual Emancipation Day celebrations, held on July 14. The date held deep significance for Black Bostonians—after the American Revolution, while white Americans celebrated their independence from Britain on July 4, Black residents of Boston chose July 14 as a day to celebrate their own freedom and survival. Decades before the Civil War, Black communities in Boston and throughout the North gathered each year to commemorate the abolition of the Atlantic slave trade, which had officially ended in 1808 under the US Constitution. These celebrations were acts of defiance and assertion, and from the very beginning, they faced violent opposition. Working-class white residents, angered by expressions of Black independence, frequently attacked the gatherings, underscoring the precariousness of Black liberty even in "free" states.

The *Appeal* made Walker a marked man. White lawmakers and slaveholders saw his words as a direct threat. In response, Southern states passed even harsher laws restricting Black literacy, banning the distribution of abolitionist literature, and increasing surveillance of free Black communities. The state of Georgia offered a $10,000 reward for anyone who could capture Walker and bring him to the South alive, and $3,000 for his assassination.

Despite these threats, Walker remained steadfast. He hoped that his words were reaching enslaved people in the South, providing them with hope. His message was one of not just resistance but also possibility. He reminded the enslaved that there was a world beyond their chains, where free Black people were fighting, speaking, and daring to imagine a future without bondage. His *Appeal* was a prophecy that foreshadowed the coming storm of war and the enduring fight for Black freedom in America.

THE FIRST AFRICAN BAPTIST CHURCH in Richmond, Virginia, where Black residents gathered in 1898 to celebrate Emancipation Day, traced its roots back to 1802, when enslaved Black people were forced to worship under the control of white congregants at what was then the First Baptist Church. Segregated by race, they were relegated to the balconies and back pews, their faith policed by the very people who denied them freedom. Black worshippers endured these constraints for decades until the white congregation built a new sanctuary elsewhere in the city. In 1841 the original church building was sold to Black congregants. They renamed it First *African* Baptist Church.

Despite gaining ownership of the building, true autonomy remained elusive. Because Virginia law prohibited assembly without white supervision, the church's first pastor was not a Black leader chosen by the congregation but the Reverend Robert Ryland, a white minister, a slaveholder, and the first president of Richmond College. Ryland's leadership was rooted in control rather than liberation. He allowed the congregation to have a Black deacon board but denied them the right to read the Bible freely. Instead, he authored a catechism for them, carefully crafted to emphasize submission to white authority.

Ryland's grip over the church extended beyond doctrine to physical space. No Black person was permitted to speak from the church's pulpit, only from a lectern placed to the side of the altar, reinforcing the message that even in their own house of worship, the Black congregants were not equals. Yet despite these restrictions, First African Baptist Church became a spiritual and communal refuge, attracting congregants from throughout the city and surrounding county.

Beyond supervised spaces like First African Baptist, as repression tightened its grip, the enslaved found deeper meaning in their clandestine meetings. The hush harbors became more than places of worship; they became spaces of learning, of planning, of resistance. Even under the shadow of violent retaliation, the people gathered. They prayed. They sang. They whispered stories of Moses and deliverance, of Haiti and revolution, of Nat Turner and defiance. They held fast to the belief that together, in faith and in unity, they were powerful. And that power—despite the laws, despite the fear, despite the brutal retaliation—could never be fully extinguished. They held on to hope. They danced, they sang, they prayed, and they wept. They passed their faith down from generation to generation, believing that one day God would deliver them. Jubilee.

SLAVEHOLDERS' FEAR

> During all my slave life I never lost sight of freedom. It was always on my heart; it came to me like a solemn thought, and often circumstances much stimulated the desire to be free and raised great expectation of it. . . . We always called "freedom" "possum," so as to keep the white people from knowing what we were talking about. We all understood it.
>
> —Ambrose Headen, a freedman from Talladega, Alabama, in a narrative recorded in *The American Missionary*, December 1878

FREEDOM WAS ALWAYS ON THE MIND of the people held in bondage. To survive, they had to pretend that it wasn't. Every day, all day, they had to pretend that they were content with their station in life. During every interaction with the people who owned them or supervised their labor, they had to act as if they didn't mind working without pay. They were forced to submit quietly to the punishments and the time away from their spouses and children. They had to tolerate the tight supervision of their every move and their constant exhaustion for someone else's benefit. As they planted and harvested in the fields, maintained the plantation house, cooked, cleaned, did laundry, maintained livestock, constructed buildings, and built the very infrastructure of the plantation South, enslaved people had to disguise their hearts' desire. At every turn, they had to disguise their desire to be free.

The ruse was effective. When Southern slaveholders looked at the enslaved, they could not see their discontent. Slaveholders believed wholeheartedly in their right to own other human beings, and slavery's everyday violence had become logical to them. White supremacy had seemingly become slaveholders' birthright. While they knew the enslaved were indeed people (they were far too intimate with the enslaved to really think otherwise), they still viewed them as less than. They saw the bodies of the enslaved as expendable and disposable, valuable only as property that could be bought and sold at auction. The human needs of the enslaved—for family, independence, and respect—were regularly and systematically disregarded.

The enslaved were free to think for themselves, to imagine what was possible if they were not in bondage. Slaveholders did not hear the clandestine conversations taking place out of earshot. They never understood the coded conversations. The whispered plans of escape. The hidden prayers passed down over the generations. The Black form of Christianity in which the enslaved were God's chosen people. The slaveholders could hear the harmonies but never understood the hidden meanings in work songs and spirituals. If they had, they would have been shocked that no matter how consigned the enslaved seemed to their condition at the very bottom of society, they "never lost sight of freedom," as Ambrose Headen noted.

Americans who held people in bondage had long been worried about the prospect of Black freedom. In his writings, president and slaveholder Thomas Jefferson called for freed Black people to be sent abroad to colonize other parts of the world. Citing "deep rooted prejudices entertained by the whites; ten thousand recollections, by the blacks, of the injuries they have sustained; new provocations," he claimed that what he called "the real distinctions which nature has made" would divide the nation if free Black people stayed in America, ending "in the extermination of the one or the other race."

In a debate about a law preventing slaveholders from manumitting their slaves published in the January 17, 1806, issue of the *Virginia Argus*, a semiweekly newspaper in Richmond, the writer reported that state legislators feared that freeing any of the slaves would lead to rebellion, not just by freed men but also by "the females of the blacks" who "would be as ferocious and formidable as the males." Legislators cautioned that "those black who are free, obtain some education; they obtain a knowledge of facts, by passing from place to place in society; they can thus organize insurrection." Although this version of the bill did not pass, Black freedom, education, and mobility haunted the nightmares of slaveholders.

Black people who were freed faced rampant discrimination. In a July 7, 1826, issue of the *Daily National Journal*, a letter to the editor complained that "thirty negroes made their appearance" in Salem, Indiana, after being set free in North Carolina and then required by law to leave the state. The Salem resident called for the removal of free Black people from the nation because he felt that free Black people were "unprepared to make good citizens" and characterized them as "destitute of every thing [sic] but bodily powers, and having no character to lose, and no prospect of acquiring one, even did they know its value. . . ." Asserting the white supremacist viewpoint of his day, the letter writer hoped that the free states would remain "free of amalgamation" and "unsullied" by the presence of former slaves. Such fear and discrimination were rampant throughout the nation. When establishing the Republic of Texas in the 1830s, lawmakers forbade free Black people from settling there. Such restrictions were never formally lifted even after Texas joined the United States in the 1840s.

Minstrel performances—the blackface images the white world fabricated to represent the men, women, and children who had once labored as slaves—were degrading depictions of Black freedom as seen from the imagination of white racists. They created the characters—Mammy, Sambo, Jim Crow, and Topsy—not just to mock black skin, black bodies, and "nappy" hair, but also to serve as a cautionary tale about a world where Black people were free. Old Black Sambo was intended to show that it was useless to try to educate Black people; he mangled the English language, pontificating but saying nothing. Mammy on the minstrel stage, portrayed by men in fat suits, showed white audiences that enslaved women didn't even want to be free; they preferred serving the families of their white slaveholders over caring for their own, and their "pickaninny" children were eaten by alligators or drowned in swamps. Jim Crow was the "wheeling stranger" who never knew how to properly behave in public. The white men who played Jim Crow on stage would depict him showing up in fine restaurants and hotels in tattered, dirty, smelly rags, talking loudly and interrupting the events held by upper-crust whites. The farce of minstrelsy was so seared into white Americans' minds that they named the laws separating Black and white people on trains and streetcars Jim Crow, fearing that the first emancipations in Northern states would spell disaster for a "civilized" nation.

Slaveholders were always fearful of Black freedom. Manumission, or the formal act of freeing a slave, was extremely rare, and in most Southern states it was strictly governed by state law. Most states required anyone manumitted to leave the state; some Southern states required that a slaveholder obtain permission from the state legislature to free someone. Enslaved people who escaped were fiercely pursued; indeed, professional slave catchers could be hired to pursue those who ran. Newspapers were full of detailed advertisements (slaveholders knew the people they held in bondage intimately) seeking those who had run away in search of a better life anywhere. Enslaved people's fight to escape bondage in the antebellum South was just a hint of what would come after, during the Civil War.

The war was begun and there were stories of fights and freedom. The news went from plantation to plantation and while the slaves acted natural and some even more polite than usual, they prayed for freedom. Then one day I heard something that sounded like thunder and missus and marster began to walk around and act queer. The grown slaves were whispering to each other. Sometimes they gathered in little gangs in the grove. Next day I heard it again, boom, boom, boom. I went and asked missus "is it going to rain?" She said, "Mary go to the ice house and bring me some pickles and preserves." I went and got them. She ate a little and gave me some. Then she said, "You run along and play." In a day or two everybody on the plantation seemed to be disturbed and marster and missus were crying. Marster ordered all the slaves to come to the great house at nine o'clock. Nobody was working and slaves were walking over the grove in every direction. At nine o'clock all the slaves gathered at the great house and marster and missus came out on the porch and stood side by side. Everything was so quiet. You could hear a pin drop everything was so quiet. Then marster said, "Good morning," and missus said, "Good morning, children." They were both crying. Then marster said, "Men, women and children, you are free. You are no longer my slaves. The Yankees will soon be here."

Marster and missus then went into the house [and] got two large armchairs [and] put them on the porch facing the avenue and sat down side by side and remained there watching.

In about an hour there was one of the blackest clouds coming up the avenue from the main road. It was the Yankee soldiers, they finally filled the mile long avenue reaching from marster's house to the main Louisburg road and spread out over the mile square grove. The mounted men dismounted. The footmen stacked their shining guns and began to build fires and cook. They called the slaves, saying, "You are free." Slaves were whooping and laughing and acting like they were crazy.

> Yankee soldiers were shaking hands with the Negroes and calling them Sam, Dinah, Sarah and asking them questions. They busted the door to the smoke house and got all the hams. They went to the icehouse and got several barrels of brandy, and such a time. The Negroes and Yankees were cooking and eating together. The Yankees told them to come on and join them, they were free. Marster and missus sat on the porch and they were so humble no Yankee bothered anything in the great house. The slaves were awfully excited. The Yankees stayed there, cooked, eat, drank and played music until about night, then a bugle began to blow and you never saw such getting on horses and lining up in your life. In a few minutes they began to march, leaving the grove which was soon as silent as a grave yard. They took marster's horses and cattle with them and joined the main army and camped just across Cypress Creek one and one half miles from my marster's place on the Louisburg Road.
>
> When they left the country, lot of the slaves went with them and soon there were none of marster's slaves left.
>
> —Mary Anderson's account of being freed in Wake County, North Carolina, as detailed in *Born in Slavery: Slave Narratives from the Federal Writers' Project, 1936–1938*, a collection of the US Library of Congress, vol. 11, part 1, *North Carolina: Adams–Hunter*

THE PROCLAMATION

In the early years of the Civil War, emancipation was far from a certainty for the Union. While abolitionists saw the war as a direct path to ending slavery, many in the North viewed such a goal as dangerous and unnecessary. The fear of disrupting the fragile political balance was so strong that even some staunch Unionists rejected the idea outright. In the pages of the pro-Union newspaper

The Daily Ohio Statesman, one writer insisted that emancipation was "impossible" and warned that it would "distract and divide the North, and alienate from it the loyalists in the South, thus jeopardizing, if not rendering hopeless, the reunion of the States." The war, as they saw it, was not about slavery but about preserving the Union.

President Abraham Lincoln, though personally opposed to slavery, initially held this same position. His priority was saving the Union, not dismantling the institution of slavery. In his famous letter to *New-York Tribune* editor Horace Greeley in August 1862, Lincoln made his stance clear: "If I could save the Union without freeing any slave, I would do it, and if I could save it by freeing all the slaves, I would do it; and if I could save it by freeing some and leaving others alone, I would also do that." His words reflected the careful political balancing act he believed was necessary to maintain Northern unity.

But the war itself made neutrality on slavery impossible. The Civil War opened the floodgates of change, forcing both the Union and Lincoln himself to confront the unavoidable reality that slavery was at the heart of the conflict. With every battle, the enslaved seized the moment, taking the matter of their freedom into their own hands. Union Major General Benjamin Franklin Butler, commander of Fort Monroe on the Chesapeake Bay, first coined the term "contraband of war" in relation to three enslaved men who arrived at the Union army lines seeking protection from the Confederates in 1861. Butler determined that the Union troops could "take possession" of the enslaved, much like they would any property of their secessionist owners. Given that Virginia had seceded and declared itself part of a foreign nation, Butler decided that the 1850 Fugitive Slave Act that would otherwise have compelled the enslaved to return to their slaveholders no longer applied. Although President Lincoln did not recognize the legitimacy of the Confederacy, he let the policy stand. Butler's wartime decision started the process by which the Civil War would become a war for emancipation.

The enslaved would not wait for political leaders to decide their fate. Across the South, thousands fled plantations and crossed battle lines, seeking refuge with Union forces. Some risked their lives running through swamps and forests to reach nearby camps, while others staged outright rebellions on plantations before Union troops even arrived. Enslaved men, women, and children turned the war into their own struggle for liberation, well before any official proclamation declared their freedom. By the time Lincoln was seriously considering freeing the enslaved in the states in rebellion, Black Americans had already been fighting for their own freedom, making emancipation not just a wartime necessity but an undeniable reality.

In September 1862, with the Civil War raging and the stakes higher than ever, President Abraham Lincoln began to take decisive steps that would alter the course of the conflict. On September 22, he signed the Emancipation Proclamation, which declared that if the Confederate states did not cease their rebellion and rejoin the Union by January 1, 1863, all enslaved people within those states would be free. Primarily not an act of moral conviction but a calculated wartime strategy, the Emancipation Proclamation struck at the very foundation of the Southern economy—enslaved labor—destabilizing the Confederacy from within. Lincoln also hoped to encourage the enslaved to continue to resist their oppressors and support the Union cause, further weakening the Southern war effort. On January 1, 1863, the bold declaration completely transformed the Union's aims. The document began:

> That on the first day of January, in the year of our Lord one thousand eight hundred and sixty-three, all persons held as slaves within any State or designated part of a State, the people whereof shall then be in rebellion against the United States, shall be then, thenceforward, and forever free; and the Executive Government of the United States, including the military and naval authority thereof, will recognize and maintain the freedom of such persons, and will do no act or acts to repress such persons, or any of them, in any efforts they may make for their actual freedom.

Though the Emancipation Proclamation did not immediately free all enslaved people, and it applied only to areas still in rebellion and not to the border states that remained loyal to the Union, it sounded the death knell for slavery as an institution. The war was no longer just about preserving the Union; it was now undeniably a fight for liberation. The Emancipation Proclamation also opened the door to the enlistment of Black men into the Union army and navy:

> And I further declare and make known, that such persons of suitable condition, will be received into the armed service of the United States to garrison forts, positions, stations, and other places, and to man vessels of all sorts in said service.

Immediately, Massachusetts and Connecticut organized Black state regiments, and the federal government organized the US Colored Troops. More than 180,000 Black men served in the Union army and an additional 18,000 served in the Union navy. The Emancipation Proclamation was transformative both for Black men who served a nation that had once enforced their enslavement and for every enslaved person who encountered the Union army, whether in the form of Black or white units. With every Union advance into Confederate territory, enslaved people made their way toward freedom. For better or for worse, Union troops became agents of emancipation.

News of the proclamation spread quickly among the enslaved, carried by word of mouth, secret gatherings, and Black preachers, who understood its transformative power. Those who knew of the decree stayed awake late into the night on December 31, 1862, waiting for the dawn of the new year—waiting for freedom. These gatherings, known as Watch Night services, became sacred moments of anticipation as Black communities filled churches and homes, praying, singing, and hoping that their long-awaited liberation had finally arrived. When the clock struck midnight, shouts of joy and songs of praise filled the air.

These first Watch Night services were among the earliest collective celebrations of Southern emancipation and initiated a tradition that endures to this day. In many Black churches across the country, congregations still gather on New Year's Eve, not only to welcome another year but to remember the night when their ancestors watched and waited for freedom.

BETRAYAL AT EBENEZER CREEK

When enslaved people on Georgia's vast plantations heard the thunderous approach of General William Tecumseh Sherman's troops during his infamous March to the Sea, they knew their moment of jubilee had arrived. For generations, they had prayed, waited, and clung to the promise that one day God would deliver them from bondage. Now, as Union soldiers stormed through the Georgia countryside, torching the infrastructure of the Confederacy, the enslaved seized their chance. Emerging from the shadows of the fields and cabins where they had toiled, they ran toward the Union lines, their voices rising in cries of "Hallelujah!" and "Jubilee!" This was not just military conquest; for the enslaved, it was divine intervention, the realization of a promise long deferred. As one historian of Sherman's March noted, "Freed people imagined their emancipation as having world-historical significance, as being rooted in ideas of rebirth and divine justice, and as pointing toward a dawning of freedom that would mend the sins of American slavery." In that moment, their liberation was not simply a legal or political act; it was also a spiritual reckoning, an affirmation that they were God's chosen people and that their suffering had not been in vain.

Their freedom, however, was not just symbolic but had a tangible impact on the Confederacy. The mass exodus of enslaved people from plantations crippled the output of the Southern economy, stripping it of its labor force and its wealth and making it nearly impossible for the Confederacy to sustain the war effort. This shift was so impactful that historian W. E. B. Du Bois called it a "general strike" in his historic text *Black Reconstruction in America*. Indeed, it was the will of the enslaved to stop laboring and start seeking freedom that tipped the scales of a brutal conflict in the favor of the Union.

The newly freed men and women were not just passive beneficiaries of Union victory; they were active agents of the war's outcome. Many provided essential wartime reconnaissance, serving as guides for Union soldiers, pointing out hidden Confederate supply caches, and relaying critical intelligence about enemy movements. Plantation owners, desperate to protect their wealth, ordered the enslaved to bury food stores, livestock, and valuables in the ground, hoping to keep them from Union foragers. But rather than complying, many enslaved people led Sherman's troops straight to the hiding places or took the goods directly to Union lines themselves. The Confederacy had built its fortunes on the forced labor of enslaved people, but in these moments, the enslaved flipped the script, wielding their intimate knowledge of the land and its resources as a weapon against their former oppressors.

As Sherman's army marched deeper into Georgia, the number of enslaved people seeking refuge in Union lines swelled to unprecedented levels. By late 1864, more than 20,000 formerly enslaved men, women, and children had attached themselves to his army, trailing the soldiers in a desperate pursuit of freedom. Their presence, however, was met with indifference—and in some cases, outright hostility—by the Union officers leading the campaign. Sherman himself, despite being the face of their liberation, was deeply ambivalent about Black people. He openly questioned their capabilities and resisted their enlistment as soldiers. But even his callousness was eclipsed by the cruelty of one of his commanders, Brigadier General Jefferson Columbus Davis, who led Sherman's 14th Army Corps.

As the army neared the Georgia coast, soldiers encountered a formidable obstacle: the deep, rushing waters of Ebenezer Creek. With Confederate cavalry in pursuit, the Union troops built a makeshift bridge to cross. But once the last soldier had made it to the other side, Davis ordered his men to destroy the bridge, leaving behind the hundreds of freed people who had followed them. Stranded in the swampy wilderness with Confederate forces closing in, the men, women, and children who had risked everything for their freedom now found themselves abandoned to the enemy. Confederate cavalry charged into the helpless crowd, slaughtering many on sight. Others, in a desperate bid to escape, threw themselves into the cold waters of the creek and drowned. The massacre at Ebenezer Creek was a horrific betrayal, a brutal reminder that the path to freedom was neither safe nor guaranteed.

Those who survived the march to Union-controlled territory found themselves facing new struggles. Refugee camps for freed people were overcrowded, undersupplied, and overwhelmed by the sheer number of those seeking shelter. Disease, hunger, and exposure took a devastating toll. The jubilation of freedom was tempered by the harsh reality that even in Union refugee camps, Black lives were often treated as expendable. The moment that the formerly enslaved had longed for had come, but the indifference and violence that met them afterward was a terrible reminder that true freedom would be a far more complicated battle. Although their suffering had not ended with emancipation, the enslaved had taken their first, perilous steps toward liberation.

FORTY ACRES AND A MULE

In spite of the betrayal at Ebenezer Creek, when General Sherman and his army marched triumphantly into Savannah, Georgia, in December 1864, they were greeted as liberators by the city's Black residents. Churches and gathering spaces across the city hosted grand celebrations, embracing December 22, 1864, as their own Emancipation Day. The First and the Second African Baptist Churches in Savannah, two of the oldest Black congregations in America, overflowed with jubilant crowds, their voices rising in praise and gratitude. For many, this was the moment they had prayed for, the culmination of years of suffering and struggle. But even as they rejoiced, they were looking ahead. Freedom, they knew, could not be sustained without land, and with emancipation now at hand, they set their sights on securing their future.

By January 1865, the freed people of Savannah had formed a clear vision of what must come next. They did not want to simply remain laborers on white-owned land under new forms of exploitation. They wanted self-sufficiency, ownership, and the means to provide for themselves and their families. They knew that it had been their hard work that had made the South prosperous, and they now wanted some of that prosperity for themselves and their children.

A delegation of twenty Black pastors led by Garrison Frazier, a former slave and retired pastor of Savannah's Bryan Baptist Church, met with Sherman and Secretary of War Edwin Stanton to try to shape the future of Black freedom. During their meeting, Stanton asked Frazier how the freed people could best sustain themselves. The reverend's answer was clear and unequivocal:

"The way we can best take care of ourselves is to have land, and turn it and till it by our own labor. . . . We want to be placed on land until we are able to buy it and make it our own." Frazier and his fellow ministers understood that without land, freedom was an illusion. The promise of liberty meant little if Black people remained economically dependent on the very white landowners who had once enslaved them.

Frazier's compelling request led General Sherman and Secretary Stanton to pen Special Field Order No. 15. Issued on January 16, 1865, the order designated 400,000 acres of confiscated Confederate land in the coastal low country of Georgia and South Carolina to be divided into forty-acre plots for the formerly enslaved. This was the birth of the famed promise of "forty acres and a mule," a policy that on its surface offered newly freed Black people a foundation for economic independence and landownership. Black leaders hoped that this order might be a form of reparations, a tangible step toward redressing the theft of their labor and their lives.

For the freed people of Savannah and beyond, this was a moment of immense possibility. The land represented more than soil; it was a chance to build a future on their own terms. They hoped that this would be their opportunity to move onto land, farm, build homes, rebuild their families, and establish communities. On February 2, 1865, those who were hopeful packed into a massive gathering at Savannah's Second African Baptist Church, jubilant about what was possible. Others noted the order did not give the former slaves title to the land. It was only a passing arrangement, perhaps just a way to keep the land productive, but not an attempt to build a positive future for free people.

In the end, the skeptics were correct: The promise of forty acres and a mule would prove to be tragically short-lived. Just months later, after the assassination of President Abraham Lincoln and the rise of Andrew Johnson, a Southern-sympathizing president who sought to restore the South's previous racial order, former Confederate landholders were allowed to take back property they had owned prior to the war, leaving thousands of former slaves landless once again. Though the government ultimately failed to fulfill its promise of forty acres and a mule, the call for land and reparations did not die; it has echoed across generations, remaining at the heart of Black struggles for justice and equality in America today.

The disappointments about the government's broken promise were not yet known when Richmond, Virginia, the capital of the Confederacy, fell to the Union on April 3, 1865. That day there was only jubilation from the formerly enslaved, and trepidation on the part of Richmond's Confederates, who stood peering out of the doorways of their grand mansions, watching their chattel walk away and fearing that their homes might go up in smoke. But the fires that burned in Richmond that day had been set by Confederate soldiers as they retreated south to Danville, Virginia, burning bridges, supply warehouses, and explosive gunpowder and munitions.

Black Richmond celebrated the victory that signaled the coming end of the war. Union soldiers opened the slave pens, where thousands of enslaved people had been brutally imprisoned, bought, and sold. President Abraham Lincoln and his youngest son arrived in Richmond to greet the troops and survey the city, riding through the capital in a horse-drawn carriage. Black Richmonders lined the route, shouting to God and praising the Lord for their freedom. A correspondent from *The Press*, a Philadelphia newspaper, described the scene: "There was a grand jubilee meeting at the [First] African [Baptist] Church, the largest building in the city, where [Confederate president] Jeff Davis has frequently convened the conspirators to plot and execute treason. The colored people turned out in full force; every seat was taken up, and all standing room was occupied; the windows were thronged; and hundreds were outside unable to get within hearing or seeing distance."

It was during that service that the first Black man would speak from the church's pulpit: "It should be remembered that no colored man had ever in that church, though belonging to that oppressed people, dared to speak to the people from the pulpit. Chaplain Stevens [chaplain of the US Colored Troops] was the first to ascend. Negro ministers were permitted to speak from the altar, but no higher." It was fitting: regiments of the US Colored Troops were among those that battled to liberate the city. As the newspaperman from *The Press* wrote, "Every one declares that Richmond never before presented such a spectacle of jubilee."

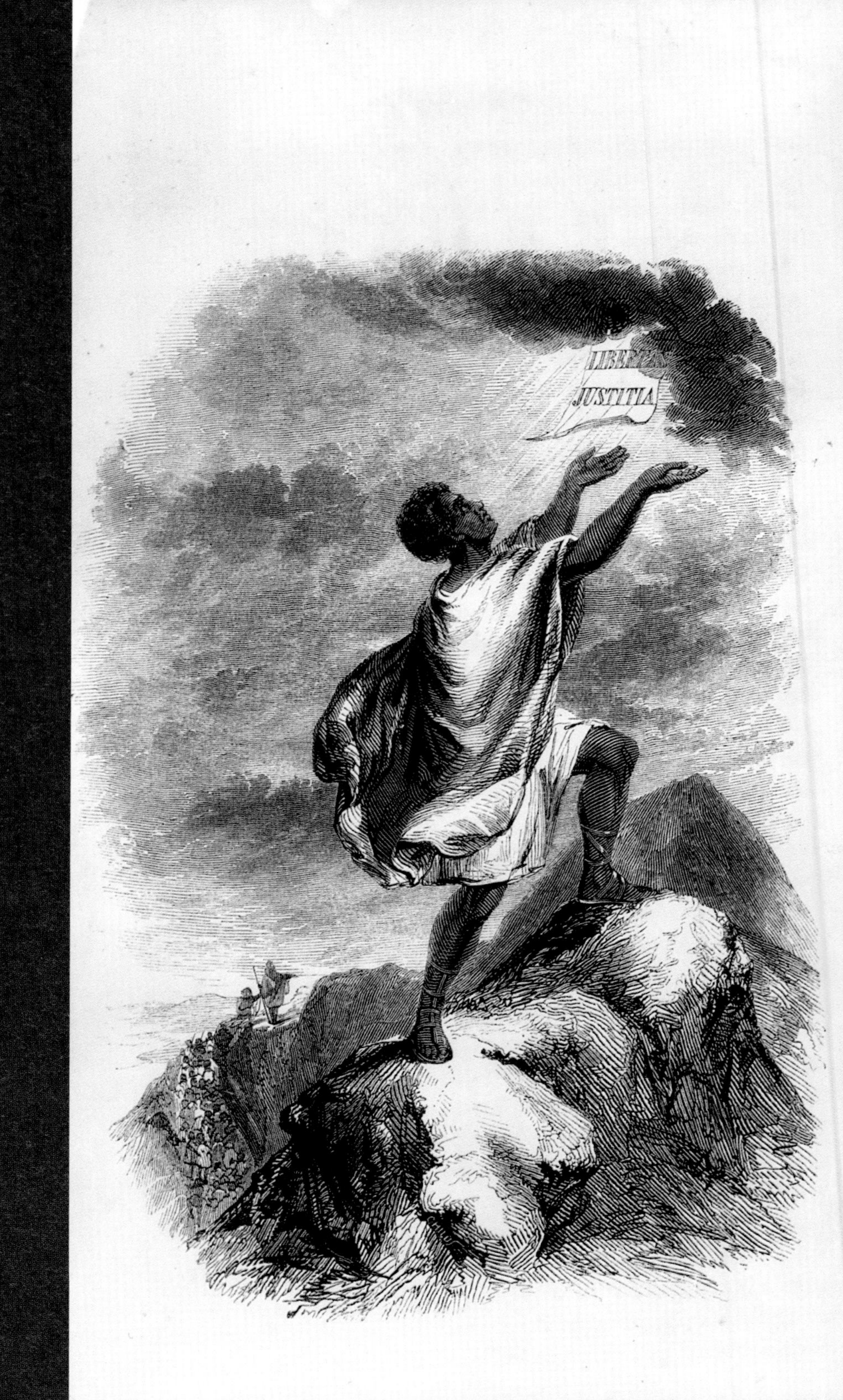
JUSTITIA

WALKER'S

A P P E A L,

With a Brief Sketch of his Life.

BY

HENRY HIGHLAND GARNET.

AND ALSO

GARNET'S ADDRESS

TO THE SLAVES OF THE UNITED STATES OF AMERICA.

NEW-YORK:

Printed by J. H. Tobitt, 9 Spruce-st.

1848.

PREVIOUS: *David Walker's Appeal* (1829). Written by a free Black abolitionist in Boston and smuggled into the South in sailors' clothing, *Walker's Appeal* was a call to arms that condemned slavery as a moral abomination, urging the enslaved to rise up against their slaveholders.

OPPOSITE: At Cumberland Landing in Virginia, self-emancipated men, women, and children gather in front of a building in a Union army encampment. Labeled "contraband of war," the formerly enslaved people undermined the Confederacy by seizing their own freedom. Fleeing plantations, aiding Union forces, and reclaiming their stolen labor, enslaved people played a pivotal role in bringing about the end of slavery.

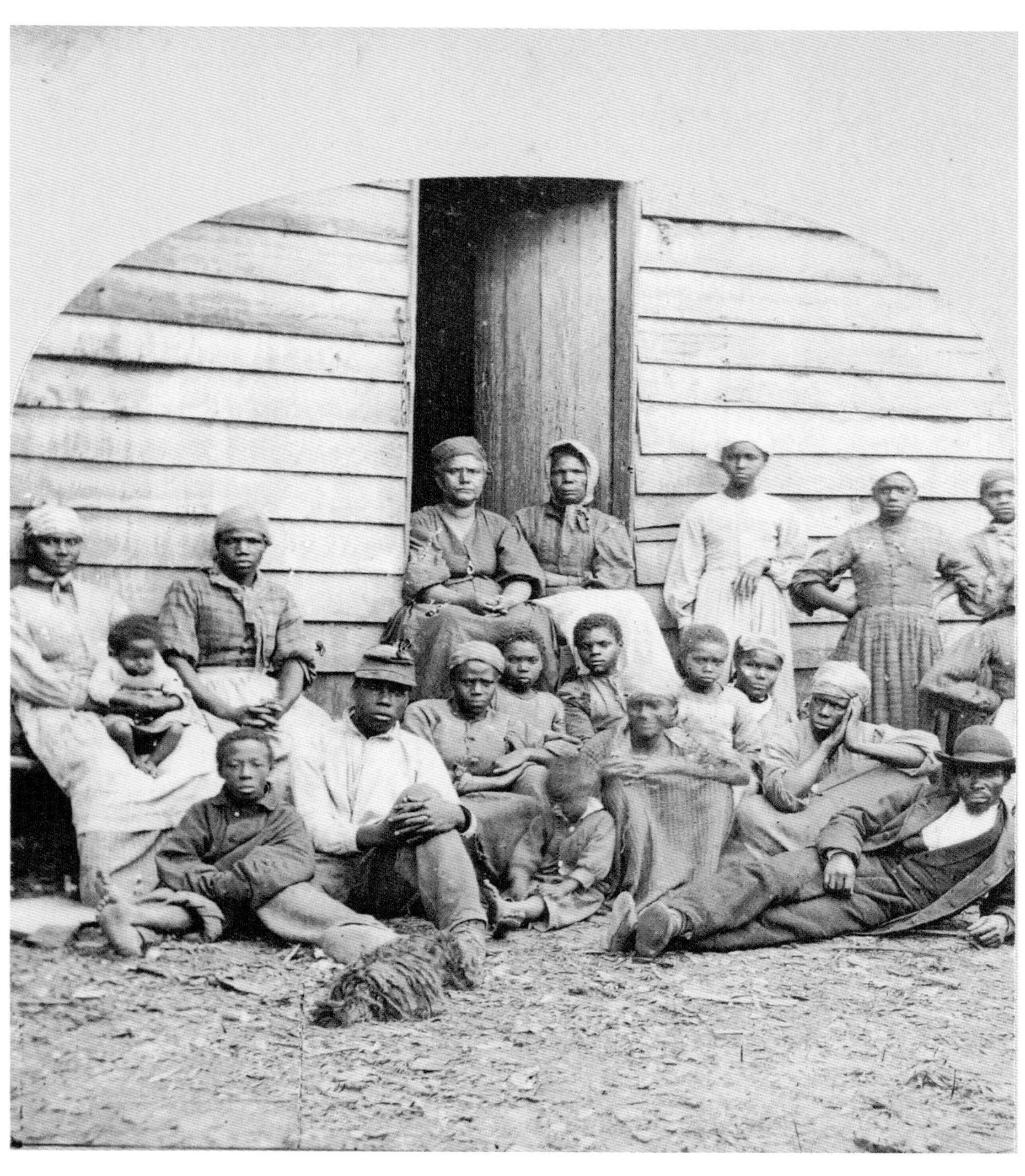

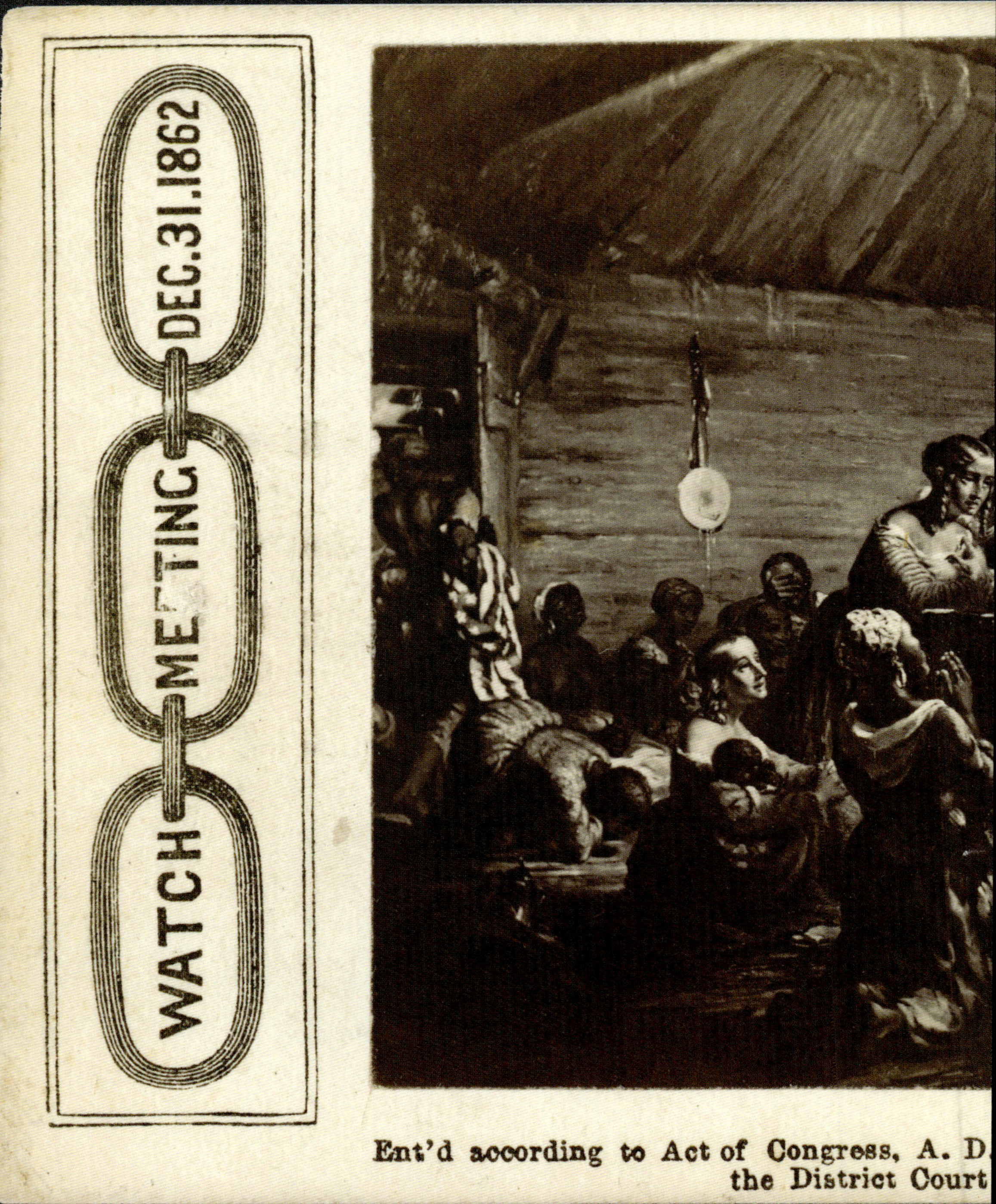

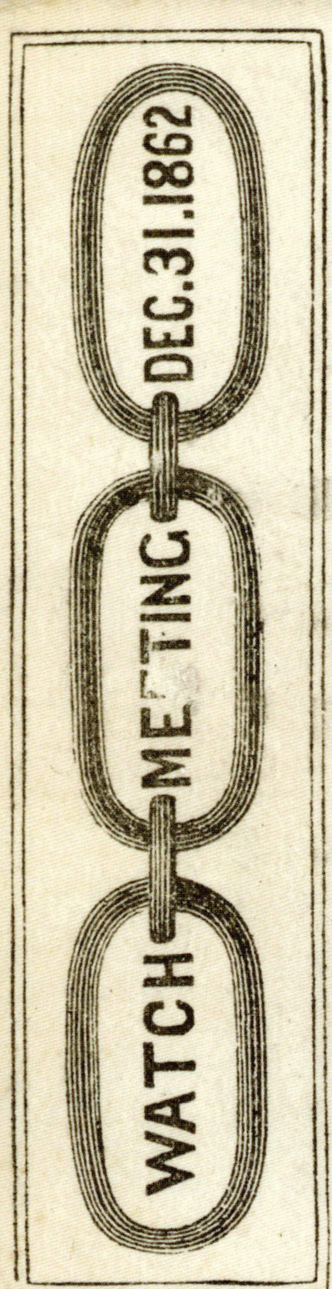

Ent'd according to Act of Congress, A. D.
the District Court

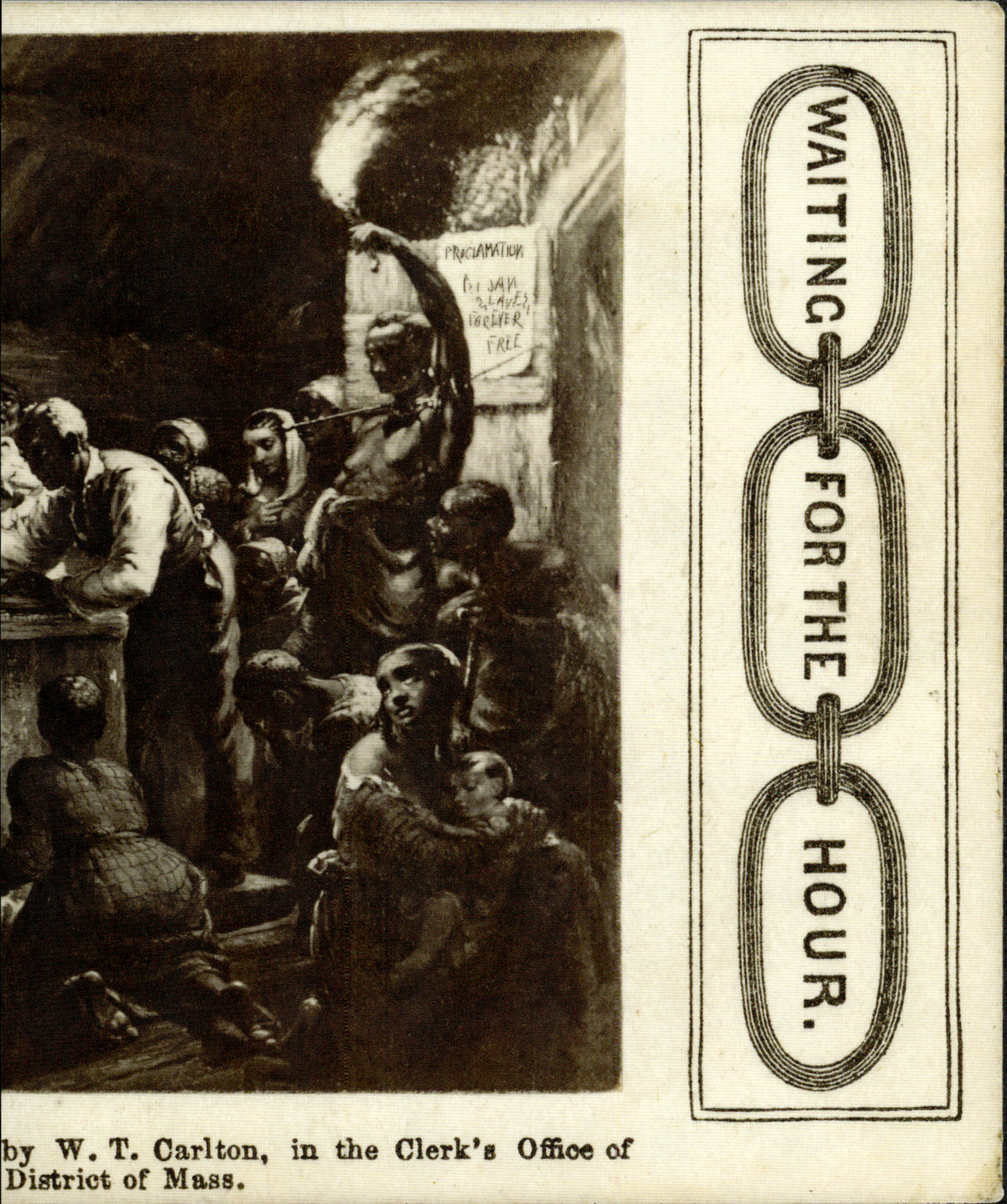

by W. T. Carlton, in the Clerk's Office of
District of Mass.

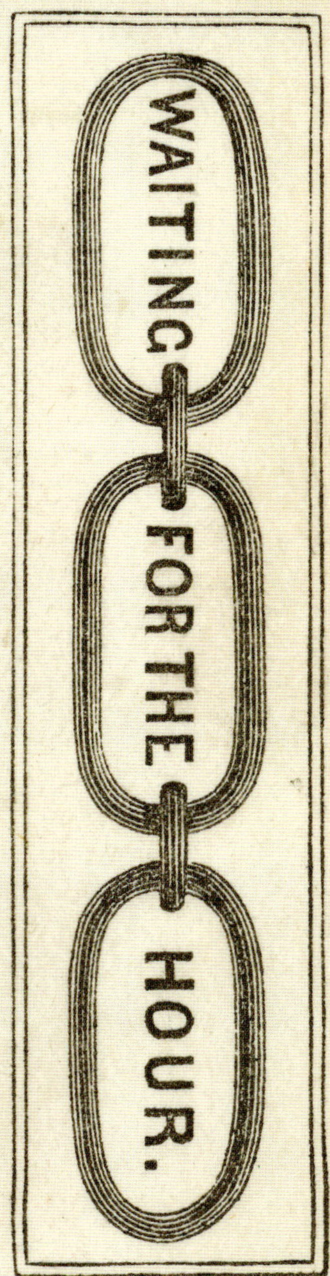

This carte-de-viste depicts Black families gathered in churches on the eve of 1863 pray ng and waiting as midnight approached, marking the moment when the Emancipation Proclamation would take effect.

The sacred occasion of gathering on New Year's Eve is still commemorated in Black churches throughout the nation, in recognition of those first emancipatory gatherings.

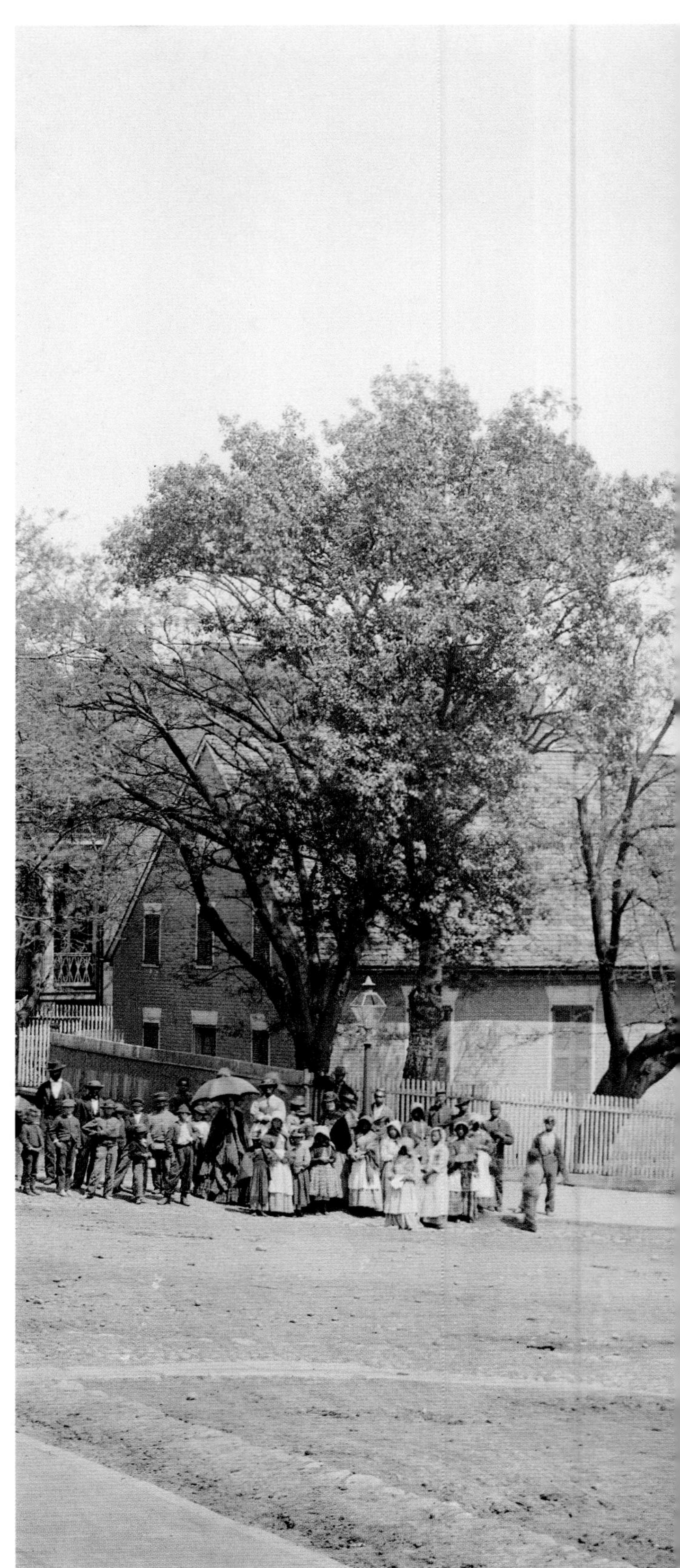

Black congregants pose outside Richmond, Virginia's First African Baptist Church after the city fell to Union troops. Once forced to worship under white supervision, Black members used the grounds after emancipation as a site for celebrating the end of slavery and the annual remembrance of Emancipation Day.

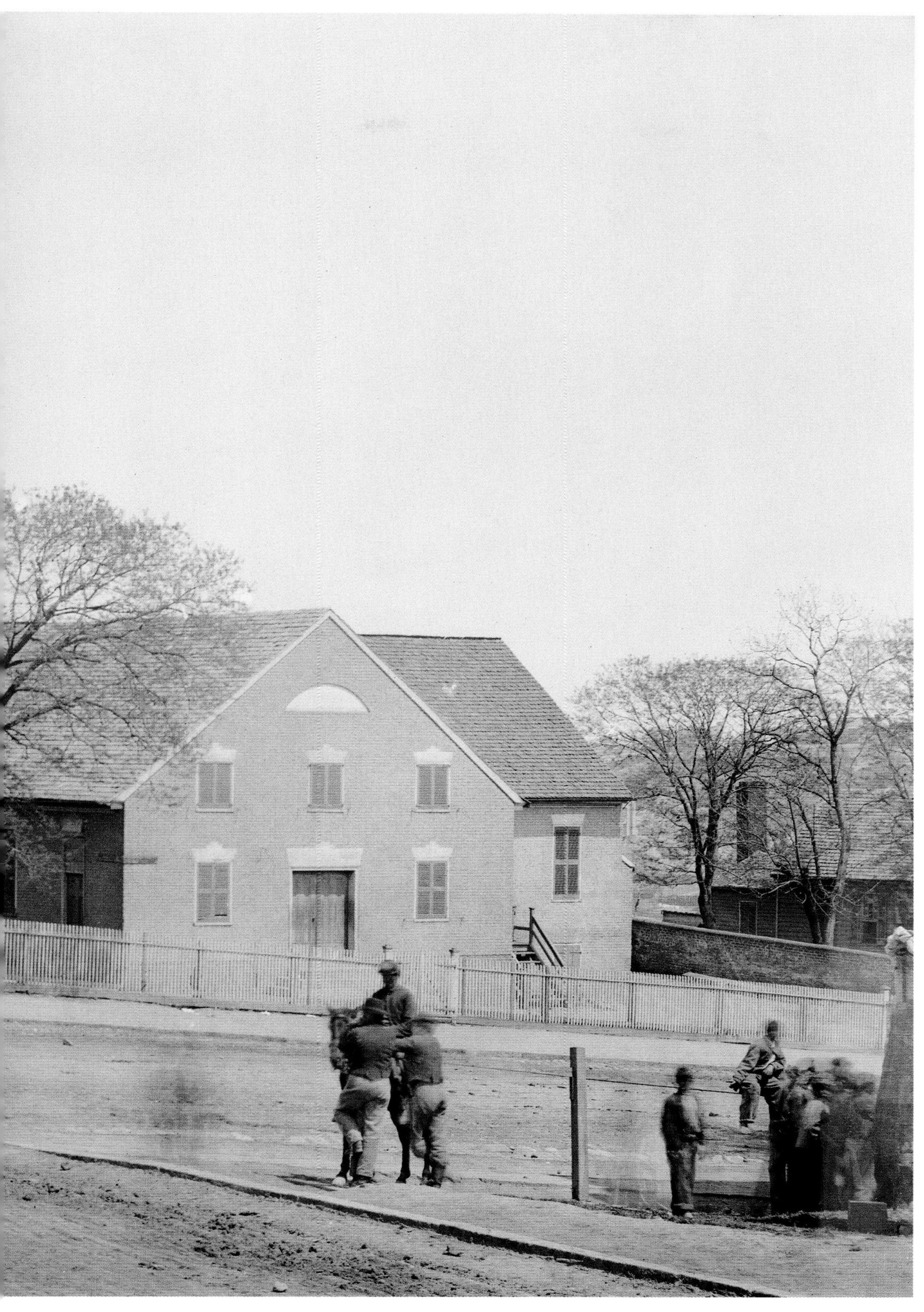

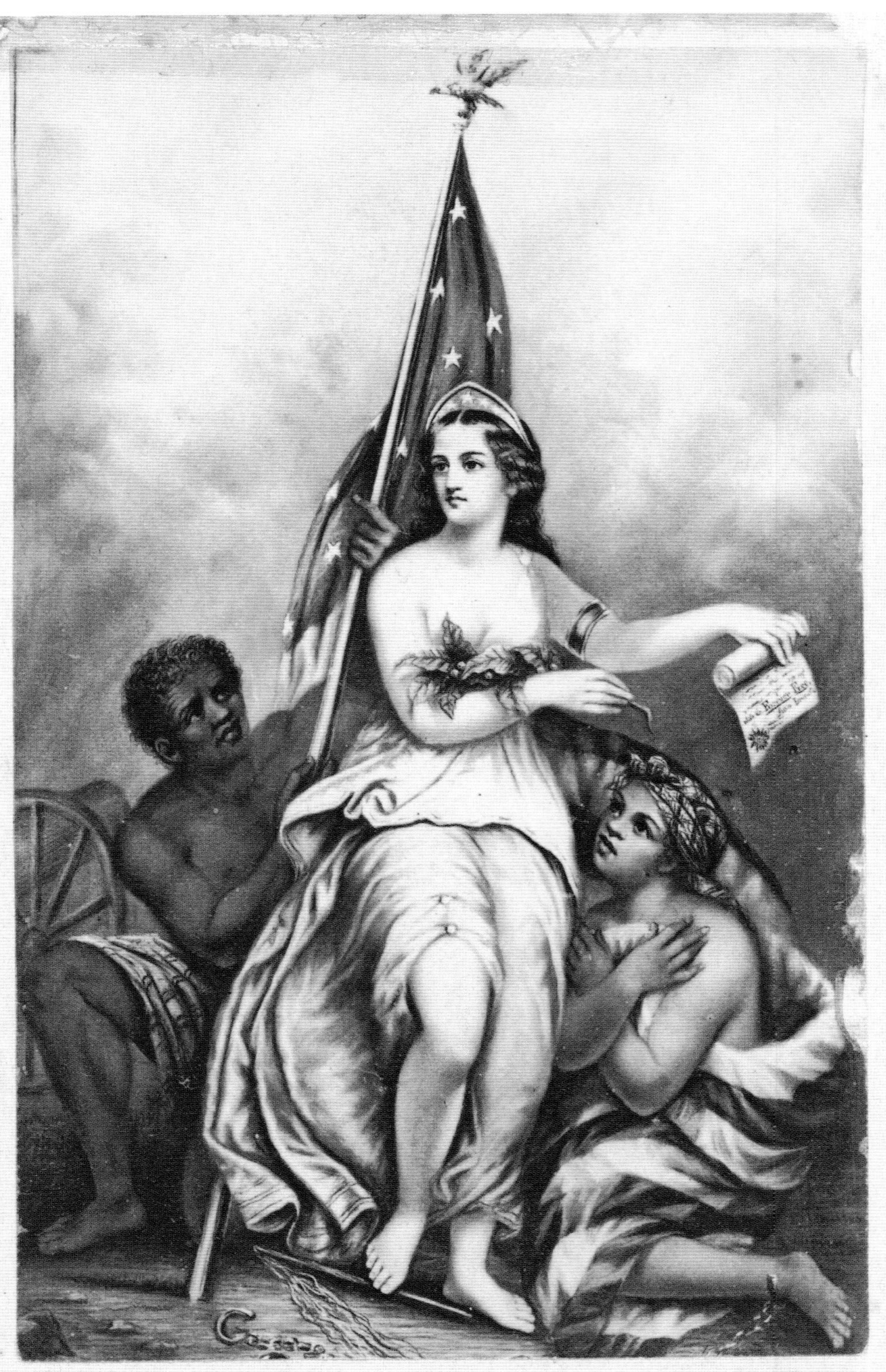

G. G. Fish, Pinx. J. P. Soule, Photo.

Entered according to Act of Congress, in the year 1863, by John Sowle, in the clerk's office of the District Court for the District of Massachusetts.

EMANCIPATION.

Published by John Sowle. 14 Summer St., Boston.

OPPOSITE: In this allegorical image, Columbia, symbolic of the United States, holds the Emancipation Proclamation above kneeling figures of an enslaved man who is holding the flag aloft and an enslaved woman draped in another flag, as chains fall away from their limbs. Produced in 1863, the image casts emancipation as patriotic and moral, aligning the cause of Black freedom with the nation's broadening definition of liberty.

FOLLOWING: This 1865 engraving by Thomas Nast commemorates the end of slavery at the close of the Civil War. At its center, a freed family gathers around a warm stove beneath portraits of Lincoln and symbols of freedom. Surrounding scenes contrast the brutality of slavery with Nast's hopeful vision for Black life after emancipation—one shaped by family, education, labor, and dignity.

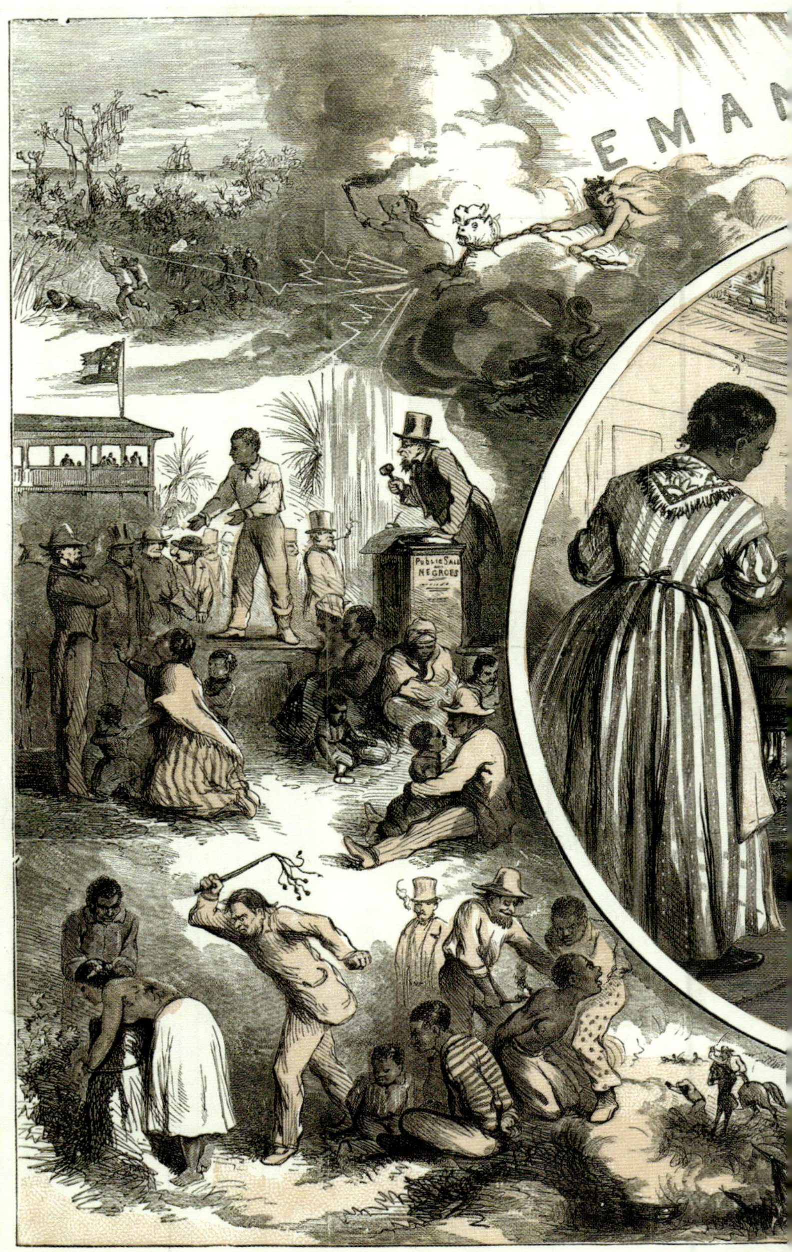

King & Baird, Printers, 607 Sansom Street, Philadelphia.

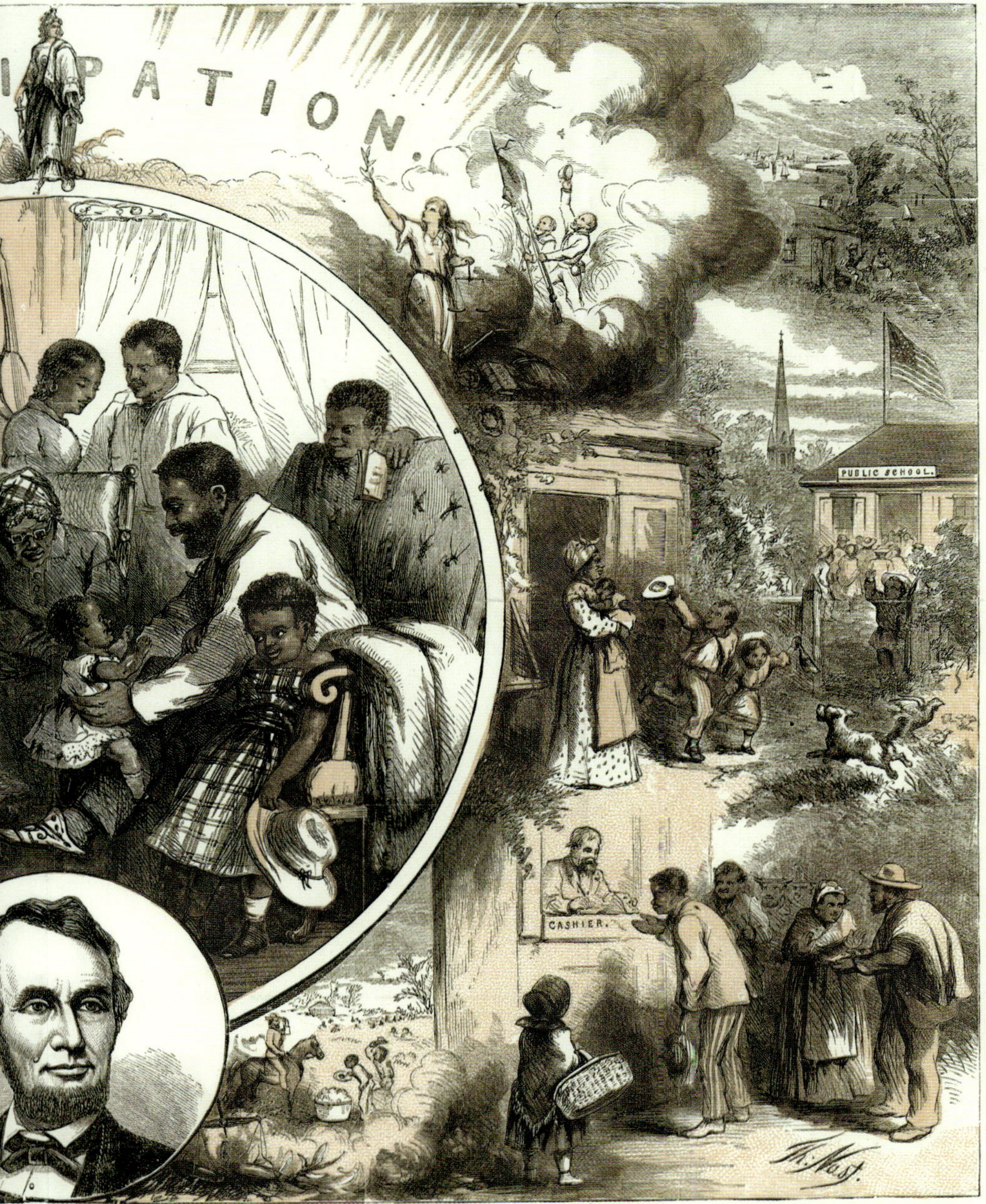

Entered according to Act of Congress, in the year 1865, by J. W. UMPEHENT, in the Clerk's Office of the District Court of the United States, for the Eastern District of Pennsylvania.

Published by S. BOTT. No. 43 South Third Street, Philadelphia, Penna.

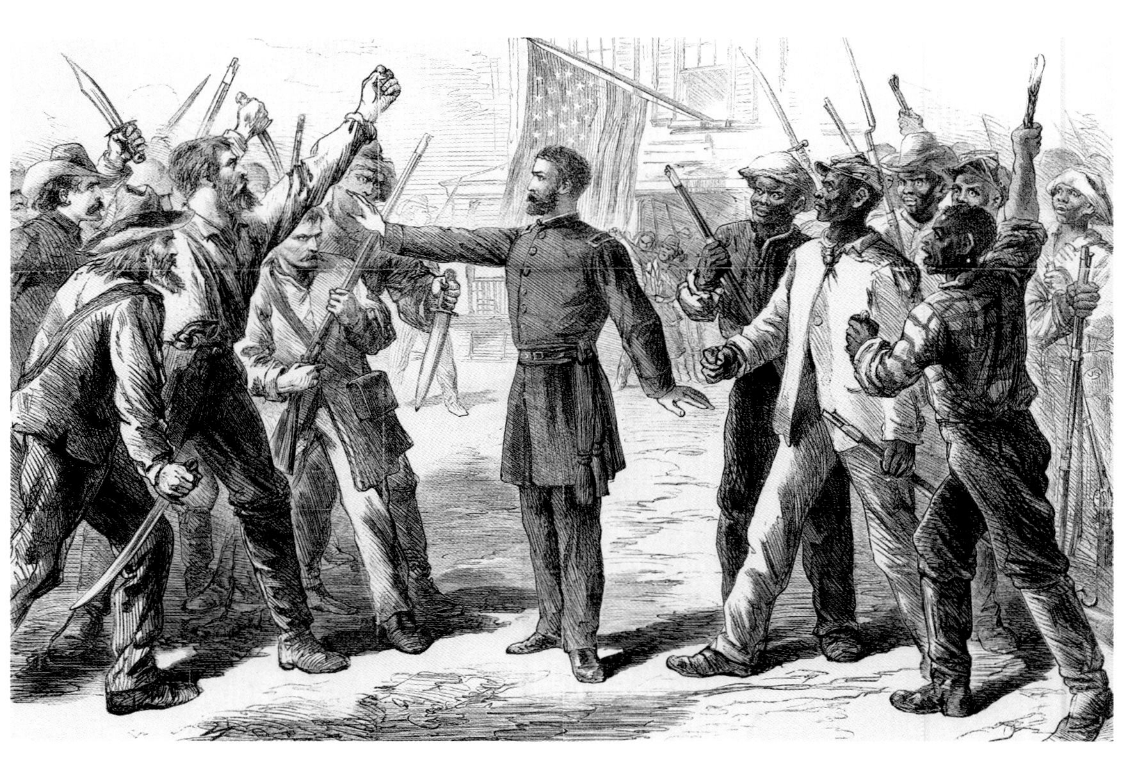

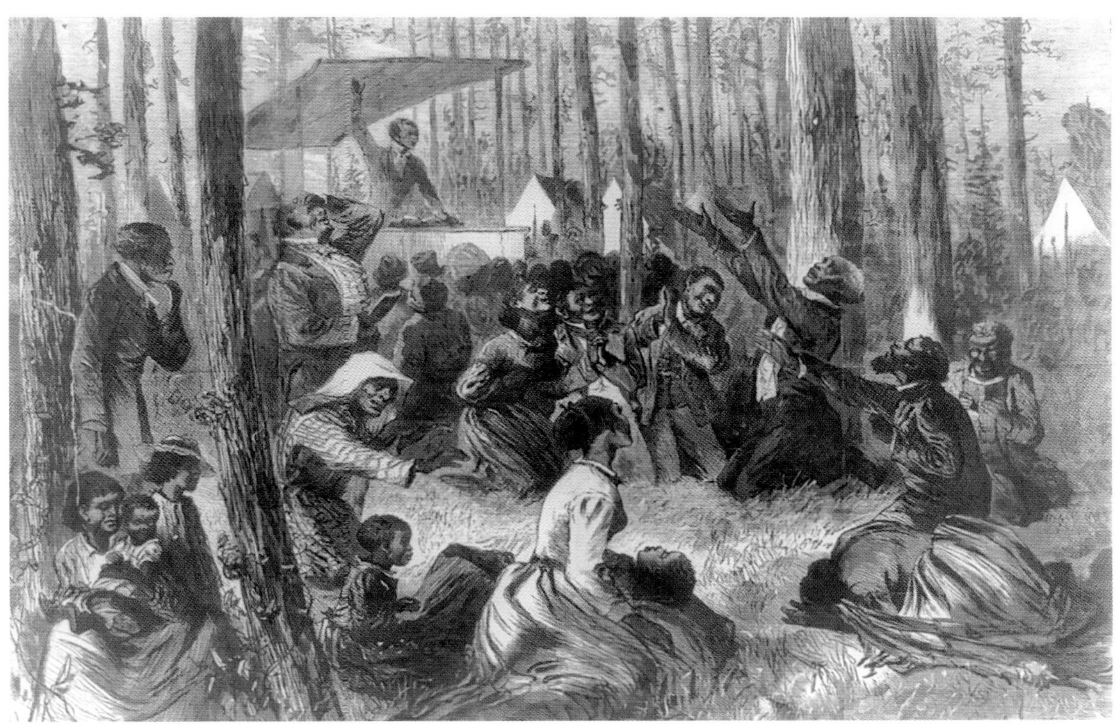

OPPOSITE: In this 1868 cartoon, a Freedmen's Bureau agent is shown mediating between formerly enslaved people and white Southerners, depicted here as equally ungovernable. Rather than honoring emancipation as a step toward Black autonomy, the image reveals the paternalistic resistance to Black freedom that persisted after the war.

ABOVE: An 1872 illustration of a camp meeting where Black worshipers gather in the woods for prayer, song, and sermons. Such gatherings were sites of spiritual resistance and communal renewal. For many Black worshippers, emancipation was not just a political shift, but also the fulfillment of a divine promise.

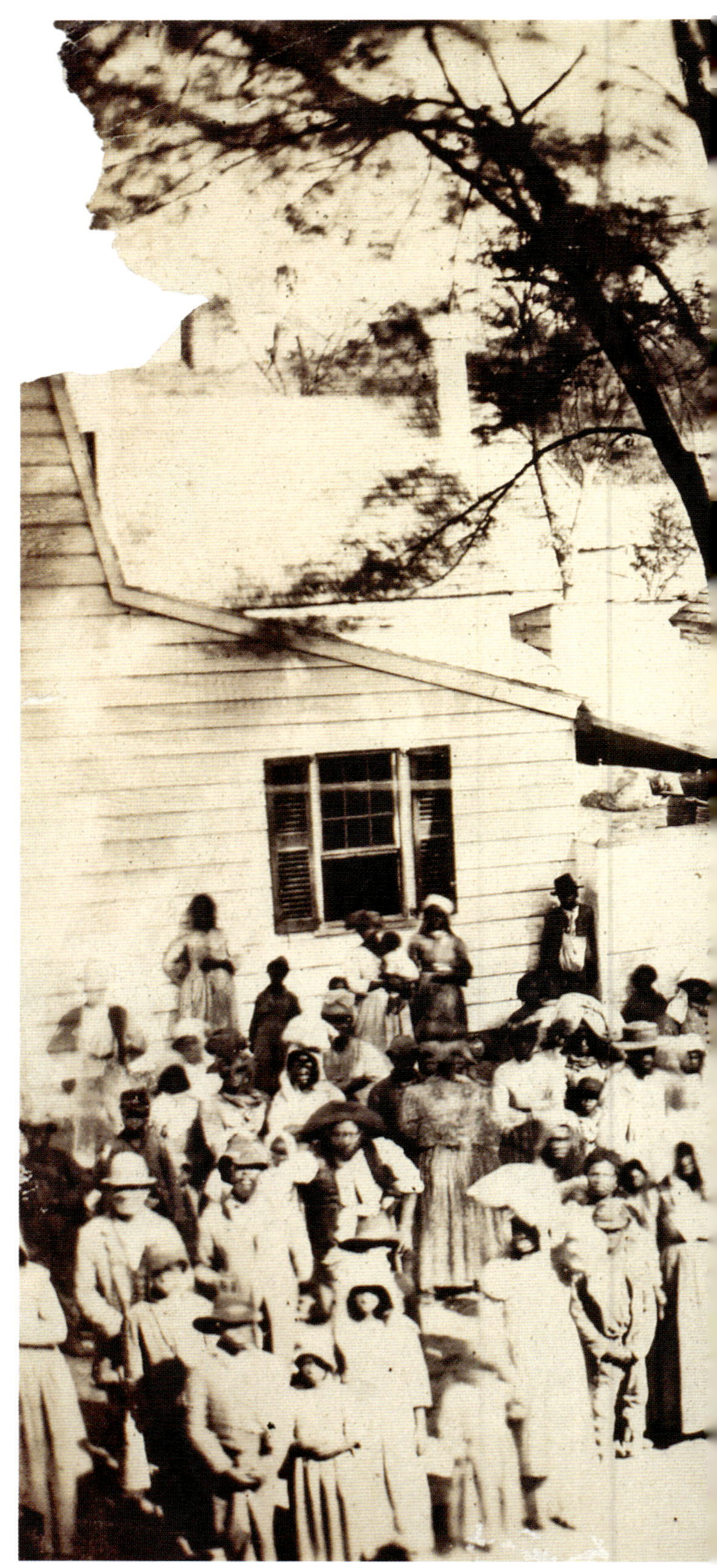

Formerly enslaved people once held in bondage by James Joyner Smith, a South Carolina slaveholder who fled Beaufort as Union troops approached. Holding their belongings, and surrounded by their kin and community, they prepare to seize their freedom.

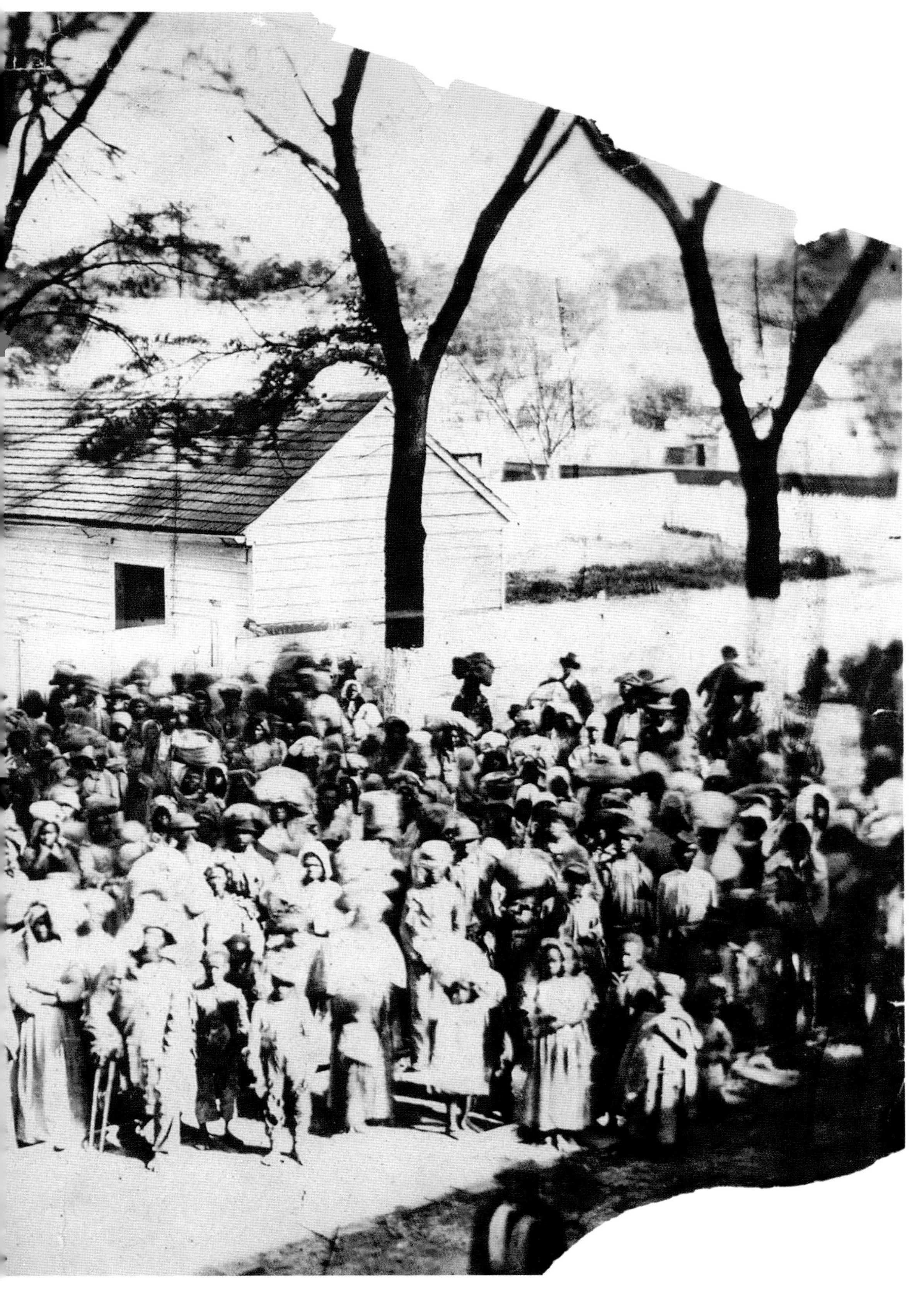

A portrait of a Black washerwoman with a hand-painted American flag pinned to her dress. She was working for Union troops near Richmond, Virginia, during the Civil War. Washerwomen were essential to both the Union war effort and to the long story of Black labor in America. Washerwomen used their own tools and drew on their own skills to clean, dry, and press clothing. Washerwomen were more than caretakers of clothes: They were entrepreneurs, cultural stewards, and survivors, sustaining armies while building lives in the shadow of the war and freedom's fragile beginnings.

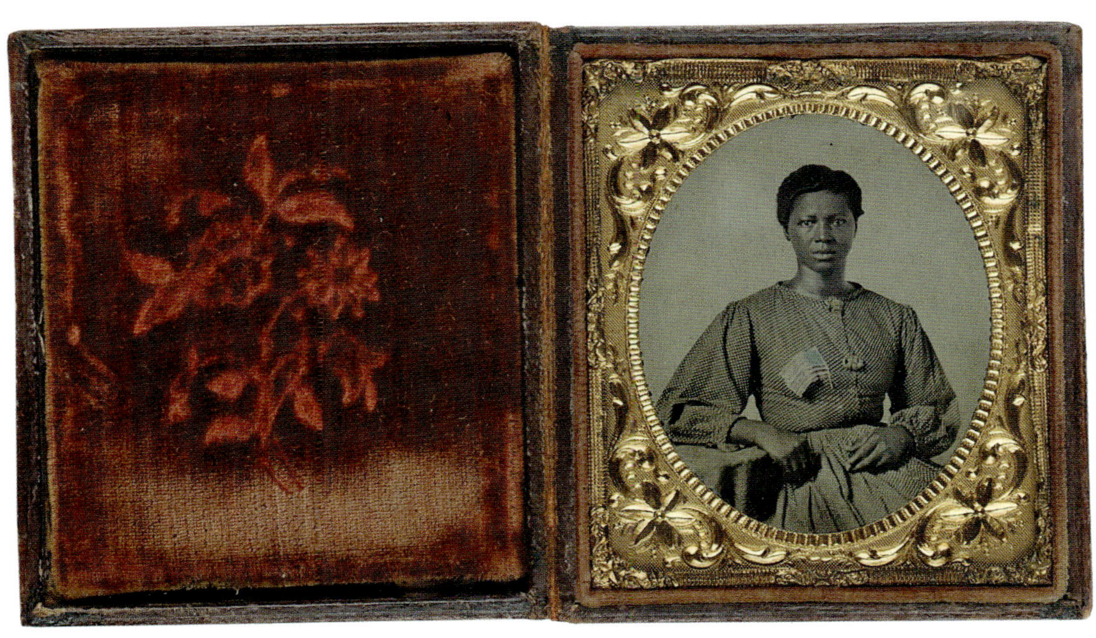

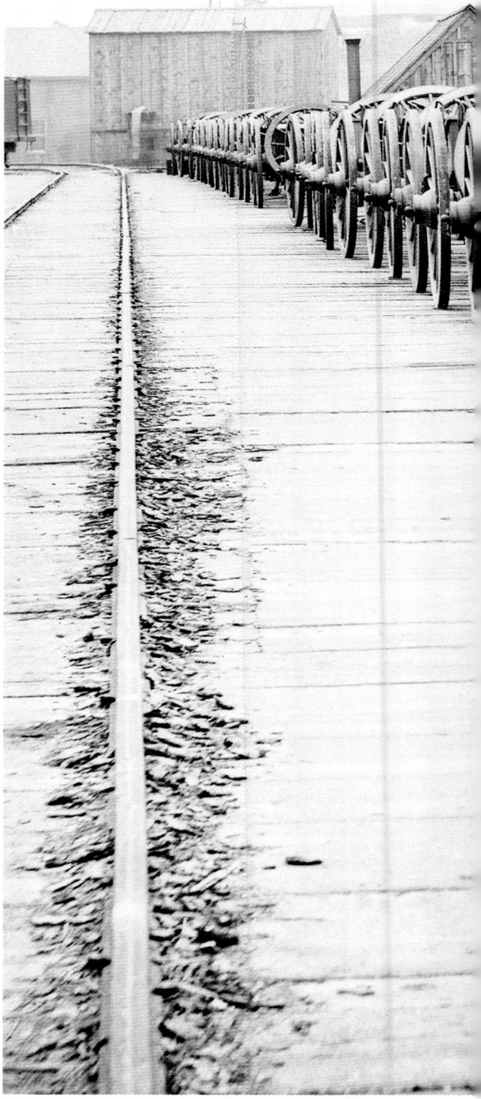

RIGHT: A Black soldier stands guard beside cannons at City Point, Virginia. The soldier's presence here reflects the vital roles Black troops played in securing Union positions, defending supply lines, camps, and the hard-won ground of freedom.

FOLLOWING: At City Point, Virginia, Black soldiers are seated on Union supply wagons in one of the Civil War's military hubs. Though previously excluded from service, Black men became essential to the war effort and the struggle for Black freedom.

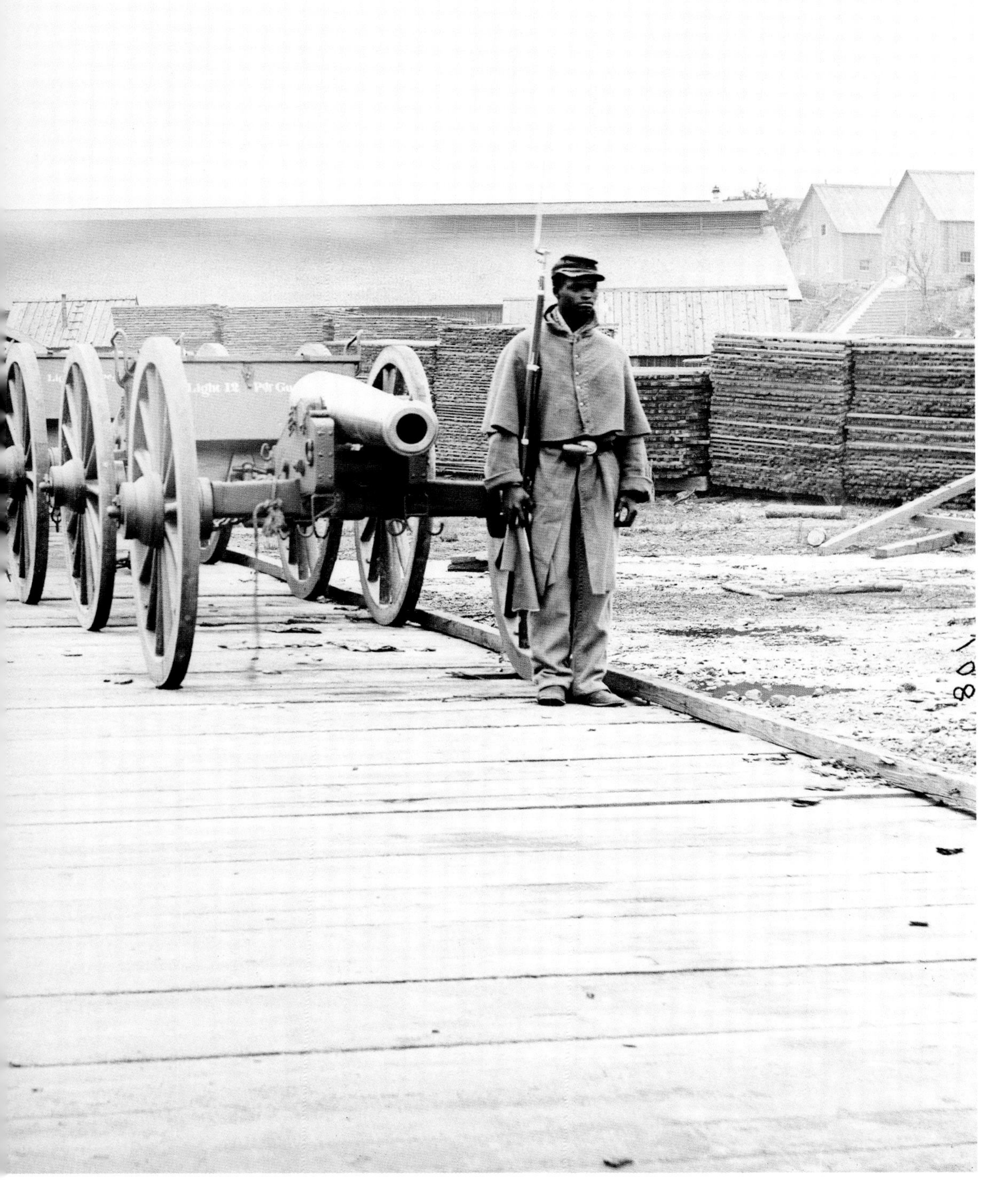

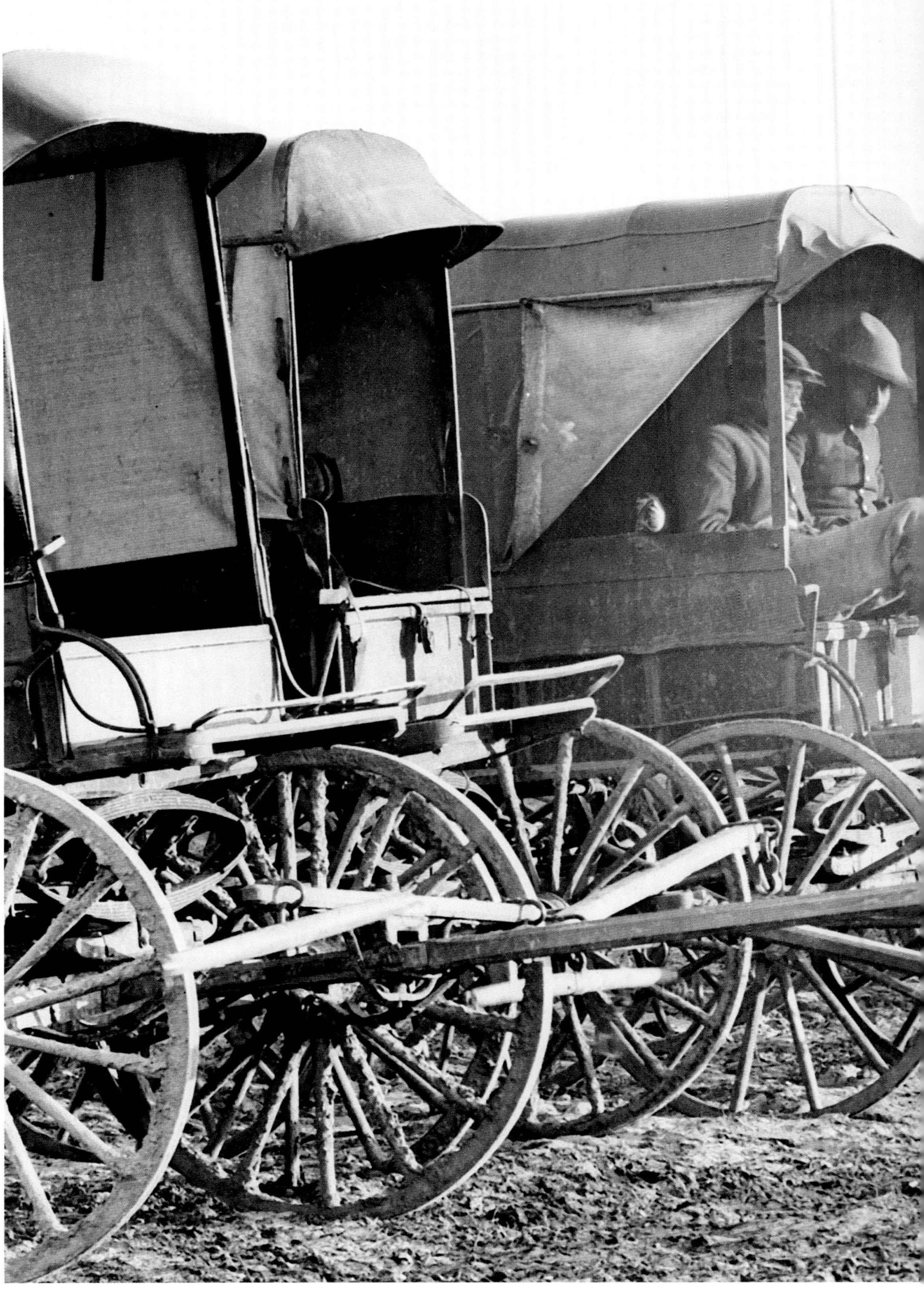

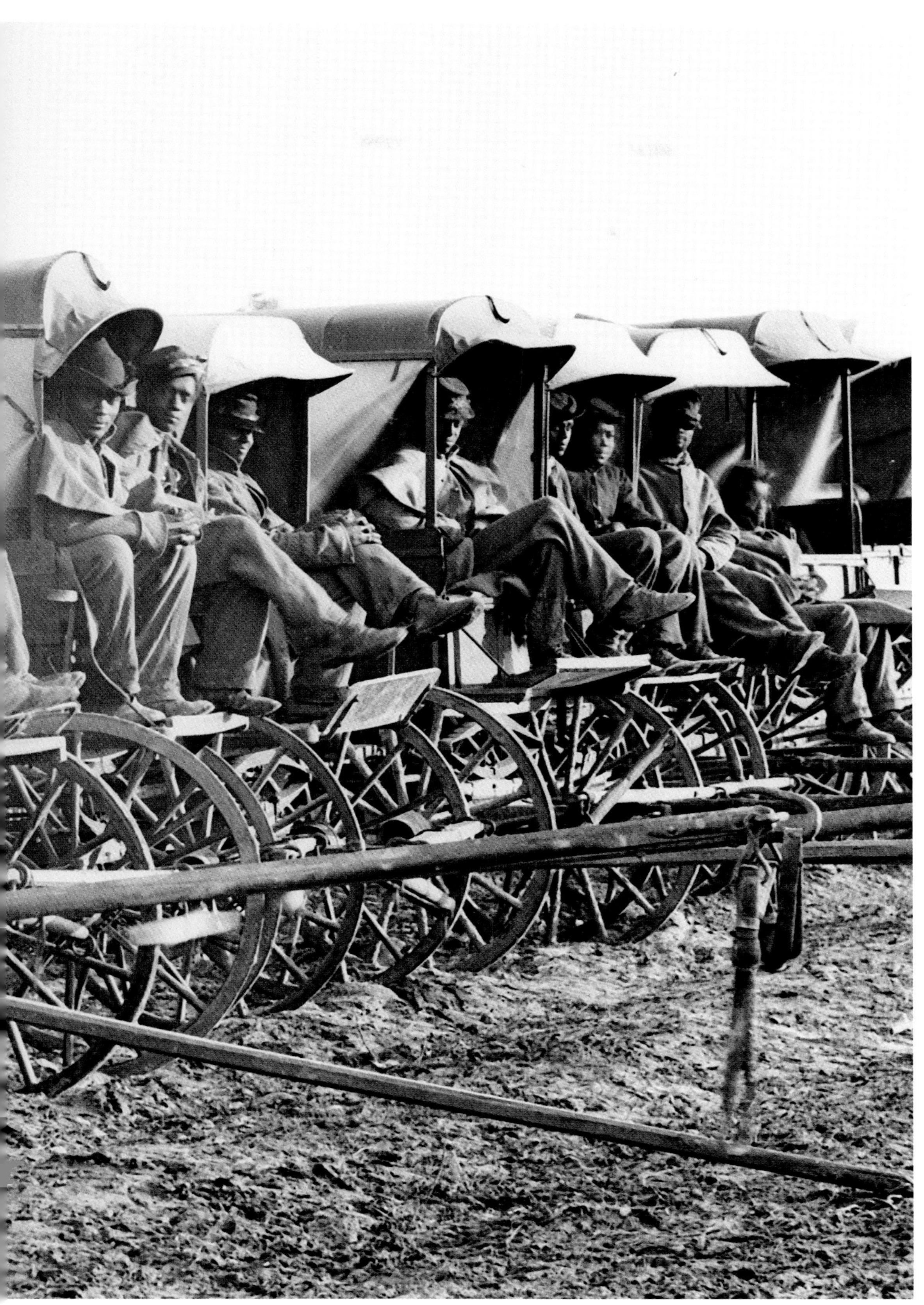

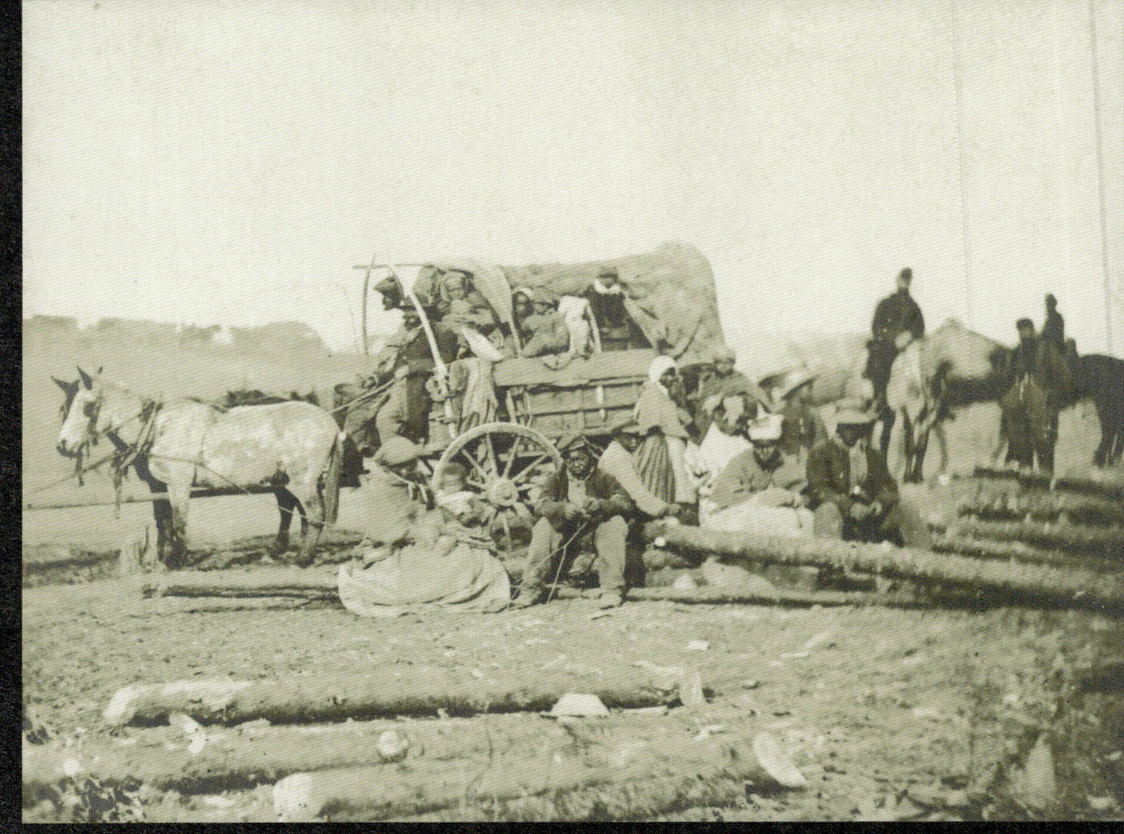

This photo shows once-enslaved men, women, and children arriving in a tattered, mule-drawn covered wagon at Union lines in the midst of the Civil War. They fled from slavery, seeking freedom and declaring their own emancipation. Known as "contraband of war," those that escaped bondage not only secured their freedom but also strengthened the Union cause, and, in the process, reshaped the course of the Civil War. Artist Alfred Waud sketched this moment, and his drawing, *An Arrival in Camp-Under the Proclamation of Emancipation*, was published on January 31, 1863, in *Harper's Weekly*. This image marked the beginning of a new chapter in the Civil War.

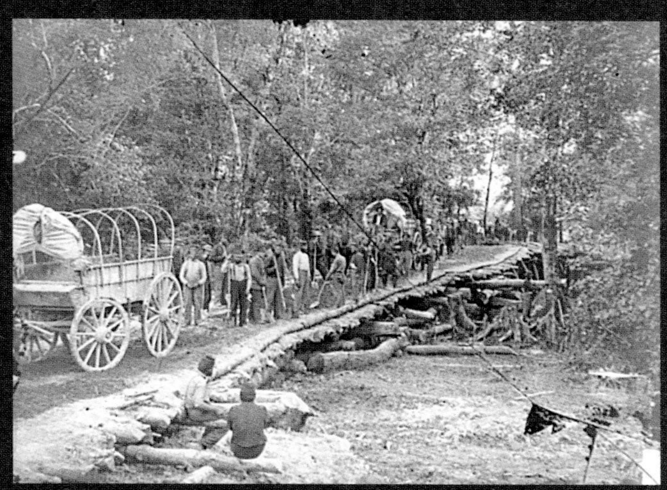

Throughout the war, Union Army engineers built temporary bridges like this one to allow troops to cross rivers where no bridge was present. During General William T. Sherman's March to the Sea, General Jefferson C. Davis ordered his troops to remove the temporary pontoon bridges over Ebenezer Creek in Georgia, causing hundreds of freed slaves—who were following the Union army—to drown.

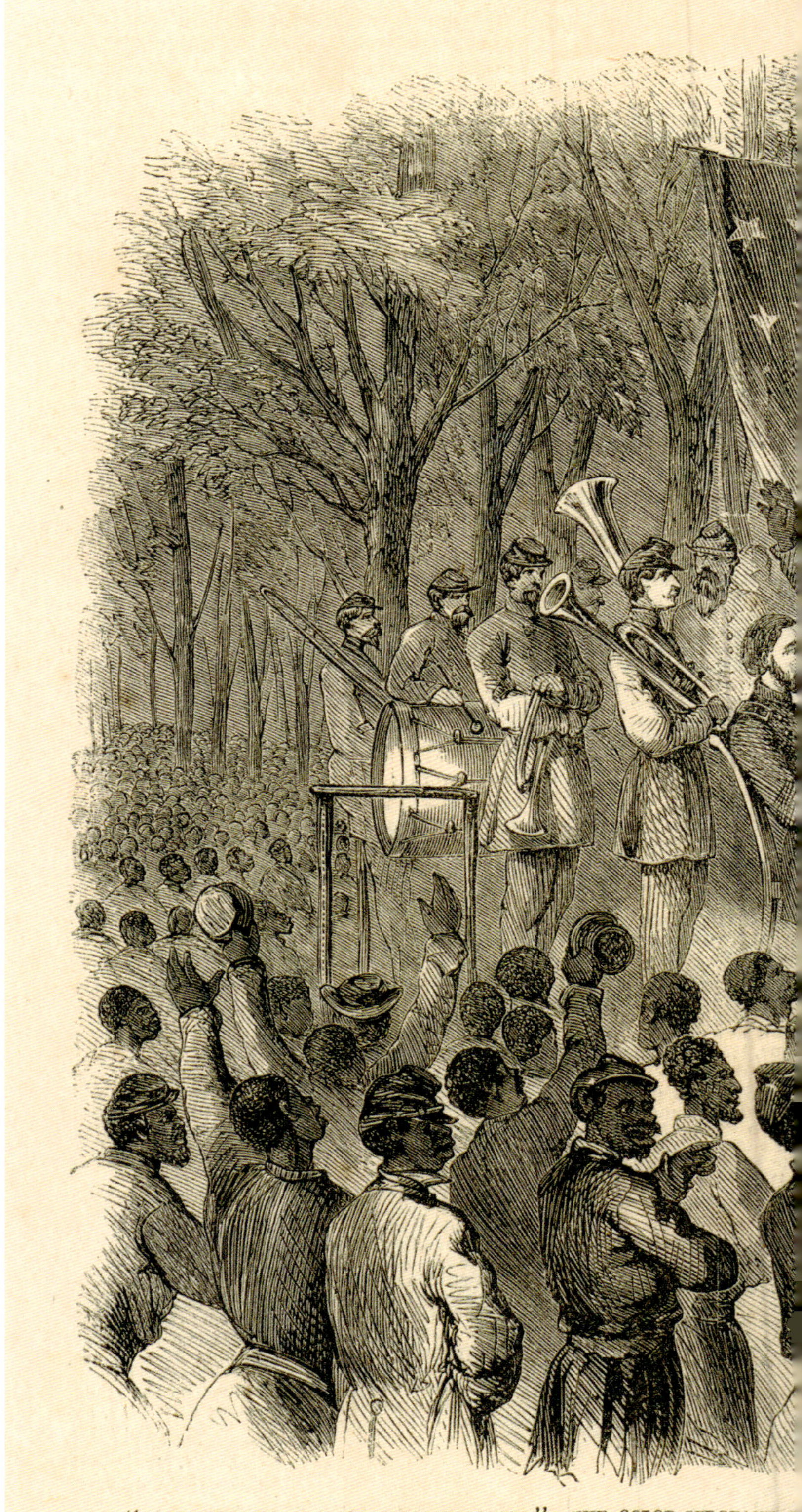

The sketch depicts January 1, 1863, the day the Emancipation Proclamation went into effect, when the Color Sergeant of the 1st South Carolina Colored Volunteers addressed his regiment after receiving the US flag at Smith's Plantation on Port Royal Island, South Carolina. Drawn from formerly enslaved men, the regiment stood as a powerful reminder of the meaning behind Black military service.

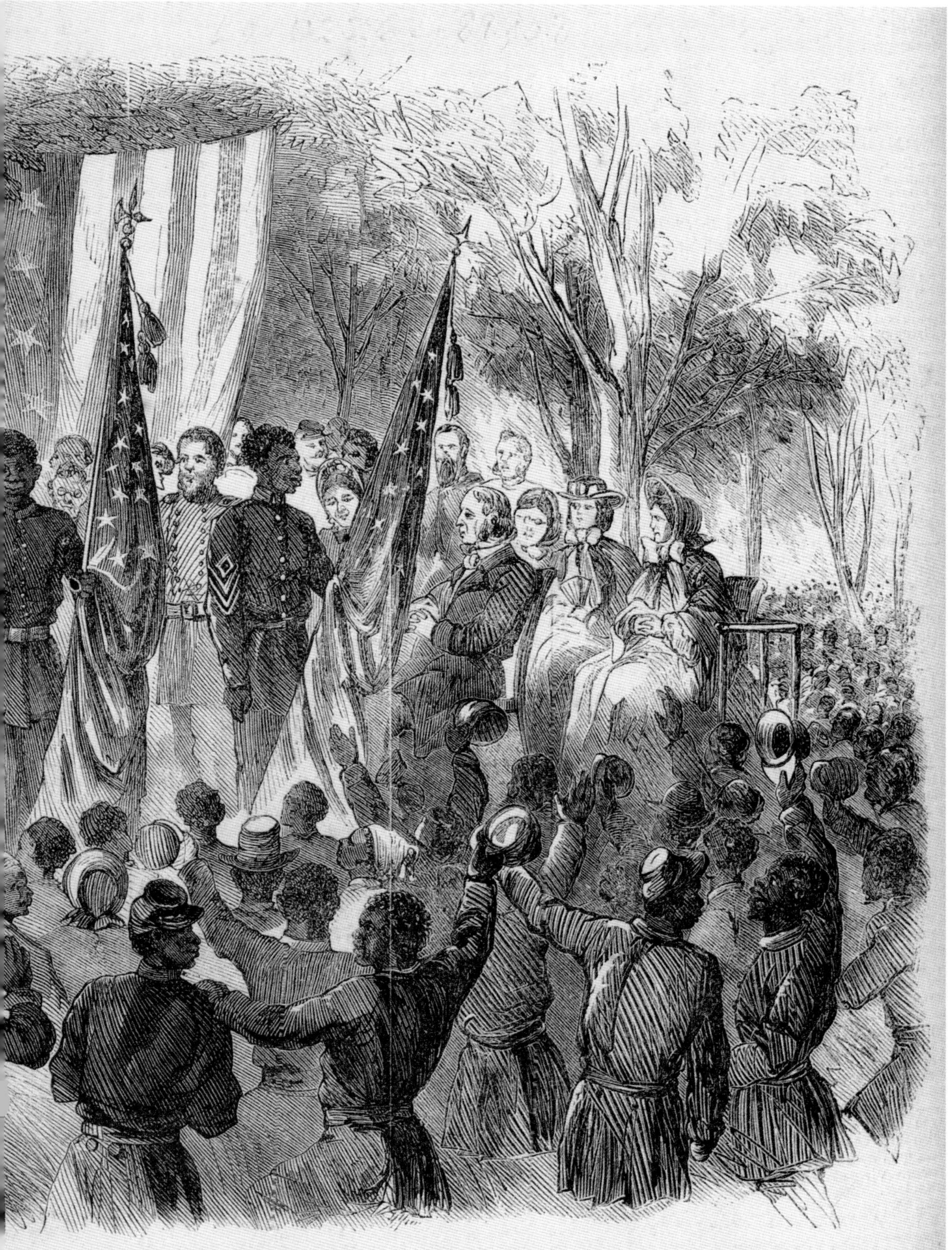

UTH CAROLINA (COLORED) VOLUNTEERS ADDRESSING THE REGIMENT, AFTER HAVING BEEN PRESENTED WITH THE
AL ISLAND, JANUARY 1.—FROM A SKETCH BY OUR SPECIAL ARTIST.—SEE PAGE 275.

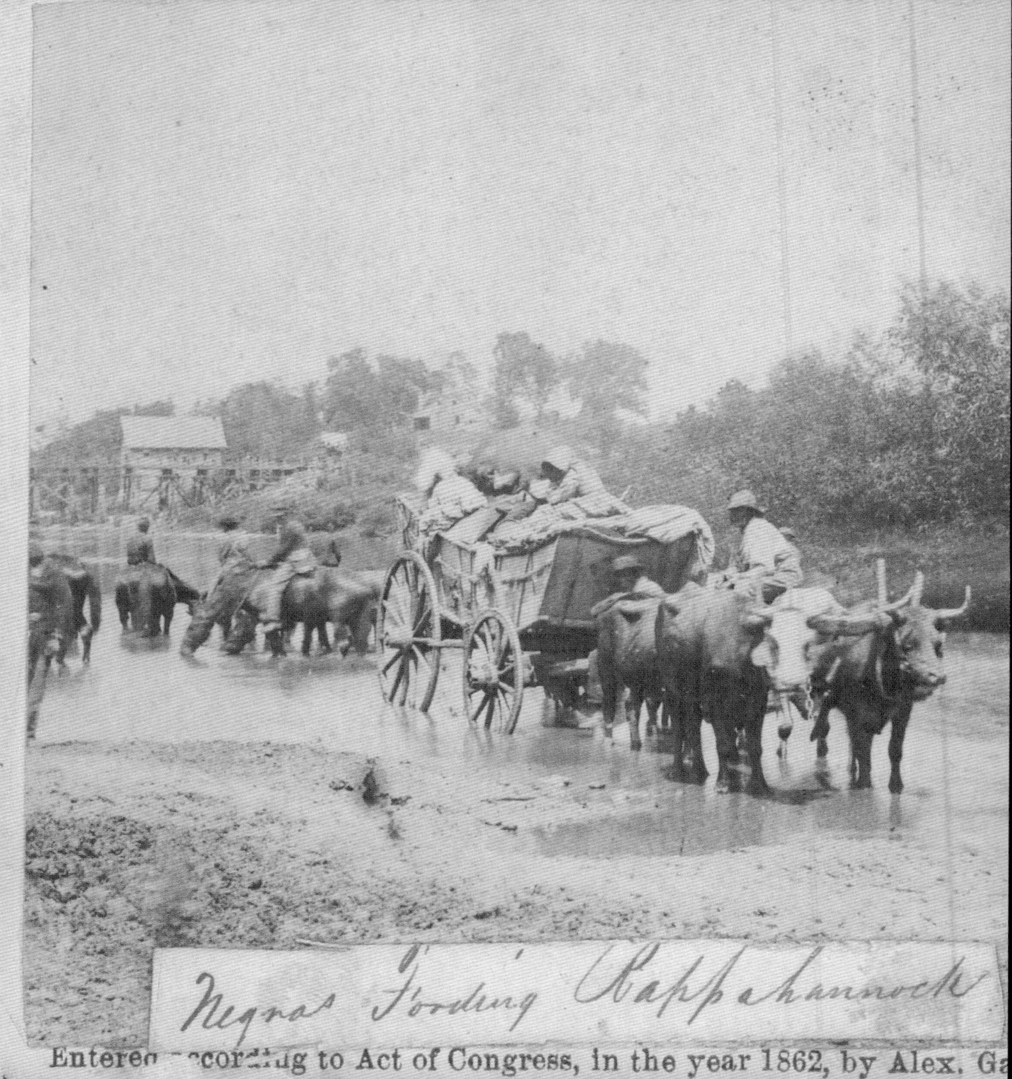
Negros Fording Rappahannock

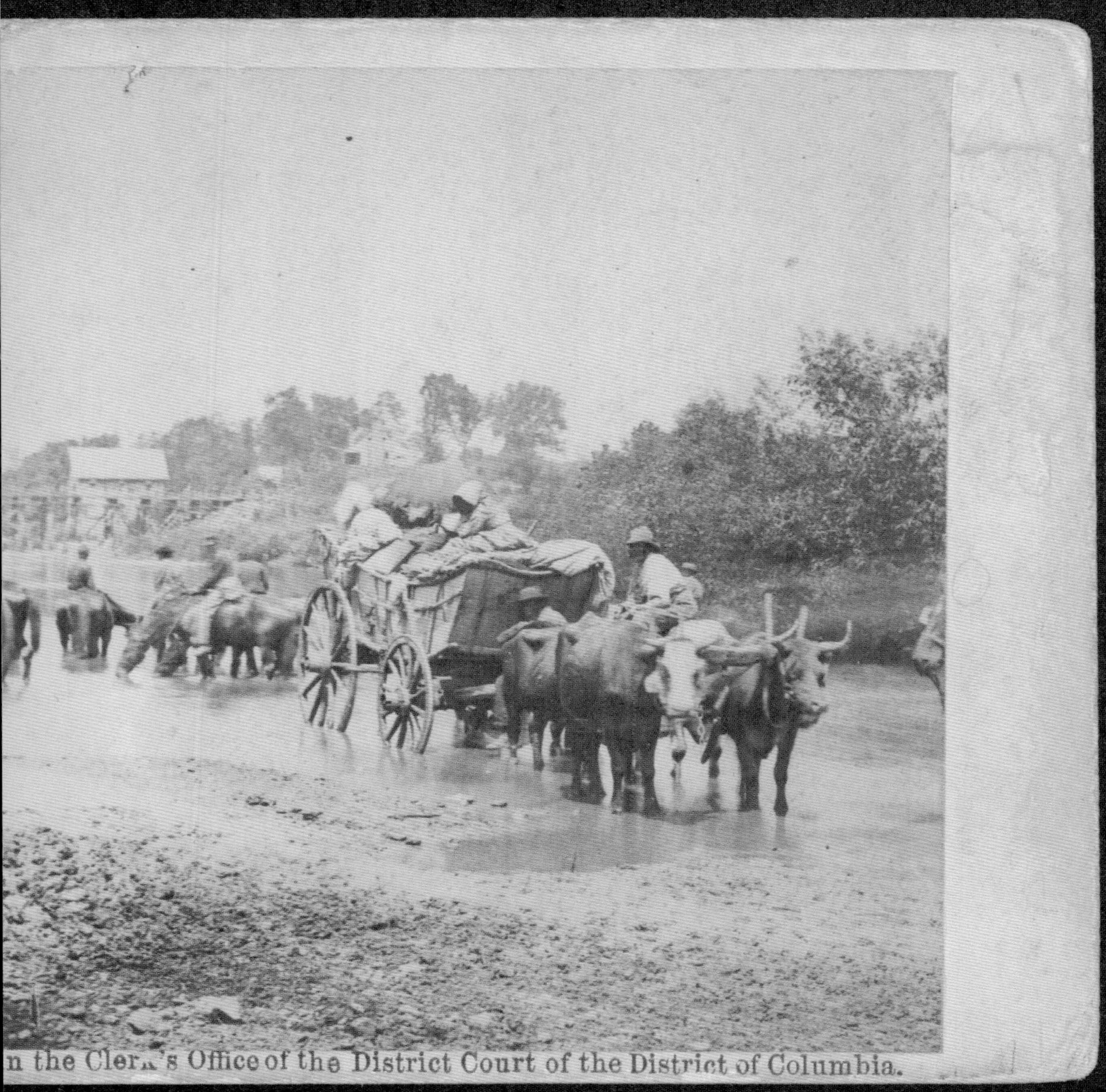

Escaping slavery in search of freedom, a group of Black Americans cross the Rappahannock River in Virginia by oxcart. Their journey reflects that of the countless enslaved people who took liberation into their own hands, risking their lives to reach Union lines during the Civil War.

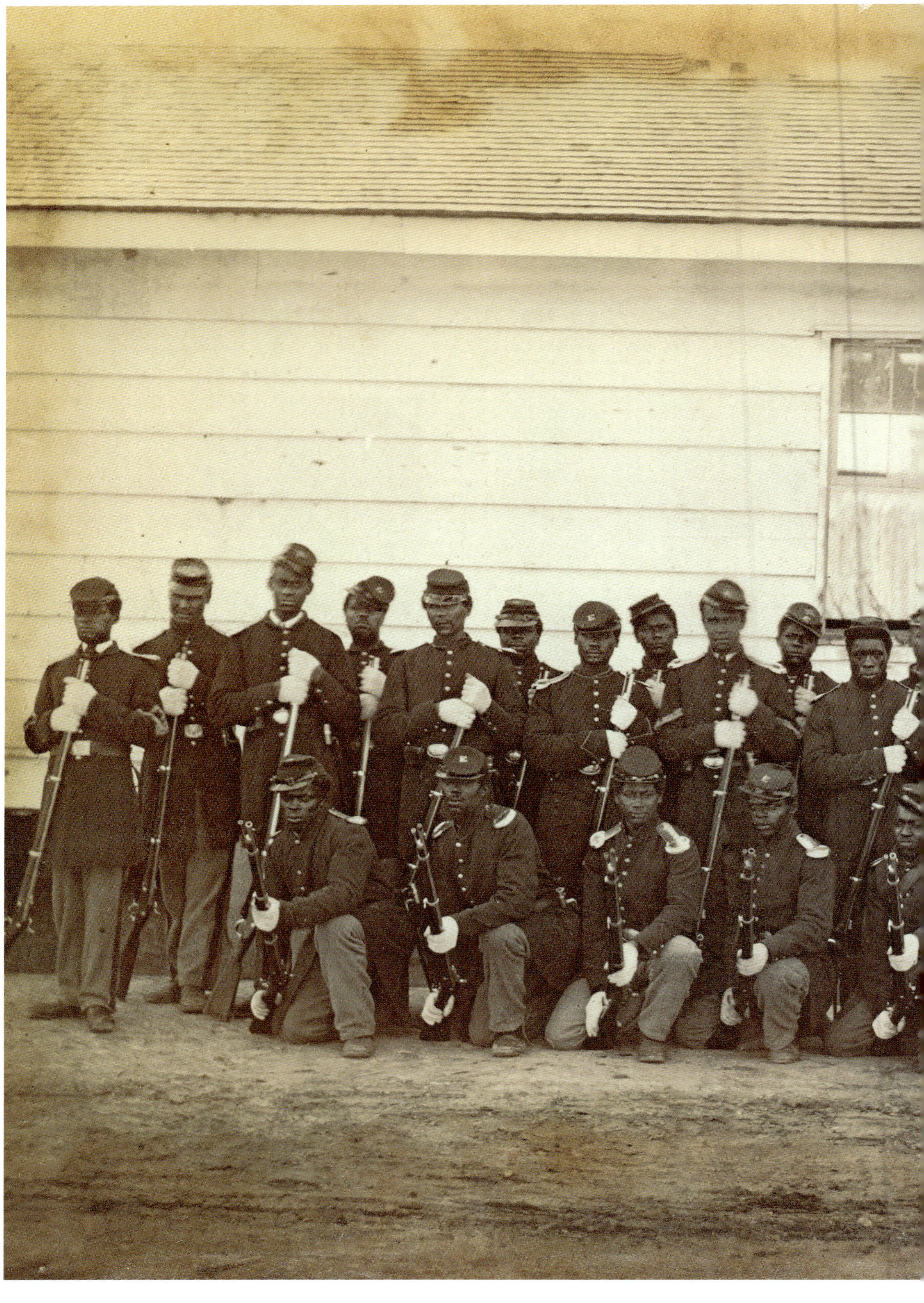

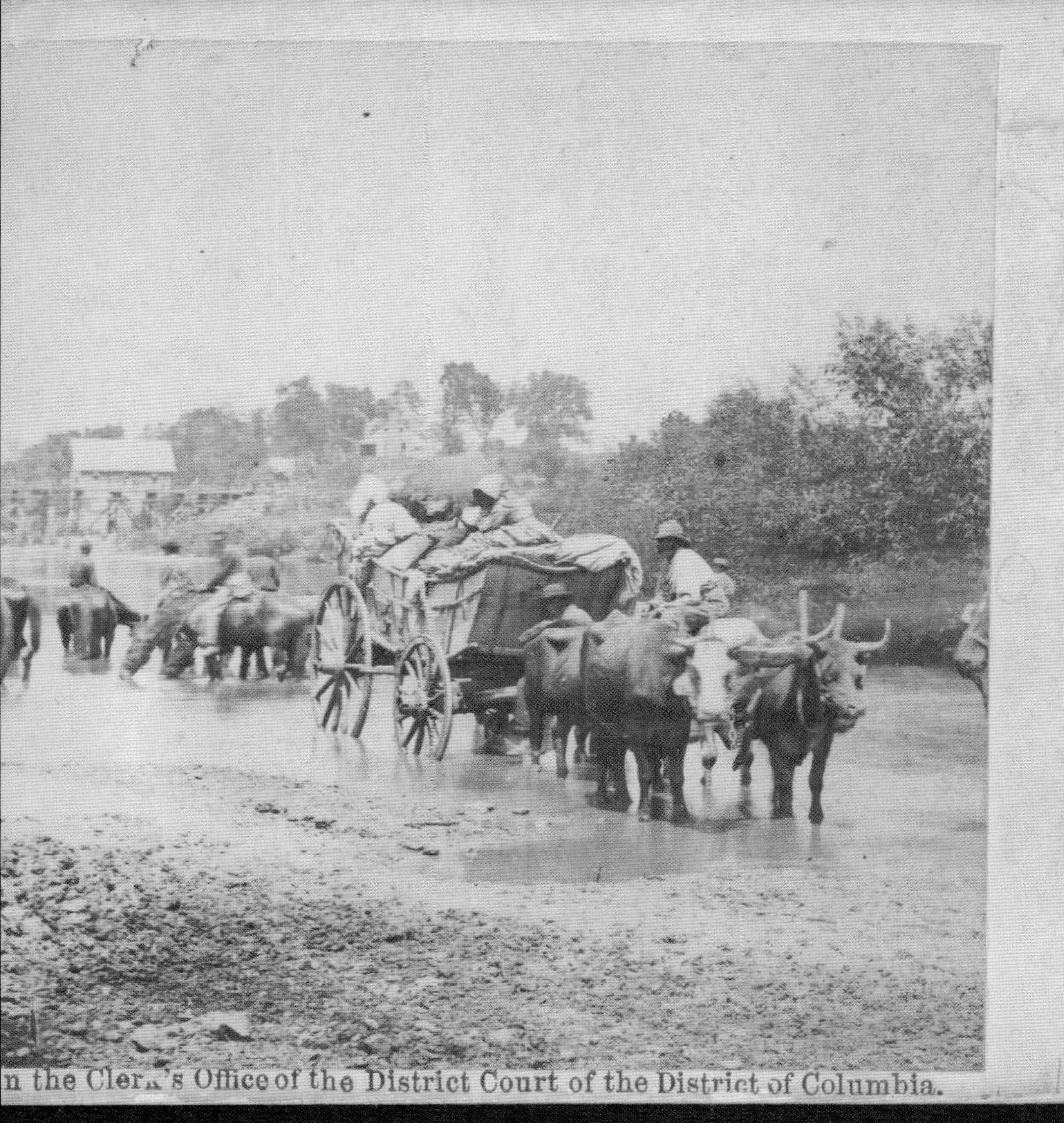

Escaping slavery in search of freedom, a group of Black Americans cross the Rappahannock River in Virginia by oxcart. Their journey reflects that of the countless enslaved people who took liberation into their own hands, risking their lives to reach Union lines during the Civil War.

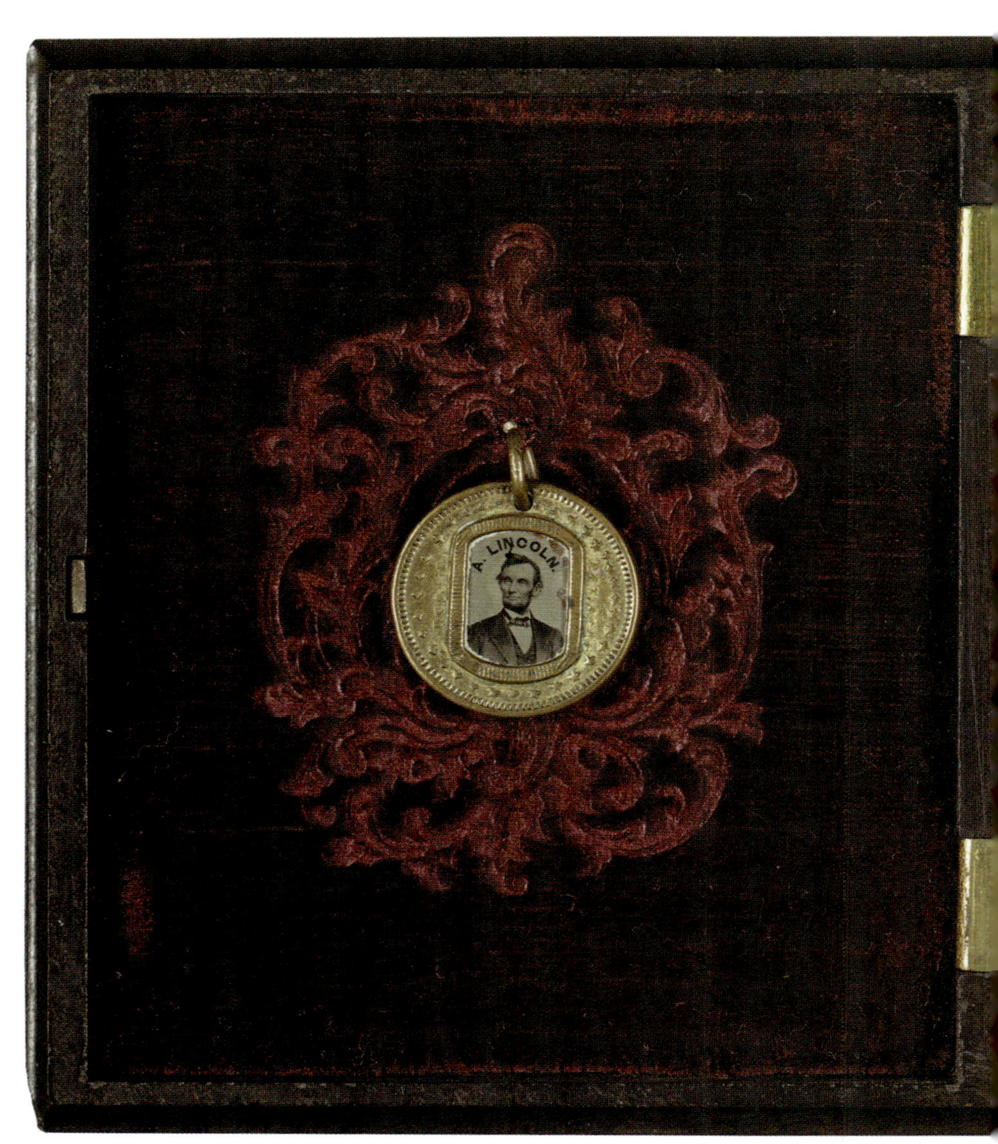
A. LINCOLN.

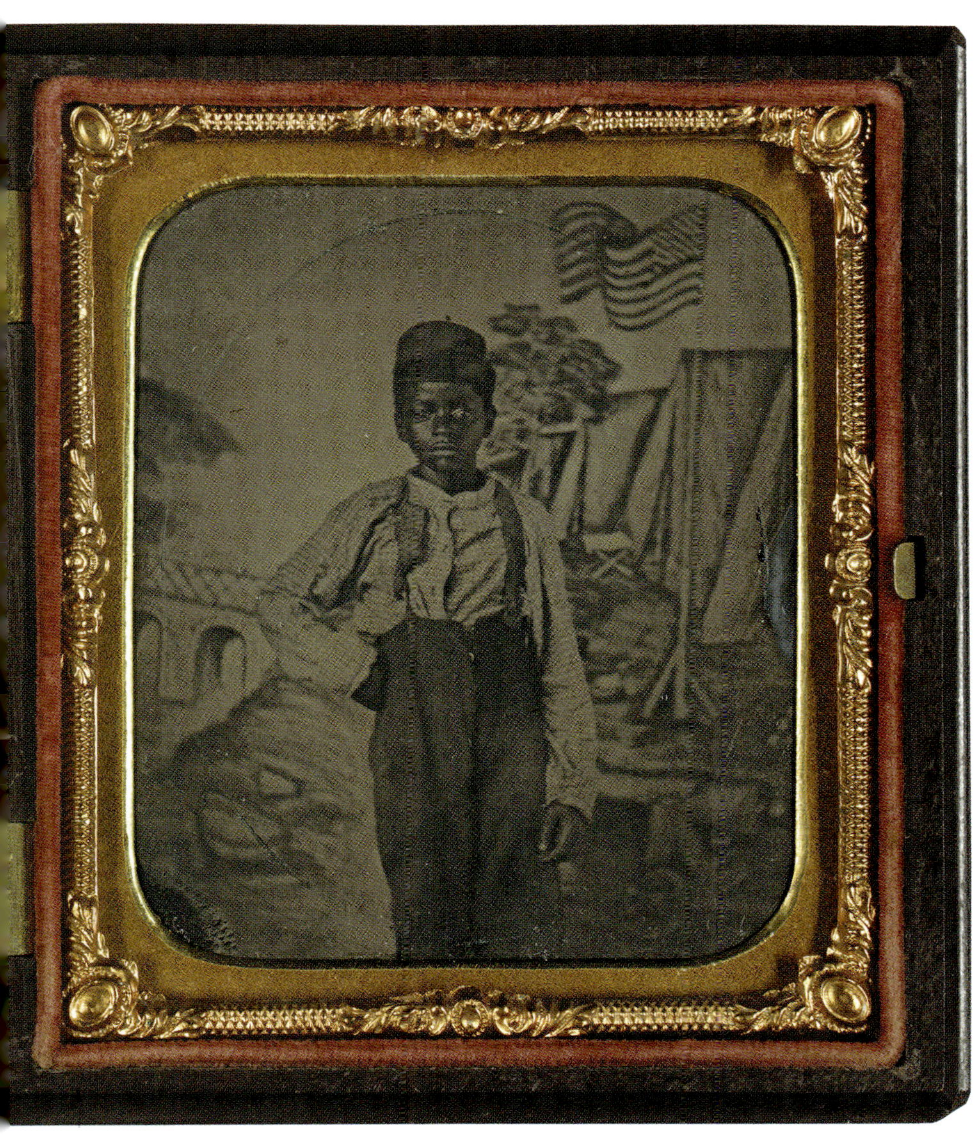

A young African American boy stands posed in front of a screen painted with patriotic wartime imagery. Though his name is unknown, the Civil War era portrait, and its frame decorated with a campaign pin bearing the images of Abraham Lincoln and Andrew Johnson, captures the spirit of determination and hope freed people had in the wake of the Emancipation Proclamation.

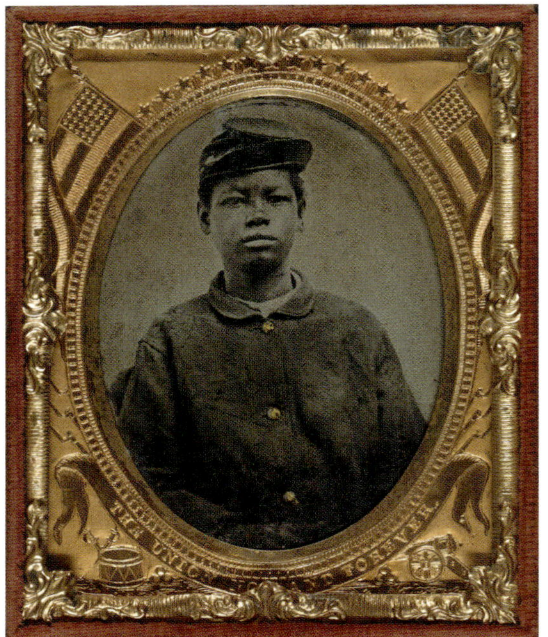

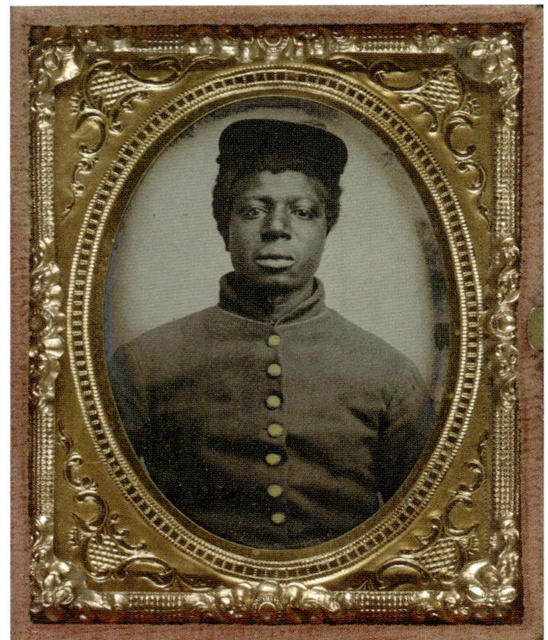

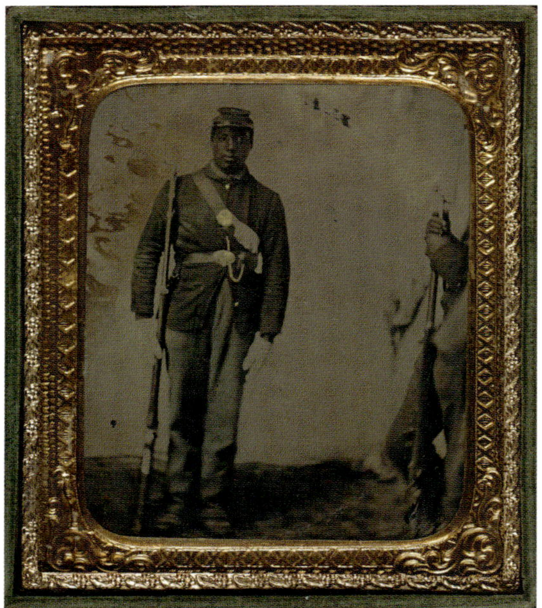

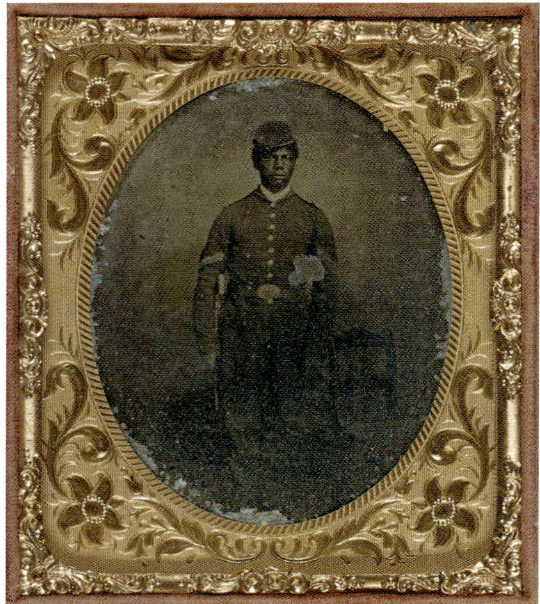

TOP LEFT AND TOP RIGHT: Two portraits of young Black boys in Union uniforms and forage caps. Both gaze powerfully into the camera's lens. Although their names are lost to time, their images are a testament to the willingness of the formerly enslaved to stand in defense of freedom.

BOTTOM LEFT: A Black soldier in formal Union uniform stands at attention. Another soldier can be seen waiting just outside of the frame.

BOTTOM RIGHT: A Black soldier in Union uniform. The single-stripe chevrons on his sleeves denote his rank as a corporal, a reminder that Black soldiers served with valor and were promoted during the war.

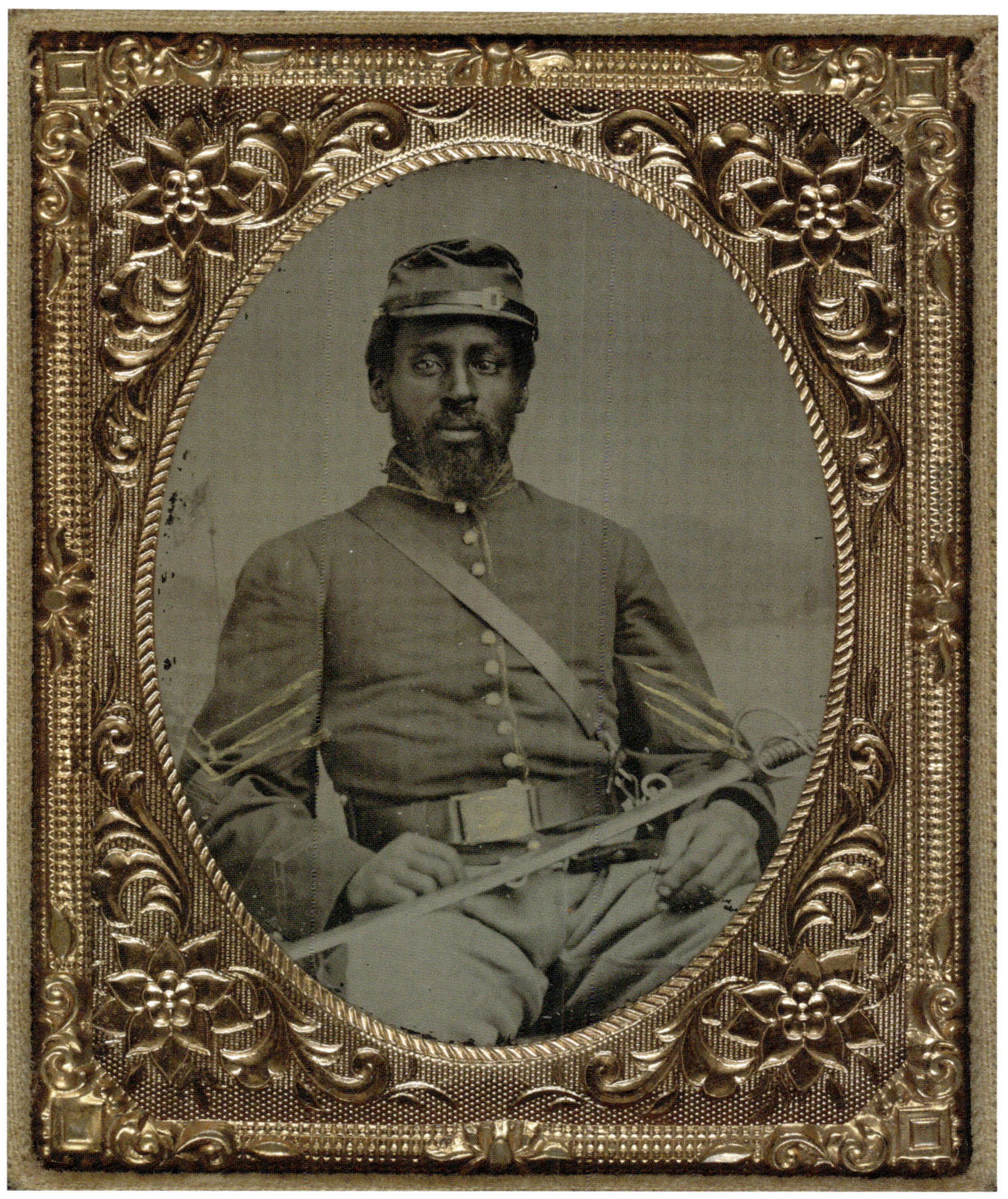

An African American soldier poses in a Union cavalry uniform, with a cavalry saber across his lap. Though his name and rank are unknown, sergeant's chevrons have been painted onto the photograph, suggesting a desire to honor his service and status. His portrait stands as a striking reminder of the Black cavalrymen who rode and fought for freedom during the Civil War, challenging the boundaries of race, rank, and remembrance.

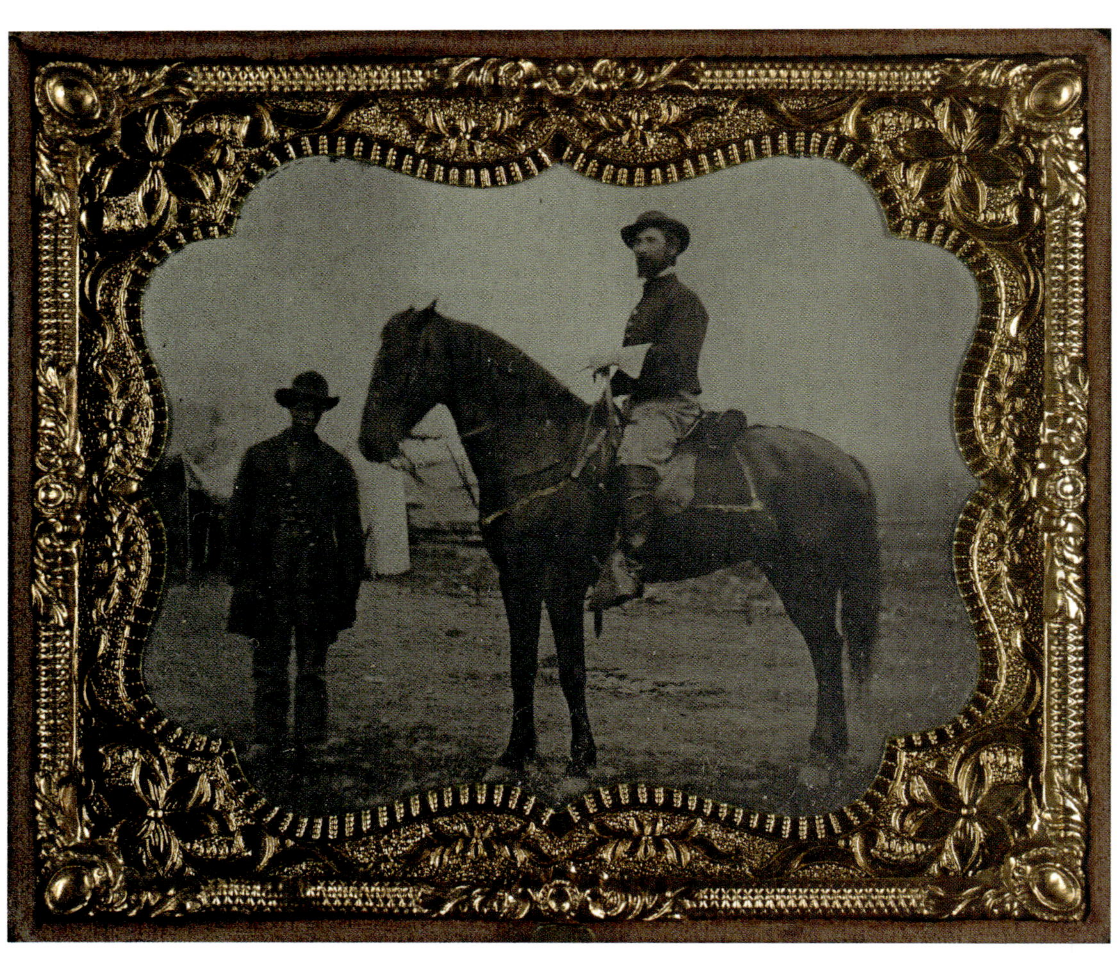

Two unidentified Union soldiers pose for this striking wartime portrait. A white soldier sits mounted on a horse, while an African American soldier stands beside him. Though dressed in uniform, the Black soldier's position—on foot, beside the horse—suggests the complex and often unequal roles Black men held within the Union Army. Some served as soldiers, others as laborers, teamsters, or body servants, all contributing to the war effort while navigating a system still marked by racial hierarchy.

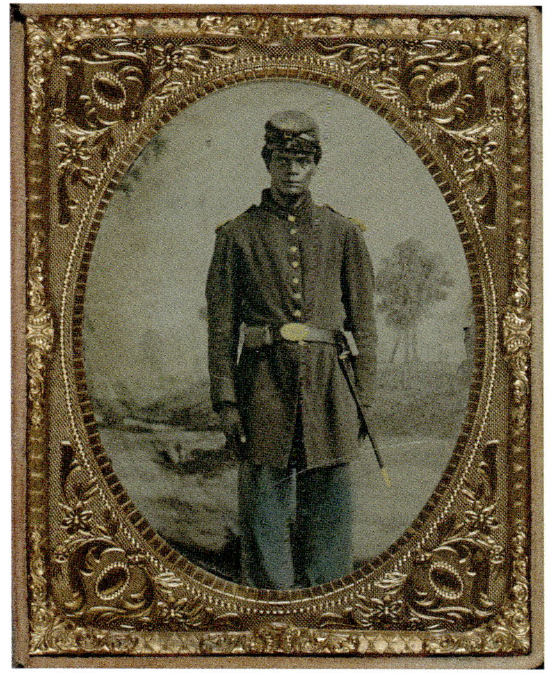

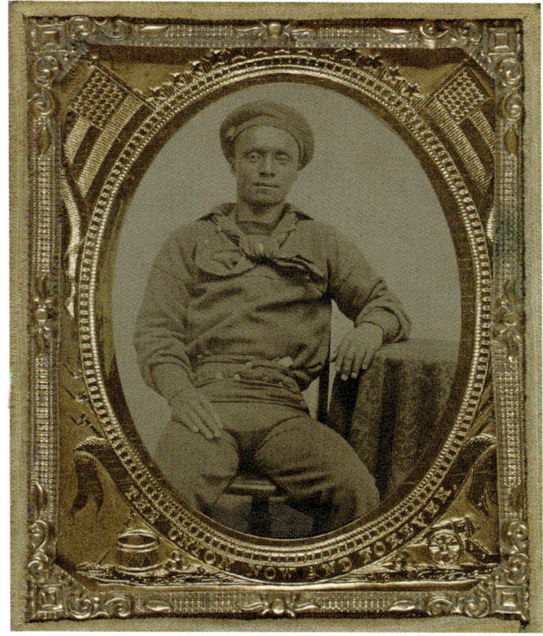

ABOVE LEFT: A Black soldier in Union uniform, wearing a forage cap marked "Company D. 103rd Regiment." Given that his name is unknown, this insignia shows that he was either a member of the United States Colored Infantry, which was organized at Hilton Head, South Carolina, or a member of the US Volunteers Service.

ABOVE RIGHT: A Black sailor in Union uniform. A reminder of the often overlooked service of Black sailors during the Civil War.

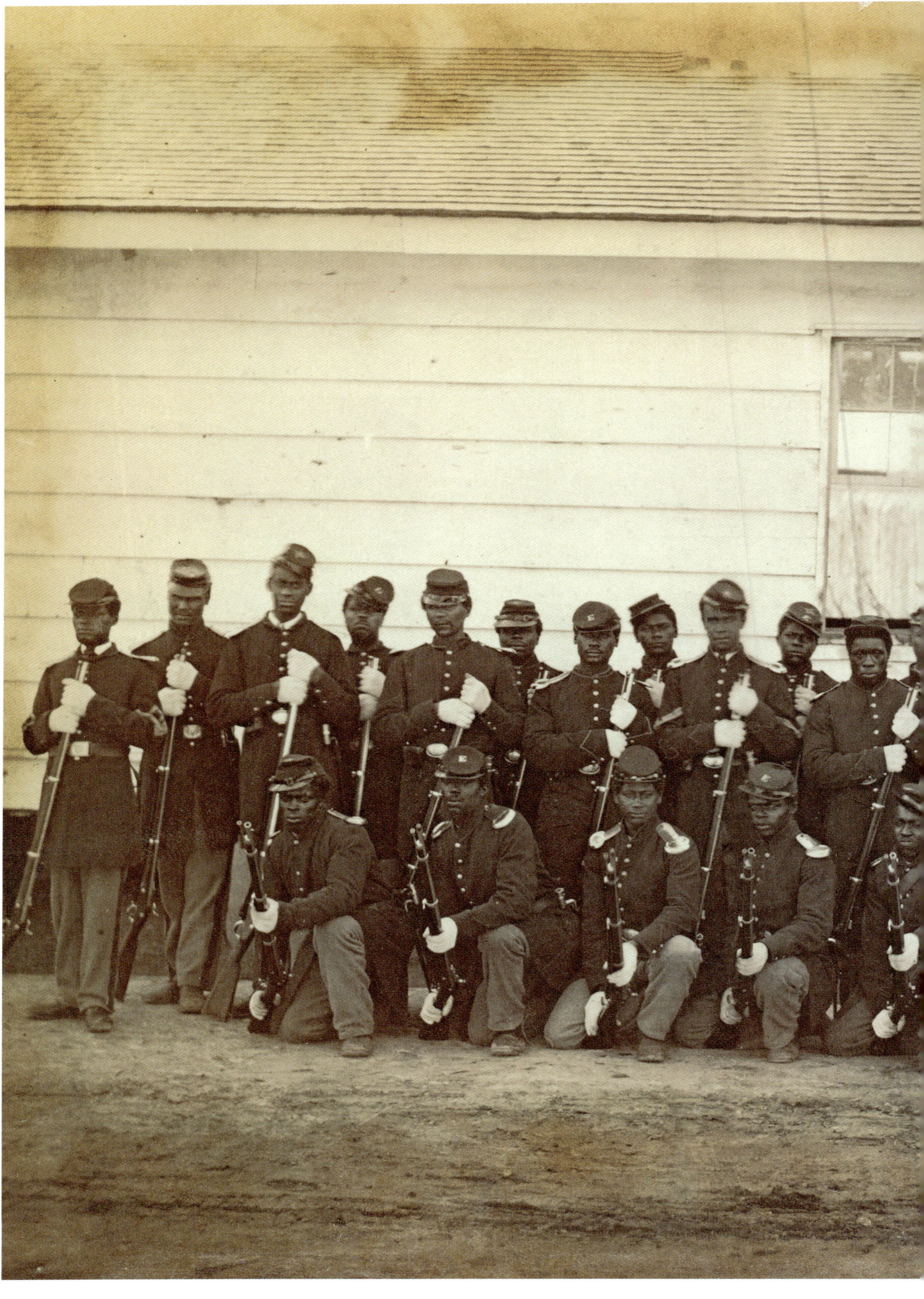

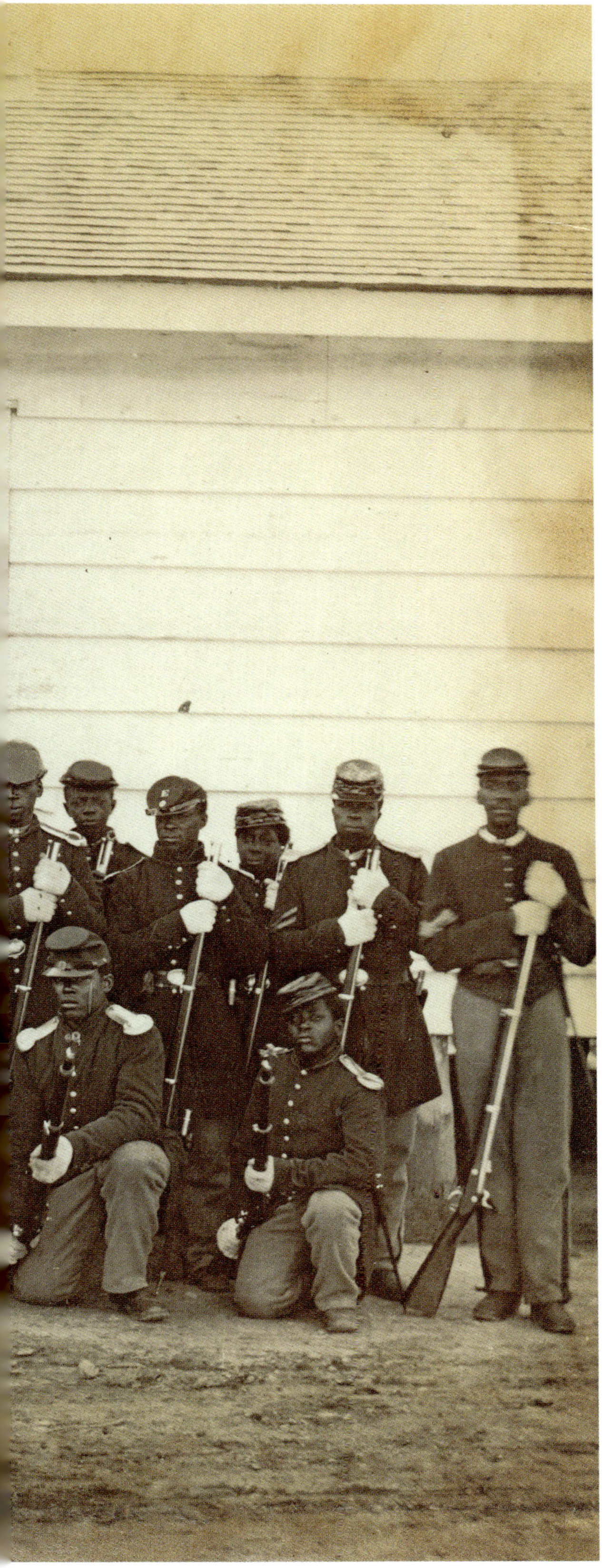

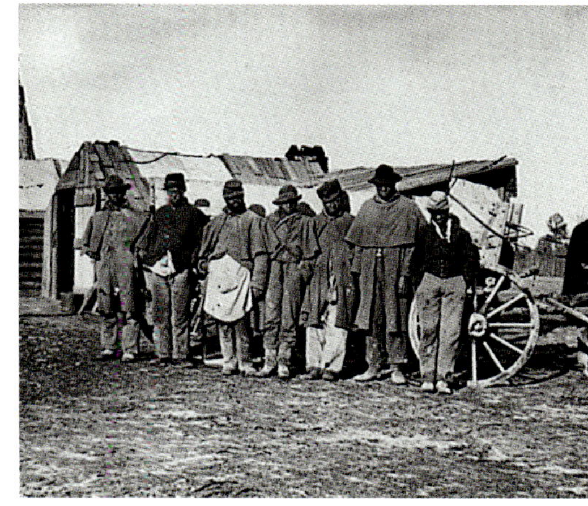

LEFT: A company of United States Colored Troops (USCT), formed during the Civil War after the Emancipation Proclamation opened the door for Black men to enlist. These soldiers represent just a fraction of the more than 180,000 African American men who served in the Union Army, many of whom had only recently escaped slavery or been freed by the advancing war. Their service, which would be celebrated year after year at Emancipation Day celebrations, helped redefine America.

ABOVE: At Bermuda Hundred, Virginia, a group of seven formerly enslaved men working for the Union Army stand in worn Union uniforms. Photographed between June 1864 and April 1865, this image is a reminder of the essential labor performed by Black men in service of the Union army. Though often dismissed as just "contrabands," their work sustaining the war effort was a powerful act of self-emancipation and service.

Head Quarters District of Texas
Galveston Texas June 19th 1865.

General Orders
No. 3.

The people of Texas are informed that in accordance with a proclamation from the Executive of the United States, "all slaves are free." This involves an absolute equality of personal rights and rights of property between former masters and slaves and the connection heretofore existing between them becomes that between employer and hired labor.

The freedmen are advised to remain quietly at their present homes, and work for wages. They are informed that they will not be allowed to collect at military posts and that they will not be supported in idleness either there or elsewhere.

By order of Major General Granger.
F. W. Emery,
Major A. A. Genl.

ABOVE: Handwritten copy of General Order No. 3, issued in Galveston, Texas, on June 19, 1865, announcing the end of slavery in Texas, now commemorated as Juneteenth.

OPPOSITE: A minstrel-style cartoon mocking emancipation that was intended to ridicule the transformative nature of the historic moment.

FOLLOWING: This illustration from *Le Journal Illustré* depicts newly emancipated Black Americans in the wake the of the Civil War, a reminder of the international interest in the end of American slavery.

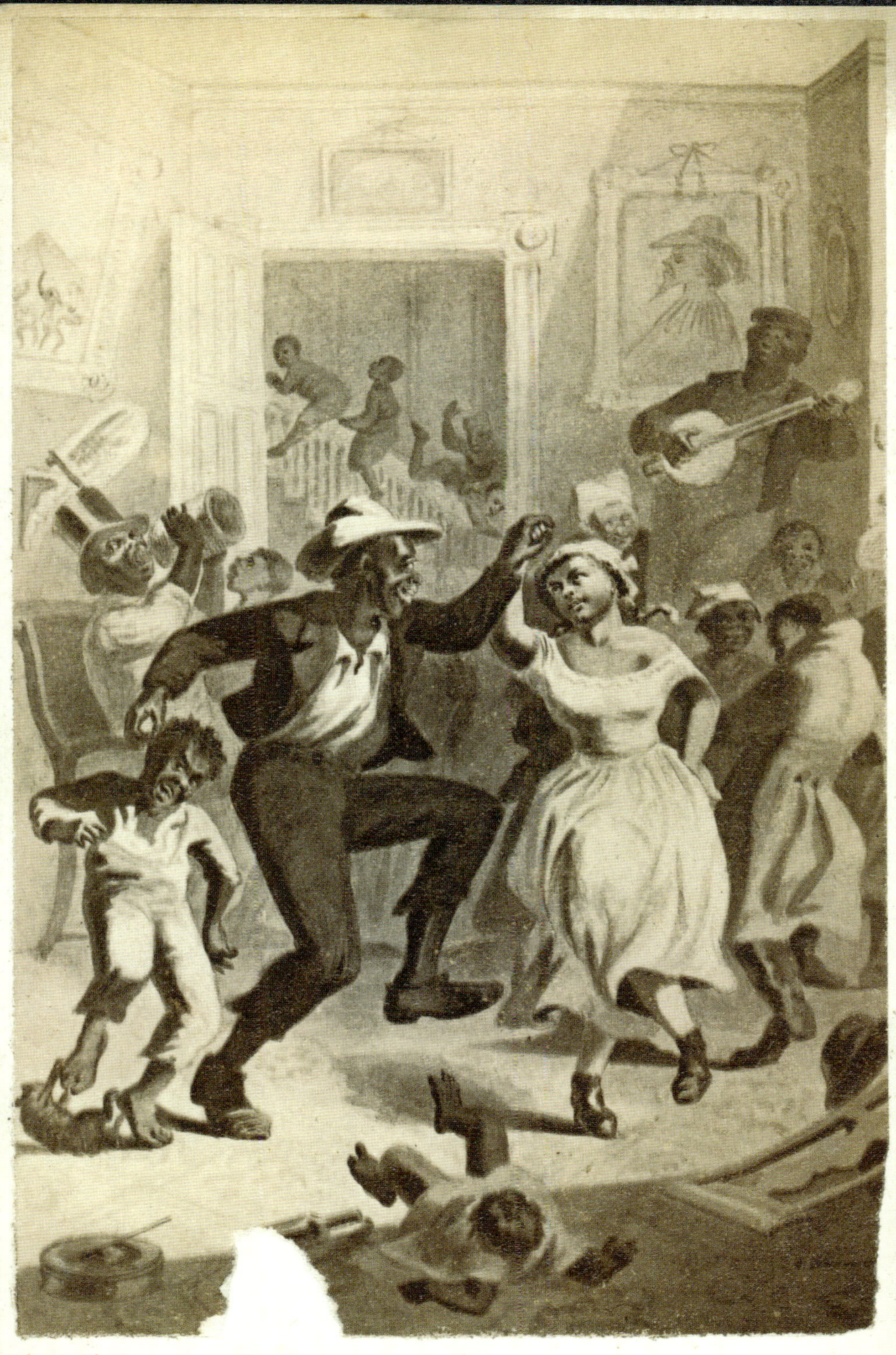

Entered, according to Act of Congress in the year 1865, by J. A. Arthur, in the Clerk's Office of the District Court for the Eastern District of Pennsylvania.

THE DAY OF JUBELO.

E. B. Bensell, Pinxt. Photo. and Pub. by Phil. Pho. Co., 730 Chestnut St.

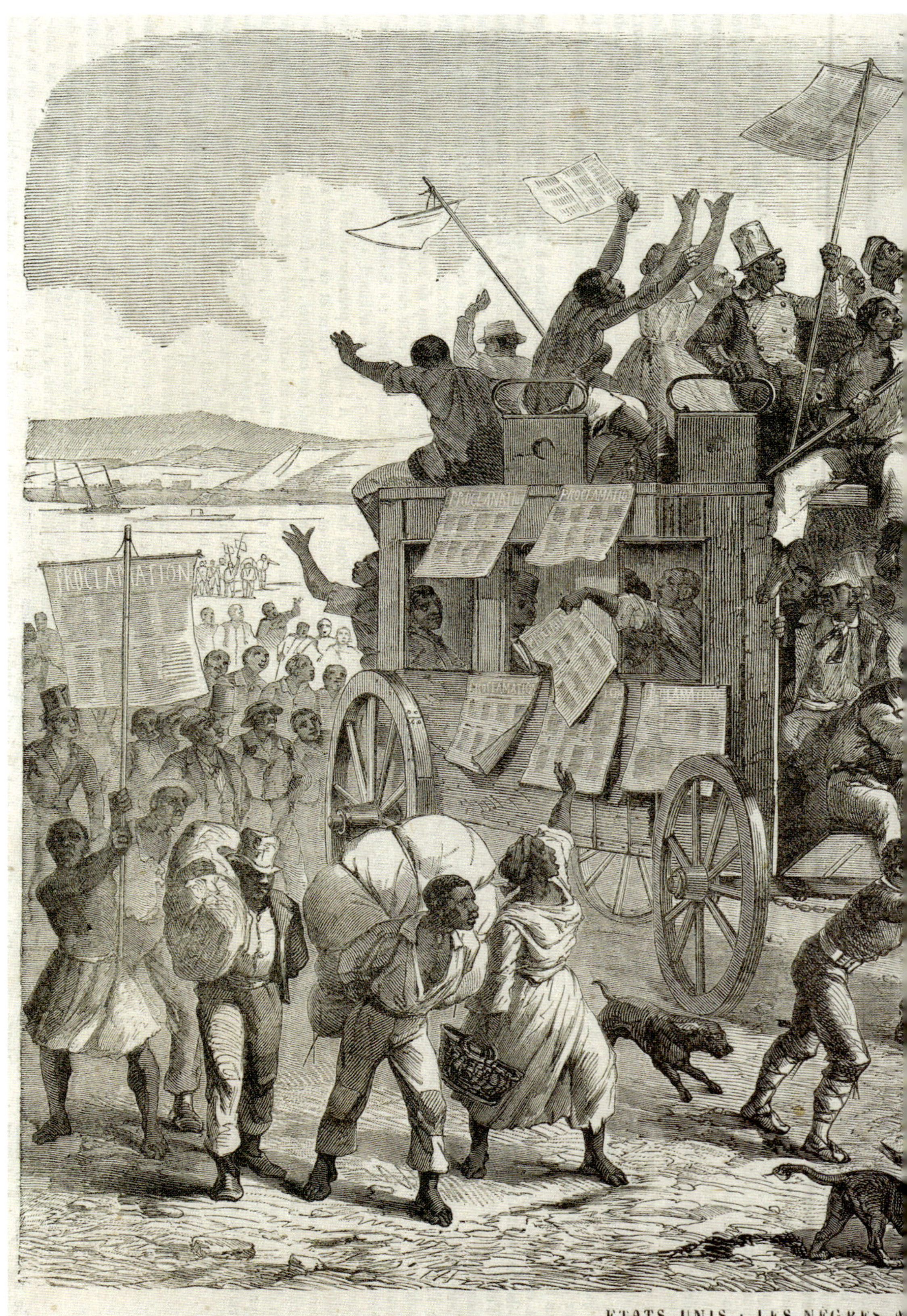

ETATS-UNIS : LES NÈGRES A

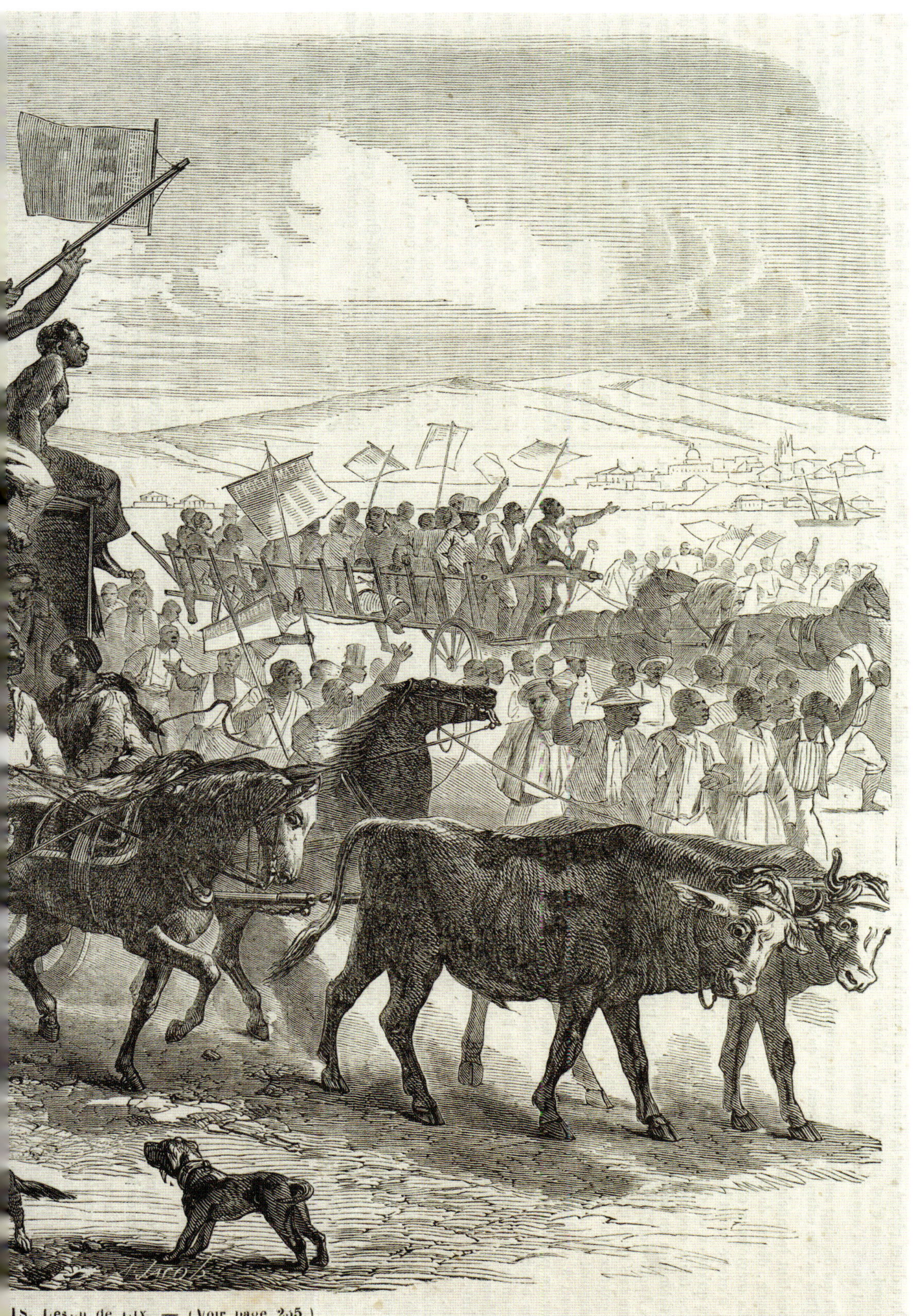

18. Dessin de Lix. — (Voir page 255.)

TEX

AND THE MEA

JUNET

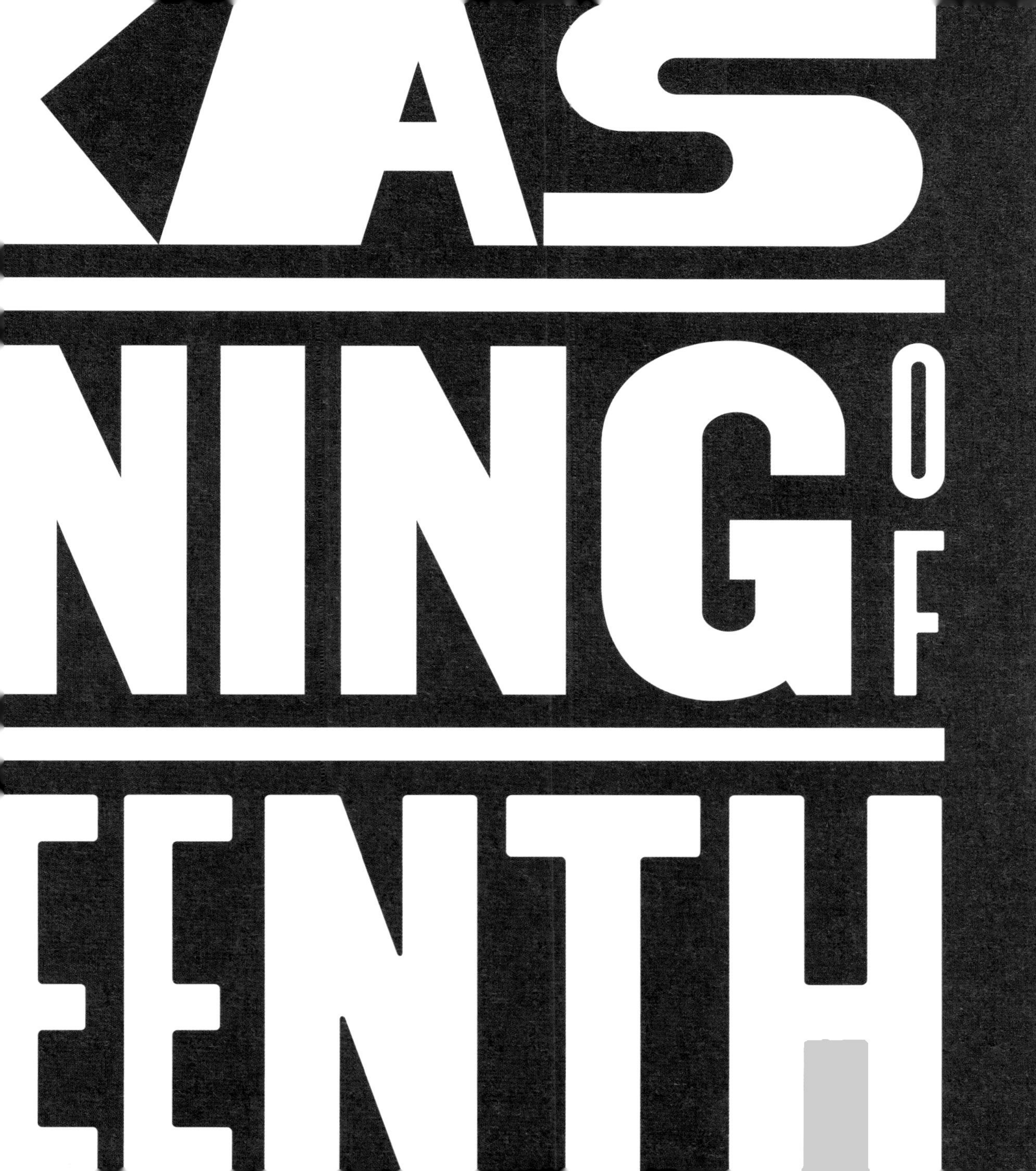

TEXAS, FIRST AS an independent republic and later as the twenty-eighth state in the Union, was founded on an unsettling and deeply exploitative vision. Its leaders and settlers saw it as an opportunity, an open frontier where American planters could push farther south and west to establish profitable plantations. But this expansion was contingent on a grim condition: The plantation owners would come only if they were permitted to bring with them their vast holdings of enslaved people.

The promise of unbridled access to land and enslaved labor fueled a rapid and brutal transformation of East Texas. The region's fertile soil and mild climate, coupled with the relentless toil of thousands of enslaved laborers, created immense wealth for white slaveholders, cementing slavery's grip on the economy and society. In many ways, Texas did not merely adopt slavery; it thrived because of it, embedding the institution even deeper into the fabric of the American South. But in spite of this terrible bargain, it would be Black Texans who would define what it truly meant to commemorate American freedom.

SPANISH TEXAS

The Spanish colonists who laid claim to the land that would later become Texas were cursory participants in the African slave trade, at least in this region of the world. Like most Europeans engaged in colonizing the West, they held Africans in bondage, though the scale of slavery in Texas under Spanish rule was relatively small. The first known enslaved African in Texas history was a man named Estevanico, the enslaved servant of Andrés Dorantes de Carranza. Estevanico was among the few survivors of the ill-fated 1528 expedition led by Pánfilo de Narváez that eventually shipwrecked near present-day Galveston, Texas. Alongside the famous Álvar Núñez Cabeza de Vaca and others, Estevanico wandered across Texas and the Southwest, enduring years of captivity among Indigenous groups, only to later escape and travel extensively—eventually reaching as far as California. His skills as a guide, interpreter, and mediator made him invaluable to Spanish explorers, but his story ended in tragedy when he was killed in present-day New Mexico in 1539.

Though Estevanico is the most well-documented enslaved African in early Texas history, he was by no means the only one. Spanish authorities permitted slavery, but Texas, on the northernmost frontier of Spain's empire, never saw the large-scale importation of enslaved Africans that defined the economies of other colonies in the Americas. The three main settlements of Spanish Texas—San Antonio, Nacogdoches, and La Bahía—collectively recorded fewer than fifty enslaved people at any given time in colonial censuses of the 1700s. However, while Texas was not a major hub of enslavement under Spanish rule, its coastline did become a gateway for the illegal smuggling of enslaved Africans. After the United States formally ended its participation in the international slave trade in 1808, Galveston became a key port for traffickers who smuggled African captives into Louisiana and Mississippi, making fortunes in the process. Spanish Texas remained sparsely populated, with few enslaved individuals or settlers. It was only after Mexico gained its independence from Spain in 1821 that the colonial projects of Moses Austin and, later, his son Stephen F. Austin brought large numbers of Anglo-American settlers and the enslaved people they held in bondage to Texas. It would be the Austins who ushered in a new and far more entrenched chapter of slavery in Texas.

American businessman Moses Austin had lost his fortune in lead mining before he turned his ambitions toward Texas. He saw an opportunity in the sparsely populated area, particularly the region that would become East Texas, envisioning a colony of Anglo-American settlers who would establish plantations and generate wealth. However, before he could fully realize his plan, he fell ill with pneumonia during his travels and, on his deathbed, urged his son Stephen to carry forward the colonization effort. The younger Austin took up the mission with zeal, negotiating with Mexican authorities to bring American settlers into Texas. Unlike Spanish Texas, which had never developed a large-scale plantation economy, Austin's colony was designed with slavery at its core. White American settlers were incentivized to bring enslaved laborers with them, receiving an additional eighty acres of land for each enslaved person they brought. By 1825, an official census of Austin's settlement recorded 440 enslaved people among a total population of 1,800. In Austin's colony, slavery was not just tolerated but essential to the economic structures.

Although the Mexican government was officially hostile to slavery and sought to curtail its expansion, Anglo settlers found ways to circumvent antislavery policies. They created a legal loophole, falsely reclassifying enslaved individuals as indentured servants for life and passing laws within their own settlements to strengthen their controls over enslaved people. It was in this time that Stephen Austin himself became one of the most vocal defenders of slavery in Texas. In 1833, he made his position unmistakably clear, writing, "Texas *must be* a slave country. Circumstances and unavoidable necessity compels it. It is the wish of the people there, and it is my duty to do all that I can, prudently, in favor of it. I will do so."

From its inception, the region that became East Texas was deeply tied to plantation slavery, and this connection would shape its political trajectory. While growing friction between the Mexican government and the settlers in Texas was driven by a complex web of economic and political grievances, the preservation of chattel slavery, meaning the ownership of another person as property, was undeniably one of the motivations for Anglo-Americans seeking independence from Mexico. In part, the fight for Texas became a struggle to ensure that slavery, along with the wealth it provided to white landholders, would continue to be unchallenged in the future.

These conflicts culminated in two wars: first, between Anglo Texas and Mexico, and later between the United States and Mexico in the wake of Texas statehood. Texas entered the Union as the twenty-eighth state and, significantly, as the last slave state admitted to the United States—a final massive expansion of the plantation economy before the country plunged into civil war.

THE ENSLAVED IN TEXAS

For the white slaveholders who migrated to Texas throughout these years, the territory represented an unparalleled opportunity for unchecked wealth-building. Many were the younger sons of wealthy plantation families who saw Texas as a blank slate where they could amass their own fortunes. Others were men who had failed elsewhere, economic strivers who had gone bust in other parts of the country and came seeking a second chance, dragging their enslaved laborers with them. But what was a fresh start for them was a brutal rupture for the Black people they enslaved. For the thousands of Black men, women, and children forced to migrate to Texas, this westward expansion was not an opportunity—it was a dislocation from their families and communities, another chapter in a cycle of separation and suffering.

For enslaved people, forced migration to Texas was not just a move, it was an act of violence. Many were "sold South" from Maryland and Virginia as part of the United States' internal slave trade. Others were handed down as property in wills or as wedding gifts. So many families were ripped apart on auction blocks: husbands torn from wives, children taken from their mothers, never to see them again. Some of those sold were loaded into unventilated railcars. Others were forced to trek across the country. Their journeys were perilous; countless enslaved people died along the way, their bodies discarded on the roadside like fallen livestock. The journey west was not as infamous as the Middle Passage, but for those who endured it, the trauma was just as deep. It was another forced migration, another crossing into the unknown, another moment when Black families had to rebuild their lives under the crushing weight of bondage. For a people who had already lost so much, this was yet another profound loss.

In the brief period between Anglo colonization and US statehood, just twenty-seven years, Texas became a stronghold of slavery. By the time of the Civil War in 1860, Texas held more than 200,000 Black men, women, and children in bondage, an astonishing number given how recently the state had been settled by slaveholders. Yet despite this vast enslaved population, freedom came last to Texas.

Because of the state's distance and vast size, the Civil War itself unfolded differently in Texas than in much of the rest of the South. Thousands of white Texans joined the Confederate army, and the majority of them left the state to fight in battles raging across the eastern and southeastern United States. Unlike the enslaved in Virginia, North Carolina, South Carolina, and Georgia, who saw a tragic and terrible theater of war play out all around them, enslaved Black people in Texas remained isolated from the war front. They did not hear the thunder of cannon fire, watch troops advance through their towns, or witness their plantations fall under the control of Union soldiers.

In much of the South, the enslaved had the opportunity to respond to the chaos of war. They escaped, followed the troops as "contraband of war," worked for the Union cause as laborers, or even joined the conflict as soldiers. Many thousands of Black men who encountered Union forces took up arms for the Union, enlisting in regiments that played key roles in the struggle against the Confederacy. Even those who were not formally enlisted were put to work digging trenches, fortifying battlefields, and aiding in the war effort. Black women also contributed, serving as nurses, cooks, and laundresses for the Union army. In contrast, Texas remained largely untouched by these developments. The relative isolation of the state in the Southwest meant that, for much of the war, slavery persisted uninterrupted. In fact, rather than confronting the possibility of emancipation, many slaveholders in the Southeast and the Deep South viewed Texas as a final refuge, fleeing there with their human property to escape Union troops and hold on to slavery for as long as possible.

Freedom, when it finally came to Texas, arrived painfully late, nearly three months after General Robert E. Lee's formal surrender to General Ulysses S. Grant at the village of Appomattox Court House, Virginia, on April 9, 1865. Even after word of that decisive moment, Confederate forces in Texas continued to resist. In fact, soldiers loyal to the Confederacy in Texas continued to fight the war. The Battle of Palmito Ranch in Cameron County, Texas, in May 1865, the last engagement of the Civil War, took place more than a month after Lee's surrender. It was only in June that Confederate General Edmund Kirby Smith finally brokered his own surrender in Galveston, Texas, the last holdout of the Confederacy.

GRANGER'S ORDER

With the Civil War finally over, the task of enforcing emancipation in Texas fell to Union Major General Gordon Granger. When he arrived in Galveston in June 1865, he penned the words, modeled on Lincoln's Emancipation Proclamation, that would forever change the lives of the nearly 200,000 Black people enslaved in Texas. General Order No. 3 declared in no uncertain terms: "The people of Texas are informed that, in accordance with a proclamation from the Executive of the United States, all slaves are free." His words went a step further than Lincoln's, proclaiming, "This involves an absolute equality of personal rights and rights of property between former masters and slaves." Granger narrowed the terms of what equality might mean, mandating that "the connection heretofore existing between them" (the master–slave relationship) "becomes that between employer and hired labor." He then regressed into stereotypes and warned the former slaves that "they will not be allowed to collect at military posts and that they will not be supported in idleness there or elsewhere." So much for total equality.

Word spread quickly of Granger's order. For the enslaved, this moment was both a culmination and a beginning, a long-overdue declaration of freedom, yet one that came with limitations and uncertainty. Many had long suspected that freedom was near, having heard whispers of Union victories and the Confederacy's decline. Others, especially those on remote plantations, remained entirely unaware of the events of June 19. Indeed, freedom did not come overnight. Some slaveholders withheld the news for weeks, refusing to comply with the order to free the people they held in enslavement until forced to do so. Others sought to coerce the newly freed into continued servitude through threats and violence. Juneteenth, as this day would later be known, marked not just the end of slavery in Texas but also the final enforcement of emancipation in the United States. Yet even as the formerly enslaved stepped into an uncertain future, the fight for true freedom was far from over.

TESTIMONIES OF FREEDOM

Decades later, in the mid-1930s, the Federal Writers' Project undertook to interview more than 2,300 formerly enslaved people, publishing their first-hand accounts of slavery in a seventeen-volume work titled *Slave Narratives*. Collected at the height of Jim Crow segregation, these interviews are notorious for the ways in which white interviewers tipped the scales toward a rosy retelling of a slave past, steeped in the romantic frame of the Lost Cause mythology. Most interviewers wrote the transcripts of the stories that the formerly enslaved shared in almost unreadable prose, uniformly rendered in a thickly accented language better suited to a performance by a blackface minstrel. Black people in the 1930s were not free to speak their minds about the past or the present. After all, this was decades prior to the modern Civil Rights Movement, and at the height of racial violence in the American South. Black interviewees could not safely tell the truth about what they thought about race or slavery. However, when read against the grain, these interviews provide brief glimpses into the truth. Given that we don't have many written accounts from the point of view of the formerly enslaved, when read carefully and collectively, these interviews can be culled for the bits and pieces that interviewees were willing to share in spite of the risk. They are important documents despite the profound bias in the texts.

Felix Haywood shared his emancipation story with a white oral historian from the Federal Writers' Project in July 1937. His account is indicative of this combination of both bias and insight. His parents, Tecumseh and Elsie Haywood, had been brought in bondage by a man named Albert Goodloe from Mississippi to Cibolo, Texas. Haywood shared his memory of the first moments of freedom in Bexar County, Texas.

> The end of the war, it come jus' like that—like you snap your fingers. . . .
>
> Hallelujah broke out—

"Abe Lincoln freed the nigger
With the gun and the trigger;
And I ain't goin' to get whipped any more.
I got my ticket,
Leavin' the thicket,
And I'm a-headin' for the Golden Shore!"

Soldiers, all of a sudden, was everywhere—comin' in bunches, crossin' and walkin' and ridin'. Every one was a-singin'. We was all walkin' on golden clouds. Hallelujah!

"Union forever,
Hurrah, boys, hurrah!
Although I may be poor,
I'll never be a slave—
Shoutin' the battle cry of freedom."

Everybody went wild. We all felt like heroes and nobody had made us that way but ourselves. We was free. Just like that, we was free. . . . Right off colored folks started on the move. They seemed to want to get closer to freedom, so they'd know what it was—like it was a place or a city. Me and my father stuck, stuck close as a lean tick to a sick kitten.

Celebrations like the one recounted by Haywood were common. Also common was the desire to stick close to family that Haywood and his father experienced. Too often Black families, particularly those brought to Texas, were separated. Freedom finally allowed the former slaves the opportunity to honor the family bonds that had been so callously disregarded by their former slaveholders.

Lu Lee's slaveholder had fled to Texas, to keep his slaves in bondage. Born on the way to Texas, she was held on one of the last plantations where they got news of their freedom. She recalled the moment of freedom as a joyous one. After her slaveholder was forced by a federal officer to read a proclamation stating that everyone was finally free, a man on her plantation named George was overcome, shouting his praises of thanks to God. She recalled that "George cried out in a powerful voice: 'Free, free my Lord. Oh! free, free, my Lord. Free, free, free. Oh my Lord. You will me free.'" This freedom was like "thunder and lightning" rolling over their heads. She recalled that she felt the thunder and lightning of freedom "roll over [her] head too," and she cried. She told an interviewer, "I thought on it something fine to be free. Better than religion." The newly freed people all came together to celebrate that night: "They set up torches and poured tallow in bottles around twisted cloth and put them on posts. They lit them all up and made a grand sight." For thousands of the formerly enslaved, these early moments of freedom shone bright like the torches Lu Lee remembered all lit up that first night.

This kind of joyous freedom was not in reach for all the freed people. As the formerly enslaved celebrated in Galveston and beyond, many paid a high price when angry Confederates turned their guns, swords, and whips on their former chattel. Former slave Andy M. Adams recalled:

> When that war was over Maser, he called me there to his back door and told me that I was free and I could do just as I pleased, so I thanked him and went down to Huntsville, Texas. Negroes they were plum thick hollering and shouting cause they were free, but that merriment did not last long, as there was a white man came down through that bunch of people on a horse fast as he could go with rag tied over his face and rode by a negro woman, just leaned over in his saddle and cut that negro woman nearly half in two and just kept riding. . . . Ever last one of us negroes that were left we went home and went in a hurry, cause we did not know how many more of us would be done just like that negro woman.

Former Texas slave Dave L. Byrd recounted the fear he experienced the moment he discovered he was a free man. His slaveholder "got news that the South had lost and the war was over." He returned to the wagon where Byrd was sitting and said, "You black devil you are free, now you can do just as you please." Byrd recalled that he "wanted to get down off that wagon and holler," but he was afraid of an angry reaction from his former master. When he walked into town, all the former slaves were jumping and shouting out on the streets, but the celebration ended quickly when "Patter Rollers"—Black vernacular for members of slave patrols known for their violence and brutality in recapturing fugitive slaves—came and attacked the celebrating crowds. Byrd said they attacked "about 100 negroes that night," beating them with cowhide bullwhips.

In line with Texas's historically tight control over the enslaved, many former Confederates preferred seeing their former chattel dead over seeing them free. For the formerly enslaved, building a life as a free people would be a hard fight in Texas. Even in the face of occupying Union armies, the establishment of the Freedmen's Bureau, and the onset of Reconstruction, former Texas Confederates went on the attack, joining riotous mobs across the state to violently attack Black people who dared assert their freedom.

In spite of the danger and the violence, Black Texans continued to acknowledge the importance of their freedom and to celebrate each year on June 19, the anniversary of their emancipation. Their celebrations were sometimes grand and sometimes as simple as gathering to worship in Black churches that were being established across the state. The celebration of the emancipation also extended into the newly founded Freedmen's Bureau schools. One poignant record of part of an early celebration comes from June 12, 1867, when the local superintendent of schools headed by the Freedmen's Bureau in Columbus, Texas, wrote to his supervisor in Galveston:

> The freedpeople of this County are to celebrate the anniversary of their Emancipation on Saturday June 24th. The Schools of this District will form a feature of the day's enjoyment in making short addresses & singing songs and hymns. It has been suggested that Prizes be distributed on that day to those of the children who have received the highest averages for good conduct and application to study.
>
> Will the Bureau furnish these say 10 or 15 handsome Bibles and a few other good Books for the occasion?

This simple letter of request expresses so much. The history of emancipation was being taught to Black children from the very beginning; clearly, the Black community intended to memorialize the history of June 19 in Texas. Also notable are the literacy and learning as means of commemoration, when just two years prior it would have been illegal for those same children to learn how to read and write, let alone be rewarded with a Bible and "a few other good Books" for being excellent students. For Black Texans, the celebration of emancipation would happen each year, extending from the schoolhouse to the church, from the fairgrounds to the thoroughfares of their towns and cities. It would be a day they were determined never to forget.

EMANCIPATION PARK

In 1872 four formerly enslaved men—Richard Allen, Richard Brock, Jack Yates, and Elias Dibble—came together with a shared vision of securing a place where Black Texans could celebrate their hard-won freedom. Pooling resources from their congregations, they purchased a ten-acre plot of land in Houston, Texas, for $800, a remarkable feat given the economic barriers and systemic racism that sought to limit Black wealth and property ownership in the post–Civil War South. With this land, they established Emancipation Park—a sanctuary for Black residents and a dedicated space to commemorate their liberation from slavery.

More than just a park, Emancipation Park became a symbol of resilience, self-determination, and the enduring importance of Emancipation Day celebrations. The founders envisioned it as a gathering place where the community could reflect on the struggle for freedom, honor their ancestors, and celebrate the promise of a future shaped by their own hands. When Emancipation Park was christened in 1872, it became the first public park in Houston and remains the oldest existing park in the state of Texas. Its creation demonstrated the deep commitment of Black Texans to preserving the memory of emancipation and ensuring that future generations would have a place to come together in joy, remembrance, and solidarity.

Despite the pervasive racial segregation that defined the Jim Crow era, Emancipation Park remained a vital hub for Black life in Houston. It served as one of the few recreational spaces where Black residents could gather freely, fostering community pride and cultural expression. Even as discriminatory policies restricted access to public facilities across the South, Black Houstonians refused to let their history be erased. The park's very existence underscores the centrality of Juneteenth and Emancipation Day celebrations in the lives of Black Texans from the very beginning.

One of Emancipation Park's founders, Jack Yates, had lived through his own harrowing journey to freedom. His agonizing fight to keep his family together captures the painful contradictions and cruel realities indicative of the history of enslavement in Texas. His story is one of sacrifice, resilience, and an unshakable commitment to those he loved. Born in bondage in Virginia, Yates learned to read and write by first listening to the lessons of his slaveholder's son and then practicing in secret. Eventually, when his slaveholder learned he was literate and skilled at math, he utilized Yates in his business. Allowed to earn money on the side, Yates purchased his freedom. Yates became free, but his wife and children were owned by a different enslaver who was determined to hold on to his human property. To evade the reach of the Emancipation Proclamation, this enslaver planned to relocate to Texas, a place where slavery still thrived. He would take Yates's wife and three children with him. Like hundreds of other enslavers who fled to Texas during the war, he saw the state as a final stronghold, a place where slavery could persist even as it crumbled elsewhere in the South.

Faced with the prospect of losing his family, Yates was forced to make an excruciating choice. Rather than risk permanent separation, he made the heart-wrenching decision to accompany his family even though it meant being re-enslaved himself. He willingly reentered bondage, choosing captivity over the unbearable prospect of losing his wife and children forever. Together, the Yates family endured the long, dangerous wartime journey to Texas, uncertain of what awaited them on the other side.

For Yates, freedom came not once, but twice. The first time, it was granted to him by proclamation. The second time, it arrived on June 19, 1865, when General Granger declared that "all slaves are free." This time, the promise of emancipation was real—Yates's entire family was finally liberated.

Yet Yates understood that freedom was more than the absence of chains; it was about building a future. Determined to carve out a new life, he settled with his family in Houston's Freedmen's Town, where in 1871 he became a homeowner and a leader in the growing Black community. He found work as a businessman and, more important, as a pastor of Antioch Missionary Baptist Church, one of the first Black churches in Houston. His leadership helped shape a thriving enclave of formerly enslaved people who sought to create stability, opportunity, and dignity in their newfound freedom.

The Yates family and others like them recognized that freedom was not a personal triumph but a communal legacy that had to be remembered. Their insistence on preserving the memory of emancipation led to the establishment of Emancipation Park. In 1916, at the height of Jim Crow segregation, the park was donated to the city of Houston as a designated space for Black residents, cementing Juneteenth in the physical and cultural landscape of the city.

EARLY CELEBRATIONS

The emancipation celebrations in Houston were not an anomaly. Each year, June 19 celebrations were held all throughout the state of Texas in communities small and large. For example, in 1883, almost twenty years after the end of the Civil War, Texas newspapers chronicled well-attended Emancipation Day gatherings throughout the state. In Galveston, there was a parade through the streets and picnics held at Pleasant Grove and Schmidt's Garden. *The Austin Weekly Statesman* noted that "in consequence of it being Emancipation Day, all prisoners confined on trivial charges in the [Galveston] city jails were discharged." Dallas hosted the North Texas Emancipation Day celebration, which was attended by more the eight thousand Black residents. The procession was an astounding two miles long and included "123 decorated wagons . . . , military companies, carriages, [and] brass bands." No one moving around the city that day could have avoided the sights and sounds of the Black freedom celebration.

In San Antonio the emancipation festivities included a thirty-eight-gun salute, one for each state in the Union in 1883, followed by a long parade "through the principal thoroughfares" of the city. The procession included the "Sunset band, . . . Travis Rifles, Excelsior Rifles, Fire company No. 3, benevolent societies, Capitol Base Ball club, Austin Light-weight Base Ball club, teachers and scholars of the Colored school, a chariot drawn by four horses, containing thirty-seven girls representing the States" and a young woman dressed as "the Goddess of Liberty." What an extraordinary sight it must have been for those who had survived slavery to see young Black people dressed in finery and representing a patriotic tableau of the nation. The main procession was followed by "eight carriages containing the orators, distinguished guests and committee men" participating in the day's formal program. The San Antonio ceremony was hosted at San Pedro Springs Park, the city's oldest, and featured prayer, a reading of General Granger's emancipation order, and several speeches. After the formal part of the day, those gathered broke into smaller family groups to picnic in the park, play baseball and croquet, shoot targets, dance, and sing. Bands played that evening for a "grand ball" that continued until three in the morning.

That same year, eight thousand gathered just outside of Brenham, Texas, to celebrate the anniversary of their freedom. In the small town of Franklin, attendees braved "exceedingly warm" weather to attend an Emancipation Day celebration that included two speeches from local Black leaders. One speaker highlighted the forty-four public schools for Black children in the county and encouraged Black attendees to seek out education for their children. The gathering included a large number of Black people and a "considerable scattering of white people." Everyone there "partook of a sumptuous barbecue."

In the town of Palestine, the 1883 Emancipation Day celebration included a "parade of colored Odd Fellows, a picnic at Gum springs, and installation of officers of a new lodge." The heavily attended event included speeches and a "social reunion" that night. Celebrations in this railroad town even included a train ride excursion for Black celebrants to nearby Long Lake. The town of Bryan celebrated with a "feast of emancipation," and the town of Calvert hosted a picnic. Five thousand Black residents celebrated in Corsicana, Texas. In fact, celebrations took place in nearly every town in East Texas, including Bastrop, Liberty, Marshall, and Round Rock.

Even as an uptick in lynching and racial violence swept the South after the close of Reconstruction, Black residents continued to celebrate Emancipation Day as an expression of their patriotism, asserting that citizenship was indeed still their birthright. During a massive celebration on June 19, 1888, in Dallas, not only did the parade include two brass bands, a drumline, floats featuring local schoolchildren, military companies, and a troop of horsemen, but participants carried banners, one of which asked, "Whar dat mule and dem forty acres?"—in reference to the federal government's historic failure to provide the land promised by General Sherman in Special Field Order No. 15. In 1898, two years after the US Supreme Court ruled in the case of *Plessy v. Ferguson* that segregation was the law of the land, Black Texans gathered on June 19 and marched in uniform through the cities and towns of the state, a reminder of the service of Black soldiers during the Civil War.

Over time, white newspapers dedicated less and less space to accurately reporting on the annual celebrations. They did, however, leave room for watermelon jokes and reprint letters to the editor complaining that Emancipation Day celebrations had become "vulgar." The *Fort Worth Daily Gazette* complained about Black workers in Austin taking the day off to celebrate: "The negroes turned out enmasse this morning to celebrate Emancipation Day. They were all in it—old and young, male and female. There is hardly a kitchen in the city that was not abandoned to its mistress to-day and to-night, and people who cannot cook are eating at the restaurants." In an account of the celebration at Cleburne, the writer said celebrations there were peaceful "with the exception of a knock-down between two darkies." Jokes, complaints that Black residents were lazy, and racial slurs were commonplace year after year.

White newspapers may have made fun of the Emancipation Day observances because they sensed the radical potential of these all-Black gatherings. Indeed, in 1915, Black celebrants in Waco, Texas, used Juneteenth as a political gathering. Speakers first held a discussion of the question, "Should the Negro emigrate to Africa or stay in the United States?" Speaker after speaker resolved that Black Americans should stay in the United States and demand their rights. Having made the patriotic reaffirmation of their place in the nation, they went on to call for support for state legislation that would increase the available land and funding for Prairie View State Normal and Industrial College for Colored Youths, expanding educational opportunities for Black students throughout the state. They followed with the demand that their right to vote be reinstated throughout Texas, supporting a state constitutional amendment that would allow residents to vote in counties other than their home county. While the proposed amendment to the state constitution had been written to allow those who were on the road to vote as absentees, Black citizens hoped that it might be a solution to the white primaries that blocked them from voting in the counties where they lived.

Indeed, white legislators throughout the South had whittled away at Black men's constitutional right to vote promised in the Fifteenth Amendment. Southern segregationists were creating more and more barriers to prevent Black people from participating in elections. While Texas did not pass laws requiring literacy tests or enacting grandfather clauses, tools commonly used in other Southern states to limit access to the franchise, they did adopt their own unique measures to suppress Black participation. In 1902, for example, Texas put in place poll taxes that required voters to pay $1.50 to $1.75 each year in order to register to vote. While that may not seem like much, at the turn of the twentieth century it was a large sum, particularly for many Black working-class voters. Additionally, the Democratic Party in Texas established "white primaries" with regulations declaring that only white citizens could vote in primary elections, turning the elections into a private, members-only club that prevented Black Americans and Tejanos from participating. So, the Black citizens who gathered for Emancipation Day in Waco in 1915 were hoping to travel to parts of the state that did not have white primary rules in place in order to reassert their constitutional right to vote. Though they were not successful in this fight—Texas's white primaries became state law in 1923—the 1915 gathering served as a reminder of the radical potential of June 19.

THE GRANDMOTHER OF JUNETEENTH

Grand public celebrations of Juneteenth continued in spite of the racist violence that plagued Texas. On one particular occasion, segregationist violence and Juneteenth intersected. Otis Flake, along with his wife, Mattie, his oldest daughter, Opal, and two sons, Otis Jr. and Hugh, had moved from Marshall to Fort Worth, Texas. Flake, a railroad porter, purchased a home at 940 East Annie Street. Before the Flake family's arrival, the neighborhood had been all white, and neighbors began menacing the family as soon as they moved in. One of their neighbors, J. C. Moore, even hired an attorney who appealed to the Fort Worth city council for immediate passage of a zoning ordinance that would formally restrict the neighborhood to whites only. The city council "declared the movement unconstitutional" but sympathized with the idea. In the end, such a law was not necessary, because just four days after the Flake family moved in, a mob of more than five hundred white attackers descended on their home. Flake had a gun and was determined to protect his family and his home, but he was told by local police that if he shot the gun, they would allow the mob to kill the whole family and "get every nigger in Fort Worth." Instead, the family was forced to watch as the mob burned down the home, dragging their furniture out and burning it in the front yard so the family would have no way to recover. Fort Worth policemen, state highway officers, and members of the local sheriff's office also watched and did little to stop the mob. White residents who were sympathetic to the Flakes were told that if they did anything to help the family, they would suffer the same fate. When a reporter from the *Pittsburgh Courier* asked a local resident about the events, he responded, "We told them not to move in the house; we warned them to get out." When asked why he objected to their presence, the man responded quickly, "We just don't want niggers that close to us." The attack on the Flake home happened on Juneteenth: June 19, 1939.

As an adult, Opal Flake Lee became focused on justice and a full recognition of the importance of freedom for Black Americans. She campaigned to make Juneteenth, the day her family suffered from a tremendous assault, a national holiday. Her advocacy work continued for decades, earning her the nickname "the grandmother of Juneteenth." In 2016, seventy-seven years after her family home was burned to the ground, she embarked on a walk from her home in Fort Worth, Texas, to Washington, DC, seeking to gain nationwide attention for her campaign. Opal Flake Lee's activism, particularly in the wake of the 2020 murder of George Floyd, moved Congress to finally make Juneteenth a national holiday, the first national holiday to commemorate Black emancipation in American history. Texas's unique legacy of celebrating freedom on June 19 suddenly became the pathway by which emancipation could finally be formally commemorated by the nation as a whole. President Joe Biden signed the Juneteenth National Independence Day Act into law on June 17, 2021.

Given Texas's Black history, grounded in harsh forms of slavery, rigid control over the enslaved, laws forbidding the settlement of free Black people in the state, segregation, lynching, and disenfranchisement, it is poignant that it was Black Texans who eventually made the celebration of Black freedom a national holiday. But the Black enslaved brought to Texas were the descendants of ancestors who had already taught them how to remake a world. Their survival in a land new to them and a system bent against them required them to remake themselves again and again. Remake family. Remake community. Remake faith. Remake pathways of collective support and resolve. Remake culture and meaning in spite of the violences they suffered. Like Jack Yates and Opal Flake Lee, and all those who celebrated Juneteenth in ways both grand and small, they were already in the habit of surviving and beginning again.

OPPOSITE: An 1860 map of the population of enslaved people in Texas shows the dense concentration of people in bondage in East Texas. The region was rapidly transformed by the expansion of plantation slavery. In just a generation, Texas became a stronghold of bondage built on the forced migration of thousands of Black people.

FOLLOWING: The last orders freeing the enslaved in Texas and ending the Civil War.

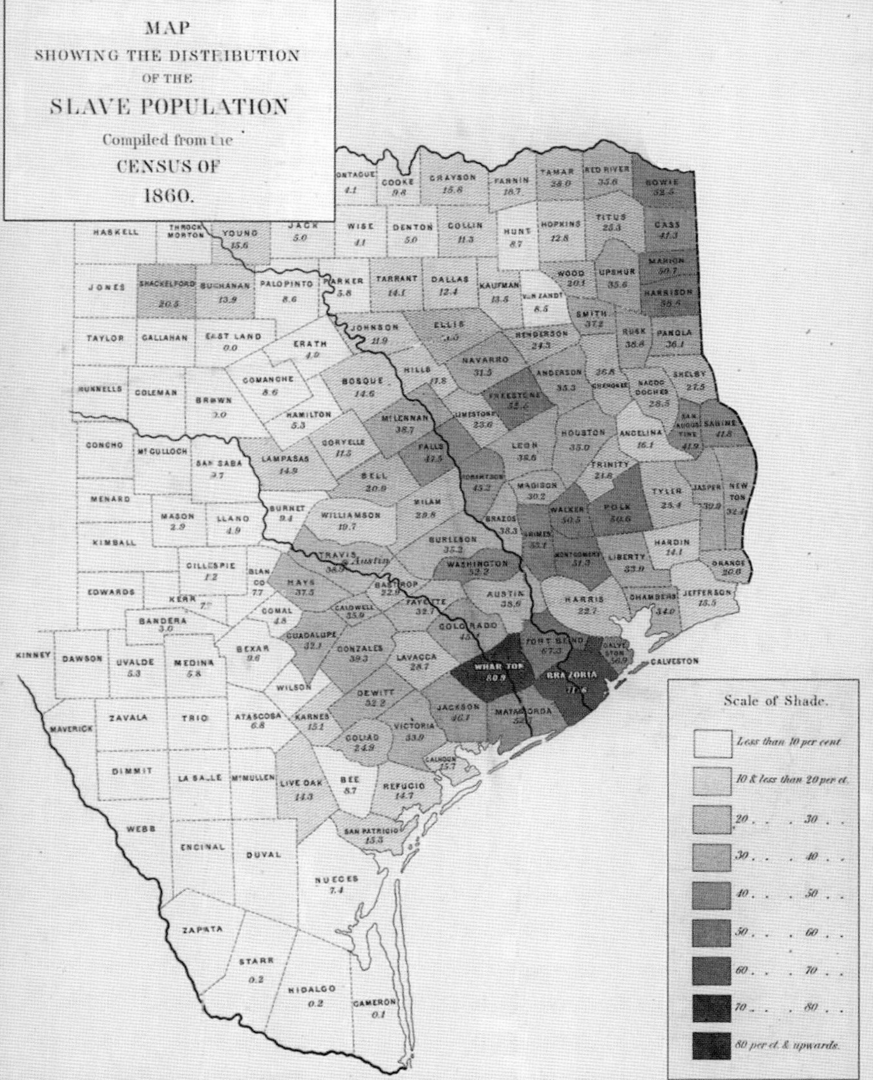

MAP
SHOWING THE DISTRIBUTION
OF THE
SLAVE POPULATION
Compiled from the
CENSUS OF
1860.
ONTAGUE 4.1
COOKE 9.8
GRAYSON 15.8
FANNIN 16.7
LAMAR 38.0
RED RIVER 35.8
BOWIE 52.5
HASKELL
THROCKMORTON
YOUNG 15.6
JACK 5.0
WISE 4.1
DENTON 5.0
COLLIN 11.3
HUNT 8.7
HOPKINS 12.8
TITUS 25.3
CASS 41.3
JONES
SHACKELFORD 20.5
BUCHANAN 13.9
PALO PINTO 8.6
PARKER 5.8
TARRANT 14.1
DALLAS 12.4
KAUFMAN 13.5
VAN ZANDT 8.5
WOOD 20.1
UPSHUR 35.6
MARION 50.7
HARRISON 58.5
SMITH 37.2
TAYLOR
CALLAHAN
EAST LAND 0.0
ERATH 4.9
JOHNSON 11.9
ELLIS
HENDERSON 24.3
RUSK 38.8
PANOLA 36.1
NAVARRO 31.5
HILLS 17.8
ANDERSON 35.3
CHEROKEE 26.8
NACOGDOCHES 28.5
SHELBY 27.5
RUNNELS
COLEMAN
BROWN 2.0
COMANCHE 8.6
BOSQUE 14.6
McLENNAN 38.7
FREESTONE 52.6
LIMESTONE 23.6
HAMILTON 5.3
SAN AUGUSTINE 41.9
SABINE 41.8
CONCHO
McCULLOCH
SAN SABA 3.7
LAMPASAS 14.9
CORYELLE 11.5
FALLS 47.5
LEON 38.6
HOUSTON 35.0
ANGELINA 16.1
TRINITY 21.8
BELL 20.9
ROBERTSON 43.2
MADISON 30.2
TYLER 25.4
JASPER 39.0
NEWTON 32.4
MENARD
MASON 2.9
LLANO 4.9
BURNET 9.4
WILLIAMSON 19.7
MILAM 29.8
BRAZOS 38.3
WALKER 50.5
POLK 50.6
GRIMES 55.1
KIMBALL
BURLESON 35.2
HARDIN 14.1
MONTGOMERY 51.9
LIBERTY 33.9
WASHINGTON 52.2
TRAVIS 38.9
Austin
GILLESPIE 1.2
BLANCO 7.7
HAYS 37.5
BASTROP 22.9
EDWARDS
KERR
COMAL 4.8
CALDWELL 35.9
FAYETTE 32.7
AUSTIN 38.6
HARRIS 22.7
CHAMBERS 34.0
JEFFERSON 13.5
ORANGE 20.6
BANDERA 3.0
GUADALUPE 32.1
GONZALES 39.3
COLORADO 45.1
FORT BEND 67.3
GALVESTON 36.9
GALVESTON
KINNEY
DAWSON
UVALDE 5.3
MEDINA 5.8
BEXAR 9.6
LAVACCA 28.7
WHARTON 80.9
BRAZORIA 71.6
WILSON
DEWITT 32.2
MAVERICK
ZAVALA
TRIO
ATASCOSA 6.8
KARNES 15.1
JACKSON 46.1
MATAGORDA
VICTORIA 33.9
GOLIAD 24.9
CALHOUN 15.7
DIMMIT
LA SALLE
McMULLEN
LIVE OAK 14.3
BEE 8.7
REFUGIO 14.7
WEBB
SAN PATRICIO 13.3
ENCINAL
DUVAL
NUECES 7.4
ZAPATA
STARR 0.2
HIDALGO 0.2
CAMERON 0.1
Scale of Shade.
Less than 10 per cent
10 & less than 20 per ct.
20 . . . 30 . .
30 . . . 40 . .
40 . . . 50 . .
50 . . . 60 . .
60 . . . 70 . .
70 . . . 80 . .
80 per ct. & upwards.

54TH CONGRESS, 1st Session. } HOUSE OF REPRESENTATIVES. { Doc. No. 369, Part 2.

THE WAR OF THE REBELLION:

A COMPILATION OF THE OFFICIAL RECORDS OF THE UNION AND CONFEDERATE ARMIES.

PUBLISHED UNDER THE DIRECTION OF

The Hon. DANIEL S. LAMONT, Secretary of War,

BY

MAJ. GEORGE W. DAVIS, U. S. ARMY,
MR. LESLIE J. PERRY, CIVILIAN EXPERT,
MR. JOSEPH W. KIRKLEY, CIVILIAN EXPERT,
Board of Publication.

SERIES I—VOLUME XLVIII—IN TWO PARTS.

PART II—CORRESPONDENCE, ETC.

WASHINGTON:
GOVERNMENT PRINTING OFFICE.
1896.

GENERAL ORDERS, No. 3. } HEADQUARTERS DISTRICT OF TEXAS, *Galveston, Tex., June 19, 1865.*

The people of Texas are informed that, in accordance with a proclamation from the Executive of the United States, all slaves are free. This involves an absolute equality of personal rights and rights of property between former masters and slaves, and the connection heretofore existing between them becomes that between employer and hired labor. The freedmen are advised to remain quietly at their present homes and work for wages. They are informed that they will not be allowed to collect at military posts and that they will not be supported in idleness either there or elsewhere.

By order of Major-General Granger:

F. W. EMERY,
Major and Assistant Adjutant-General.

GENERAL ORDERS, No. 4. } HEADQUARTERS DISTRICT OF TEXAS, *Galveston, Tex., June 19, 1865.*

All acts of the governor and legislature of Texas since the ordinance of secession are hereby declared illegitimate. All civil and military officers and agents of the so-called Confederate States Government, or of the State of Texas, and all persons formerly connected with the C. S. Army in Texas, will at once report for parole at one of the following places, or such others as may be designated hereafter, to the proper U. S. officers to be appointed: Houston, Galveston, Bonham, San Antonio, Marshall, and Brownsville. Although their long absence from their homes and the peculiar circumstances of their State may palliate their desertion from their organizations, this order will be strictly and promptly complied with. The above-mentioned and all other persons having in their possession public property of any description whatever, as arms, horses, munitions, &c., formerly belonging to the so-called Confederate States or State of Texas, will immediately deliver it to the proper U. S. officer at the nearest of above-mentioned places. When they cannot carry it, and have not the means of transporting it, they will make to the same officer a full report of its character, quantity, location, security, &c. All persons not complying promptly with this order will be arrested as prisoners of war, sent North for imprisonment, and their property forfeited. All lawless persons committing acts of violence, such as banditti, guerrillas, jayhawkers, horse-thieves, &c., are hereby declared outlaws and enemies of the human race, and will be dealt with accordingly.

By order of Major-General Granger:

F. W. EMERY,
Major and Assistant Adjutant-General.

GENERAL ORDERS, No. 5. } HEADQUARTERS DISTRICT OF TEXAS, *Galveston, Tex., June 19, 1865.*

Until the arrival of the proper Treasury agents in this district all cotton may be turned in to the quartermaster's department for shipment to New Orleans or New York, there to be sold to the U. S. purchasing agents. In case of such consignment bills of lading will be given and the owner will be permitted to accompany his property for

Juneteenth celebrants at Emancipation Park in Houston, Texas's Fourth Ward, a space established in 1872 by formerly enslaved people to mark the anniversary of their freedom. Reverend Jack Yates, pictured on the far left, was one of the park's founders, and a towering figure in Houston's Black community. His daughter, Sallie Yates, is seated at the center dressed in black. This historic photo captures not only a day of celebration, but a legacy of determination to upbuild a space where emancipation could be freely remembered with joy and dignity.

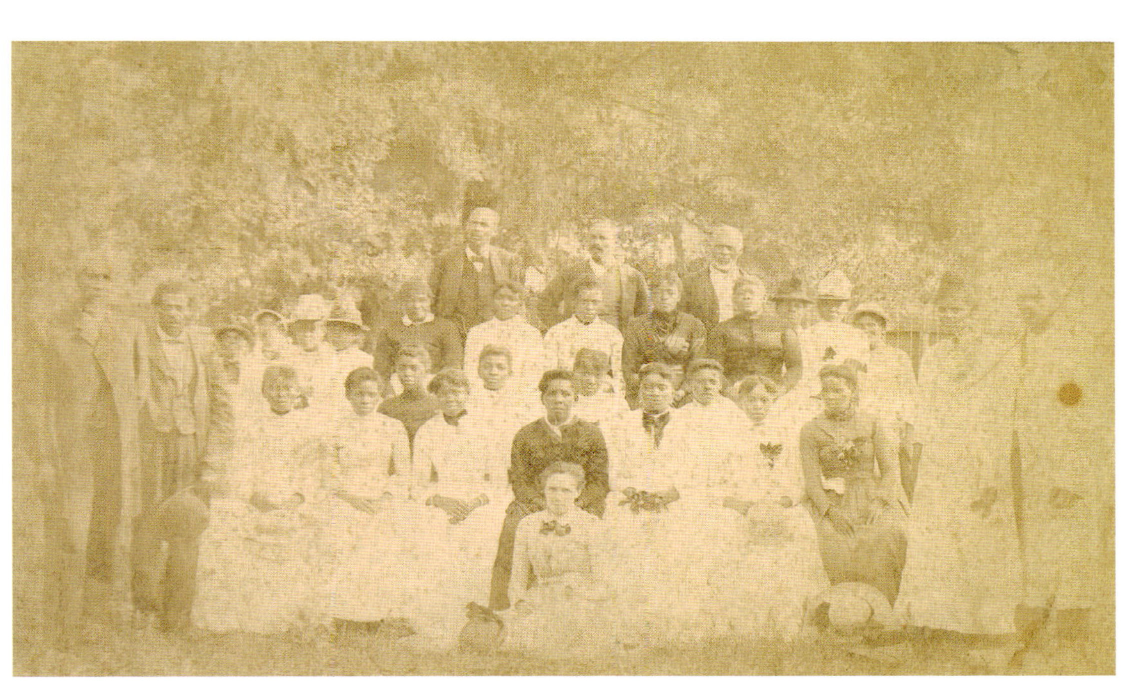

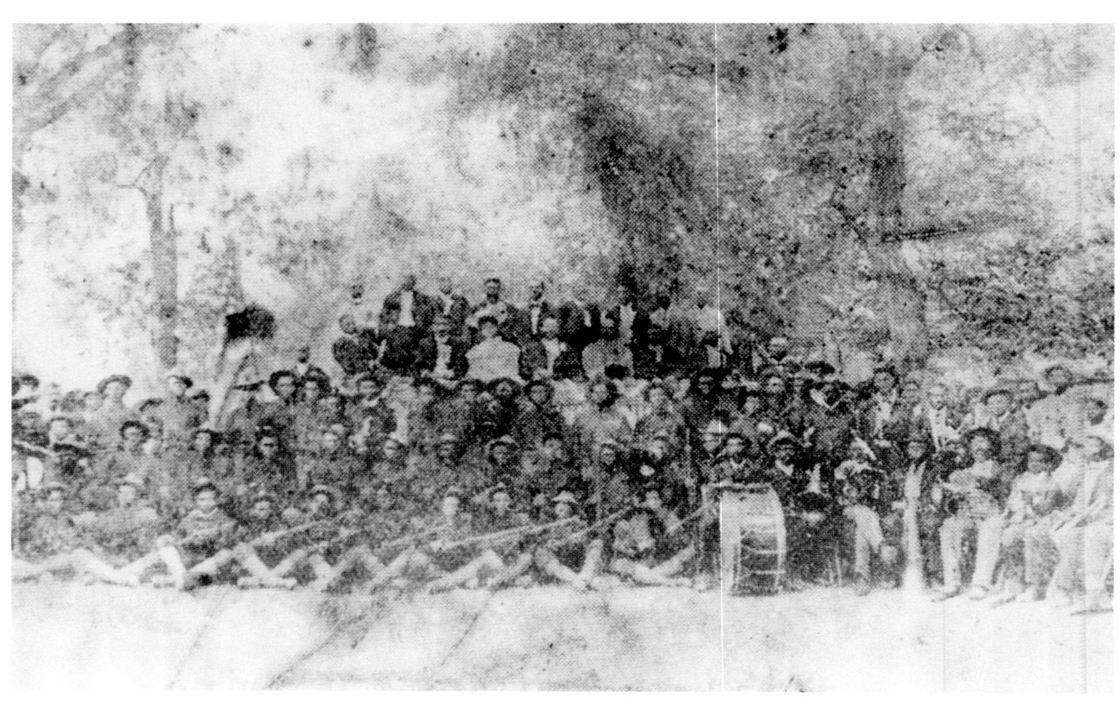

ABOVE: Marching bands and Black militia men were an important element present at most early Juneteenth celebrations. The Morris Givens Band and Negro National Guard at Juneteenth Celebration at Wheeler's Grove, Texas, June 19, 1900.

OPPOSITE: A chef pit-barbecuing meat at the Emancipation Day Celebration on June 19, 1900. Food, particularly traditional barbecue, was a central part of Juneteenth celebrations.

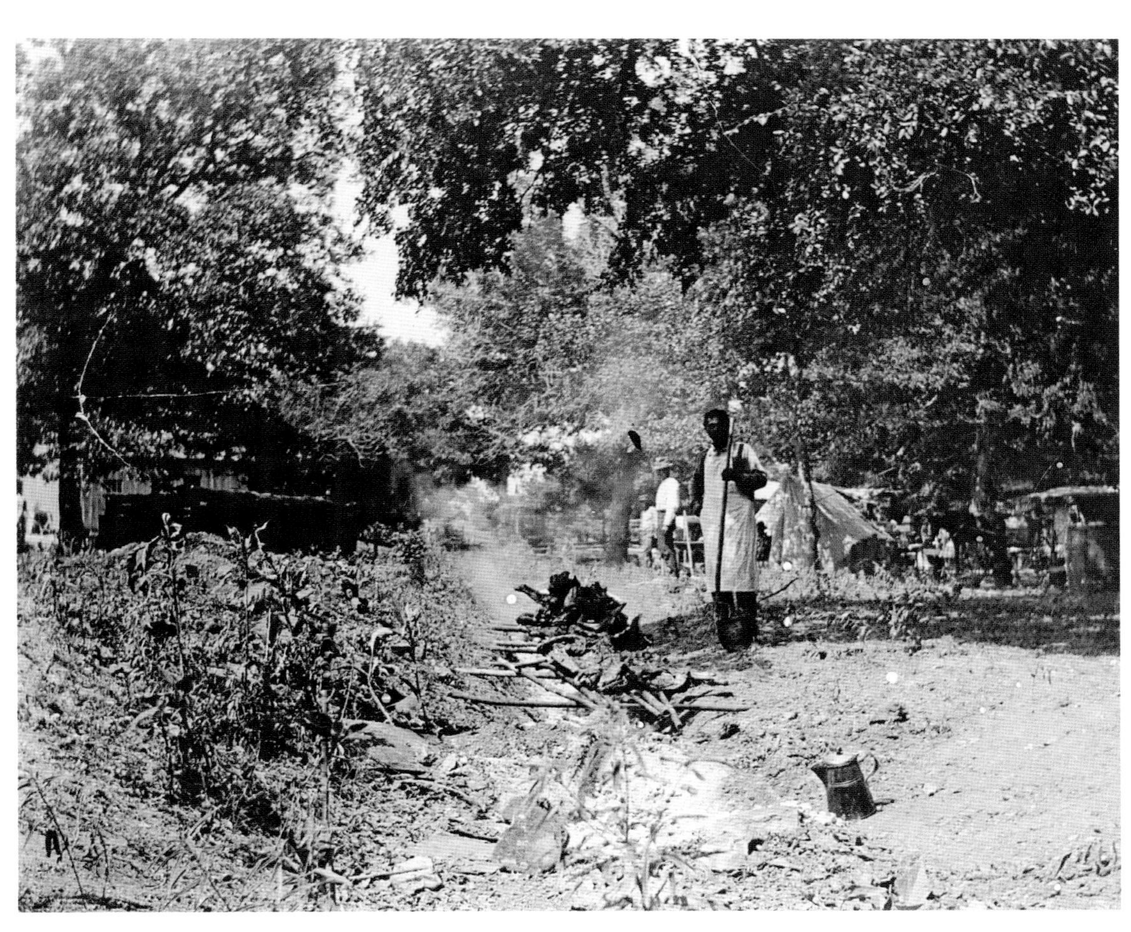

Three young boys, in their Sunday best suits and hats, at the Emancipation Day celebration in East Woods Park, Austin, Texas, June 19, 1900. While the photographer may have been trying to capture a stereotype of Black children eating watermelon, they also inadvertently captured the intergenerational nature of Juneteenth celebrations.

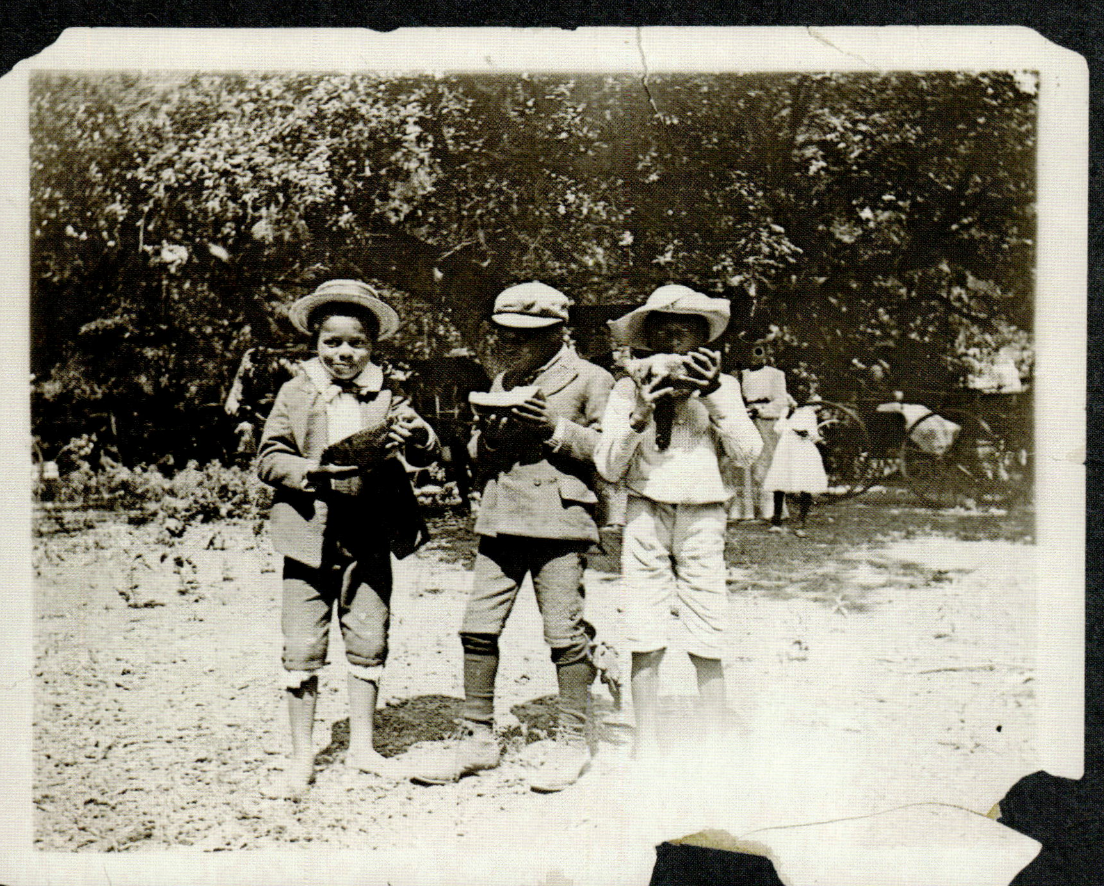

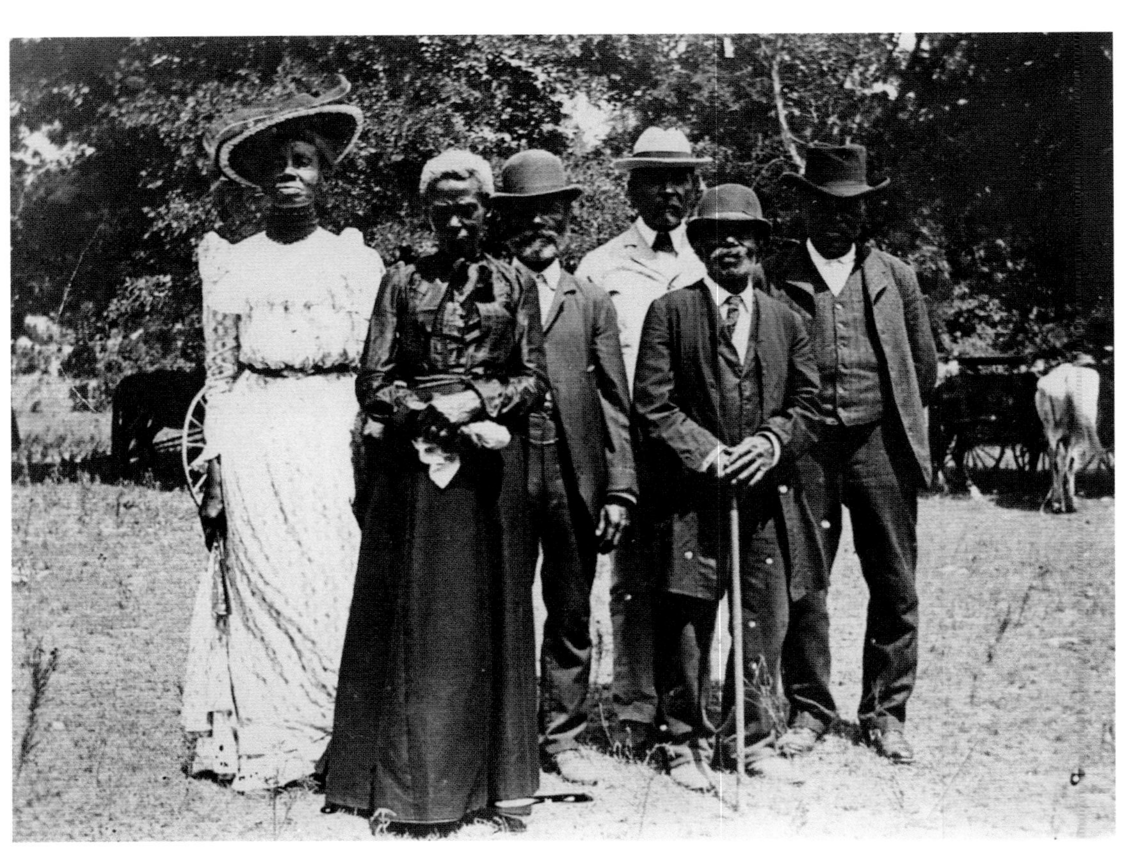

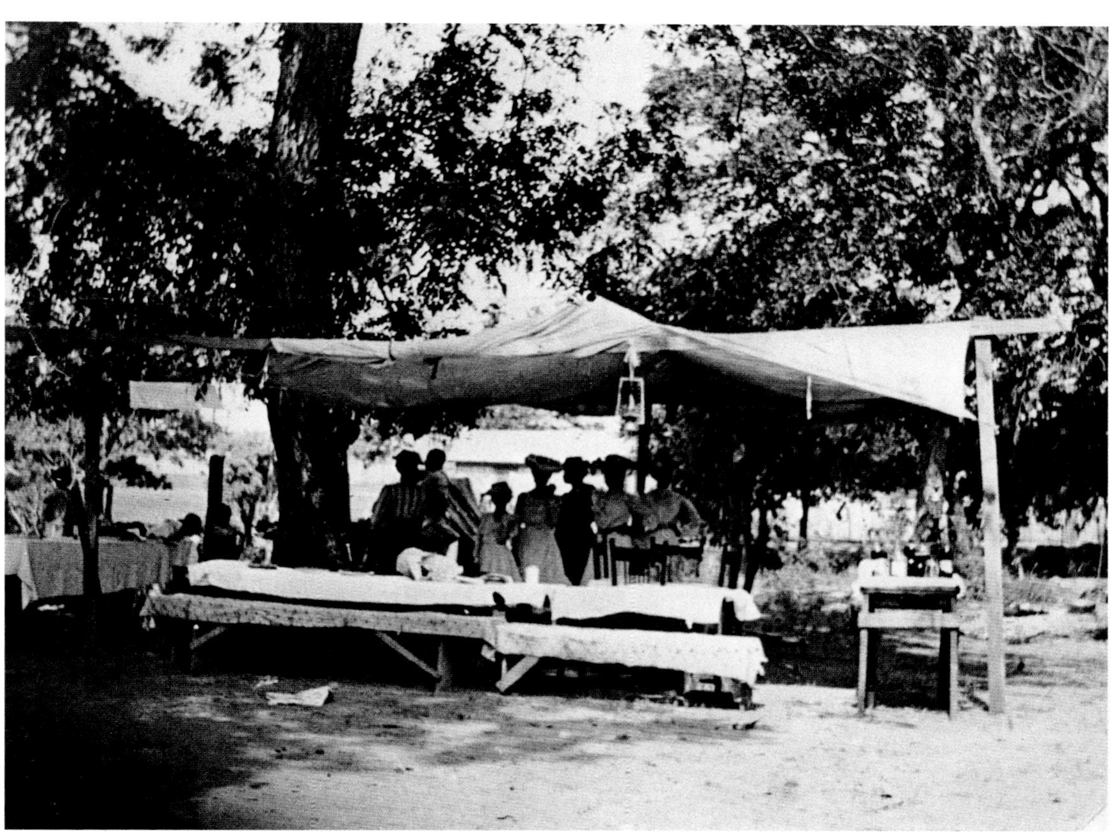

OPPOSITE: Elder celebrants gather for a picture during the Emancipation Day celebration, June 19, 1900, held in Austin, Texas. Although their names were not preserved along with the photograph, we know that the photographer is Grace Murray Stephenson since she kept a diary of the day's events.

ABOVE: One thousand nine hundred Juneteenth celebrants gathered under a tent in the park near Austin's East Woods on East 24th Street. Dressed in hats and high collars, they marked the day with music, prayer, food, and fellowship, hallmarks of the annual celebration.

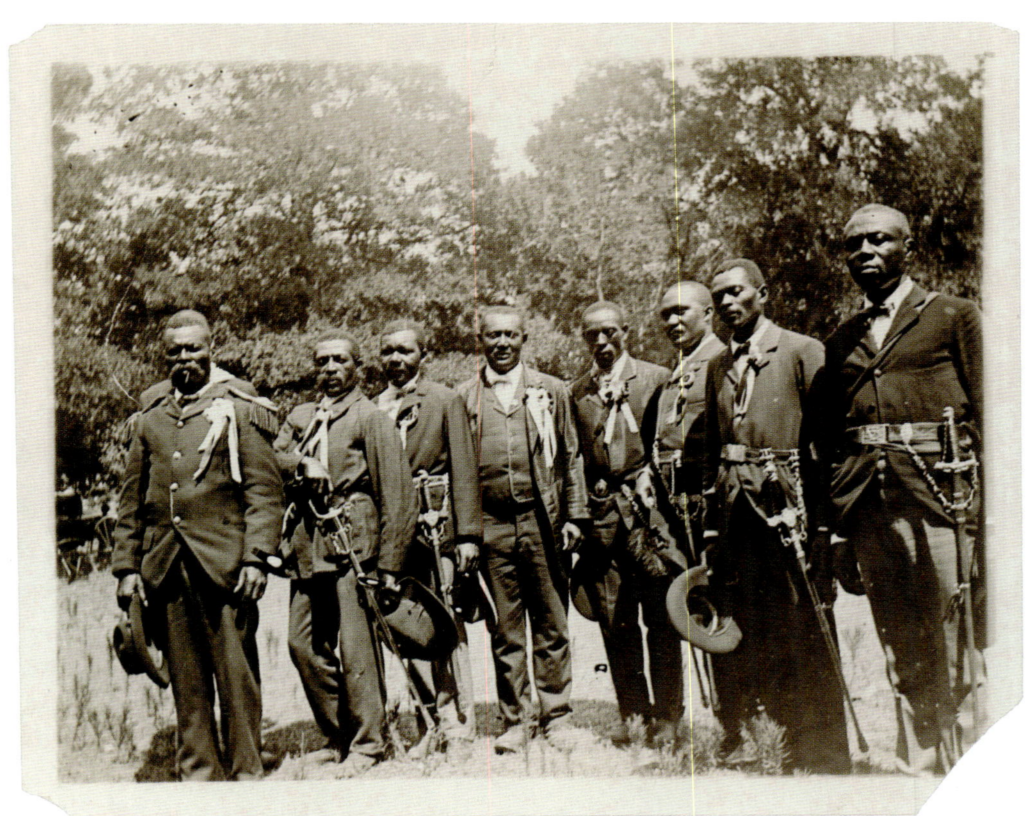

ABOVE: Black militiamen posed with ceremonial swords on their hips, June 19, 1900, after marching in the Emancipation Day Juneteenth procession. Their display of military pride was a reminder of the legacy of Black military service during the Civil War, when thousands of Black soldiers fought for freedom, playing a vital role in the Union victory.

OPPOSITE: The Grand Marshal of Austin, Texas's 1900 Emancipation Day parade, pictured in a ceremonial white uniform and carrying a sword. Although his name was not recorded with the photograph, he was likely a formerly enslaved elder. The formal dress and weaponry served as symbolic reminders of how Black Texans fought for their freedom and continued to organize to defend freedom's promise amid the rise of Jim Crow.

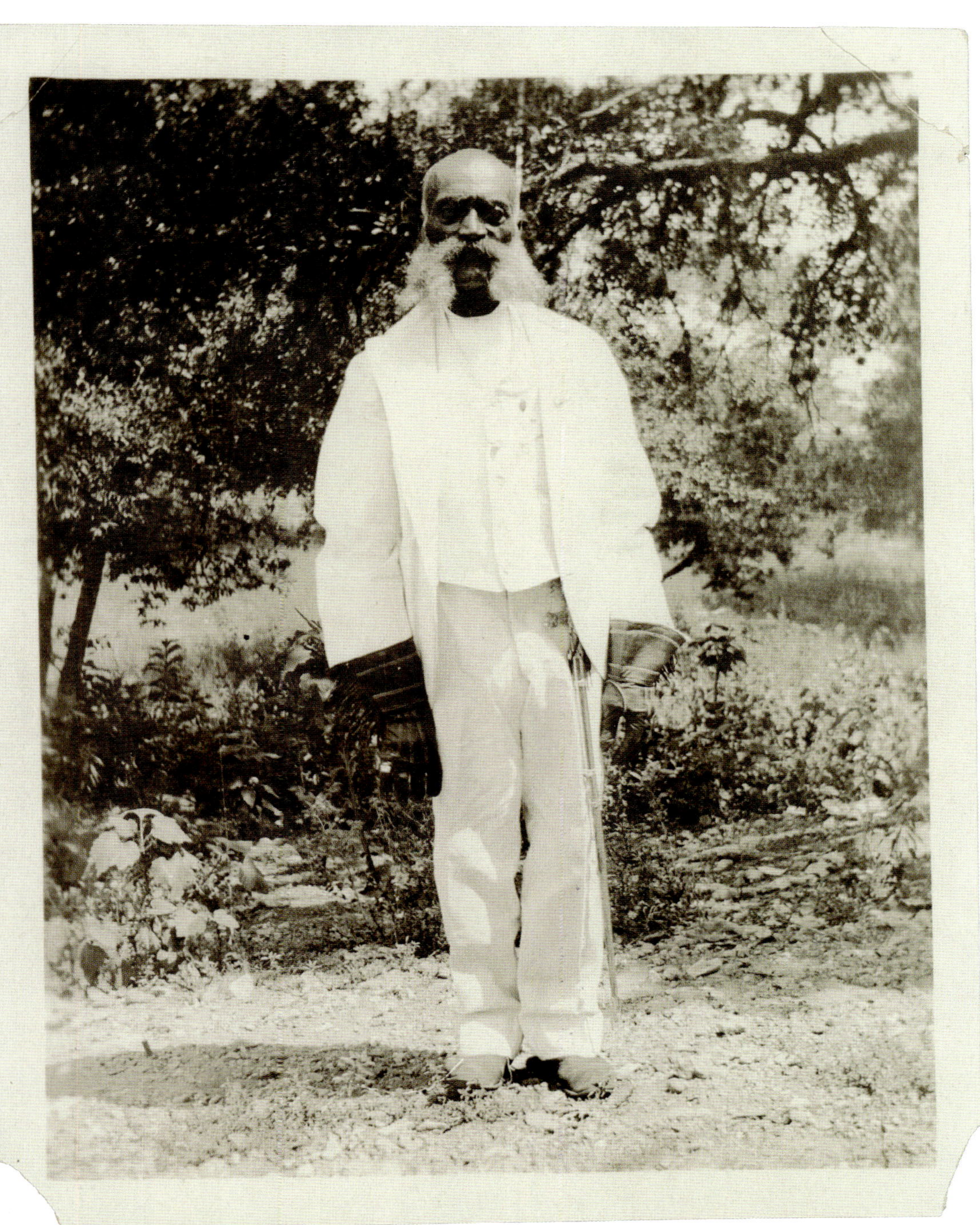

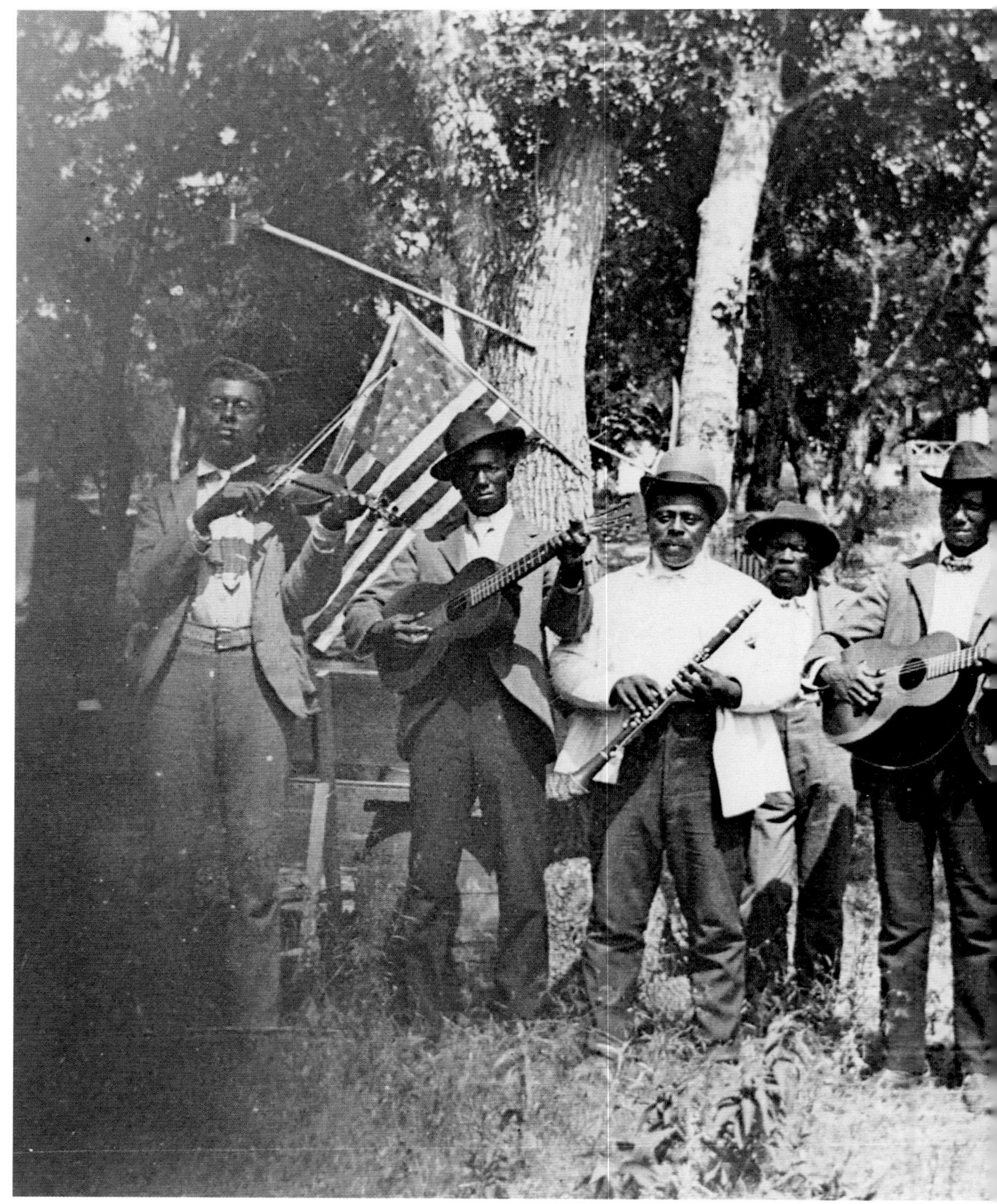

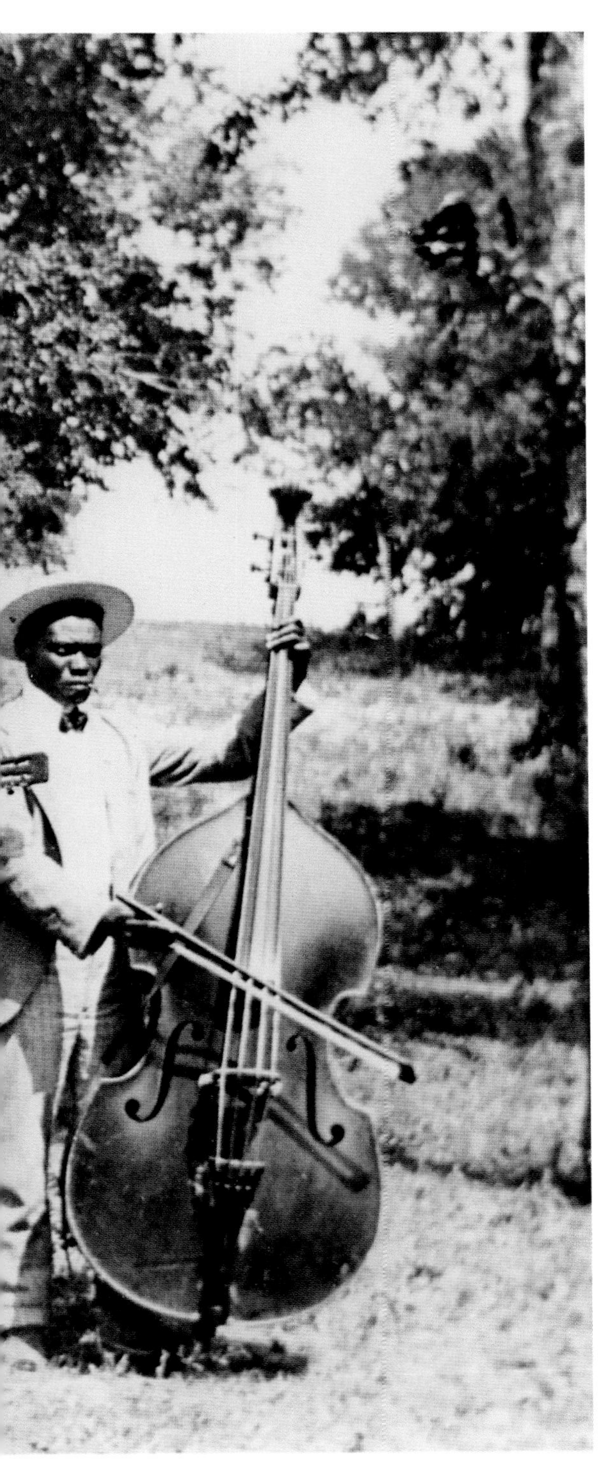

A band that participated in the Emancipation Day Juneteenth Celebration in Austin, Texas, June 19, 1900. This picture shows a group of six men with instruments including a cello, violin, woodwind instrument, and two guitars. While enslaved, Black musicians were often musically trained in order to entertain white audiences, but in freedom, their creativity and musicianship uplifted Black audiences during celebrations like Juneteenth.

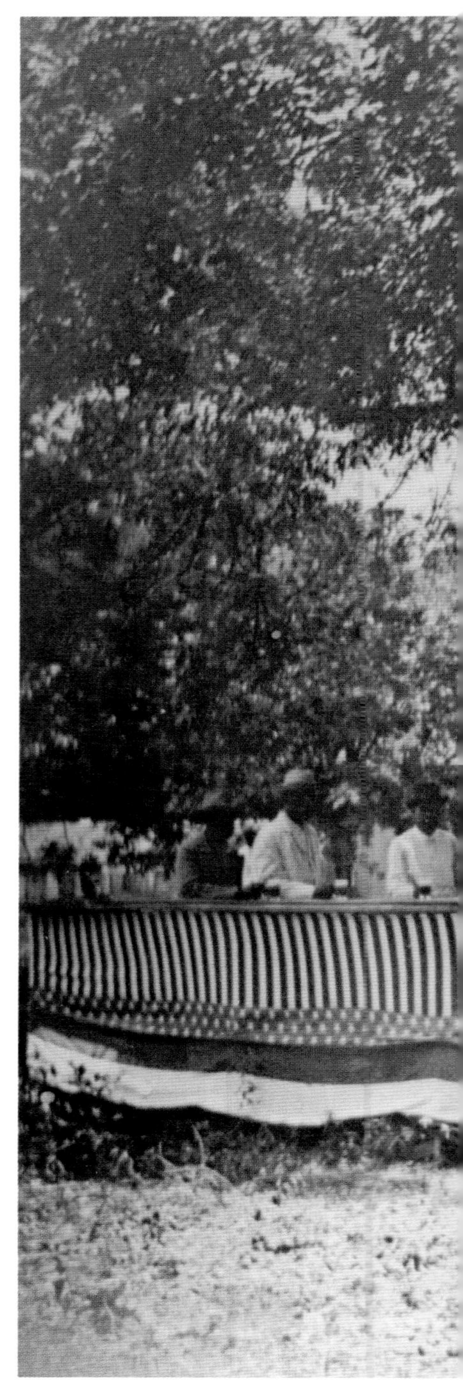

American flag bunting and the stars and stripes decorate a stage at the Emancipation Day Juneteenth Celebration at Eastwoods Park, Austin, Texas, June 19, 1900. Black celebrants rightfully claimed the symbolism of the American flag as their own during celebrations of Black freedom.

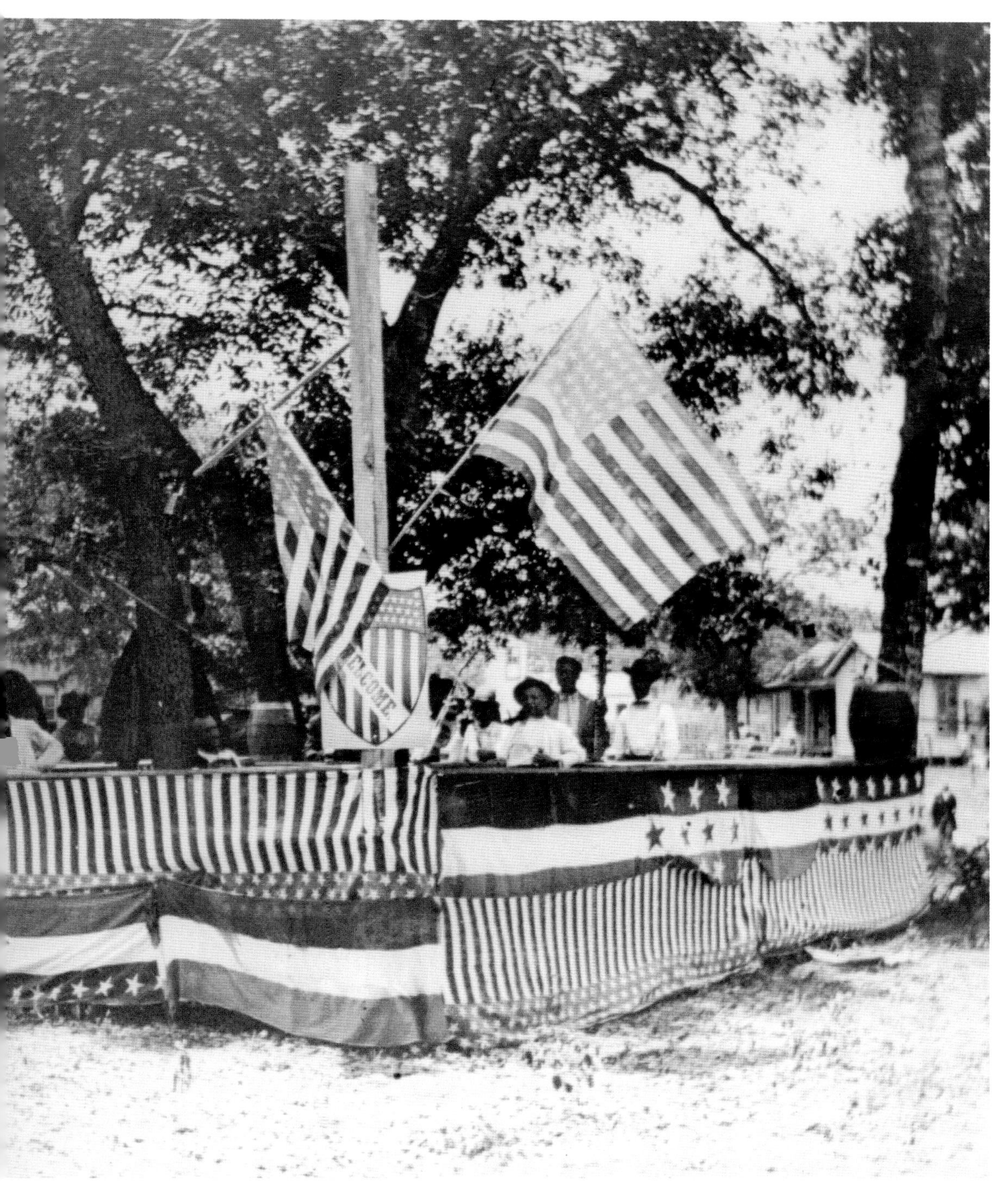
ELCOME

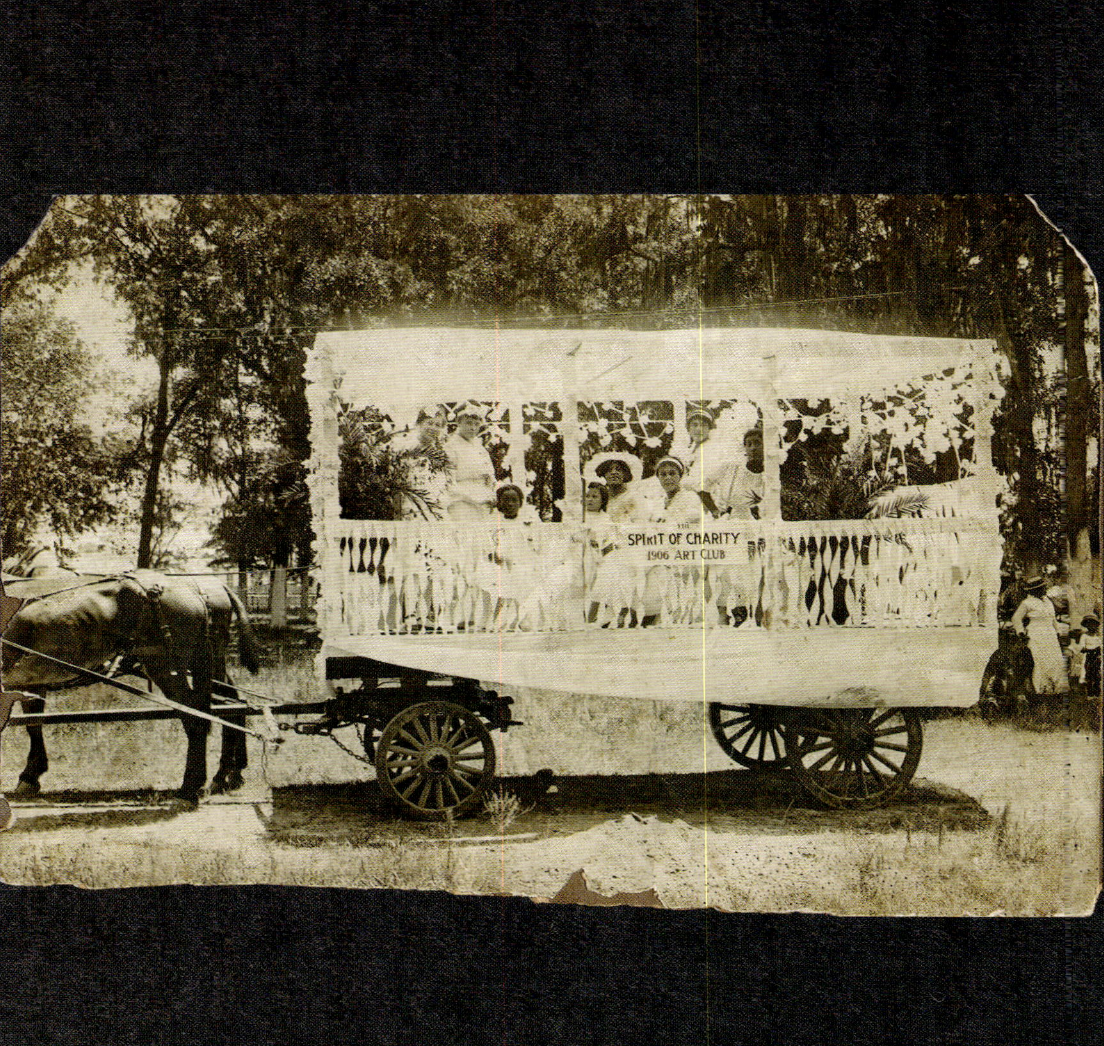
THE
SPIRIT OF CHARITY
1906 ART CLUB

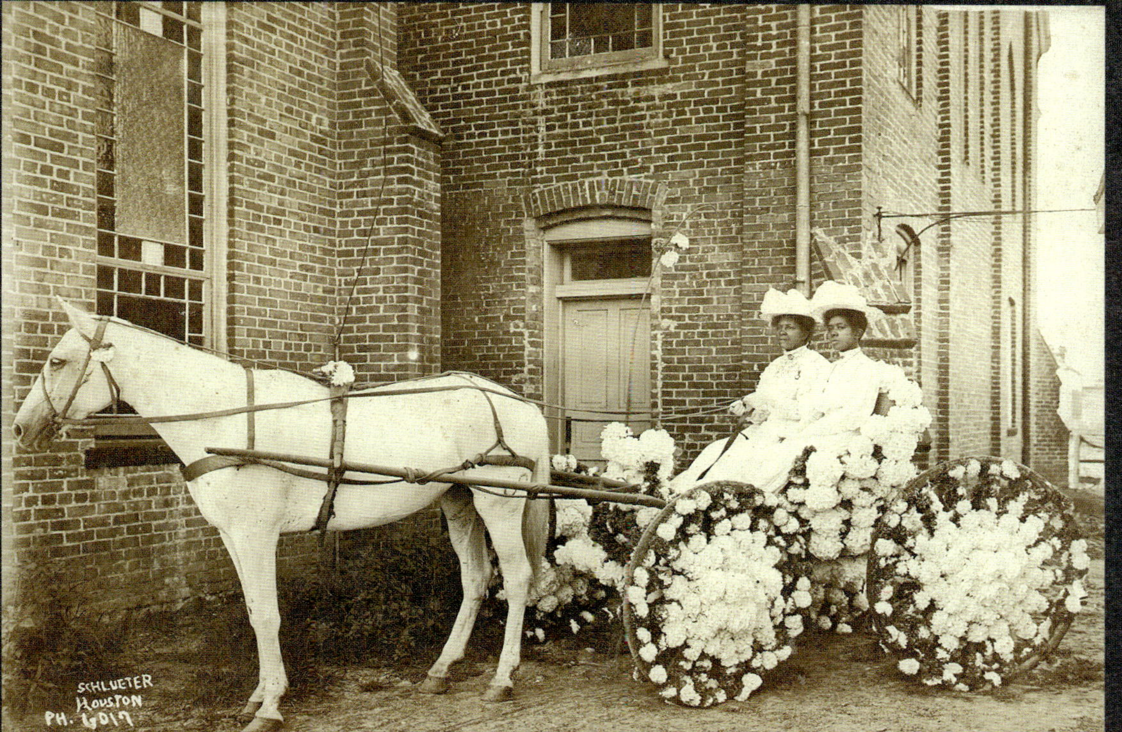

OPPOSITE: Adorned with fresh white flowers, this float in Houston, Texas's 1906 Juneteenth parade included six elegantly dressed Black women and two young girls, all in radiant white dresses, hats, and headpieces, riding next to a banner that reads "The Spirit of Charity 1906 Art Club." Hitched to two horses, the float was part of a floral-themed procession that blended beauty and artistry. These women and children embodied the dignity and creativity that defined Black freedom celebrations at the turn of the century.

ABOVE: Martha Yates Jones and Pinkie Yates, daughters of Reverand Jack Yates, one of the founders of Houston's Emancipation Park, in a buggy lavishly adorned with flowers for the June 19, 1908, Juneteenth parade. The buggy sits in front of Antioch Missionary Baptist Church, the congregation that Reverand Yates pastored. Once re-enslaved so that he could remain with his wife and children when they were taken to Texas, Reverand Yates and his family's story is one of extraordinary devotion and resilience. This photograph captures the beauty and pride Jack Yates's legacy made possible.

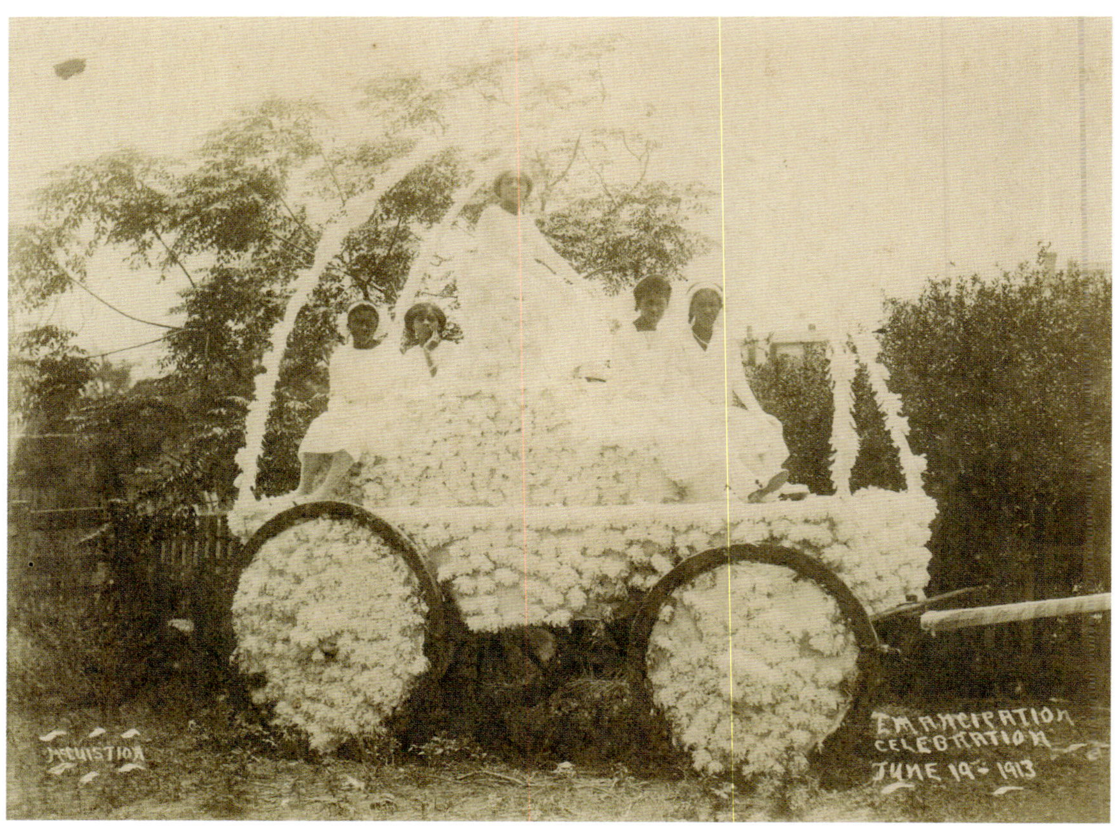

ABOVE: A group of women pose on an elaborately decorated carriage in Corpus Christi, Texas's Emancipation Day celebration, June 19, 1913. Dressed in all white and surrounded by hundreds of white flowers, the young women appear to be serving as a royal court for the woman seated at the top wearing a crown. The careful adornment of the wagon in blossoms reflects the love and detail Black people poured into Emancipation Day celebrations, creating something lovely for themselves in a world that so often demanded they serve others.

OPPOSITE TOP: Local businessman Daniel Newton Leathers driving an elaborately decorated one-horse carriage in the Corpus Christi, Texas, Emancipation celebration, June 19, 1913.

OPPOSITE BOTTOM: A man and two women ride in a flower-covered carriage in Corpus Christi, Texas's 1913 Juneteenth Day. Behind them, a towering stilt walker parades in the background.

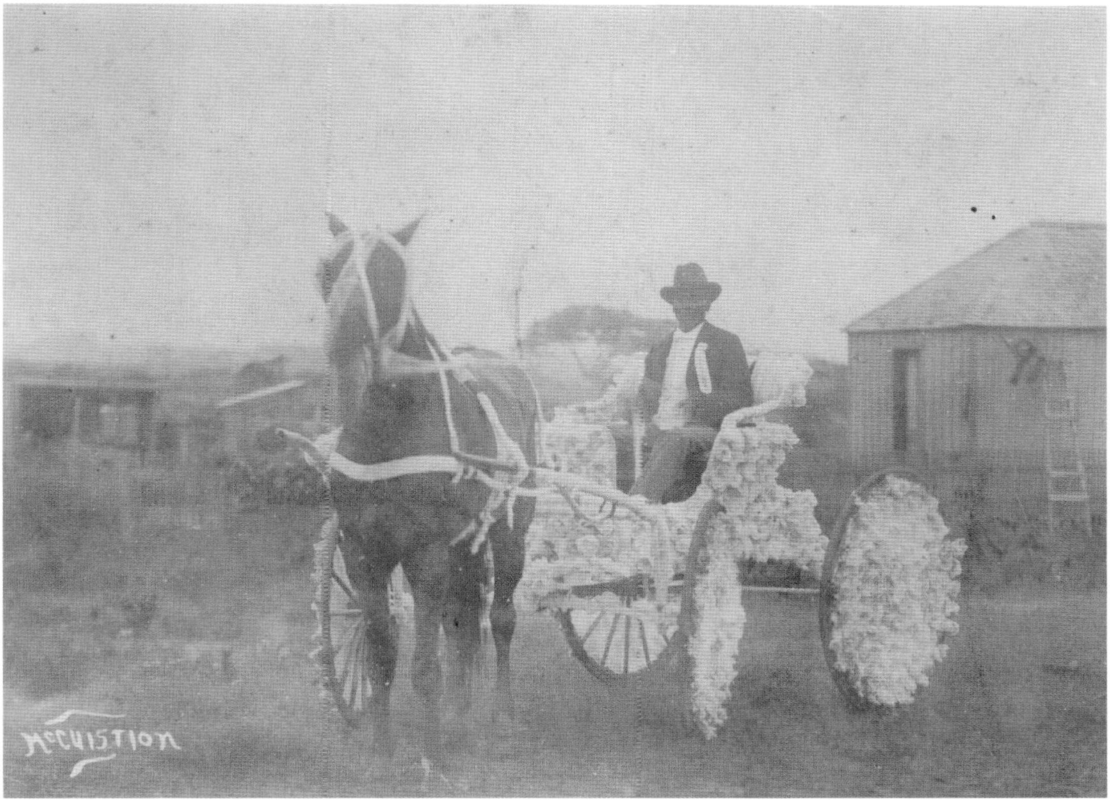

McCUISTION

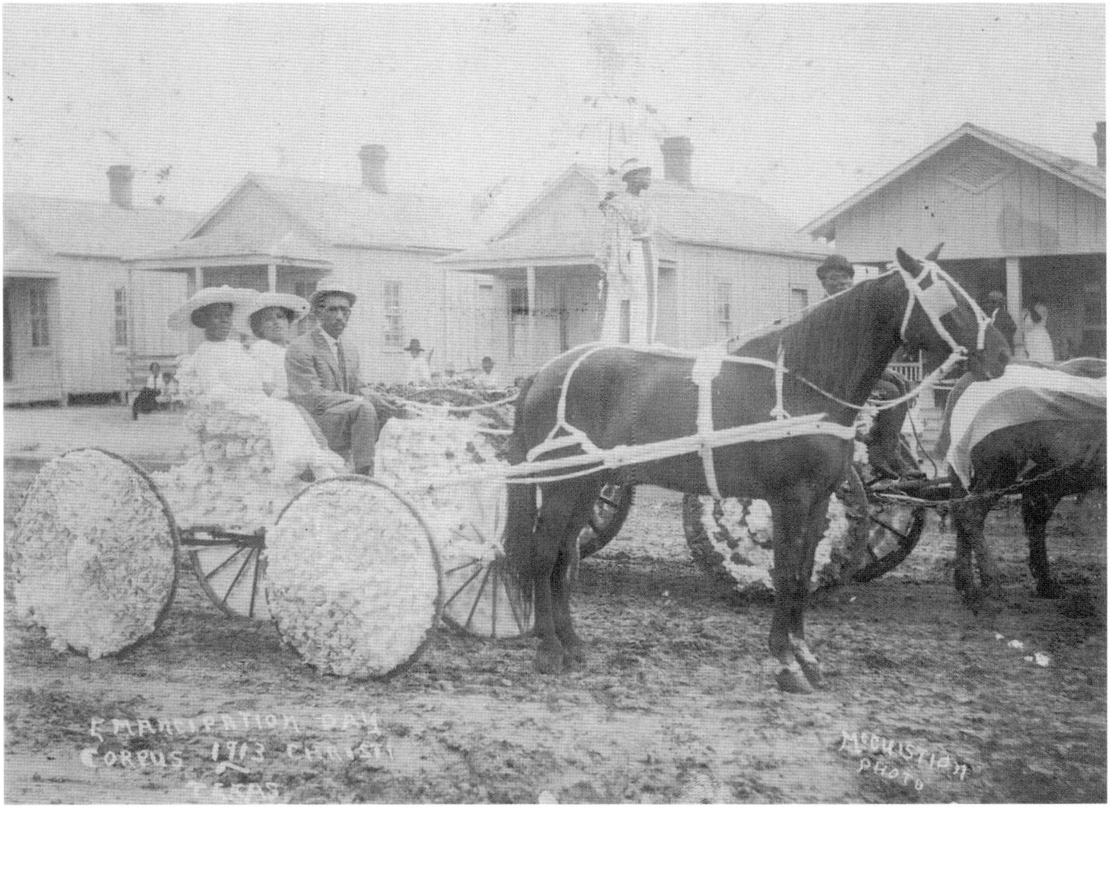

EMANCIPATION DAY
CORPUS 1913 CHRISTI
TEXAS
McCUISTION
PHOTO

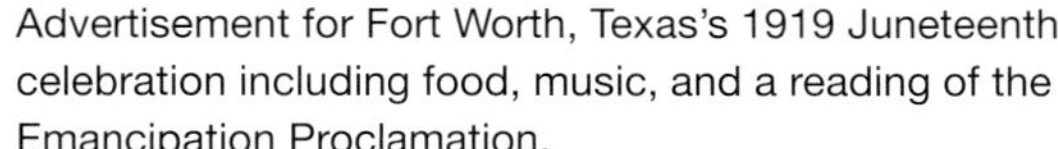

Advertisement for Fort Worth, Texas's 1919 Juneteenth celebration including food, music, and a reading of the Emancipation Proclamation.

Office Hours 7:30 A. M. to 6:30 P. M.

Phones Res. Res. 3910 Office Lamar 3801

Dr. R. E. Gilton

SURGEON DENTIST

Extraction Done Carefully and Easily

913½ Calhoun Street — Fort Worth

Office Phone L. 4082 — Res. Phone L. 4178

American Mutual Benefit Association

Incorporated

PAY SICK, ACCIDENT AND DEATH FOR SAME MONEY

I. C. BUTLER, District Superintendent

Office 911½ Jones Street — Fort Worth

PHONE—L. 4671 — NATHAN SMITH, Mgr.

FRED EARL TAILOR

Cleaning, Pressing and Repairing

First Class Shine Parlor in Connection

207 A. East Ninth Street

Texas Bottling Co.

First Class Soda Waters

Quick Deliveries

Phone L. 242 — 9th and Jones Streets

CROWN BARBER SHOP

J. W. SMITH, Prop.

307 E 9th Street

Phone Lamar 6083

J. T. Jeffrey Undertaking Co.

BEST AUTOMOBILE AMBULANCE

SERVICE IN THE CITY

OPEN DAY AND NIGHT

Cor. 10th and Gay Streets

Phone—Lamar 1157

The Limousine College

—of—

BEAUTY CULTURE

Scalp Specialist, Manicurist and Massage. I positively guarantee to stop falling hair and start the hair growing at once.

Diplomas given with the course of "The Limousine System." Ladies are invited to visit our Parlors.

MADAME A. B. GRIFFIN

I. E. MARTIN, President.

313 E. 9th Street — Fort Worth, Texas

Call—Lamar 2528; Lamar 4488

Preston's Capital Rent Co.

Stand 9th & Jones Streets

Rosedale 5611 — 961 East Rosedale

Frank Forte

ICE, COAL & WOOD

Our Service is Unexcelled

Buy Victory Bonds

Service That Is Complete

Not Comparable

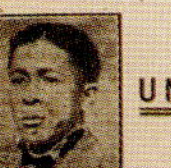

PEOPLES UNDERTAKING COMPANY

1014 E. FIRST ST — PHONE L. 1771

C. MORROW, Manager.

PHONES: Day: L. 4062; Night: L. 2267, R. 6455 — Polite Service Rendered

Union Undertaking Co

Funeral Directors and Embalmers. — Calls Will Be Answered

Promptly Day or Night. Call and See See Our Beutiful Show Room

H. B. HARDEE, Embalmer — I. C. BUTLER, Manger

S. R. PRINCE, President — J. H. WINN, Treasurer

910 Grove Street — Fort Worth, Texas

Temple Drug Store

W. M. McDONALD & SON, Props.

YOUR TRADE SOLICITED

WE TRY TO PLEASE

Phone L. 6009. If Busy L. 5109

I. HARROL MOSELY, Mgr.

105-5-7 Ninth Street — Prompt, Free Delivery

1865 54TH ANNIVERSARY 1919

EMANCIPATION PROCLAMATION

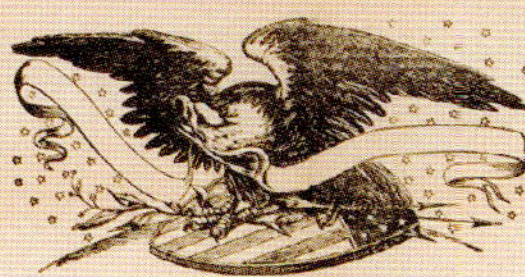

Thursday and Friday

JUNE 19-20 1919

At Herman's Park, Fort Worth, Texas

Take Stockyard Car. Get off on Viaduct. Walk down steps, turn to the left onto Gravel Walk, into the Beautiful Park

Barbecue will be under the management of Mr. O. C. Crook.

Bring your Basket and enjoy an Old Time Juneteenth Dinner

AMUSEMENTS

Big Bowling Alley, Free for Children's amusement and pleasure. K. of P. Brass Band will furnish music Day and Night. Matinee, Dancing that will be enjoyed by all

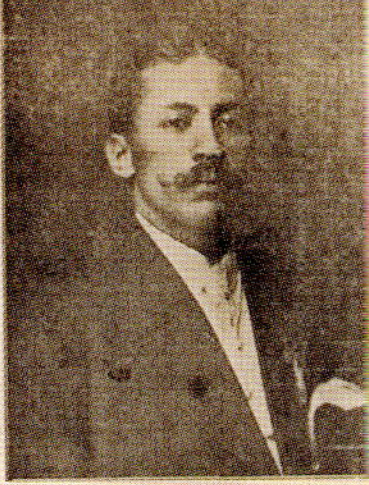

O. C. CROOK, Fort Worth, Texas

FREE GATES until Evening. After which an Admission of 30c will be Charged. Old Folks Free Day and Night Special Attention will be Given Ladies and Children at the Park

Ladies' Rest Room with all Conveniences

Play Ground for the Children

CALL LAMAR 2013 OR LAMAR 5103 — SEE NATHAN JOHNSON FOR REAL ESTATE BARGAINS — OFFICE 101 E. NINTH ST

SPEAKER OF THE DAY

HON. W. H. GRIGGS

Followed by Other Prominent Speakers

ESTABLISHED 1872 — WAPLES-PLATTER GROCER CO WHOLESALE GROCERS IMPORTERS. COFFEE ROASTERS — DENISON, FT. WORTH, DALLAS

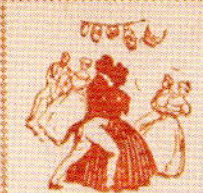

ON THE NIGHT OF THE 20TH

A SPECIAL BALL

In-Honor of Our Out-of-Town Pleasure Seakers. Come and Meet the Strangers

OLLIE TRIBUE & BILL GILLIAN, Floor Mgr's

THERE WILL BE REFRESHMENTS OF ALL KINDS

There will be Visitors from all Surrounding Towns

For Stand Privileges See O. C. Crook, Manager. Phone Lamar 7167

—Eat at The—

Dunbar Cafe

"The Place Where You Get What You Want, and Like What You Get."

REED & SLOAN, Props.

907 Jones Street

Compliments of

Northern Texas Traction Co.

"THE LINES OF GOOD SERVICE"

H. T. BOSTICK,

General Passenger Agent

SHEPARD'S STEAM DYE WORKS

THE BEST PLACE

To Have Your CLOTHES CLEANED.

Phone Lamar 2089. — 409 E. 9th St

The Ft. Worth Hornet

A Progressive Race Paper

Our Motto: "Equal Rights to all, Special Privileges to None."

Our Aim: 10,000 subscribers by Sept. 1, 1919.

J. I. DOTSON, Managing Editor

910 Jones Street — Phone L. 1947

Offices Hours: 7:30 A. M. to 6:30 P. M. Sunday by Appointment

Phones: Residence, Rosedale 287; Office L 4082

Dr. N. T. Wallis

DENTAL SURGEON

411½ E. 9th Street

McGARS PLACE

—For all Kinds of—

Soft Drinks, Finest cigars Always on Hand.

911-A Jones Street — Phone L 7107

Hampton & Co.

Up-to-date Groceries, Meats and Drugs

3rd and Crump Streets

When in FORT WORTH Stop at

The New Avenue Hotel

40 Nice Clean Rooms, A Nice Cafe, Barber Shop, Tailor Shop and Shine Parlor in Connection

QUICK AUTO SERVICE

Phone L. 2267

1712 Jones Street — G. T. OUSLEY, Prop.

W. S. CROSBY, M. D.

Physician and Surgeon

411½ E. 9th Street — L. 2674

All Work Guaranteed

Fort Worth Mechanical

Shoe Repairing Shop

1006 Houston St. — Mike Brant, Prop.

WE CALL FOR AND DELIVER — PHONE LAMAR 6887

THE

WHITEWAY DAIRY

S. C. Crook, Prop.

Buy Victory Bonds

Statement of the Condition of

TEXAS STATE BANK

of Fort Worth, Texas

As made to the Commissioner of Insurance and Banking, at Austin, Texas, at the Close of Business March 4th, 1919

Resources	
Loan and Discounts	$1,850,107.83
U. S. and Other Bonds for Investment	158,300.00
U. S. Certificates of Indebtedness	190,000.00
War Saving Stamps	5,627.21
Banking House	205,393.47
Furniture and Fixtures	16,179.98
Customer's Bond Account	87,550.00
Revenue Stamps	200.00
Interest in Depositors Guaranty Fund	20,829.57
Cash on Hand and in Banks	1,077,475.99
	$3,510,166.05
Liabilities	
Capital Stock	$200,000.00
Surplus and Undivided Profits	77,727.56
Bills Payable	150,000.00
Deposits	3,082,438.49
	$3,510,166.05

CELEBRA

BLA

FREE

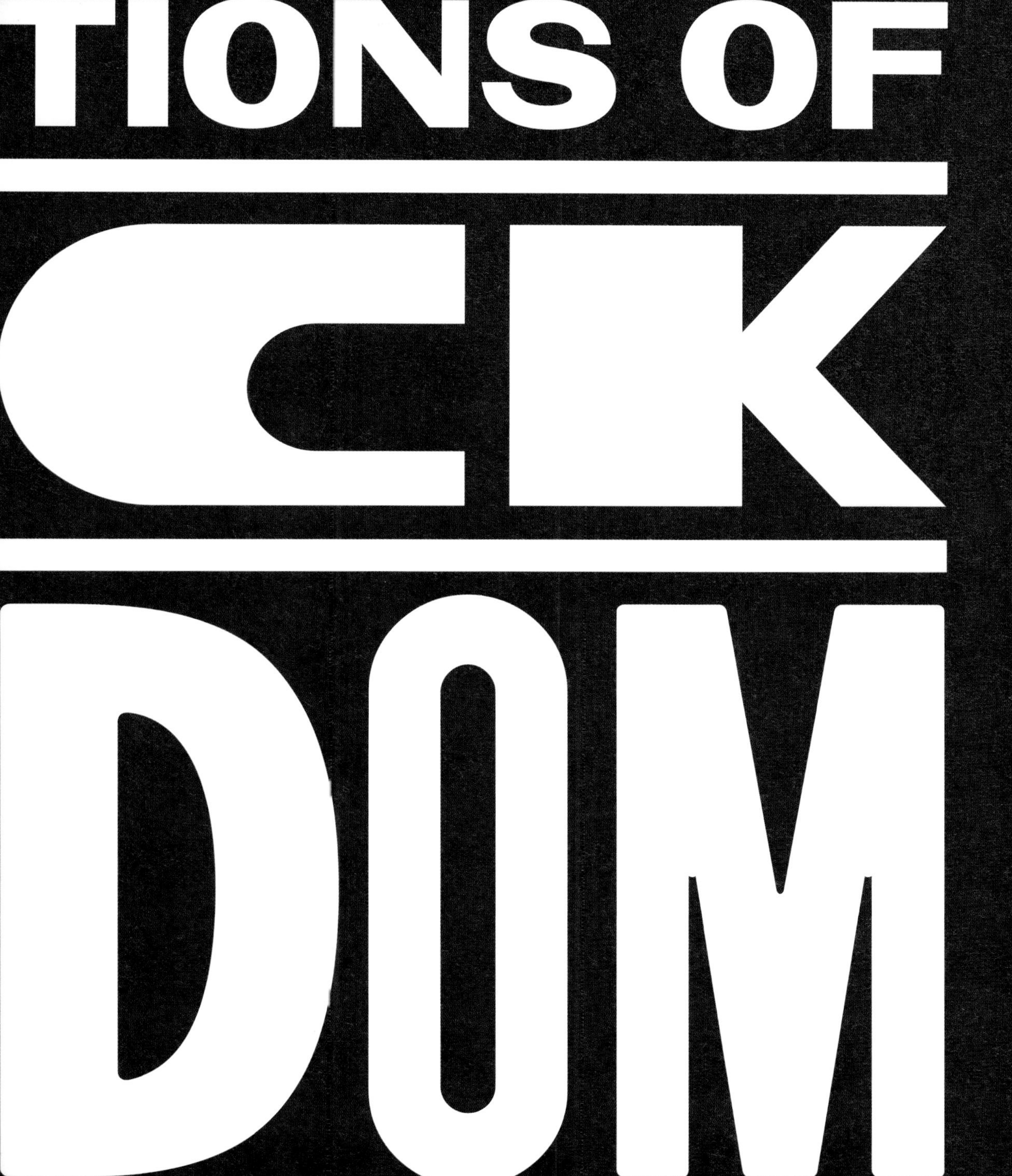
TIONS OF
CK
DOM

IN A VOICE FROM THE SOUTH, Raleigh-born educator and intellectual Anna Julia Cooper reflected on the liminal space into which she was born, caught between enslavement and the distant promise of freedom. Born in 1860 to an enslaved mother and most likely her white enslaver or a member of his family, she spent her early childhood in the midst of war. On the plantation where she was held in bondage, the enslaved believed that as an infant she was "nearer Heaven" and possessed a spiritual power to divine "which side is goin' to win de war." She could not say what her cries foretold, but Cooper's story endures as a testament to the enslaved community's unwavering hope for liberation. Her life as a brilliant intellectual underscores the profound injustice of slavery—that millions of people, people with minds capable of teaching, writing, and leading, were all summarily condemned to toil beneath a cruel and false hierarchy. Yet those who stood both near and far from heaven in 1860 would soon turn the vision of freedom into a reality, carrying forward an unshaken readiness to teach, to write, and to guide the nation toward a more expansive understanding of liberty and citizenship.

From the very first moments of emancipation, Black communities across the country celebrated their newfound freedom. These early commemorations were not just gatherings but powerful expressions of long-suppressed emotions, born from generations of suffering under the brutality of slavery. They reflected the sheer jubilation of freedom's arrival, the deep pain of bondage, and an unwavering belief in a future filled with possibility.

In Raleigh, North Carolina, the city where Anna Julia Cooper was born, newly freed Black residents asserted their presence in a profound way by taking over the city's Fourth of July festivities in 1865. Their celebration was particularly significant given Raleigh's role in the final days of the Civil War. As one of the last major cities to see the conflict come to an end, its fate was closely tied to the fall of the Confederacy. Just a few hours north was the Confederate capital of Richmond, Virginia, which fell to Union forces on April 3, 1865. Less than a week later, on April 9, General Robert E. Lee surrendered at Appomattox Court House in Virginia. With the Confederate cause crumbling, North Carolina's Confederate governor, Zebulon Vance, began to negotiate the surrender of Raleigh, sending officials to meet with Union General William

T. Sherman. That surrender was finalized at Bennett Place, a farmhouse in nearby Durham, on April 26, 1865, effectively marking the end of the war in the state. By June 1865, the war was over all over the nation.

Against this backdrop, Black Raleighites reclaimed Independence Day in 1865, their first collective opportunity to formally celebrate freedom, as their own. The Fourth of July had long been meaningless for people who were not free. As Frederick Douglass so famously stated in 1852:

> What, to the American slave, is your 4th of July? I answer, a day that reveals to him, more than all other days in the year, the gross injustice and cruelty to which he is the constant victim. To him, your celebration is a sham; your boasted liberty, an unholy license; your national greatness, swelling vanity; your sounds of rejoicing are empty and heartless; your denunciation of tyrants, brass fronted impudence; your shouts of liberty and equality, hollow mockery; your prayers and hymns, your sermons and thanksgivings, with all your religious parade and solemnity, are, to Him, mere bombast, fraud, deception, impiety, and hypocrisy—a thin veil to cover up crimes which would disgrace a nation of savages. There is not a nation on the earth guilty of practices more shocking and bloody than are the people of the United States, at this very hour.

So, the July 4 celebration was transformative for the city of Raleigh and for the South. The ex-slaves were boldly redefining a holiday long associated with American liberty into a powerful statement about their freedom and their rightful place in the nation's future. Still reveling in their newfound freedom, they made that year's Fourth of July a powerful Emancipation Day celebration, seizing the moment to redefine independence on their own terms. Their grand procession through the city's streets was a striking assertion of their presence, dignity, and calls for full citizenship.

In the decades before emancipation came to the American South, free Black communities in the North held annual freedom celebrations, not as a way to separate themselves from those who were still held in bondage in the South, but to keep reminding the nation that emancipation was a possibility for all. Because Northern slavery had been abolished gradually in the decades leading up to the Civil War, Northern emancipation occurred at different times, through various legislative measures, and by different means across state lines. There was no single date that marked freedom's arrival in the antebellum North. But when the British Empire officially freed more than 670,000 people held in bondage across its West Indian colonies on August 1, 1834, Black Americans moved in solidarity to adopt August 1 as a day of collective commemoration. August 1 became a diasporic holiday, one that connected their struggle for freedom with that of others across the Atlantic world. The peaceful legislative end of slavery in the British colonies offered both a beacon of hope and a potential model for how abolition might come to the American South. They called it Freedom Day.

Northern Black communities embraced annual August 1 celebrations, which were filled with speeches, sermons, parades, and community gatherings. Freedom Day became the most widely observed Black holiday in the antebellum period. For a time, it unified Black Americans in the North around the shared cause of abolitionism and a common hope. That embrace of a single holiday for celebration would begin to shift, however, with the coming of the American Civil War and the staggered, complex, and hard-fought victories of emancipation that unfolded in the South. Southern Black communities would embrace their own local and national dates of significance in their struggle for freedom, just as Black Raleigh took over the celebration of the Fourth of July.

Even during the Civil War, cities that were held by Union forces early on in the war effort had Watch Night ceremonies and Emancipation Day celebrations. But after the war's conclusion, it was not uncommon for Black celebrations to take place on a variety of dates, even within the same city. As historians James Oliver Horton and Lois E. Horton noted, speaking about Richmond, Virginia:

> African Americans also quickly began to celebrate four holidays after the Civil War: New Year's Day, George Washington's birthday, April 3 as their own emancipation day, and the

Fourth of July. Black militias paraded on these and other occasions, while black parades for occasions such as funerals and conventions were frequent occurrences, often featuring the uniformed members of various benevolent societies. By the beginning of the twentieth century, most of these activities had been restricted to black neighborhoods, although parades were known to march from one black neighborhood to another through the center of town.

RALEIGH'S FIRST EMANCIPATION DAY

Several grand celebrations were celebrated each year in most cities of the South. White observers were often hostile to these Black celebrations, which served as reminders of the day when the world was turned upside down and "the day of the time server had passed."

A local white newspaper, *The Daily Progress*, chronicled Raleigh's first Fourth of July–turned–Emancipation Day celebration with open hostility, interweaving the account of the day's festivities with insults and derision. Yet despite the paper's clear bias, its report remains one of the only surviving records of that historic day, preserving vivid details that would otherwise have been lost to time. Remarkably, even the antagonistic writer could not deny the power of the celebration that day; as the report admitted, "It is an undeniable fact that the celebration of the Fourth of July by the colored people of Raleigh and vicinity was a success beyond the expectation of every one." The parade was described as "orderly" and followed its planned route "without interruption or disturbance." The streets came alive with "music playing, banners flying and penants [sic] streaming," and onlookers crowded in from every side. According to the writer, the event "elicited many remarks, and we heard but few except in praise."

Black people traveled from far and wide to take part in the festivities. "For days previous to the Fourth," the reporter noted, "the road from the country leading to Raleigh [was] lined with freedmen coming to participate." Dressed in their Sunday best or clothing crafted especially for that day, they sought to make a powerful impression. The reporter observed that many parade-goers were dressed in "fine linen covering, brogan shoes or fine cloth shoes," though he also mocked that the newly freed people were wearing "homespun clothes and other inconsistencies of dress, including of course the African predilection for gay colors." Despite his condescending tone, the writer acknowledged that the parade-goers defied the negative stereotypes that plagued Black people, observing that "they tramped through the dusty streets in the sweltering sun regardless of everything but a desire to appear well, attract attention, and preserve order."

An estimated 3,000 Black men and women filled the streets that day, with at least 2,000 marching in the procession. The atmosphere was jubilant as crowds gathered around the musicians, eagerly following them along the parade route. Parade participants carried extraordinary banners chronicling the history being commemorated and celebrating their hopes for the future that were unfolding on that hot July day. One banner carried by the Equal Rights League included the red, white, and blue of the American flag and stated, "No Slave lives beneath this flag." Several banners were printed with Lincoln's words, a particularly poignant memorial in the wake of his assassination just two and a half months earlier. The immortalized words of Lincoln's Emancipation Proclamation of January 1, 1863, were sewn into a banner's fabric: "And upon this act, sincerely believed to be an act of justice, warranted by the Constitution upon military necessity, I invoke the considerate judgment of mankind, and the gracious favor of Almighty God." Two banners carried by Black parade participants drew on Lincoln's second inaugural address. The first commemorated his words forewarning the nation that the struggle of the Civil War and the fight to end slavery would be a long and brutal one, costing many lives in order to meet the cause of justice: "If God wills that this mighty scourge of war continue until all the wealth piled by two hundred and fifty years of unrequited toil shall be sunk, and until every drop of blood drawn by the lash shall be paid by another drawn with the sword, as was said three thousand years ago, so still it must be said—the judgments of the Lord are true and righteous altogether." Another featured the words of reconciliation that Lincoln used to close the address: "With malice towards none, with charity for all," a powerful statement of forgiveness for people who had suffered the profound violence of intergenerational slavery.

A group of Black Union veterans carried a red, white, and blue banner bearing a simple but powerful message: "We fought for the Flag: Port Hudson, Milliken's Bend, Olustee, Fort Wagner." The places named were those battles in which Black soldiers had fought. The banner was both a declaration and a testament, a history lesson unfurled in fabric. Though it had few words, it spoke to the soldiers' valor, implicitly noting the sacrifices they had made in the pursuit of freedom, and it spoke volumes about the powerful legacy of Black service to the Union cause.

The Battle of Milliken's Bend in June 1863 had been one the first true tests of Black troops in combat during the Civil War. Many of the soldiers who fought there had only recently been freed from slavery, and they had barely completed their training before they were thrust into battle against experienced Confederate forces. Although the battle was a Union victory, it came at a high price; more than 420 Black soldiers were killed, and more than 100 were said to be missing. But numbers hid a terrible truth: The Black men who were captured by Confederate forces were not held prisoner, as white Union soldiers were, but instead were executed or sold back into slavery. Yet despite the risks Black soldiers faced, their bravery was undeniable. While many people had argued that Black men were useful only as laborers and servants to the Union cause, news of Black men fearlessly standing their ground on a battlefield shattered doubts about their capabilities as soldiers and proved to Union leadership that they had been correct to enlist Black men.

At Port Hudson, Black soldiers of the 1st and 3rd Louisiana Native Guard had participated in a grueling but strategically important campaign between May and July of 1863. Their fierce resistance helped the Union gain control over the Mississippi River, cutting off an important supply route to Confederate forces. This victory, though a costly one, helped hobble the Confederacy's power.

The Battle of Fort Wagner in July 1863 became legendary thanks to the heroism of the 54th Massachusetts Volunteer Infantry, one of the first state regiments of Black volunteers. They fought bravely during a nearly impossible charge at a heavily fortified Confederate stronghold on Morris Island, near Charleston, South Carolina. They sustained heavy loss of life, but the sacrifices of the 54th led to the enlistment of more Black troops from the North, marking their place in history.

In February 1864, the 54th also fought the Battle of Olustee, a small but brutal engagement in Florida. Once again Confederate forces, seeking retribution against free Black men, slaughtered the wounded and captured Black soldiers.

Black soldiers fought for the Union not to preserve the nation as it was, but to transform it. To change what might be possible for millions of people held in bondage. They paid an immeasurable price for their service. But in that Fourth of July–turned–Emancipation Day parade in Raleigh, North Carolina, they would not let their legacy be erased. The veterans' single, simple banner held high through the streets on that bright day commemorated a history of tremendous sacrifice. It was a declaration of their rightful place in the national story of valor and sacrifice that defined the Civil War.

While white Southerners claimed that Black citizenship and voting rights would endanger the "safety" of white women, their rhetoric was laced with hypocrisy. They framed their opposition to Black political participation as a defense against the imagined threat of rape and violence from Black men, while conveniently ignoring the generations of sexual violence that white enslavers had inflicted upon Black women. They labeled this supposed threat "social equality," using it as a rallying cry to resist even the most basic rights for newly freed people.

The Daily Progress made sure to note that white women of Raleigh did not participate in the city's Fourth of July festivities at all. The newspaper sought to explain their absence, portraying it not as a sign of disdain or lack of patriotism, but as an aversion to the new and unfamiliar presence of freed Black people in public spaces. The writer painted a picture of a city transformed beyond recognition:

> It was not contempt or even indifference to the day, but an indisposition to encounter the jostling crowd in the streets. Up to the beginning of the war Raleigh had been an inland, rather retired and very quiet place: the people were quiet and not very demonstrative, and even on festive occasions they seldom were brought into contact with strangers. But now, the streets being entirely filled with soldiers, negroes, men and women, and strangers from the four quarters, and notwithstanding the strictness of the military rule. . . . It is no prejudice towards the Union officers and soldiers, no indifference to the fourth of July, but simply because the change from a quiet, country town to the noise, bustle, crowd and confusion of a city has been so sudden that they do not yet feel at home in the seething, rushing, boiling cauldron. The ladies of Raleigh are not less patriotic than others, but the habits, tastes, and diffidence of education and association cannot be overcome in a moment.

The imagery of a once "quiet" Raleigh suddenly transformed into a "boiling cauldron" of movement that endangered white ladies was revealing. The same Black men, women, and children who had always lived in Raleigh and its surrounding counties in involuntary service to those same white women were suddenly now a threat. Unshackled and asserting their rights, they had been transformed into dangerous strangers. One banner carried in the parade directly countered the hysteria and hyperbole of white fears. Its message was simple and precise: "Equal Rights before the Law: the only equality we ask."

In those few words, Black Raleighites made their demands unmistakable. They were not threatening racial chaos nor the social upheaval some white Southerners used to stoke fear; they were simply advocating for the same legal rights afforded to any American citizen. But even this modest, measured request was met with resistance. The false notion that the mere presence of free Black people posed an existential danger would, in the decades to come, fuel the rise of racial violence, including the lynchings of thousands. The equal rights banner foreshadowed the long battle for Black rights and violent backlash that accompanied it.

The banners carried in Raleigh's Fourth of July parade of 1865 were not just the building blocks of Black memory but declarations of Black aspirations for the future. They spoke not just to the struggles of the present but to the hopes for the future. One such banner emphasized what the freed people would pass down to their children, reading, "We will teach our children to love the Union." After enduring a system that denied them the right to teach their own children, the opportunity for education and agency was an important way forward. They saw the Union as their path to ensuring a lasting freedom, and they intended to raise their children with an unshakable allegiance to it. It was a vision of a future in which their descendants would never be as vulnerable as they themselves had been as slaves.

Another banner bore the words of William Woods Holden, North Carolina's provisional governor, appointed by President Andrew Johnson after the Confederacy's defeat. It was a simple but important statement: "You may now learn to read yourselves, and also instruct others." Literacy had been forbidden to enslaved people, with laws in place to prevent them from acquiring even the most basic education. Now a new generation would be able to put those repressive laws behind them, and young people like Anna Julia Cooper would have opportunities to be scholars and teachers. Learning was one of their most important missions as a free people.

A final banner recorded in *The Daily Progress*'s account of the day drew on the Old Testament verse from Isaiah 13:12: "And I will make a man more precious than gold; yea, a man more precious than the golden wedge of Ophir." It was God's warning to man that pride and wickedness would be judged, resulting in the death of so many people that humanity itself would become a rare commodity. The former slaves viewed the war and its immense loss of life as part of God's reckoning upon a sinful nation. They who had long endured the brutality of their oppressors saw the Civil War as not just a military conflict but a moral and spiritual reckoning, one in which the wickedness of slavery had been judged. Their presence in the streets that day, marching as free men and women, was itself proof that the judgment had come, and that their suffering had not been in vain.

The parade that day led to the grounds of the Peace Institute. Originally founded as a Presbyterian school for girls, the institute featured a grand main building that had been commandeered during the war to serve as the site of Raleigh's Confederate hospital. After the surrender, the building was repurposed again, this time as the headquarters of Raleigh's branch of the Freedmen's Bureau. The crowd seated themselves on benches in front of a grandstand, on the lawn under towering trees, while speakers were seated on the stage.

The program that day began with a solemn prayer from Reverend Mingo G. Croom, a respected Black minister from the African Methodist Episcopal Church (which later became St. Paul AME Church), who set the tone for the event with an invocation that called upon divine guidance and strength for the newly freed. (The people speaking at and organizing the early celebrations of the Black freedom were also strategizing about upbuilding community. Reverend Croom, for example, would later become a trustee of Raleigh's Oberlin Cemetery and one of the homeowners in one of the first Black communities to be founded by freed people in Raleigh.)

Following Reverend Croom's prayer, A. M. Allen of the Christian Commission took the stage to recite the Declaration of Independence, whose words of liberty and equality had for too long rung hollow for the enslaved. On this day, however, the "self-evident" truths that "all men are created equal" and that they are "endowed by their Creator with certain unalienable Rights" rang out with new possibility. As the crowds of free people celebrated their emancipation, they were also making a set of demands for full equality and citizenship. Next, C. A. Scott, a Black leader from Randolph County, read aloud a proclamation from the governor. The presence of these official declarations—both the Declaration of Independence and the governor's proclamation—underscored the significance of the moment, as newly freed people claimed their rightful place in the state and the nation.

An abolitionist and correspondent for the *New-York Tribune*, Elias Smith, delivered an oration that was well received by the crowd. He reaffirmed the importance of advocating for Black rights. Although a cynical reporter from *The Daily Progress* wrote that the freed slaves likely did not fully understand his "big words," Smith's speech was a clear moment of recognition and encouragement for the freed people. The audience of freed people had been listening on the sidelines for a long time. They understood the importance of rights as the best way to make their freedoms long-lasting.

After the speeches, the ceremony concluded like a church service with a communal singing of a Christian doxology and a blessing of benediction from Reverend Croom, bringing a spiritual close to the formal portion of the event. But the day's celebrations were far from over. Beneath the shade of the trees, a feast was laid out on long tables, offering an "excellent collation" for all who had gathered. The meal, prepared with care, provided a moment for reconnection and joy as families and friends shared in the significance of the day.

In the days following the celebration, its organizers convened at the Peace Institute to formally express their gratitude to those who had supported the event. They extended thanks to the board of trustees of the Peace Institute for generously allowing them the use of their grounds. Recognizing the importance of military protection during this time of transition and uncertainty, they also expressed deep appreciation to the leaders of the Union forces in Raleigh for ensuring the safety of the Black community as they celebrated their first true Independence Day. Finally, the committee issued a special acknowledgment to the various organizing committees of the day's festivities. They particularly praised the freedwomen who had worked tirelessly as cooks and seamstresses, crafting banners, fitting uniforms, and preparing food to ensure the success of the day's program. Women who had long labored to feed and beautify for the benefit of others had finally had the opportunity to do their work for the upliftment of their own people. Their behind-the-scenes dedication had brought the celebration to life, ensuring that the newly freed people of Raleigh could properly mark this historic moment.

Looking back on that Raleigh celebration, it is difficult to fully comprehend the depth and scope of what the celebrants were experiencing. These were individuals who had only recently been subjected to the chains of bondage, traded and sold like property at Raleigh's slave market. They had witnessed the world upended as the chaos of war unfolded around them. Many of them had joined the Union cause, fighting and dying as soldiers for freedom, or fleeing from those who had once held them as chattel. When freedom finally arrived, they found themselves liberated in body but in a world that had not yet changed enough to make them equal citizens. In that moment of new freedom in 1865, when Union soldiers still patrolled the streets, they were free to move, free to celebrate, free to express their joy in a moment that had long been anticipated.

Yet even in their newfound freedom, they remained surrounded by those who had bought and sold them, separating them from their families, friends, and communities. They were still among those who had punished them for expressing any hint of independence. The ever-present threat of retribution remained a cloud on their horizons. Their skies were also clouded by their memories of the tragedies they had endured, mourning those who had died in bondage, and those who had died in the fight for freedom. And yet they insisted on claiming that space to celebrate. To move in joy with one another. After all, they had dreamed and prayed and waited for freedom. They were determined to celebrate it when it came. They did not allow the brutalities of the past to overshadow their right to celebrate the dawning of a new life. They lived in a time of fear and triumph, so the celebrations were a reminder, to themselves and to the world, that they were choosing to turn the page and begin again in joy.

The newly freed also sought to make their experiences part of the historical record. They marched under banners marked in red, emblazoned with the words of the president who had finally advocated for their freedom. His life was tragically cut short, but his legacy remained in their memory of his words. They did not idolize him as a god, but they remembered him as a human being who had laid the groundwork for what freedom should mean. His words would continue to guide them in their fight for justice and equality.

These celebrants knew exactly what they wanted because they had suffered long enough under the boot of oppression. They had endured enough to understand what it meant to stand tall, and now they were determined to demand it. Land, family, autonomy, education, and mobility were their aspirations. The spirit of this Fourth of July–turned–Emancipation Day parade was shared by free people throughout the nation; emancipation celebrations would be celebrated far and wide. Black people from all walks of life would make these days into public declarations of what they believed they deserved and what they would continue to demand in the years to come.

Anna Julia Cooper, born in bondage in the midst of the Civil War, would carry that spirit forward. She was educated in Raleigh, as part of the first class at St. Augustine's Normal School and Collegiate Institute. "When hardly more than of kindergarten age it was my good fortune to be selected for a scholarship by Dr. J. Brinton Smith, founder of St. Augustine's Normal School at Raleigh," she recalled. Smith's plan was "to train [students] as teachers for the colored people of the South." The school sheltered her "from the many pitfalls that beset the unwary" and provided a level of "shelter and protection" from the myriad ways that left too many young black women with little protection. St. Augustine shaped Cooper into an educator; at the age of ten she began teaching other students, with her pay going toward defraying her tuition. She remembered the school as her "world." Cooper would go on to write *A Voice from the South*, the first Black feminist text in American letters, and a poignant take on the particular burdens Black women were forced to endure. The vision that Cooper and millions of other formerly enslaved people had of the world was expansive. They would continue to claim their rightful place in a world they had fought to create for themselves.

EMANCIPATION DAY IN SAVANNAH

Celebrations like those held in Raleigh, North Carolina, in 1865 were not uncommon. Emancipation would be celebrated regularly throughout the nation. Communities selected different days, different times, and different ways to mark the occasion of their freedom, but the power of remembrance reverberated throughout the nation, no matter the manner or date chosen.

In Savannah, Georgia, where General William T. Sherman's March to the Sea concluded and where the historic promise of "forty acres and a mule" took shape through Special Field Order No. 15, the Black community developed a powerful tradition of commemorating emancipation. Each year on January 1, they gathered to mark Emancipation Day, honoring the date in 1863 when the Emancipation Proclamation took effect. Over the years these celebrations came to be acts of public memory, pride, and resistance.

In preparation for the January 1888 celebration, twenty-five years after emancipation, *The Savannah Tribune*, the city's most prominent Black newspaper, announced the planned program for the day's festivities as a "grand event in . . . history." That year's festivities would showcase the developing strength and organization of Savannah's Black community in the decades since emancipation. Twelve separate Black military units would march in the parade, including the Savannah Light Infantry, the Union Lincoln Guards, and the Savannah Hussars, each a testament to the ongoing legacy of Black military service in defense of freedom.

In addition to the military companies, ten civic and mutual aid organizations planned to participate, including the Savannah Lodge, the Ulysses S. Grant Association, the Leading Aid Social Club, and the Workingmen's Union Association. These lodges, social clubs, and labor associations were more than ceremonial. In the decades following emancipation, when Black communities were systematically denied access to insurance, mutual aid organizations formed the backbone of collective support. Funded through member dues, they offered aid during illness, supported families in times of bereavement, and helped members who were injured or had lost their jobs. These groups offered protection and solidarity, and in the public space of the Emancipation Day parade, their presence affirmed the progress Savannah's Black residents had built for themselves despite the formidable challenges. They not only supported the living but also preserved the collective memory of slavery, the Civil War, and the long struggle for freedom, ensuring that emancipation would be remembered not as a gift bestowed, but as a hard-won victory to be honored and defended.

The grand parade, with thousands of Black participants proudly marching through the streets of Savannah, eventually led to the park where the formal

Emancipation Day ceremony was held. This gathering was not just a celebration but a solemn occasion, rich with symbolism and purpose. The program opened with a prayer and a reading of the Emancipation Proclamation, traditions that anchored the day in both spiritual reflection and historical significance.

At the ceremony that year, the Reverend E. K. Love, former slave and pastor of Savannah's historic First African Baptist Church, delivered what was described as "a powerful and eloquent address." His speech captured both the hope and the heartache of Black life in the post-Reconstruction South. By 1888, more than a decade had passed since federal troops were withdrawn, the Freedmen's Bureau dismantled, and the radical possibilities of Reconstruction abandoned. White supremacists, emboldened by the retreat of Northern lawmakers, were reviving their grip on Southern politics and public life. Across the region, Black civil rights were being stripped away. In just a few short years segregation would be codified, and racial terror would be an evermore menacing threat.

In that climate, Love chose his words carefully. He delivered a message that was at once bold in its moral vision and cautious in its tone, a rhetorical balancing act that would become familiar to Black leaders in generations to come. At moments, his speech voiced sentiments that would later be famously echoed by Dr. Martin Luther King Jr. at the 1963 March on Washington. "I hope the day is rapidly coming," Love declared, "when my brethren will cease to hate me because I am black—will cease to judge me by my color, will take my color, which is but air, out of the scale of justice and throw me, the real man, therein and let me stand or fall by what I am."

Yet Love also made gestures designed to temper white fears. With racial tensions high and Southern white leaders denouncing calls for "social equality," Love sought to reassure his white listeners. He downplayed the role of President Lincoln and, in a surprising turn, even offered some qualified praise for Jefferson Davis, the former president of the Confederacy. Speaking candidly, Love stated:

> Our people have learned to think that Abraham Lincoln was the greatest champion of our cause. But such is not true. The thing that was uppermost in the mind of Mr. Lincoln was the salvation of the Union. So far as Mr. Lincoln was concerned the Emancipation Proclamation was purely a war measure—for he would "save the Union with or without freeing the slaves." From this single statement, it must be clear to you that our freedom was not first in Mr. Lincoln's mind, yet I thank God for Mr. Lincoln for his election which had much to do with kindling the fire between the two sections which resulted in a bloody war whose crimson stream washed away the black stain of slavery.

Then, in a dramatic and provocative twist, Love turned to Jefferson Davis. While acknowledging that Davis had fought for a cause he believed in, albeit wrongly, Love credited his resistance to the Union cause with indirectly hastening Black liberation. He said:

> Had the southern Confederacy placed a coward at its head, we would not have been freed as the results of that four years of bloody war. If Jeff Davis had not been a brave, great man fighting from what he conceived to be, a principle of right and justice (although he was wrong) he would have accepted Lincoln's offer of surrender in ninety days. If he had accepted, it is hard for me to see from a human standpoint how or when we would have been freed. The odds were against Jeff Davis. He confronted a greater army than his, far more skilled in the science of war and far more skilled in the manufacture of arms and with all the power the shattered government had, at its back. This would have been a sufficient inducement for perhaps any body but Jeff Davis to have accepted Mr. Lincoln's (inglorious offer). I call it inglorious from my stand point, for had Jeff Davis accepted it I do not see how I could have been freed. The truth of it is that God was using both Abraham Lincoln and Jeff Davis to bring to light this child of freedom the birth of which we celebrate to-day.

Even as he called for mutual respect and cooperation between Black and white Southerners, Love was careful to reaffirm the racial boundaries expected by his white listeners. "The sensible Negro and the sensible white man," he argued, "should meet on mutual grounds and away with this foolishness and mutually work to make this country glorious." But then he quickly clarified the limits of these "mutual grounds": "This does not include [racial] intermarriage nor co-education." He added, "The Negro does not want that any more than the white man does. He wants his share of the public money for education and to marry his own women, they are good enough for him." Rather than demand full integration, Love emphasized Black self-sufficiency. "I trust that when we shall celebrate our Emancipation next year," he said, "we will be able to look with pleasing pride upon some great enterprise owned and operated by Negroes and for Negroes." In a time of increasing hostility and narrowing possibilities, Love's speech reflected the immense challenges Black leaders faced. Given the climate, the continued observance of Emancipation Day itself was an act of collective resistance.

As Black rights increasingly came under attack, the speeches given by Black leaders during emancipation programs may have grown more tempered, but the determination of participants did not. For decades, the Emancipation Day procession in Savannah had been led by the First Battalion Infantry of the Colored Georgia State Troops, a unit that had come to symbolize Black manhood and citizenship. Within Savannah's Black community, the battalion had stood as a proud institution since the Civil War, a visible assertion of Black loyalty and dignity in uniform. But white state authorities, threatened by armed and organized Black men, began to deliberately withhold funding from the regiment, forcing the men to raise money themselves for uniforms and even for the construction of their own armory. Despite their willingness to serve, they were denied the opportunity to fight in the Spanish American War of 1898, their requests to serve rejected by state authorities. State legislators ended the unit in 1904, abolishing all Black regiments in Georgia and effectively silencing the battalion's presence in the public sphere.

The unit's absence was deeply felt by the Black population in the city. Without the Colored Georgia State Troops, Emancipation Day crowds became more defiant. In 1906, marchers were determined to defend the dignity of the celebration against any attempts to belittle it. When a white man tried to force his way through the procession, he was beaten back by onlookers. Later, when a streetcar conductor attempted to drive his car directly through the parade route, threatening to crash through the assembled marchers, he was pulled from the car and he, too, was forcibly removed by the crowd. What had once been a festive occasion had become a battleground for recognition and respect. In 1906, as Jim Crow legislation was becoming more ubiquitous throughout the South, Black Savannahians made it clear that they would not accept an attack on Emancipation Day. Their numbers, stretching over twelve city blocks, were a visual representation of the refusal to cede any ground. Even as segregation and lynching took hold of the South, they would stand for their freedom.

MEANINGS OF EMANCIPATION

Black Emancipation Day celebrations were never just festive gatherings. They were deeply theological, intellectual, historical, artistic, and political declarations of existence and belonging. In public parks, on parade routes, in the midst of brass bands and oratory, Black communities gathered to bear witness, not only to what had been survived, but to the truths that had always been known.

At the heart of these gatherings was a Black theology rooted in the long night of enslavement. For generations, Black faith had been driven underground, hidden from slaveholders who feared its power. It was dangerous for enslaved people to imagine themselves as the chosen ones in the biblical story of Exodus—God's people unjustly held in bondage. But with emancipation, that faith emerged from the shadows. Jubilee had come, just as it had come for the Hebrew slaves, and Black people were ready to claim it. Celebrations of emancipation were thus grounded in a faith tradition that saw dignity where the world had tried to deny it, and a divine promise of liberation where the law had once demanded bondage. These were not simply parties; they were sacred ceremonies in which freedom was named, remembered, and demanded again.

In these moments of celebration, Black oratory stood as a bold rebuke to the lie of Black intellectual inferiority. Under slavery, reading and writing had been criminalized. Slaveholders had made them illegal precisely because of their power as tools of liberation. To read is to interpret the world. To write is to communicate, to plan, to resist. Emancipation Day orators reclaimed these tools in full view of the public, their eloquence a declaration that Black minds had never been empty, only forcibly silenced. Their very presence behind a podium was a radical act—proof of brilliance in the face of a society that insisted Black people could not think well or for themselves.

History itself was on trial in these celebrations. While white Southerners and white Americans at large commemorated their version of the past with monuments, speeches, and national holidays, those rituals excluded the labor and lives of Black people. The central role of slavery in building the nation was elided, whitewashed, or wholly denied. These white commemorations, however grand, never paused to remember the day freedom came for *all* Americans. But Black communities remembered. They made space for their own public memory—for the naming of ancestors, for stories passed down, for marking the moment when the legal claim to human ownership was finally broken. Jubilee celebrations, Emancipation Days, and Juneteenth were not just acts of memory; they were counter-histories, insistent that the nation must reckon with the truths it tried to forget.

And they were beautiful. In an age when the dominant portrayal of Black life came through the grotesque distortions of blackface minstrelsy, when white performers in burned cork caricatured Black people as lazy, foolish, childlike, or monstrous, emancipation celebrations offered a different kind of stage. Black communities crafted a response to these dehumanizing images. They wore uniforms. Donned their Sunday best. Marched in formation. Danced with grace. Spoke with power. The public display of Black dignity, joy, and refinement was a profound rejection of the nation's most popular myths about Black life.

Perhaps most crucially, these celebrations laid claim to space. In a time when new laws were rapidly resegregating the South, policing Black presence in and access to public life, Emancipation Day was an unapologetic assertion of belonging. Black people filled the streets, occupied parks, lined parade routes, and made clear that this was their country too. They had built it. Their labor, their suffering, their victories were woven into the fabric of the nation. To celebrate freedom publicly was to demand recognition and refuse erasure. It was to say, with joy and conviction: We are still here. We are not out of place.

In every sermon, every march, every song, and every spectacle, Black people transformed the tools they had once used to beautify the lives of others—music making, dressmaking, floral arranging, cooking, storytelling—into gifts for themselves and their communities. Emancipation celebrations were moments of self-determination and love. They made Black life beautiful, on their own terms. And in doing so, they gave us all a blueprint, not just for remembrance, but for imagining freedom anew.

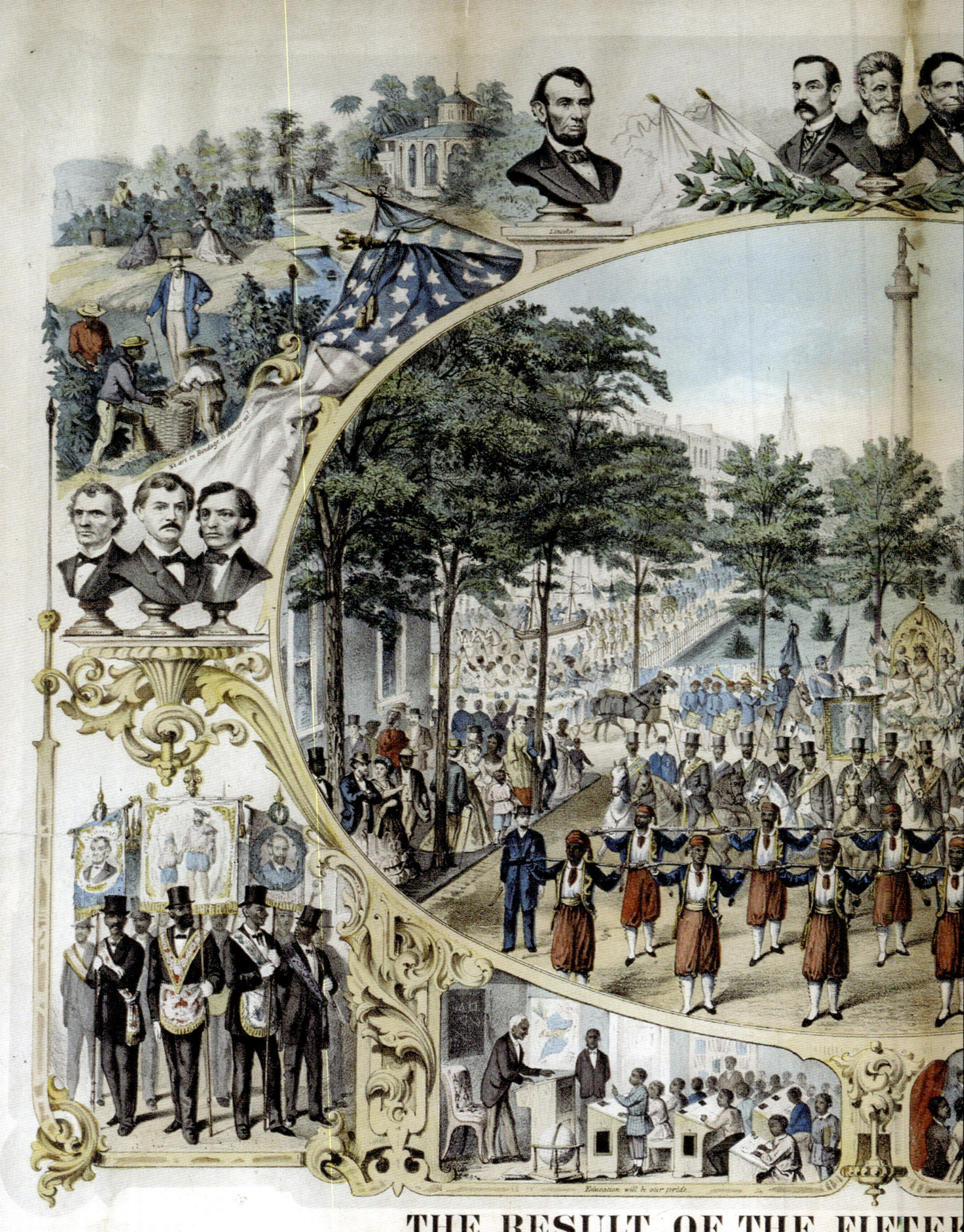
Lincoln
Education will be our pride
THE RESULT OF THE FIFTEE
And the Rise and Progress of the African Race in America and its final
BALTIMORE, PUBLISHED BY METCALF & CLARK,

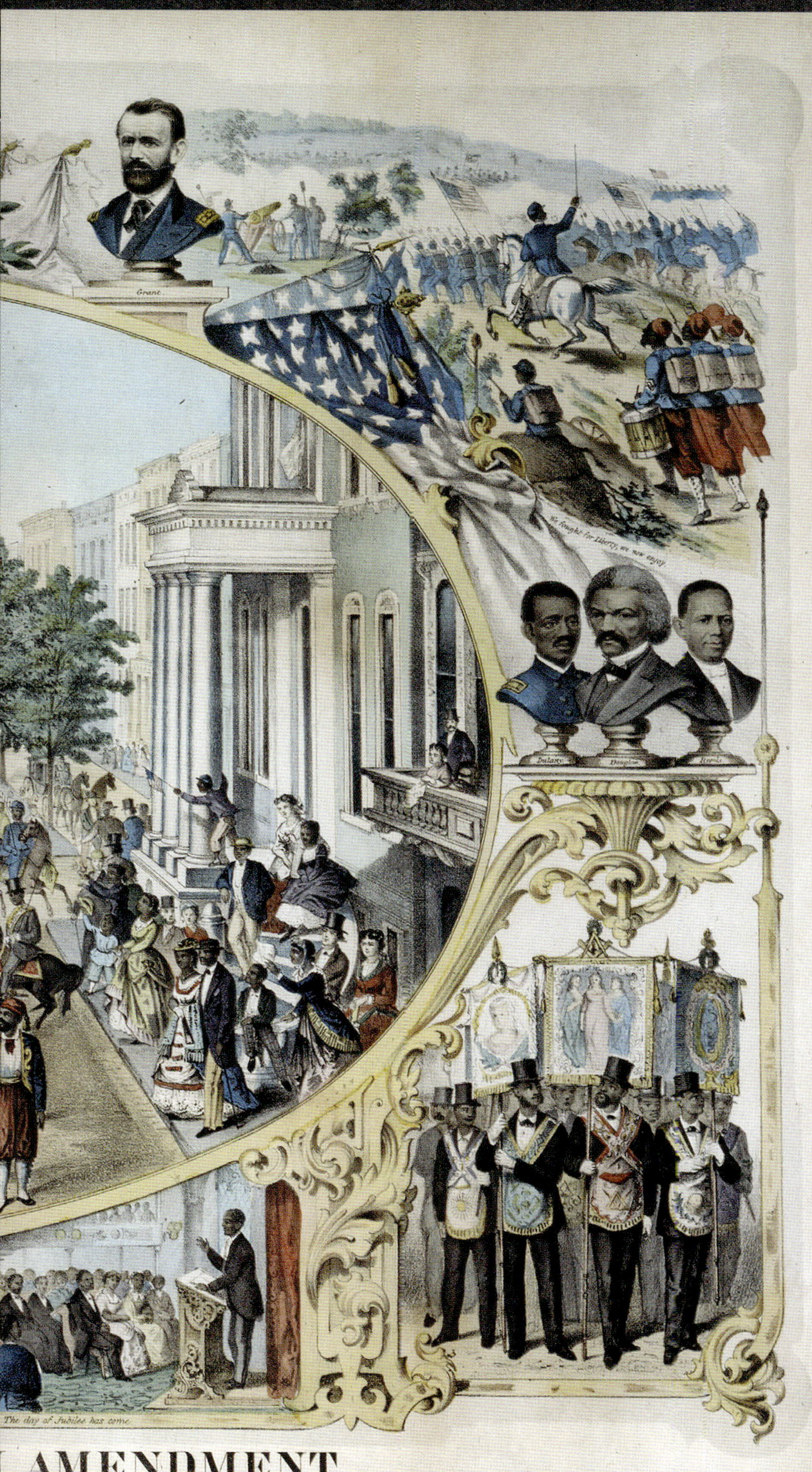

An elaborate commemorative print celebrating the passage of the Fifteenth Amendment and the May 1870 parade in Baltimore celebrating the historic addition to the Constitution that turned formerly enslaved Black men into eligible voters.

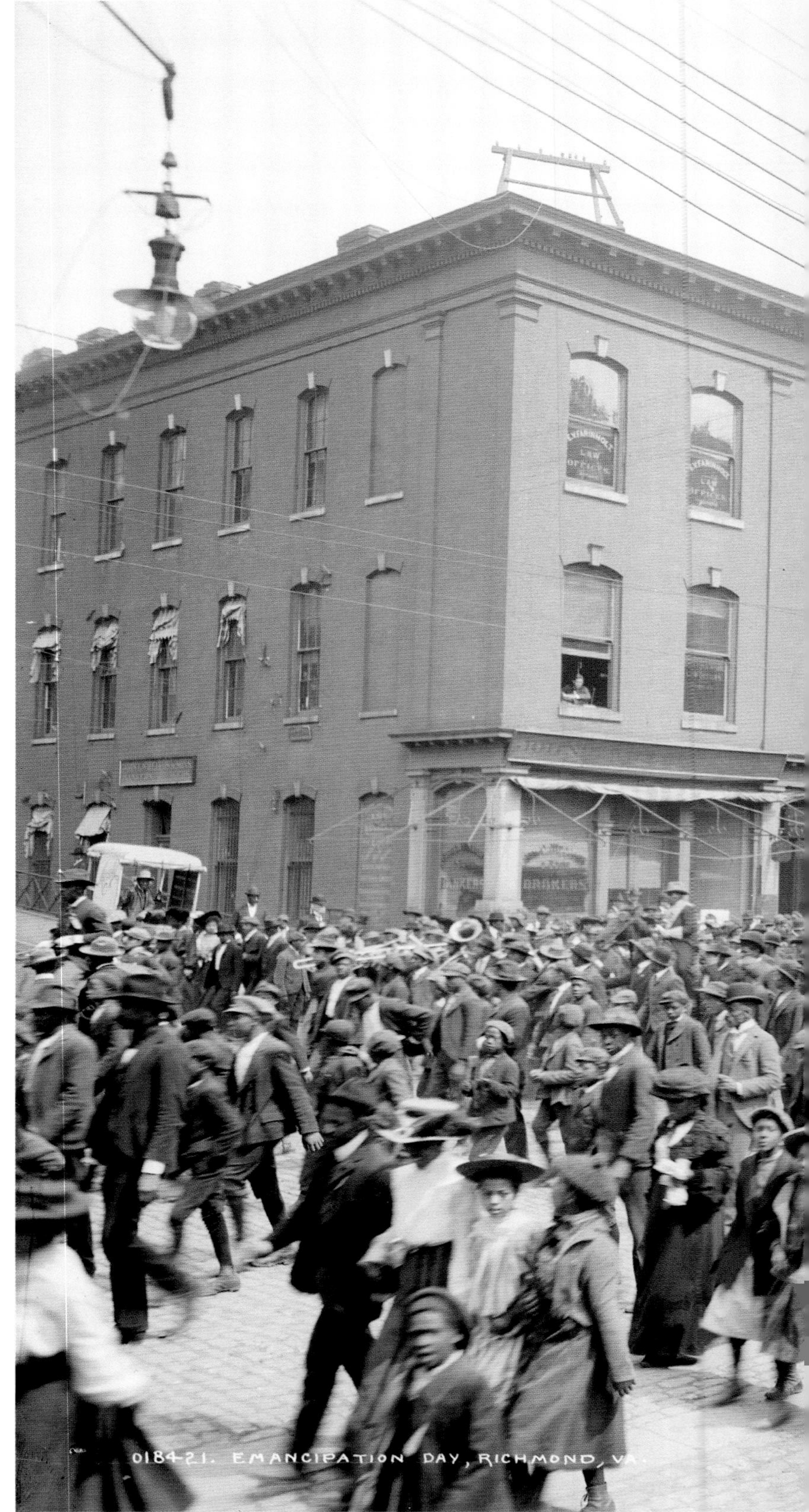

The 1905 Emancipation Day parade makes it way down Main Street in Richmond, Virginia, with a streetcar sitting in the middle of the crowd. At the time of this photograph, Black Richmonders were in the midst of a sustained boycott of the city's segregated streetcars, walking to school, work, and church rather than paying for second-class treatment. The parade tied the history of emancipation to their ongoing fight for dignity and full citizenship.

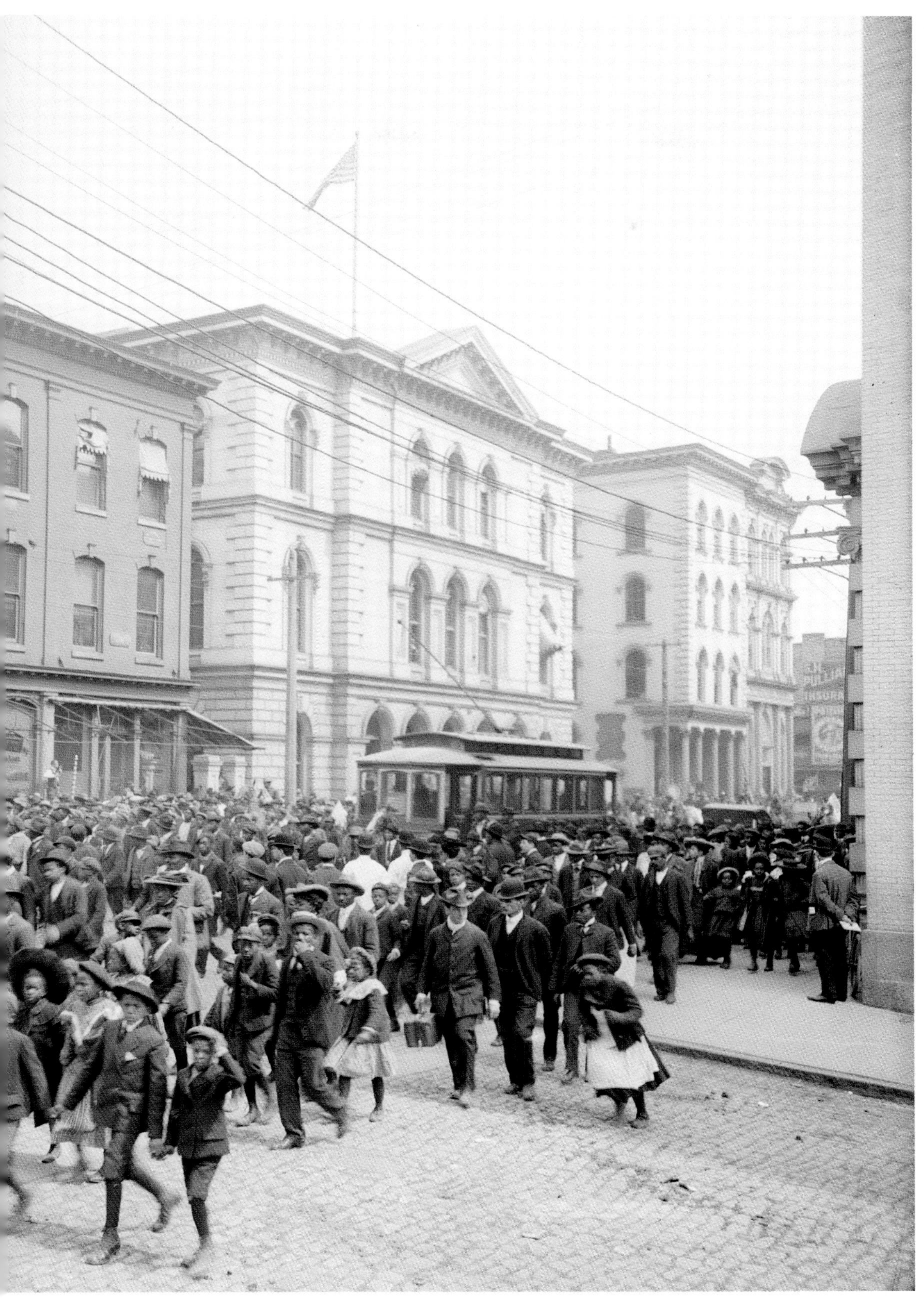

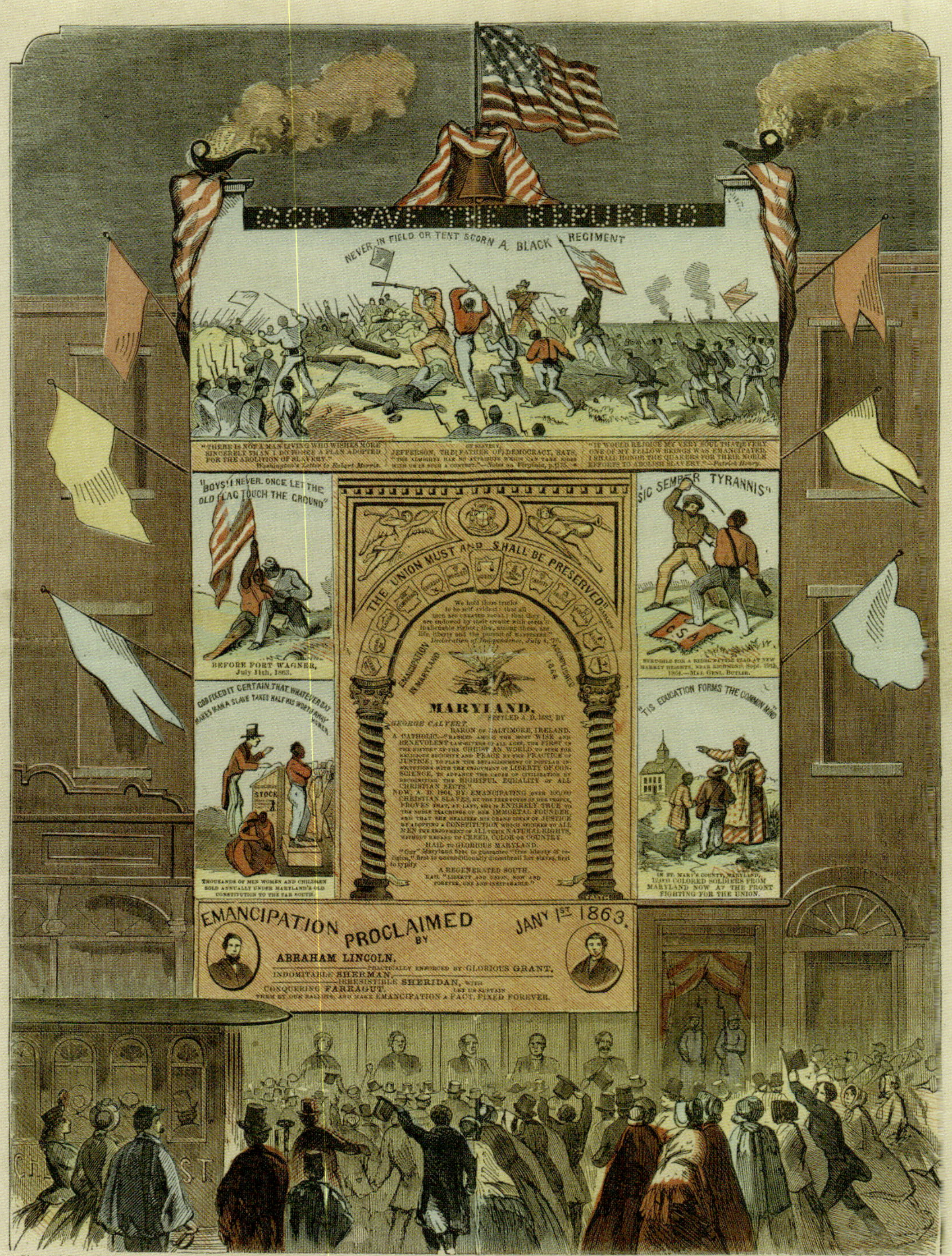

View of Transparency

IN FRONT OF HEADQUARTERS OF SUPERVISORY COMMITTEE FOR RECRUITING COLORED REGIMENTS,

Chestnut Street, Philadelphia,

IN COMMEMORATION OF EMANCIPATION IN MARYLAND, NOVEMBER 1, 1864.

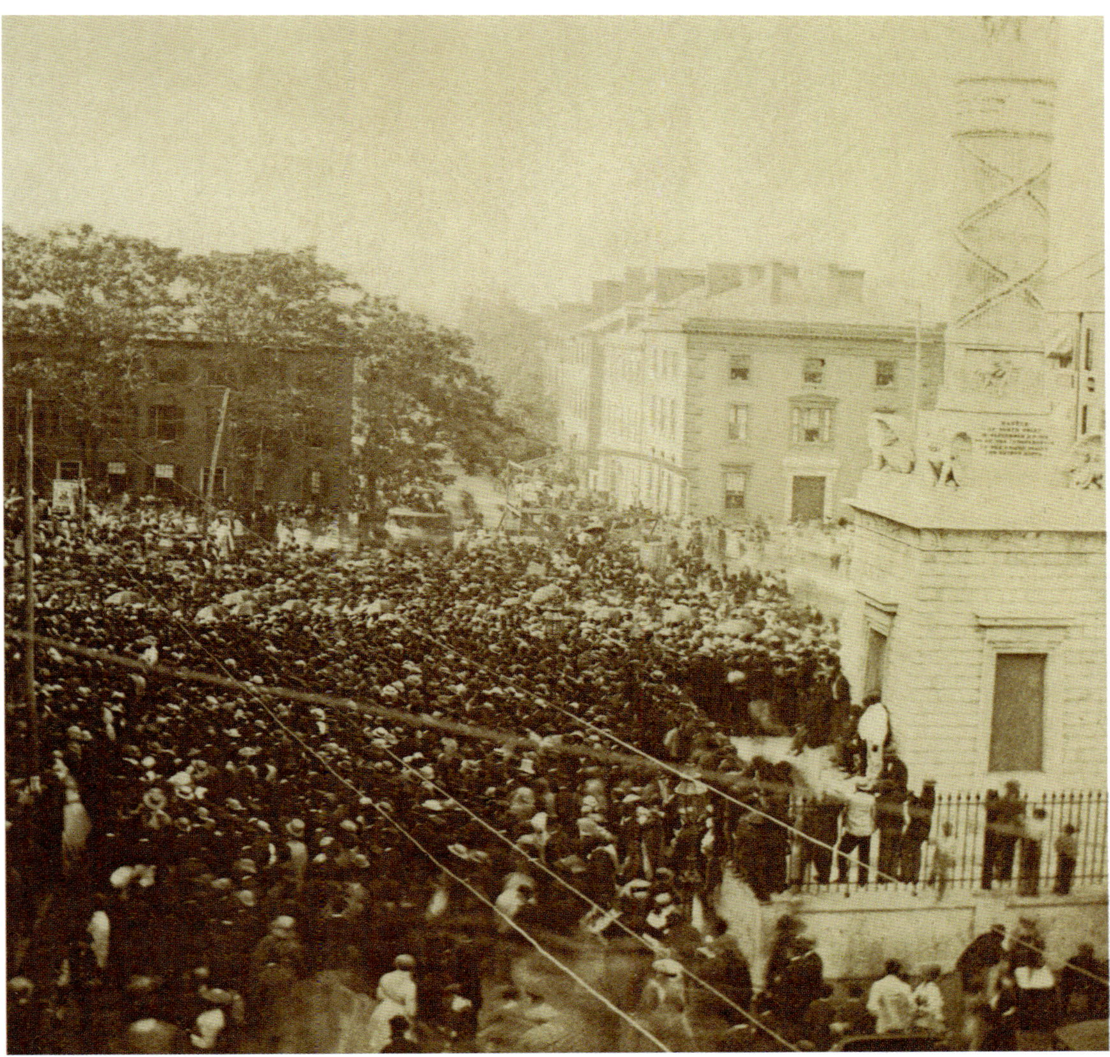

OPPOSITE: This transparency, displayed in 1864 at the Philadelphia federal recruitment office, illustrates the emancipation of Maryland's enslaved following the passage of a new state constitution on November 1, 1864. The tableau contrasted the evil of slavery with the significance of emancipation in this Union state. Although Maryland never succeeded with the Southern states, more than 33,000 men, women, and children were in bondage there at the time of the Civil War.

ABOVE: Photograph of a massive and jubilant crowd of spectators gathered in Monument Square in Baltimore, Maryland, on May 19, 1870, celebrating the passage of the Fifteenth Amendment to the US Constitution, which gave African American men the right to vote. Lasting several hours, the mile-long parade included several Black organizations and was witnessed by more than 20,000 attendees.

Handsewn dress believed to have been worn by Tempy Ruby Bryant, a formerly enslaved woman, and passed down through the generations in her family. Carefully and lovingly preserved, the garment is a personal look at Black women's lives at the moment of Emancipation, and a reminder that everyday people cared to commemorate their past.

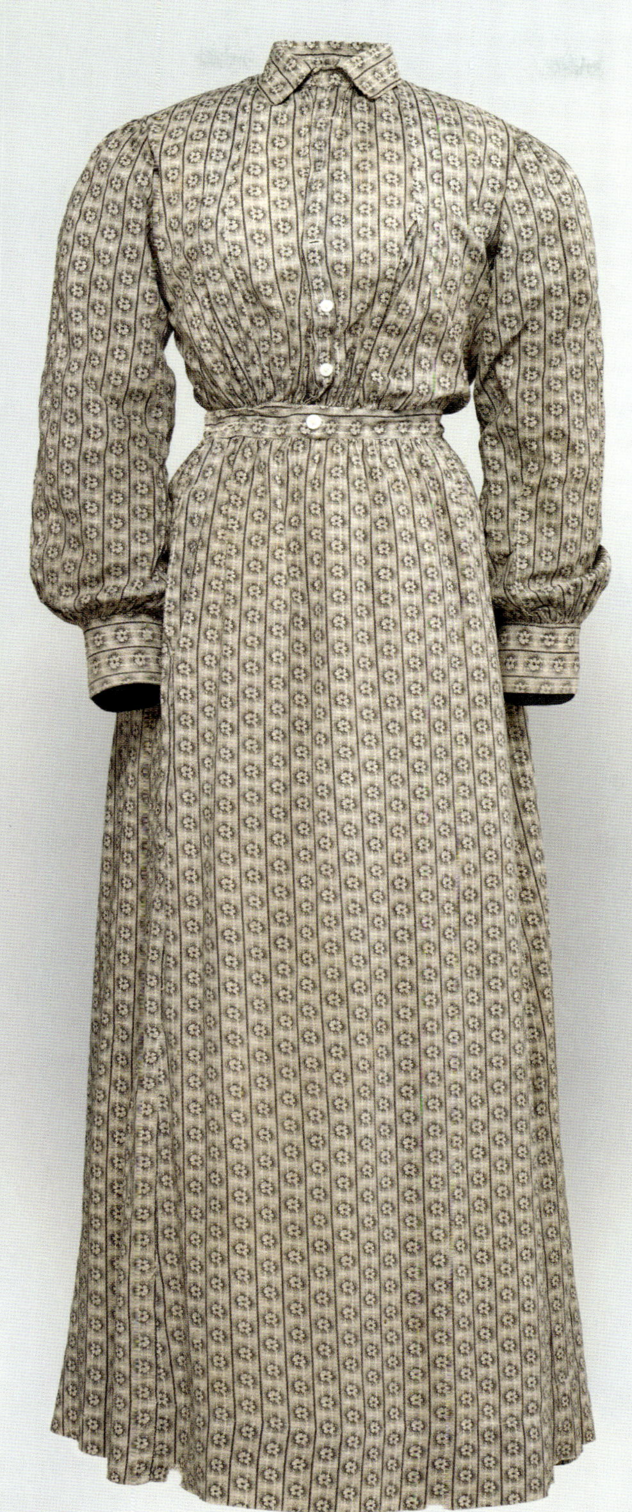

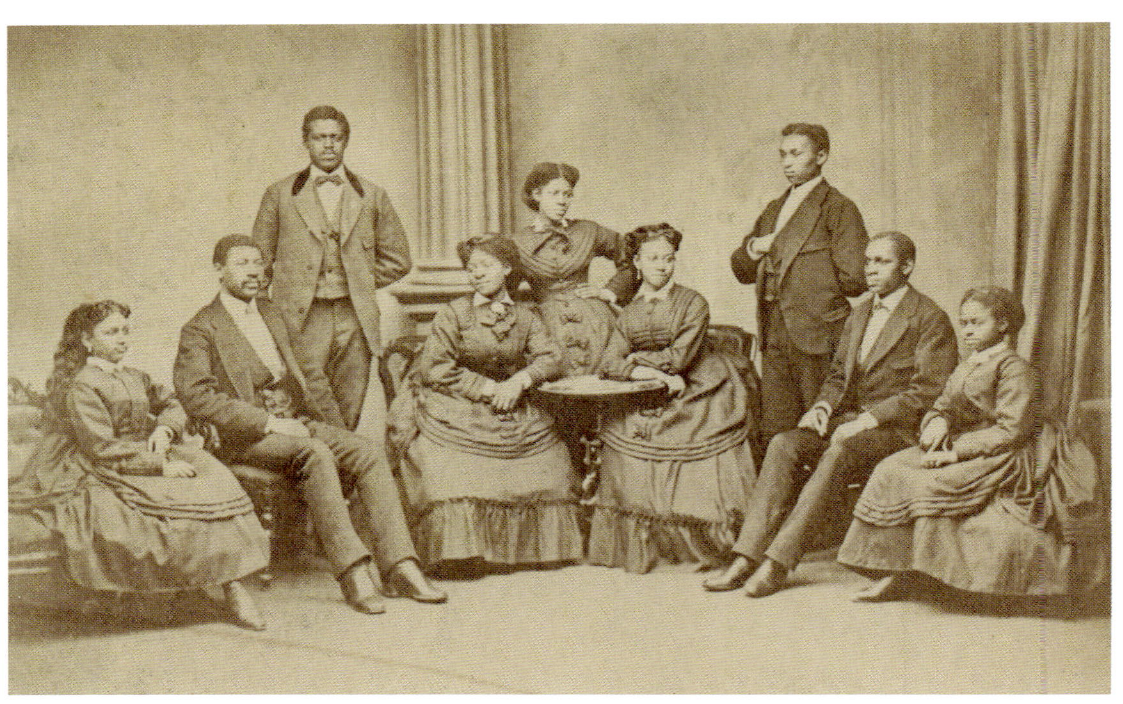

ABOVE: Studio portrait of the Fisk Jubilee Singers, pioneers in bringing the spirituals of the enslaved to audiences worldwide. Pictured from left to right: Minnie Tate, Greene Evans, Isaac Dickerson, Jennie Jackson, Maggie Porter, Ella Sheppard, Thomas Rutling, Benjamin Holmes, and Eliza Walker.

OPPOSITE: An invitation from Raleigh, North Carolina's Black leaders to attend the city's 1872 Emancipation Day celebration. Its formality stands as a testimony to the dignity and ceremony with which Black celebrants marked their freedom anniversaries. Honoring the memory of emancipation with both gravity and joy, they crafted festivities that were as serious as they were celebratory.

NINTH ANNIVERSARY
OF THE

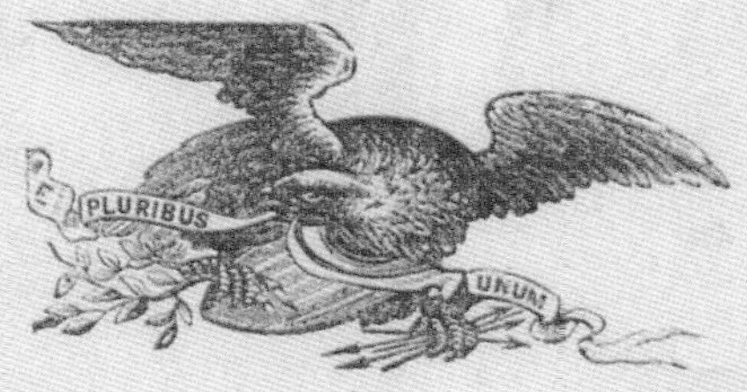

Proclamation of Emancipation.

Sir:

You are cordially invited to attend the Celebration of the Ninth Anniversary of the Proclamation of Emancipation, on January 1st, 1872.

Exercises will take place at Metropolitan Hall, at 12 o'clock.

Respectfully,

FRIDAY JONES,
Chairman Committee of Arrangements.

NORFLEET JEFFERS, Sr.,
President of the Day.

HENRY LANE,
Chief Marshal.

Chas. N. Hunter
Secretary.

Emancipation Day in Plymouth.

Great Mass Meeting of the Citizens from Several Surrounding Counties.

To the Editor of The Era:

Early on the morning of the 1st, hundreds of citizens were observed coming into Plymouth from the surrounding country, all intent upon joining in the patriotic manifestations in honor of the Anniversary of Liberty, when "the hands of the slave were freed."

Every careful observer was struck most forcibly by the great order, decorum and dignity, which the colored citizens observed on this ever-memorable occasion. All seemed to be respectful, quiet and happy, while no disturbance of any kind whatever, marred the enjoyment of the day.

At 10 A. M., the call was sounded and those desiring to join in the procession assembled at the place designated, and formed in regular order under the direction of the Marshals and their Aids.

The speaking took place from a stand erected on the Court House square.

The Chairman of the meeting, Benj. Bryant, of Bertie, called the vast assemblage to order, and the exercises of the day commenced with prayer by Rev. J. C. Coleman.

The following letter was then read by W. R. Haughton, of Chowan, addressed to the Commettee of Invitation from Dr. P. John, of Elizabeth City:

OFFICE OF THE NORTH CAROLINIAN,
Elizabeth City, N. C., Dec. 29, 1871.

Business engagements of a character I cannot postpone make it impossible for me to accept your kind invitation to address you on the 1st prox. But for these I should certainly be with you and aid by my presence and my voice in celebrating an event that is destined to be memorable in American history. To me the day will always be one of special interest. From my childhood I have been opposed to the system that held you in Slavery. When quite a boy I read the narrative and personal history of that remarkable man of your race Frederic Douglas. His struggles for freedom, his aspirations for knowledge, his longings for a higher and better condition awakened my sympathies and aroused in me a determination to do what I could to ameliorate the condition of the colored people of this country, not because of their color but because they were denied the rights of our common humanity. To me it became a question of *principle*. I believed the Bible doctrine that of one blood God created all the nations of the earth, and hence that the black man was not outside the pale of humanity, and that being a man he had the impulses, feelings, desires and aspirations of all other men. Aye, and taking the patroit founders of the Republic at their word when they declared "that *all* men are created equal; that they are endowed by their Creator with certain enalienable rights; that among these are life, LIBERTY *and the pursuit of happiness,*" I felt that it was an injustice and a wrong to deprive any portion of God's children of any one of these blessings, and hence from that time forward, with my voice, my vote and my pen, I cooperated with the men and the party whose efforts at last were crowned with a success unparallelled in the world's annals—saving a Republic and adding

SWEET POTATOES.—Boil them till done; then peel and cut in logitudinal slices, and pour upon each slice, as you lay it in the sauce-dish, gravy made in the following manner: of sugar and butter take one cup each; add half a cup of hot water, and boil till it is thick.—This sauce is a great improvement to the sweet potato, and removes the dryness of that vegetable.

HOW TO COOK BEANS.—Sort and wash them, and cover with lukewarm soft water to which a pinch of soda has been added. Let them soak, adding at times a little hot water, for half a day; pour off this water and fill with boiling water, allowing them to simmer till nearly soft; place in an earthern baking-dish, and in the middle of the beans bury a piece of salt pork; for a quart of beans a piece as large as a good-sized egg is sufficient.

COCOANUT PIE.—Grate the white part of the cocoanut, mix it with milk, and let it simmer ten minutes over the fire; allow a quart of milk to a pound of cocoanut; beat eight eggs thoroughly, and mix them with four tablespoonfuls of white sugar and a glass of wine; then stir this into the milk; add two teaspoonfuls of melted butter, a small cracker, and half a nutmeg; turn the whole into deep pie-plates lined with paste; bake immediately.

CUSTARD PIE.—Allow three well beaten eggs to a pint of milk, in which a stick of cinnamon or a bit of lemon-peel has been boiled; add a little salt and nutmeg, and pour the custard into a deep plate lined with a thick paste; bake one hour, or till done.

PASTE FOR PIES.—One pound and a half of flour, half a pound of butter; wet it with cold water enough to make a stiff paste; work it well, and roll it out two or three times.

EMANCIPATION CELEBRATION—IMMENSE GATHERING AT METROPOLITAN HALL.—Those who participated will long remember the demonstration in honor of the ninth anniversary of President Lincoln's Emancipation Proclamation, which took place on the 1st inst. The great day of liberty was announced at 7 o'clock, and the celebration commenced by the ringing of the city bells. The hasty step, and cheerful countenence of the passers by, indicated that something out of the usual course was to take place. At 10 o'clock Chief Marshal Henry Lane and his assistants repaired to the A. M. E. Church on West street, at which point a procession was formed which moved up West to Hillboro', down Hillsboro' to Salisbury St., up Salisbury to Edenton, down Edenton to Blunt, down Blunt to South, up South to Fayetteville, up Fayetteville St., to Metropolitan Hall. Here the crowd was immense. The spacious Hall was densely filled by nearly 3,000 people, representing all classes, colors, parties and sex. Here we beheld a scene which we have long desired to see. The slave and his former master side by side doing homage at the shrine of liberty. It was, indeed, a sublime spectacle. May the day speedily come when all will honor and celebrate this great day. The

OFFICERS

of the day were as follows:

Norfleet Jeffers, Sr., President.

C. I. Proctor, T. Bradford, H. C. Jones, and R. Sheppard, Vice Presidents.

Charles N. Hunter, Secretary.

Rev. Wm. Warrick, Chaplain.

Henry Lane, Chief Marshal.

great boon of liberty, &c. Unborn generations would learn to honor and bless his memory. Mr. B. proceeded in a plain, practical manner to impress upon his audience the great importance of education and economy. Men to become men, and nations to become nations, must be enlightened—must be educated. If we would have our influence and usefullness felt and appreciated, we must acquire knowledge, *knowledge is power*. Upon the subject of economy, he spoke of the Freedman's Savings Bank, its utility; the great work which it has already done, and what it is still doing. The great and increasing success of this noble enterprise has far exceeded the expectations of its warmest friends. Chartered by Congress just before the death of Mr. Lincoln, one of his last official acts was to sign the charter, and add his hearty endorsement to this enterprise. The National Savings Bank was destined to become a great and powerful institution. Though millions had passed through its vaults, yet its work had just begun. We should encourage and support it and labor to extend its branches in every part of the country. He urged them to deposit their hard earned money where it would be perfectly safe, and at the same time yielding them interest. At the conclusion of Mr. Brodies remarks, the Choir sang, "Land of the free:" when

R. C. Badger, Esq., was introduced, who was followed by Mr. C. N. Otey, of Howard University, Hons. S. F. Phillips and J. H. Harris. All of whom made able and eloquent speeches. During his remarks, Mr. Phillips spoke in high terms of the address delivered by Mr. Otey. He had not heard a subject more ably treated by the seniors of Chapel Hill. He was proud that Raleigh could boast of so talented a young colored man. He trusted that many such would spring up among the colored race. After the speaking was over, the following resolutions were offered and unanimously adopted:

RESOLUTIONS.

WHEREAS, It is proper that we should celebrate this day as the day which history will point to, as the day upon which the fetters of slavery were stricken from four millions of colored slaves; and, whereas, It is important that this day should be celebrated by our people just as the Fourth of July is celebrated by all Americans, that Emancipation day may ever be fresh in the memories of the *New Freemen* of America; and, whereas, We should by all honorable means endeavor to perpetuate the name of ABRAHAM LINCOLN by celebrating this day, therefore,

Resolved, That we return thanks to the Government of the United States for the blessings of Freedom which we now enjoy.

Resolved, That it is the imperative duty of the colored people to so conduct themselves, as to prove to the world that they are worthy to exercise the great and inestimable rights of a free American citizen.

Resolved, That while we have unbounded codfidence in the great National Union Republican party, the instrument in the hands of the Almighty by which the colored people were made free; and while we believe it to be the duty of every colored voter *now* to support that party by his ballot and influence, yet we desire the time to come when we may cast our ballot for either party, and rest assured that our rights are secure; that we will hail such a day as one of "peace on earth and good will toward men."

Resolved, That the name of Lincoln is forever sacred in our hearts; that we deplore his untimely death, but that his deeds will live when the mountains shall have descended from their lofty prominence to the level of the plains; and the influenee of this great Republic shall have destroyed the last vestige of Kingdoms and Empires.

Resolved, That our confidence in Gov. W. W. Holden is unchanged; that he deserves

ABOVE: Article from the *Carolina Era* recounting the 1872 Emancipation Day celebration in vivid detail, estimating a crowd of 3,000. The day began at Raleigh's St. Paul AME Church, where participants gathered to worship and pray before processing through the city streets to Metropolitan Hall.

OPPOSITE: Born enslaved in Raleigh, North Carolina, Anna Julia Cooper was an educator, author, and activist who championed Black women's rights.

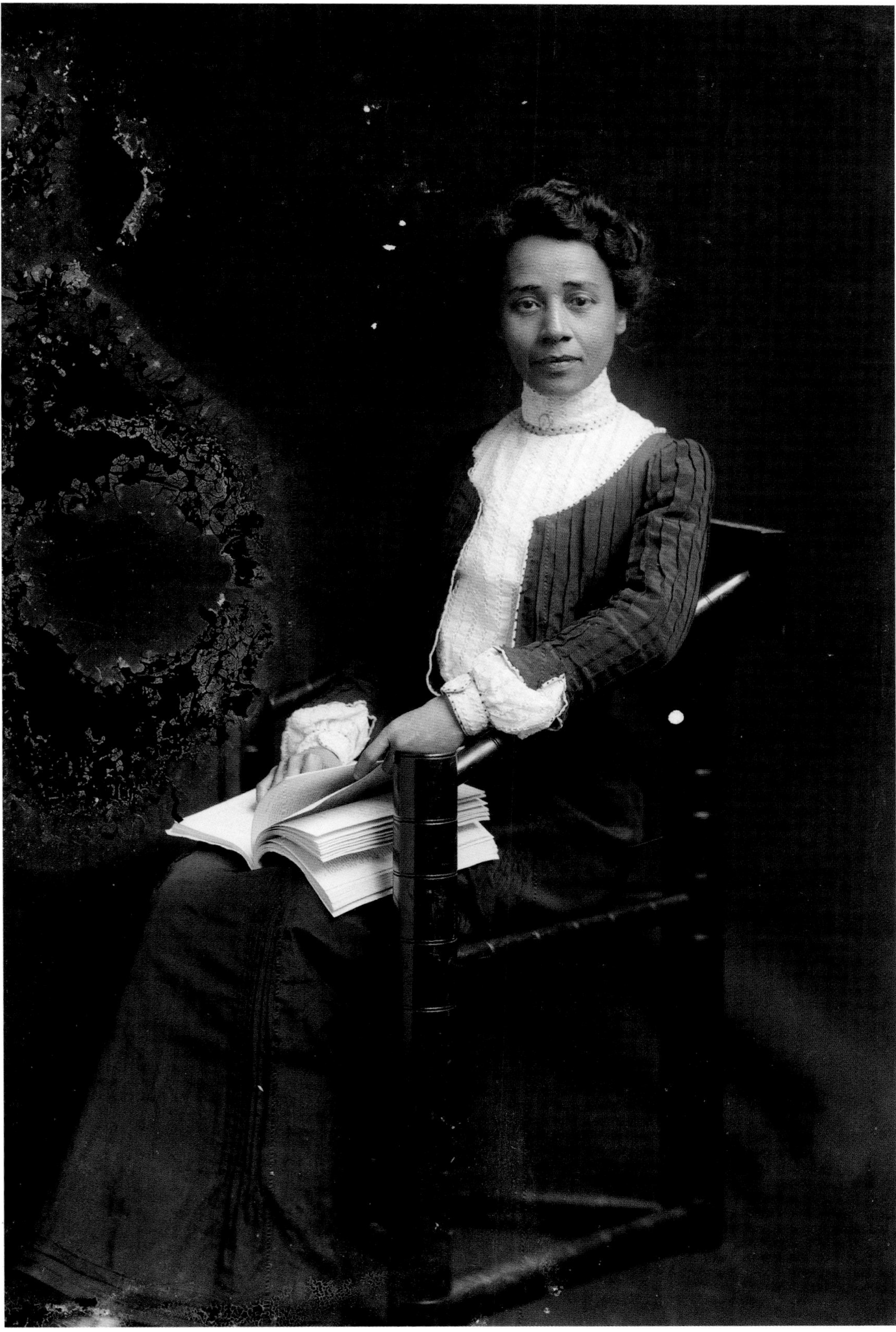

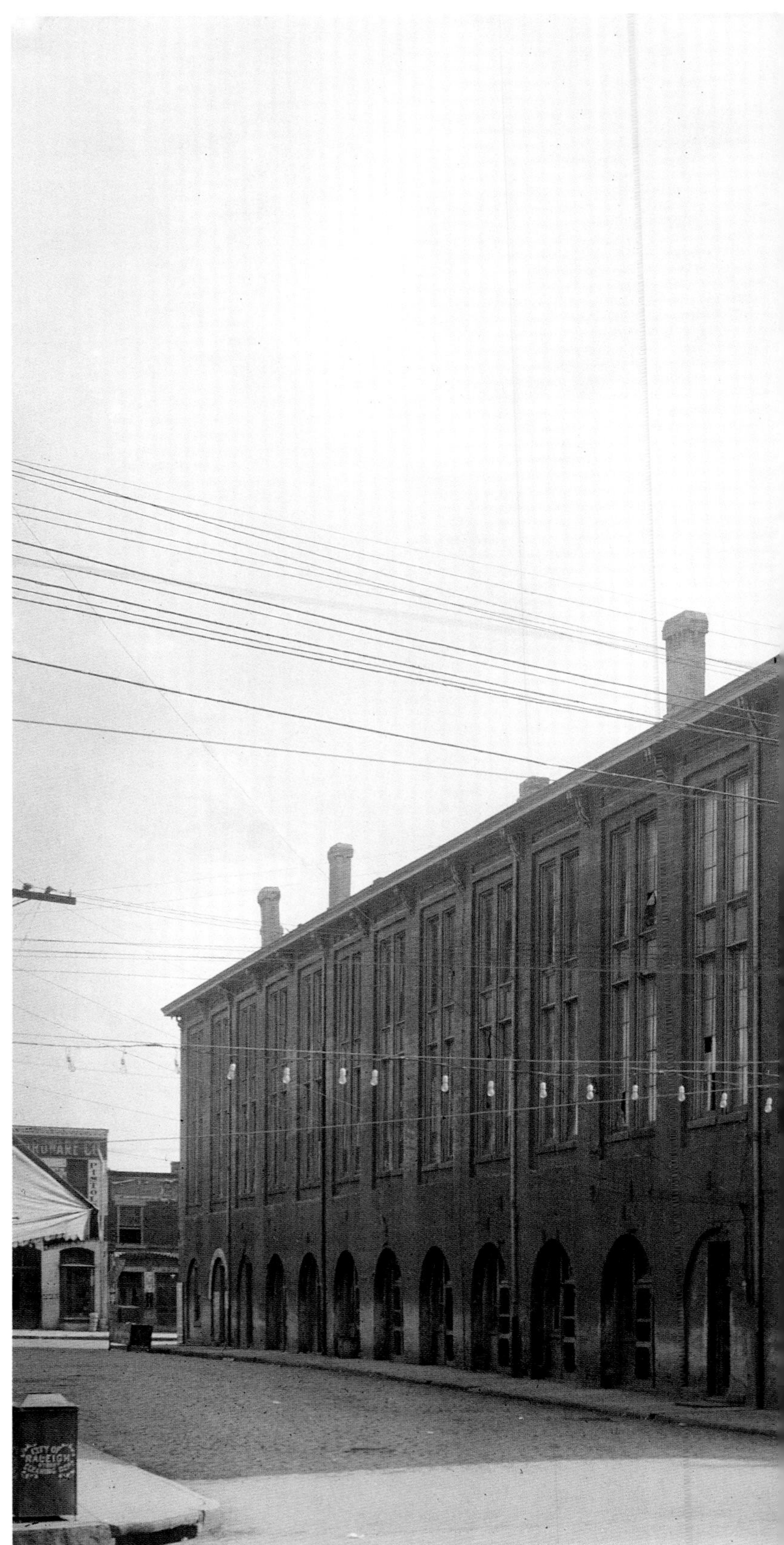

City Market, known locally as Metropolitan Hall, as it appeared in October 1914. The hall hosted Raleigh's January 1, 1872, Emancipation Day celebration. Built in 1870 and demolished in 1920, the building stood at 227 Fayetteville Street, a powerful reminder of how Black communities claimed prominent public spaces to celebrate and mark the meaning of their freedom.

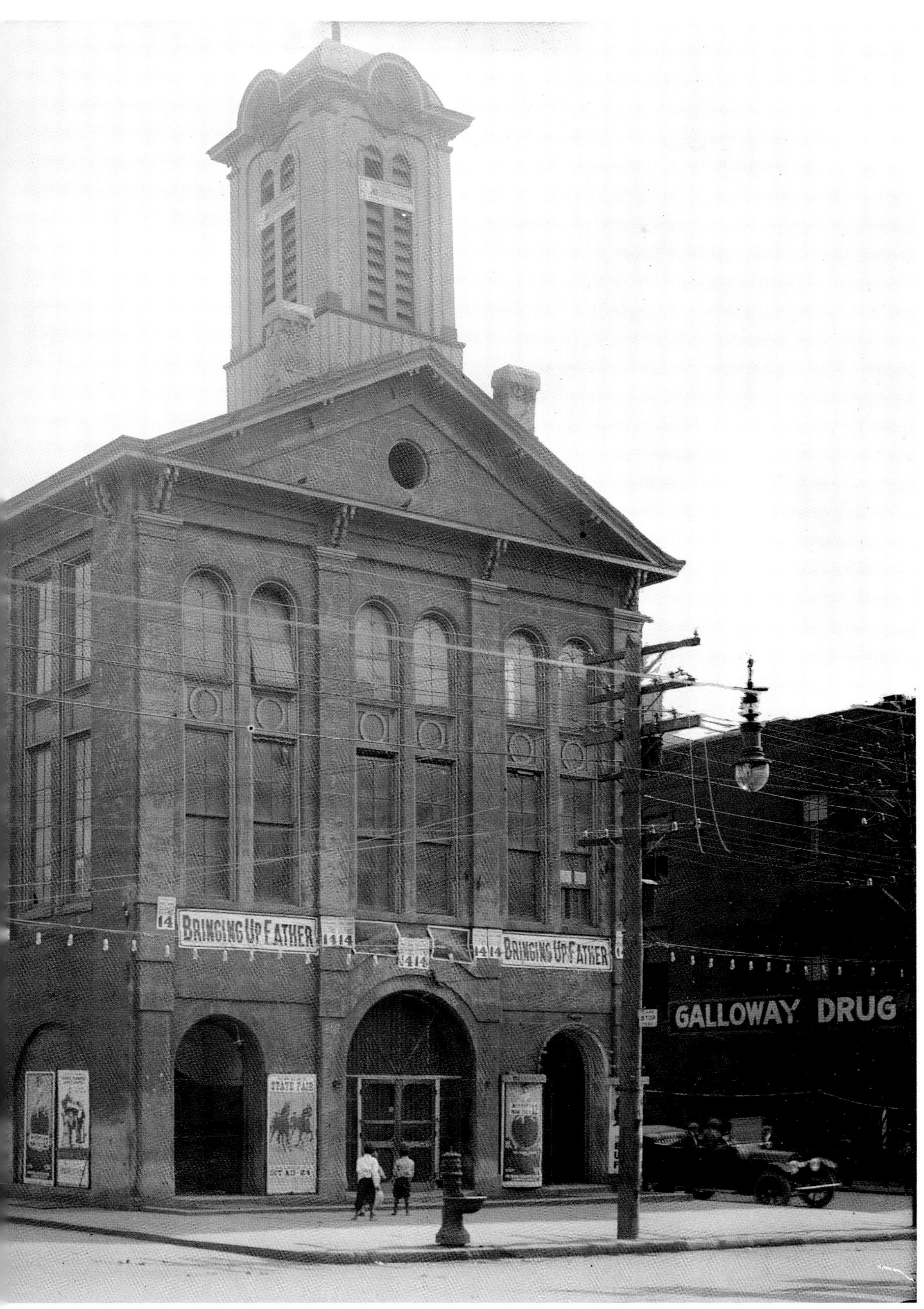
BRINGING UP FATHER
14
1414
BRINGING UP FATHER
STATE FAIR
GALLOWAY DRUG

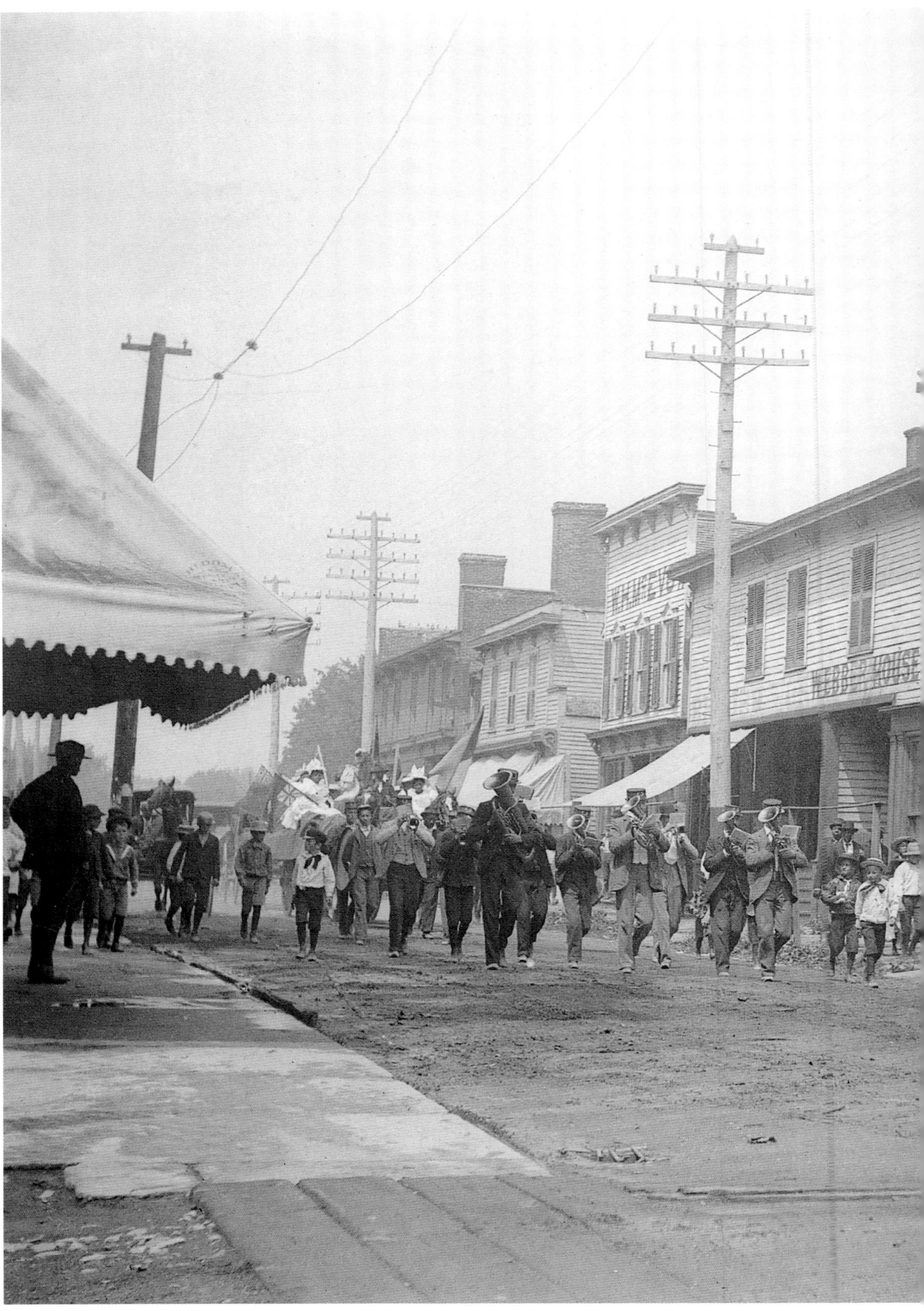
HOUSE

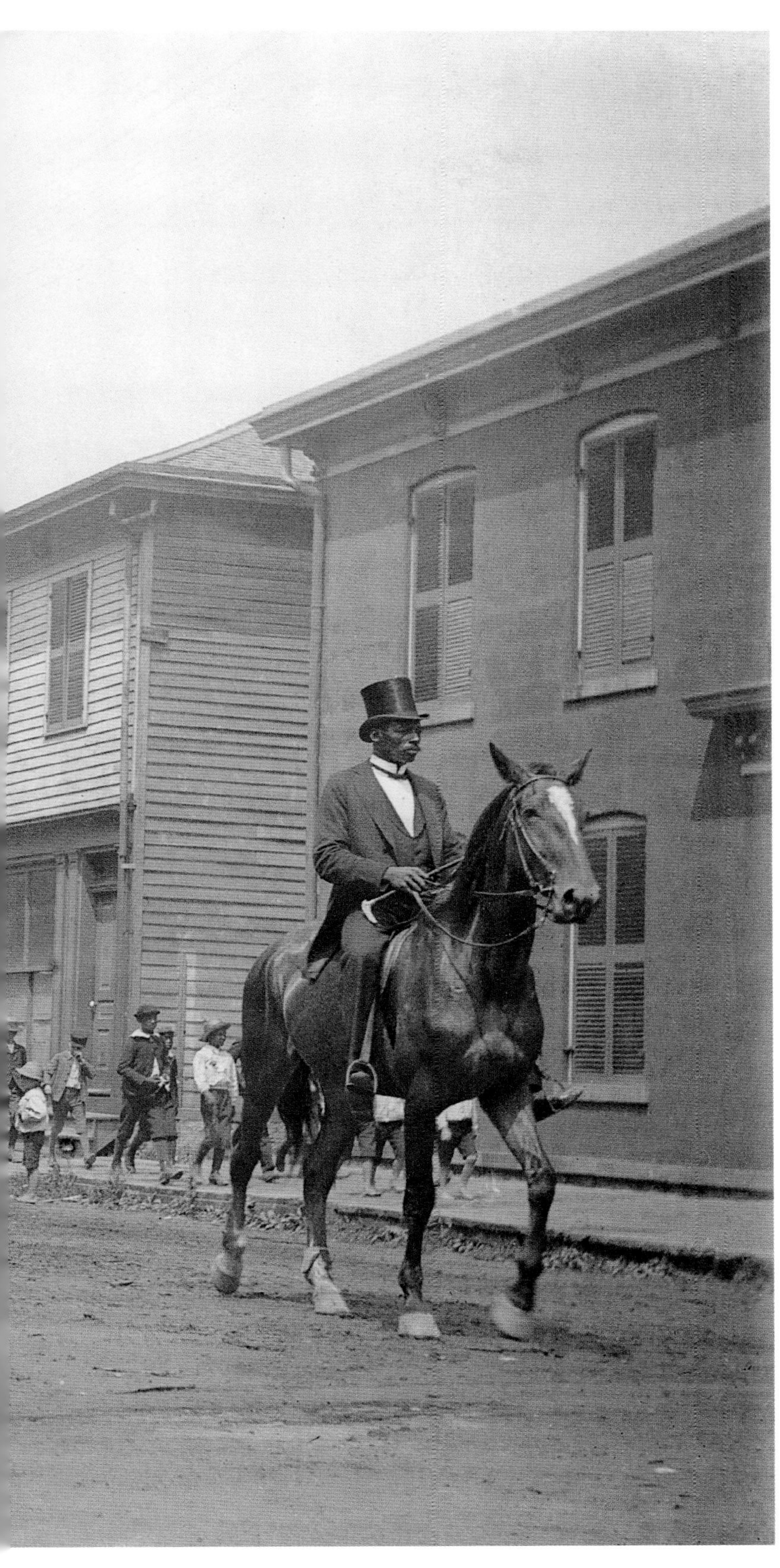

Emancipation Day Parade, Amherstburg, Ontario, Canada, 1894. Grand Marshal Moses Brantford, Jr. leads the procession down Dalhousie Street in a top hat and tails, riding horseback. More than 1,000 attendees from across Ontario and nearby Detroit gathered to mark August 1. Once a major landing point for freedom seekers fleeing US slavery, Amherstburg remained a site for cross-border emancipation celebrations well into the twentieth century.

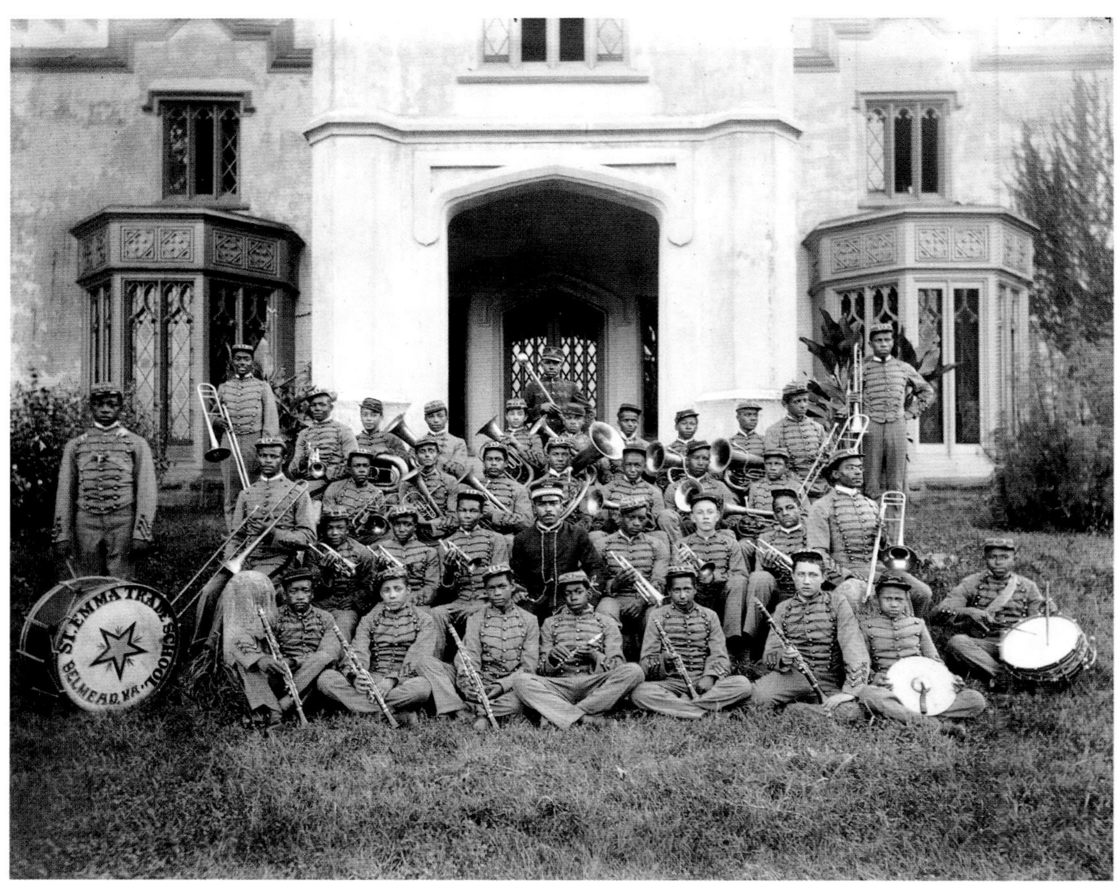

ABOVE: Dressed in crisp military uniforms, the young men of the St. Emma Industrial & Agricultural Institute band pose before their school at Belmead Plantation, Powhatan County, Virginia. With the dignified postures of a military band, they stand in the tradition of the bands that led Emancipation Day parades through southern streets, filling the air with the music that marched freedom forward.

OPPOSITE: Marching in formation on former plantation grounds, the young men of the St. Emma Incustrial & Agricultural Institute band claimed the space that had once been used to hold their forebears in bondage and created the sounds that celebrated freedom.

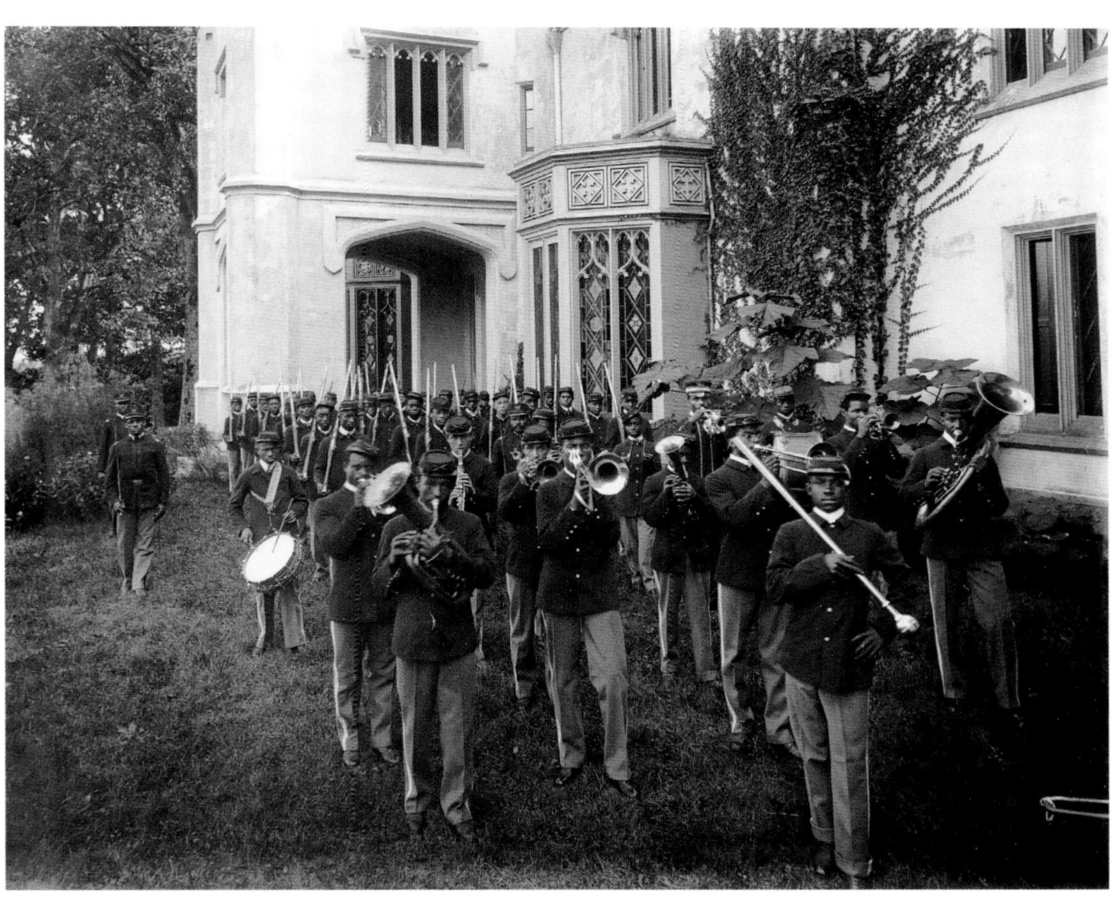

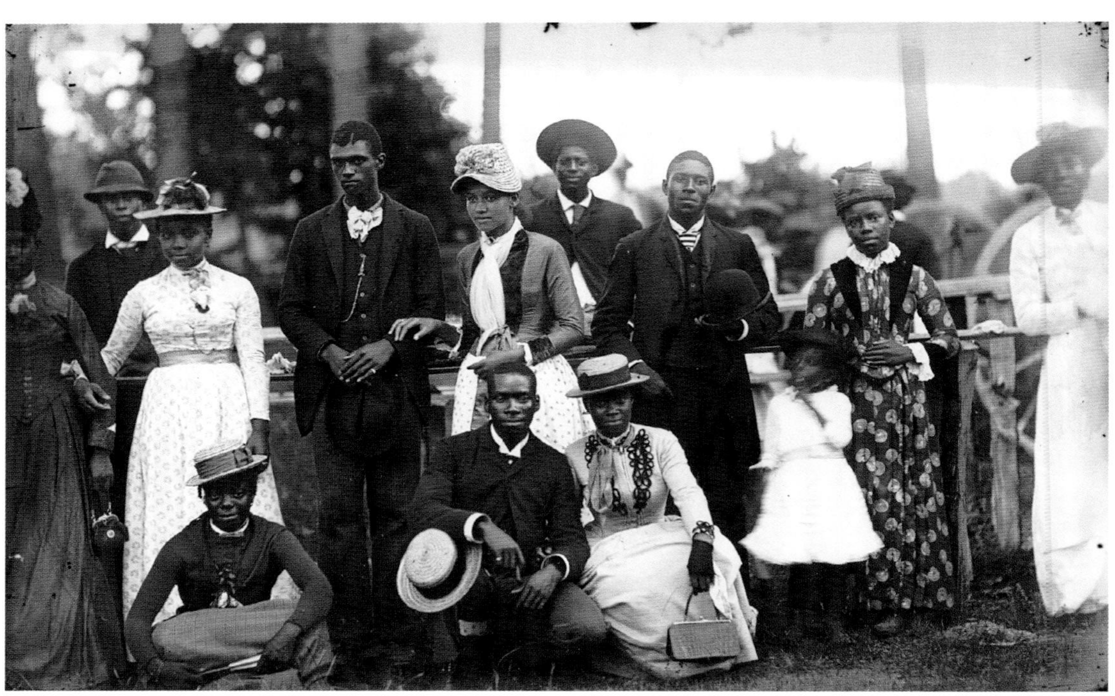

ABOVE: Dressed elaborately in their Sunday best, a group of Black celebrants gather near Bon Air in Chesterfield County, Virginia, for a church picnic. While the reason for this late-1880s gathering was not recorded by the photographer, the image of Black men, women, and children so beautifully outfitted for this occasion speaks to the formality of moments of joy and remembrance in the decades after the Emancipation.

OPPOSITE: A vendor serving ice cream at the Bon Air, Virginia, gathering. Scenes like this were common at Emancipation Day celebrations, where food, fellowship, and the dignity of everyday work were celebrated.

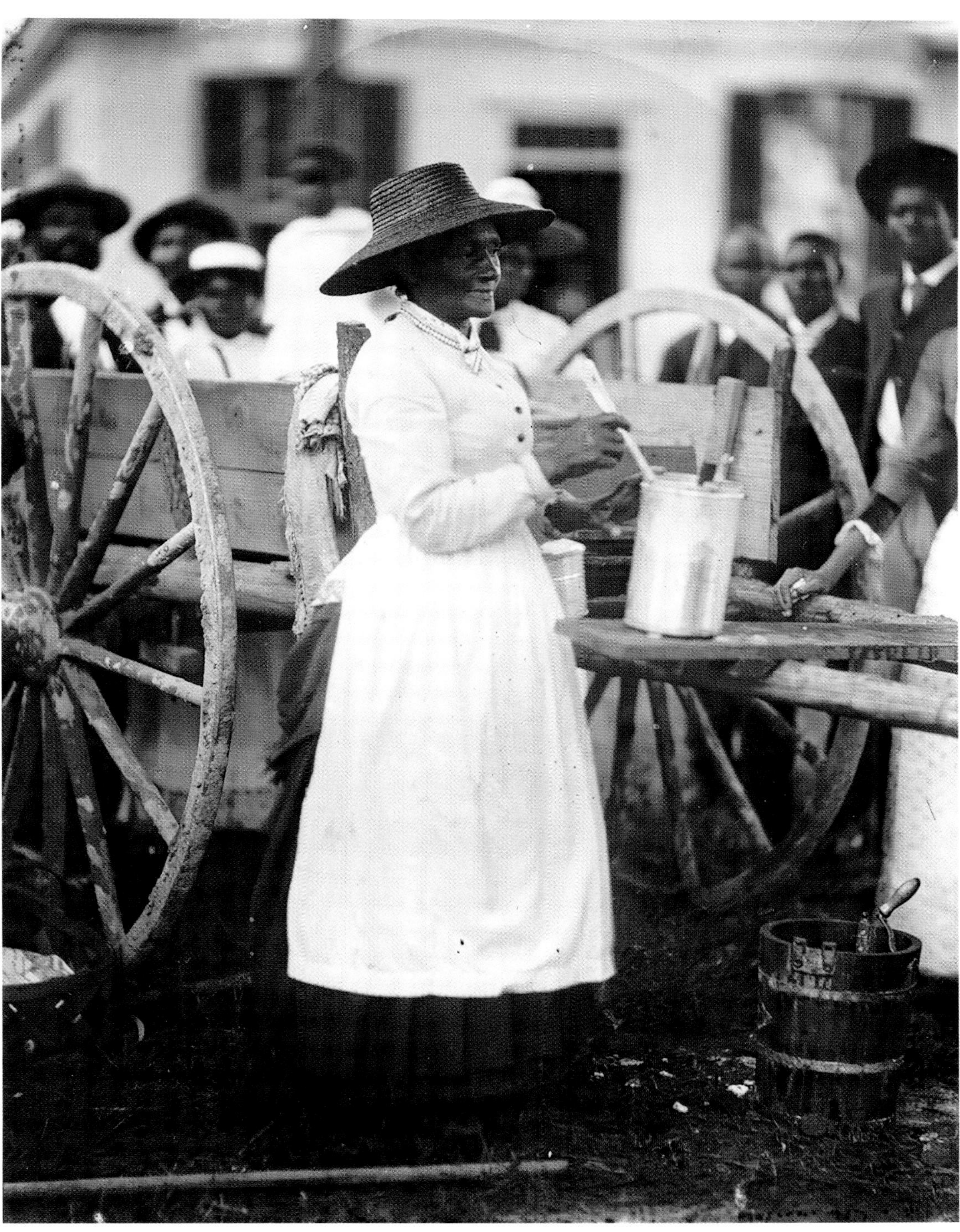

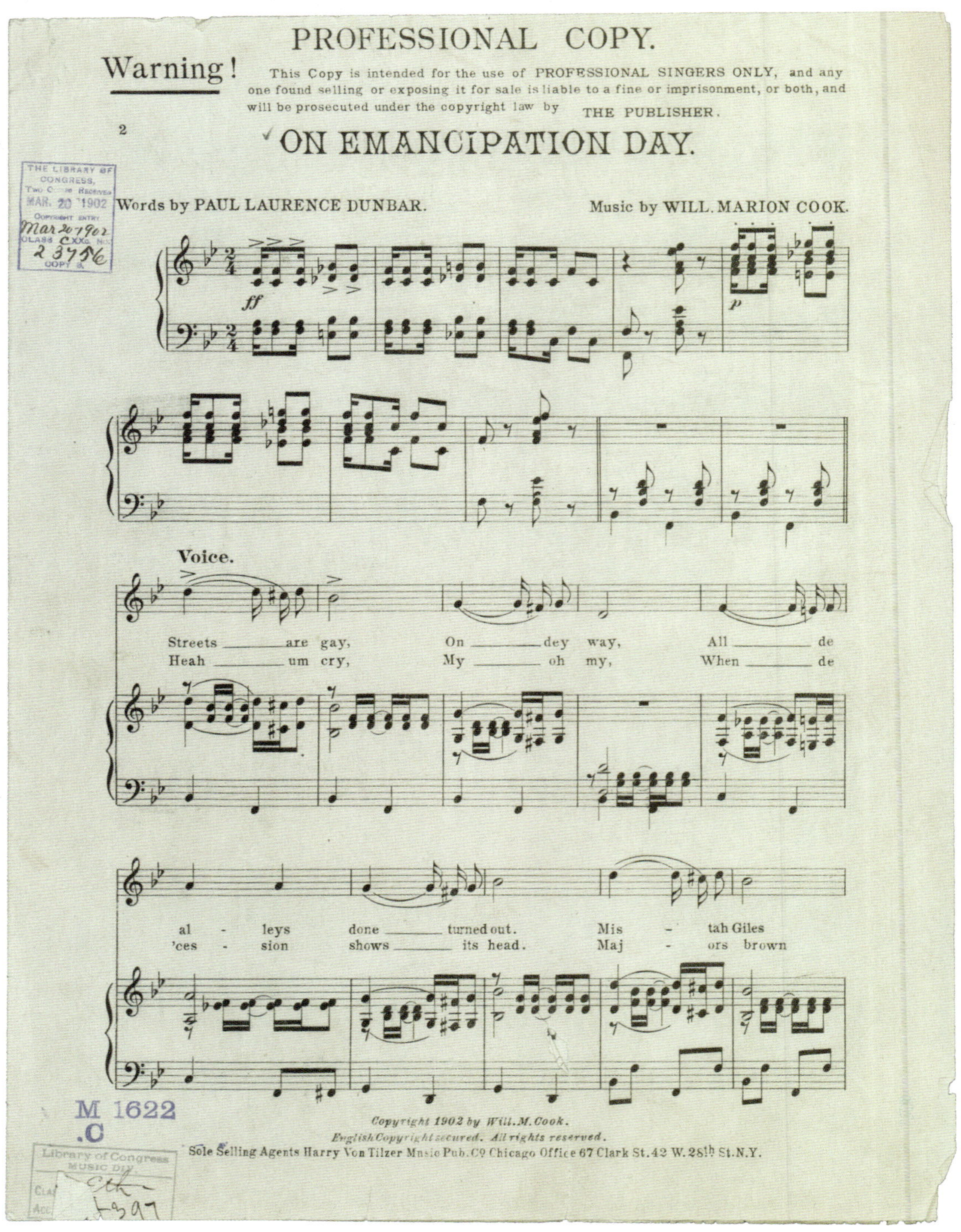

Sheet music for "On Emancipation Day," composed by Will Marion Cook with lyrics by Paul Laurence Dunbar. The 1902 song, with its minstrel-style dialect, was the finale of Cook's musical *In Dahomey*, which in 1903 became the first all-Black musical to play on Broadway.

PRESS NOTICE

THE HAMPTON NORMAL AND AGRICULTURAL INSTITUTE

HAMPTON, VIRGINIA

Emancipation Day at Hampton Institute

Hampton, Va., Jan. 2—Two thousand representative colored people of Hampton and vicinity gathered on New Year's Day in the Hampton Institute Gymnasium, at two-thirty, to celebrate the Forty-seventh anniversary of the Emancipation Proclamation. Rev. A. A. Graham, pastor of Zion Church, Phoebus, Va., was the presiding officer. The best white and colored people came together to hear the wonderful story of Negro progress during the years of his freedom. The audience was made up of prosperous-looking, intelligent, attentive, and responsive people.

The chief address was delivered by President J. A. Cotton, of Henderson Normal Institute, Henderson, N. C., who spoke on "The Negro's Opportunity for the Future."

ADDRESS OF DR. COTTON

Dr. Cotton grouped his remarks about four topics: cash, culture, character, and Christianity. He emphasized the importance of training Negro men and women who will prove themselves dependable and fearless in doing what is right. He urged the colored people to serve God aright by helping their fellow-men.

He declared that the Negro race and the nation are dying for the want of love — love that means self-sacrifice and service which is Christlike.

DR. FRISSELL SPEAKS

Dr. H. B. Frissell, principal of Hampton Institute, spoke eloquently concerning the fitness of celebrating the anniversary of the Emancipation Proclamation on ground which has been dedicated for over forty years to the upbuilding of the Negro and Indian races through agricultural and industrial training. He referred to the excellent work which is being done by Hampton students who have gone out like Christian soldiers to fight against ignorance, superstition, and sin. Where men had given their lives for freedom, it was fitting, he declared, that Negro men and women should reconsecrate their lives to noble service.

Dr. Frissell expressed the hope that year by year the colored people would gather at Hampton Institute and learn anew that through great tribulation men come to their best.

NEGRO PROGRESS

Rev. A. A. Graham said that he was glad the young people of Hampton Institute, who are the hope of their race, could face the older people and hear the story of emancipation. He outlined the Negro's uphill climb and the marvelous transformation in the colored people through less than fifty years of freedom. It was significant, he declared, that on the old battlefields there had sprung up institutions for the proper education of Negro youth. He referred with pride to the handwork of colored women which was on exhibition at the Hampton Institute Gymnasium and to the thirty-horse power automobile outside of the Gymnasium which had been built "from the ground up" by a Negro youth of Hampton.

David Owl, a Cherokee Indian, who is a Hampton student, brought the people a simple, straightforward, manly message of congratulation on their progress.

Tandy W. Coggs, a colored student at Hampton Institute, spoke on "Negro Education" He declared that the educated Negro has been showing the people that thinking and doing go together. He showed that General Armstrong's belief in the capacity of the Negro for progress, which led to the founding of Hampton Institute, had been well grounded.

INTERESTING PROGRAM

Mr. Tressler Scott, of Hampton Institute, led a chorus of fifty-voices in the singing of three selections, including "Fairy Land" and Native Land." Rev. J. W. Patterson, of Hampton, offered the invocation. The Emancipation Proclamation was read by Nannie Williams, of Hampton. The Hampton Institute Band played a selection and a medley. The audience sang "My Country 'tis of Thee" and "O Freedom." The benediction was pronounced by Rev. John H. Gray, of Hampton.

The Hampton Institute Battalion, commanded by Capt. Allen Washington, associate commandant, met the large gathering of colored people in Hampton and escorted them to Hampton Institute.

KINDLY SEND MARKED COPY TO W. A. AERY, HAMPTON INSTITUTE, VA.

The press notice of the 1911 celebration of Emancipation Day at Hampton Normal and Agricultural Institute in Hampton, Virginia. With over two thousand Black and white residents in attendance, the day's formal celebration featured a parade, speeches, and patriotic songs.

SEVENTEENTH ANNUAL

EMANCIPATION DAY CELEBRATION.

AT NICODEMUS, KS.

AUGUST 1ST, 1904.

The Committee intends to make this celebration the best ever held. A first-class program will be rendered, consisting of Music, Recitations, Drills, etc. Exercises commence at 1:30 p. m. with an appropriate song and prayer by Rev. L. C. Newby.

MASTER OF CEREMONIES, HON. G. W. JONES, OF HILL CITY.

ORATORS OF THE DAY.

Hon. E. W. Hoch, Republican nominee for governor writes he will be present if possible. Hon. H. O. Caster, of Oberlin, Kans., Populist candidate for congress, Hon. Alvin Law and Jas. Gordon and other prominent speakers from home and abroad. Rec., Miss Olive Kackley.

MUSIC BY CORNET BAND. AN IDEAL PLACE TO CELEBRATE.

ENTERTAINMENTS.

Horse Races, Foot Races, Bowery Dances, etc. Whitney's Merry-go-round, one of the largest in the state will be on the grounds. There will be a matched ball game between the first nine of Hill City and Edmond, Kas. This will be the most interesting game of the season. The Grove one mile southwest of town has been prepared and the celebration will be held there as in the past. There will be free ice water on the grounds. It is the intention of the committee to make this celebration the most successful one ever held at Nicodemus. Remember that a concert and social will be held up town in the evening by the members A.M.E.church.

ALL TOWNS CORDIALLY INVITED TO ATTEND WITH US.

Committee on Program: Mrs. Hattie Scroggins and Miss Perle E. Jones. Marshals and Peace Officers: John VanDuval, J. C. Coleman, C. C. Hall and A. G. VanDuval. For further information apply to R. B. Scruggs, Allen Thomas and Henry Wilson, committee.

Flyers advertising the 1904 and 1908 celebrations of Emancipation Day in Nicodemus, Kansas. Founded in 1877 by Black migrants fleeing to the Midwest from the violence and economic repression of the post-Reconstruction south, Nicodemus was part of the Exoduster movement, the first large migration of Black southerners to the Midwest. Notable were the celebrations taking place on August 1, which marked the date Great Britain abolished slavery in its colonies in 1834, tying this midwestern Black town to an international celebration of Black freedom.

TWENTY-FIRST ANNUAL

EMANCIPATION

Day Celebration

At Nicodemus, Kansas, August 1st, 1908.

THE COMMITTEE

intends to make this Celebration the best ever held. A first-class program will be rendered, consisting of Music, Recitations, Drills, etc. Exercises commence at 1:30 p. m., with an appropriate song and prayer by Rev. Ramey.

Master of Ceremonies, Hon. W. L. Sayers, Hill City, Kansas

Orators of the Day:

Hon. W. A. Reeder, of Logan, W. S. Fleming, of Oberlin, W. B. Ham, of Stockton, J. R. Connelly, of Colby, candidates for Congress; Hon. Wm. Wells, of Hill City, Fred Robertson, of Atwood, A. B. Jones, of WaKeeney, candidates for State Senator; Dr. C. W. Washington, of Nicodemus.

MUSIC BY THE MORLAND CORNET BAND.

Entertainment

Horse Races, Foot Races, Bowery Dances, etc. Young Bros., Merry-Go-Round, one of the largest in the state, will be on the ground in the evening of July 30. There will be matched ball games. These will be the best of the season.

On the evening of August 1, an entertainment will be given, consisting of Music and Recitations, under the management of the First Baptist Church.

The Grove, one mile southwest of town, has been prepared and the celebration will be held there as in the past. It is the intention of the committee to make this celebration the most successful one ever held at Nicodemus.

Base Ball Games

In addition to the celebration proper on July 30th and 31st there will be matched ball games at the grove. On July 30th the Nicodemus 2nd team and the local team will play for a liberal purse. It is conceded that Damar, Nicodemus, Palco and Hill City are four of the best teams in Northwest Kansas.

On July 31st the opening game will be played between Nicodemus and Damar. August 1st at 10 a. m. Palco and Hill City and at 4 p. m. Nicodemus and Damar. Come one, come all and see the greatest games of the season. James Merritt and Chas. Vaughn, Mgrs.

All Towns Cordially Invited To Attend And Help Make Merry The Day.

COMMITTEE ON PROGRAM: Mr. S. C. Geary and others. MARSHALLS AND PEACE OFFICERS: John VanDuval, James Hilden, A. G. VanDuval and C. E. Bradford.

For further information apply to R. B. Scruggs, Allen Thomas and Henry Wilson, Committee.

A group of African American men, women, boys, and girls standing on the steps to a building during a Juneteenth parade. Two girls in the back are holding signs that read "Good Samaritan."

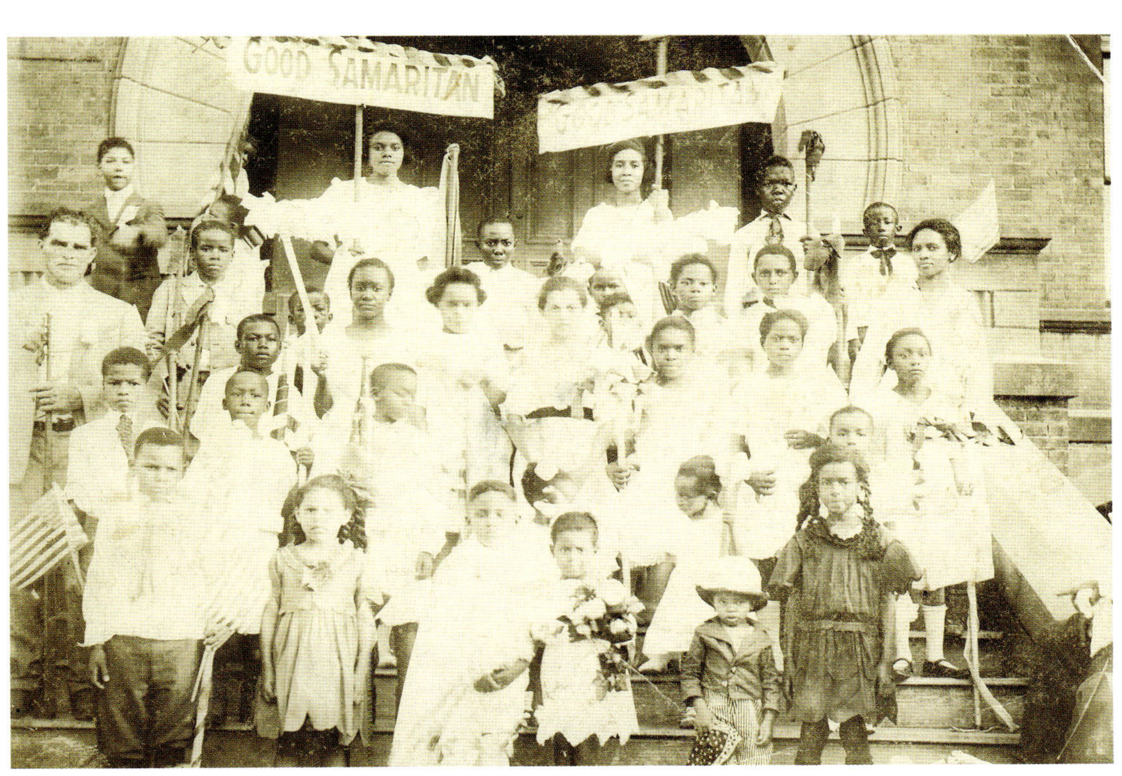
GOOD SAMARITAN

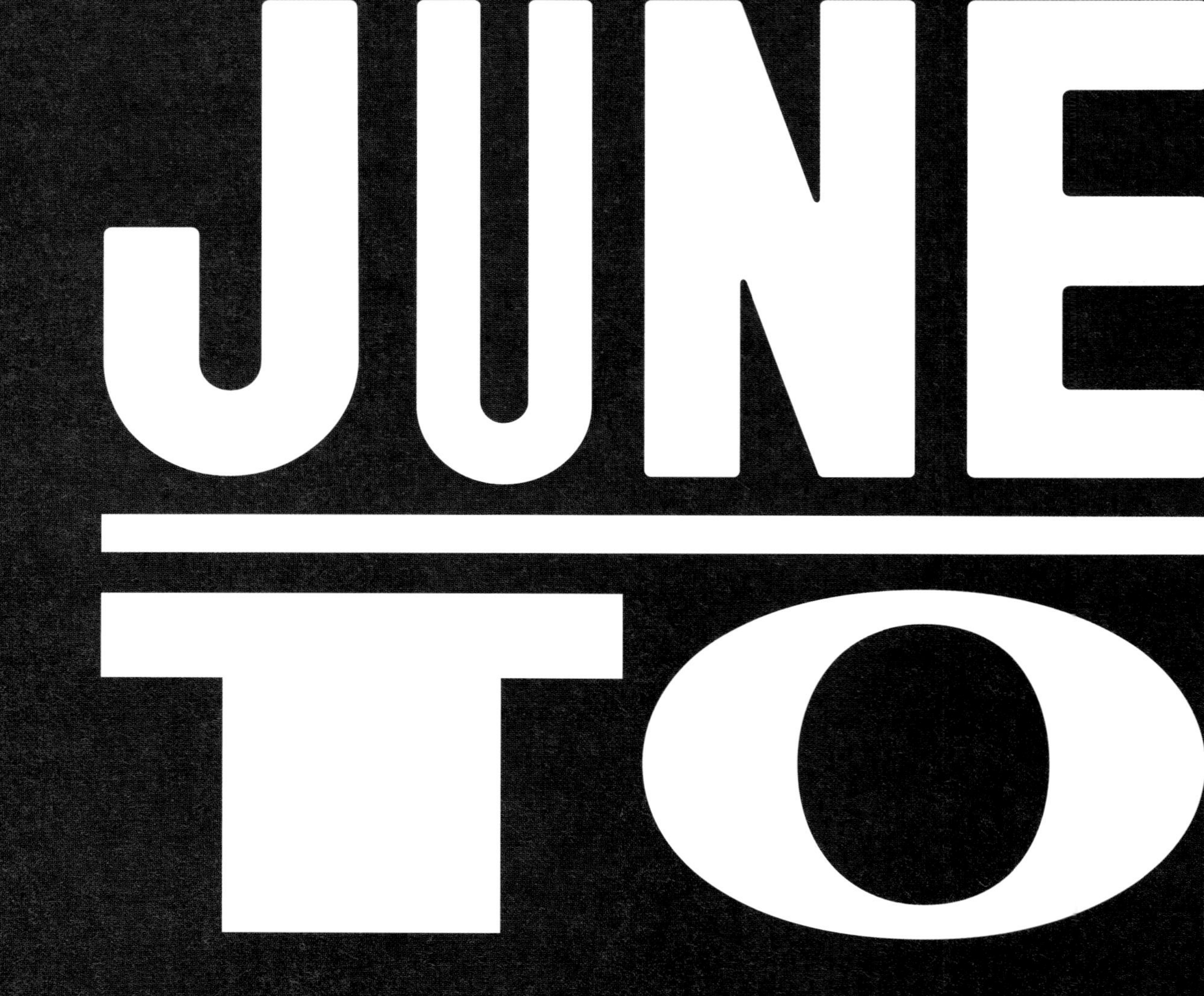
JUNE
TO

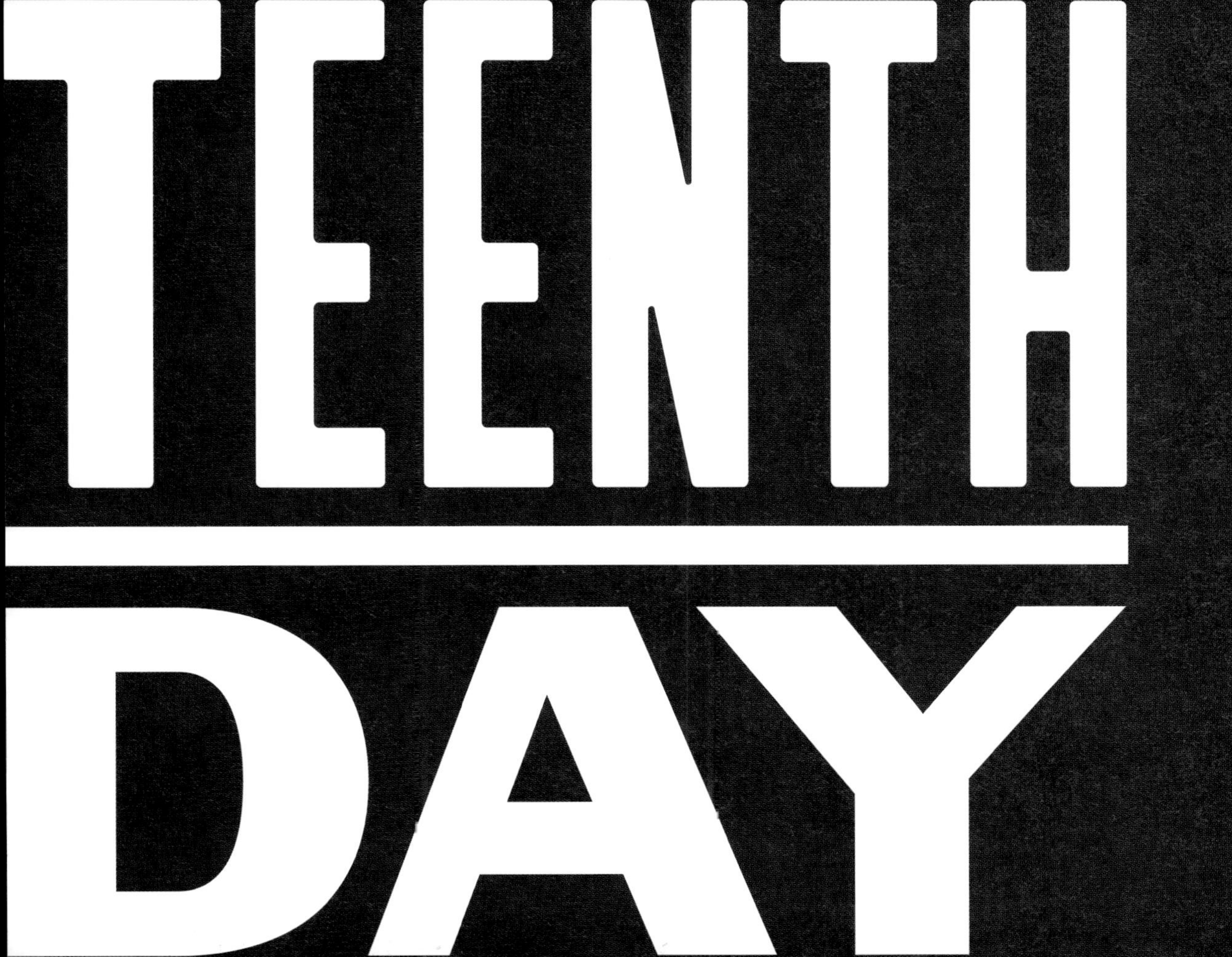
TEENTH
DAY

SLAVERY FIRST ENDED in the nation's capital, Washington, DC, when President Abraham Lincoln signed the District of Columbia Compensated Emancipation Act on April 16, 1862, freeing the thousands of enslaved people in the district. In a striking and singular gesture, the federal government offered up to $300 per person to former enslavers as compensation for the loss of their "property" in slaves—but nothing in recompense to the enslaved for their years of unpaid labor. No such payment would ever again be made to slaveholders in the United States, and no reparative payments were ever made to those who had been slaves. The DC law stood as both a peculiar anomaly and a quiet dress rehearsal for the Emancipation Proclamation that would follow the next year, an experiment in dismantling slavery within the shadow of the White House.

By 1866, Black Washingtonians had begun commemorating this landmark in history, naming April 16 as their Emancipation Day. But unlike other emancipation celebrations that emerged across the country, observances in the District of Columbia carried a unique proximity to presidential power. Each year, organizers made sure that the parade route passed directly by the White House, and celebrants would gather in Lafayette Square in full view of the executive mansion. Presidents from Andrew Johnson to William McKinley stood witness to thousands marching in remembrance of their freedom, claiming recognition from those in power. From the beginning, Black leaders in the district sought out that acknowledgment, not out of deference, but as a political assertion. These commemorations forced lawmakers and the people of the nation's capital to remember, stitching the memory of emancipation into the very fabric of the nation.

The DC celebrations are a reminder that the road to national recognition for Juneteenth did not begin in 2021. It stretches back more than 150 years, through parades in Washington, DC, and all the way down to the local traditions of Black families who never stopped celebrating their freedom. From the earliest Emancipation Day commemorations in the shadow of the White House to Watch Night services in churches to Juneteenth cookouts in Texas and beyond, Black Americans have insisted that freedom be remembered, not just in books or speeches, but in public space, in song, and in tradition. That insistence has never been passive. It has been grounded in resistance, creativity, and faith. Though the federal recognition of Juneteenth in 2021 marked a powerful shift in national memory, it was not the beginning of the story. Nor does it mark its culmination.

Juneteenth has always been more than a holiday. It is rooted in the ancestral memory of survival. It is carried in the joy of children waving flags and elders seated in folding chairs beneath the summer sun. It is the taste of barbecue. The sound of sermons reverberating off the wooden walls of rural churches, the rolling sound and high knees of a Black marching band, and family stories passed down over the generations. It is the story of a people who refused to forget, even when the nation preferred that they did. Juneteenth, like all Emancipation Day traditions, does not rely on federal acknowledgment to be deeply felt. With or without the federal holiday, these celebrations have endured because of the Black dedication to resistance and memory across generations. The celebration itself is a form of freedom.

In the decade before the federal recognition of Juneteenth, the National Association for the Advancement of Colored People, an institution born of struggle and sustained by a sacred commitment to justice, put forward a call for a national "Jubilee Day" on January 1 of each year. Not only did the NAACP support the tradition of emancipation celebrations early in the twenty-first century, but its 2014 resolution calling for "the observation of a Holiday in recognition of the Emancipation Proclamation of 1863" was a reminder that the nation had failed to acknowledge the depth of the meaning behind emancipation. The association insisted that what happened on January 1, 1863, should not be confined to footnotes and forgotten speeches but should be lifted up, year after year, as a moment of national reckoning and renewal.

As the NAACP made clear, the Emancipation Proclamation was simply the first mile of a long and unfinished journey: "The emancipating of said slaves was not an end within itself, but the beginning of a long struggle for equality and justice that continues today." The association reminded the nation that "the history and story of the slaves who were emancipated has not been fully and completely told, nor properly recorded or represented," and called on the country to research, gather, and archive the fragments of this history. Given the sacrifices made by the enslaved to make this country what it is today, it was past time to honor their lives. The NAACP's call for Jubilee Day foreshadowed the importance of Juneteenth's federal recognition, part of a long tradition of demanding that the nation remember.

And through it all, Texas never stopped remembering. Just as Juneteenth celebrations weren't halted by threats of lynching and segregation in the early twentieth century, they were not abandoned by the generations that won civil rights victories in the late twentieth century. Texans kept remembering—and as they migrated to other parts of the nation, they kept the tradition alive wherever they went. Juneteenth was a spirit they carried with them, from Oakland, California, to Oklahoma City, Oklahoma, and beyond. A reminder that freedom was not conferred; it was insisted upon, generation after generation, in ways both grand and quiet.

And that insistence lives on today.

Juneteenth is about family. It's community. It's personal and ancestral. It didn't require federal recognition to survive. It lives on in the hearts of the descendants of those who heard the news of their freedom at last, on June 19, 1865.

Juneteenth attempts to trace the shapes of memory. The sound of brass bands echoing down dusty roads. Girls with ribbons in their hair. Elders dressed in white gathered beneath wide oaks and tall steeples. Poems and prayers. Testimonies about what each generation survived. Family photo albums filled with pictures of loved ones gathered around picnic tables. These celebrations themselves are living testimonies, evolved and adapted, persisted and reemerged, even as laws were passed to suppress Black rights. People continued to remember, even in the face of erasure. They built beauty in the margins and claimed public space, refusing to shrink.

Black people from New York to Texas expressed creativity through pageant and parade. The quiet power of a sermon. The joy of a cookout. Black people throughout the generations were makers: red velvet cakes, freedom quilts, flower arrangements, photography. A new generation has taken up the torch—through protest, through performance, through poetry. A reminder that this history is living.

And in every image, every archival flyer or program booklet, every lovingly rendered outfit and intentional ritual, there is this same core truth: Black people never needed permission to gather, to sing, to dance to shout or to remember.

The freed people did not wait for someone to declare it appropriate to celebrate the day on which they walked away from the fields and into their futures. They didn't seek approval to play the drums or sing the spirituals. They didn't need a law to tell them that their freedom mattered. They knew.

Juneteenth, and every Black freedom celebration, was for Black people, by Black people, in celebration of Black people, and in memory of Black people. They were all sacred practices.

Even as the world tried to ignore these commemorations, Black people made sure the story continued. Passed it down, one gathering at a time. Through family reunions and block parties. Through community centers and churches and school assemblies.

So yes, it matters that Juneteenth became a federal holiday. That schoolchildren across the country read about General Granger's arrival in Galveston. That television specials, museum exhibits, and op-eds now wrestle with the meaning of this day. But none of it was necessary for Black Americans to keep the flame alive.

We were already marking the day, teaching our children, remembering the ones who never lived to see freedom but dreamed it anyway. We were already free in the ways that mattered most: in spirit, in imagination, in resistance, in joy. That's the heart of Black freedom. The ability to make meaning and beauty even when the systems around us refuse to do so. The creativity to shape tradition from what we've endured. The audacity to laugh, to wear bright colors, to dance in the street, even when we are mourning.

Because we understand that mourning and celebration are not opposites. Grief and joy, struggle and pride, the past and the possible—all live side by side in our traditions.

When we celebrate emancipation, we do more than remember a historical event. We testify that our ancestors' freedom was not theoretical. It was embodied. It was practiced. It was cooked and sung and stitched and shouted. We honor them by keeping those traditions alive.

We will continue to gather. We will continue to remember who we are. Our ancestors imagined freedom before it came. And when it did come, delayed, distorted, and incomplete, they continued to fight to shape it into something more.

This book traces that creative inheritance. It shows the richness of our traditions—not just in the past, but today. Ways of making meaning. Ways of surviving the unthinkable. Ways of keeping the memory alive.

So even as we commemorate Juneteenth with new national attention, we must remember what came before. The generations who carried the celebration through years of silence. The communities that kept the memory alive even when it wasn't fashionable or federally recognized. The elders who insisted that we not forget. Their work is why we're here.

The celebration of Juneteenth today is a vow to gather, again and again, and say: We are still here. Still marching. Still building on what they began. Still imagining more. Participating in the sacred. Keeping the promise of freedom real for those yet to come. As long as we remember, as long as we celebrate, and as long as we struggle, jubilee is not past. It is ongoing. It is ours.

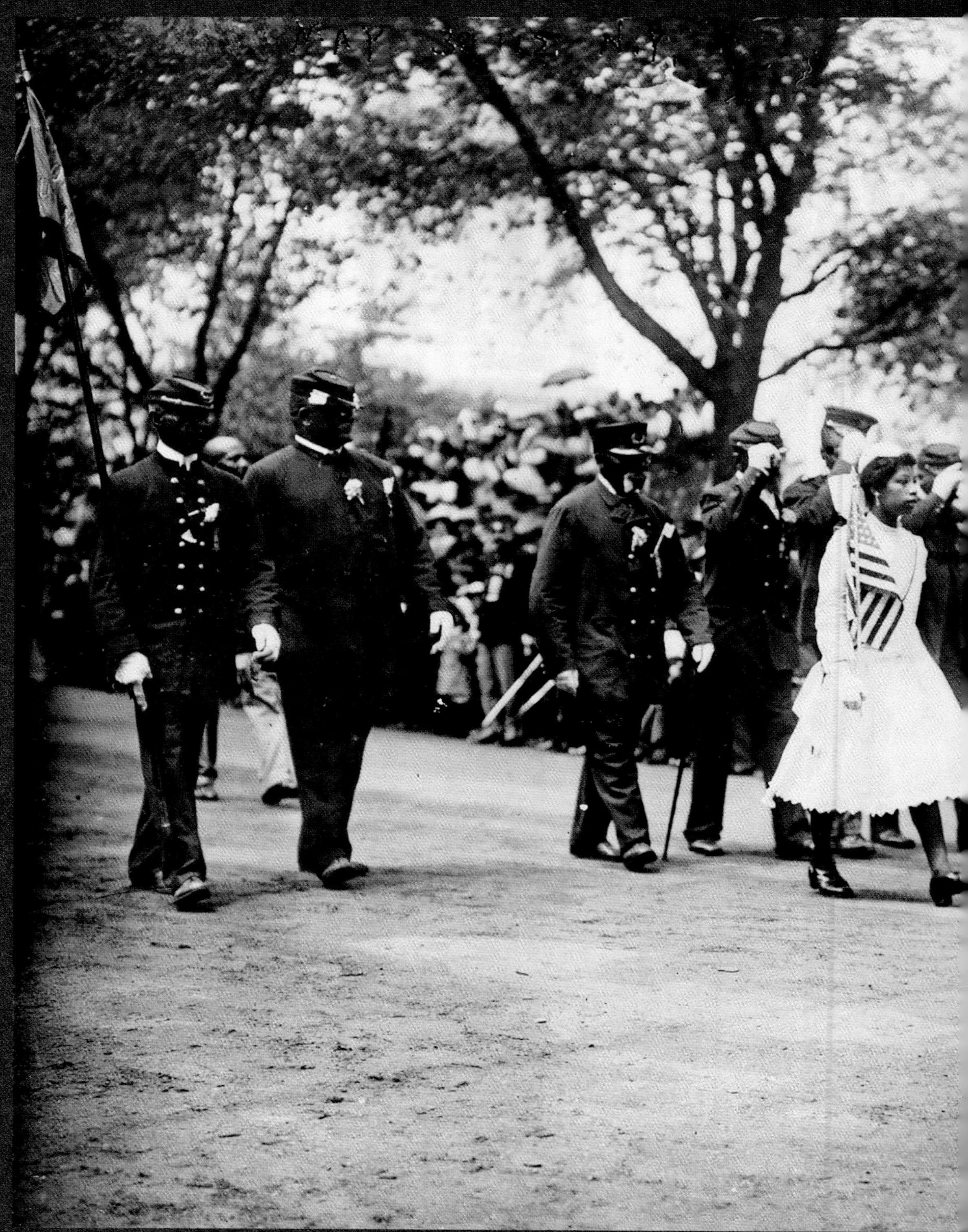
MAY
NY

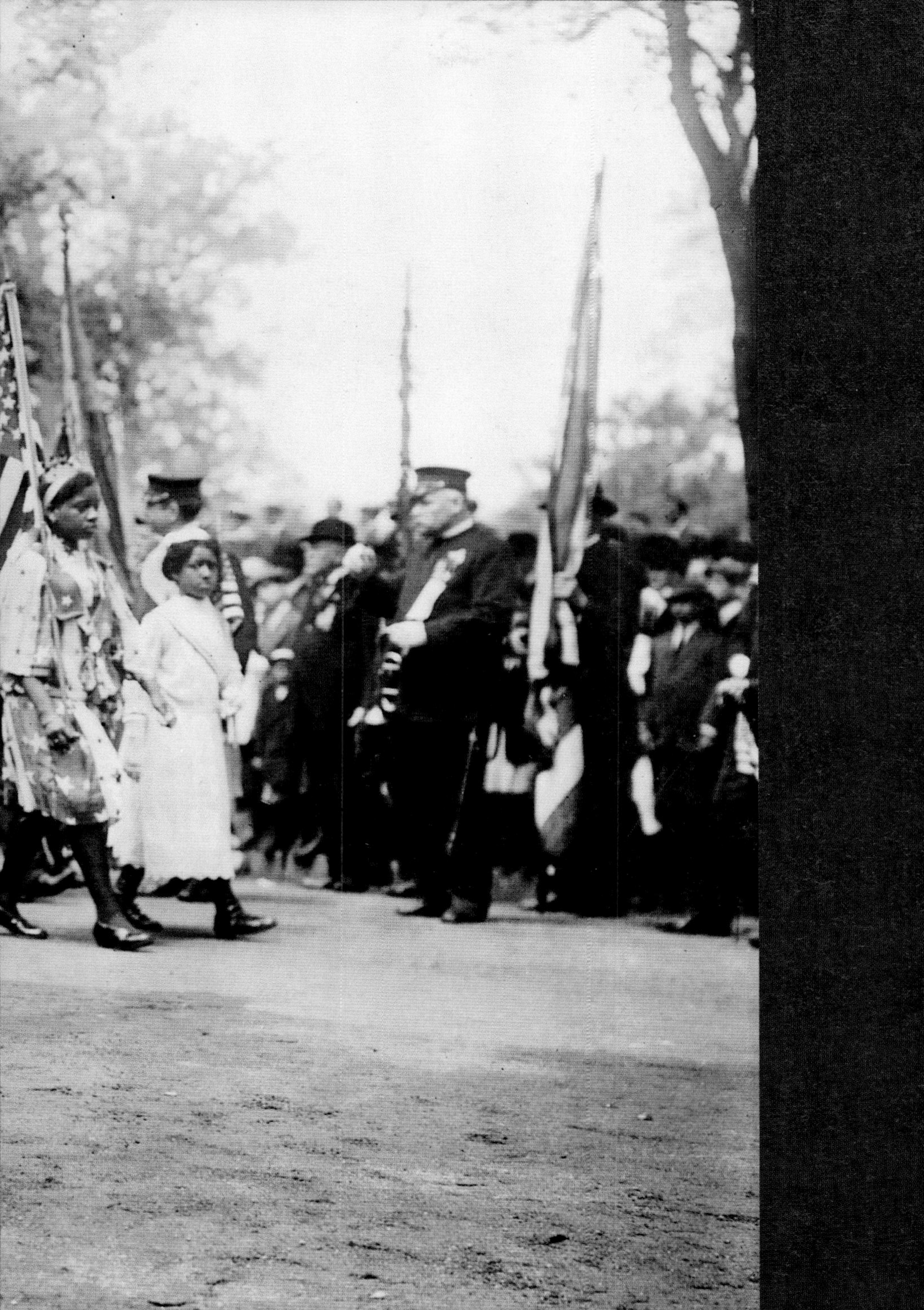

PREVIOUS: Black veterans representing the Grand Army of the Republic (GAR) march proudly through the streets of New York City on May 30, 1912, to celebrate Memorial Day. Black Civil War veterans were the driving force behind much of the remembrance of emancipation and the long struggle to be recognized as full citizens of the nation that they fought to preserve.

RIGHT: The Martin family gathered in front of their home in Oakland, California, to celebrate Juneteenth. The holiday first celebrated in Texas had become a tradition of kinship, collectivity, and remembrance wherever Black families migrated.

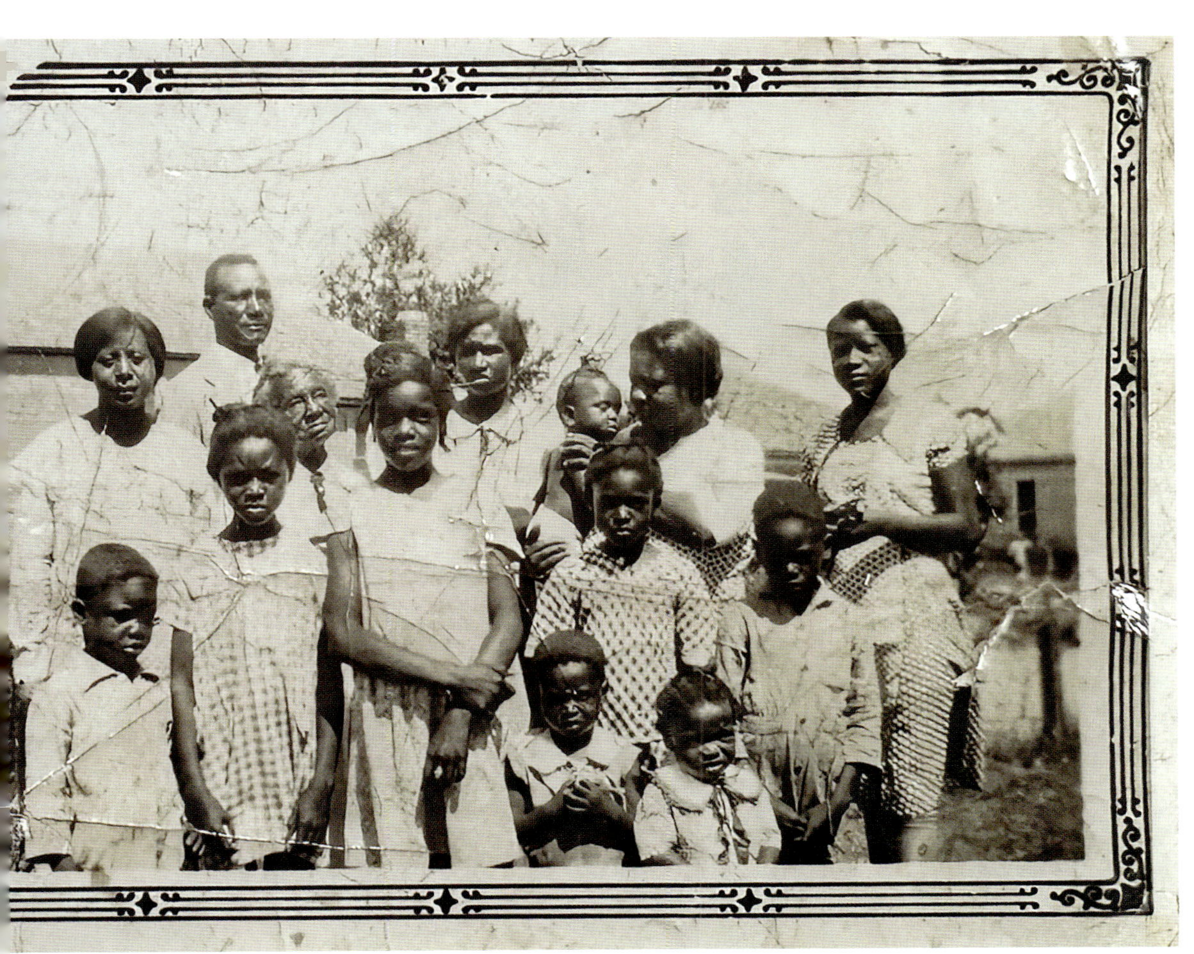

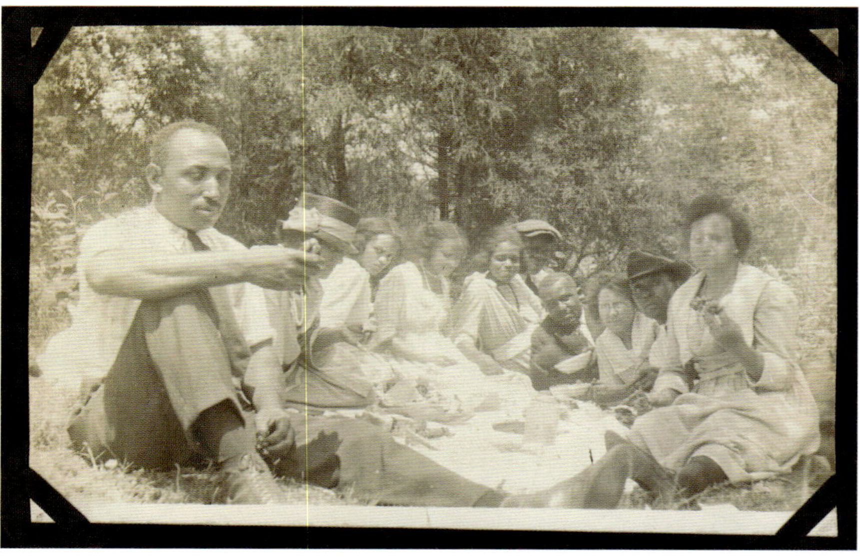

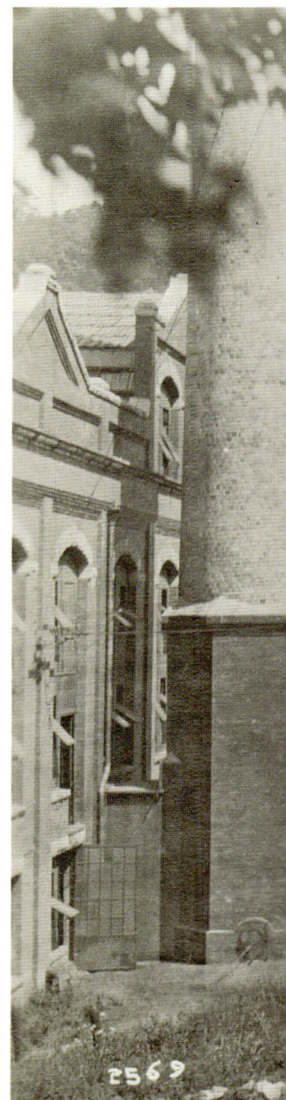

ABOVE: Family picnics like this one were held across the country to celebrate Juneteenth and Emancipation Day. Gatherings both grand and simple provided wonderful opportunities to come together, eat, and remember.

RIGHT: A parade, led by men on horseback and marchers in ceremonial white suits, winds its way up a steep, hilly street through a Kentucky town. The title handwritten on the photograph mounting reads, "Emancipation Day Parade, 1924." Early in the twentieth century, there were hundreds of emancipation parades, both grand and small, throughout the nation.

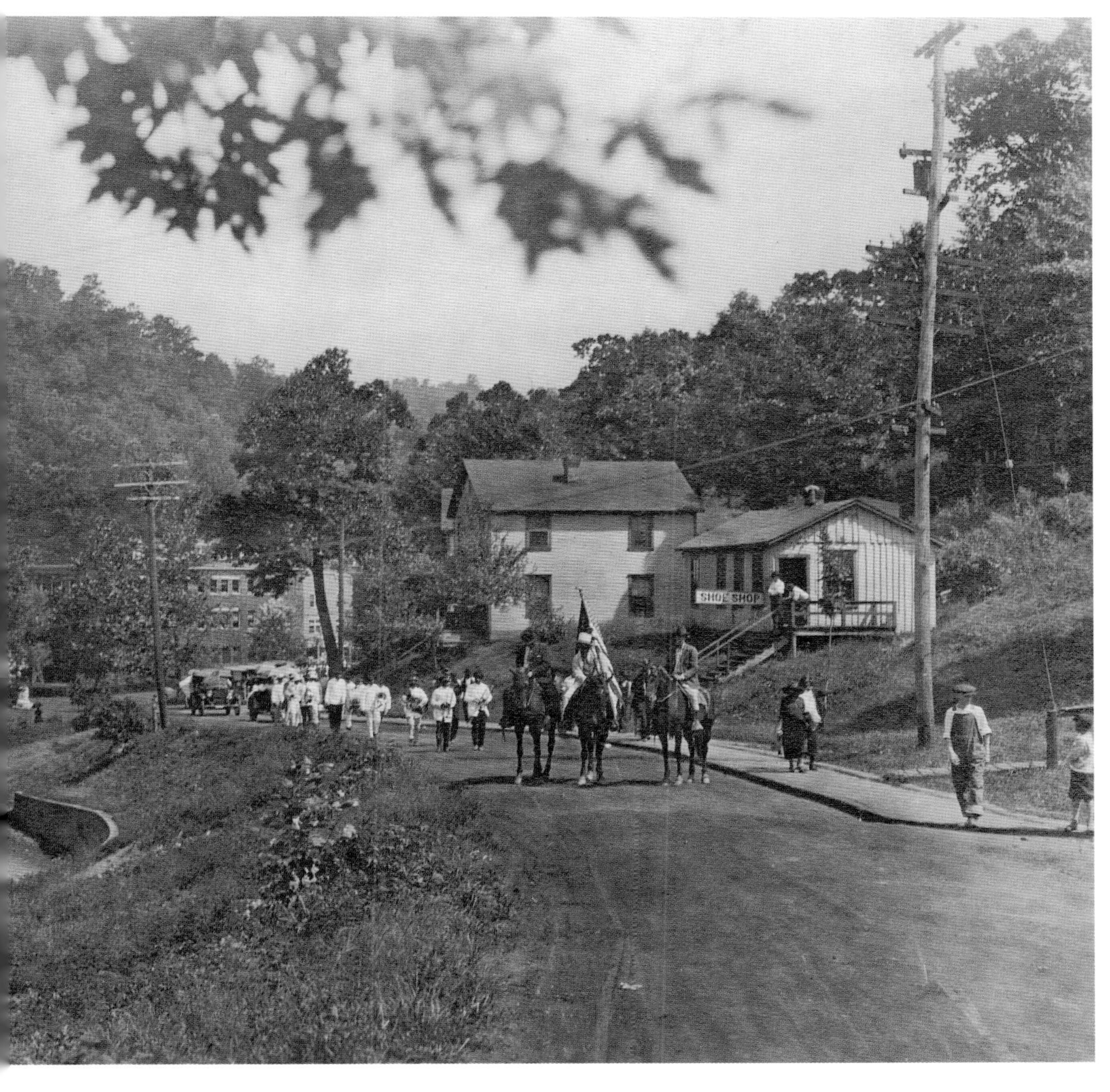
SHOE SHOP

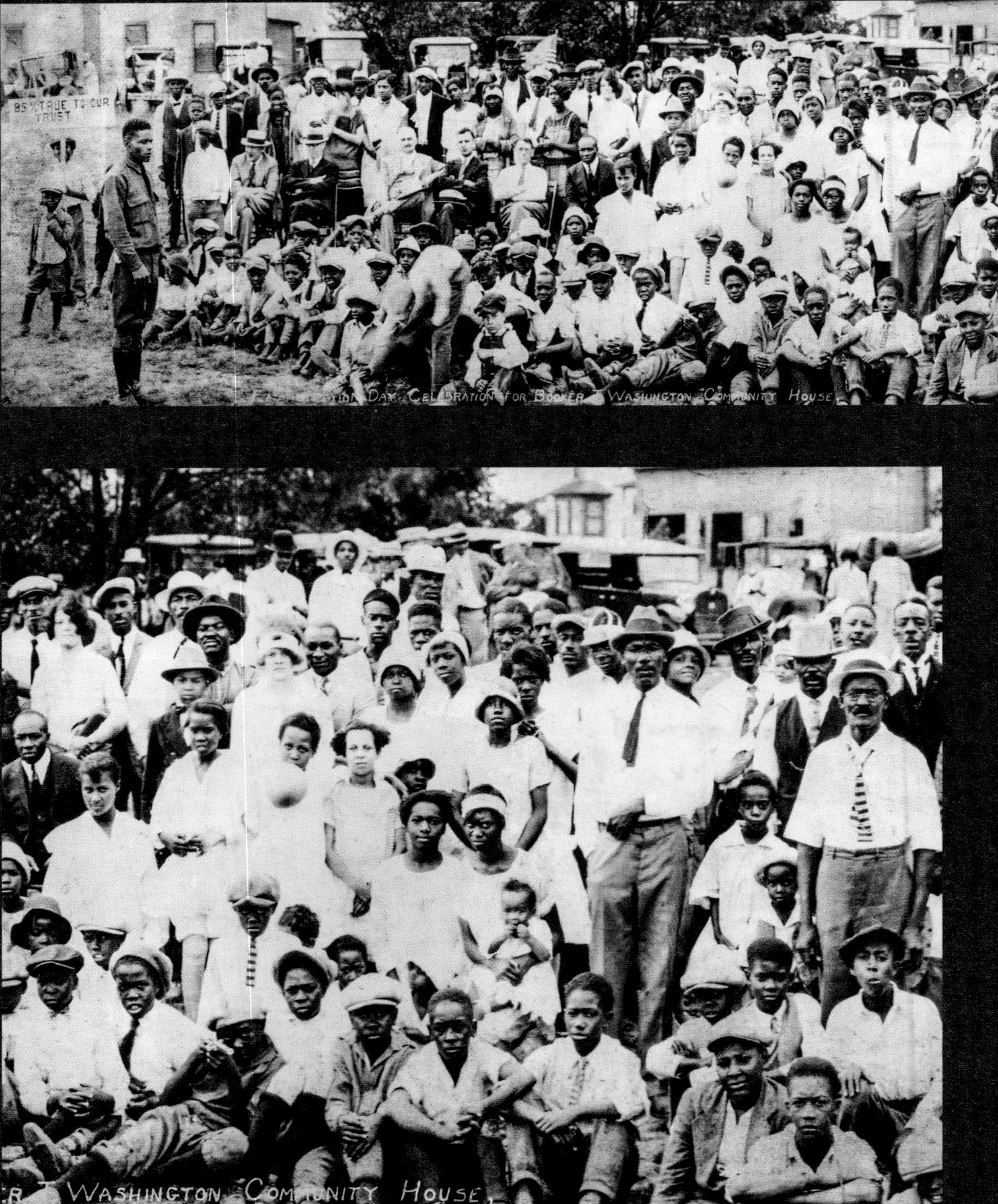
85% TRUE TO OUR TRUST
DAY CELEBRATION FOR BOOKER T. WASHINGTON COMMUNITY HOUSE
R T. WASHINGTON COMMUNITY HOUSE,

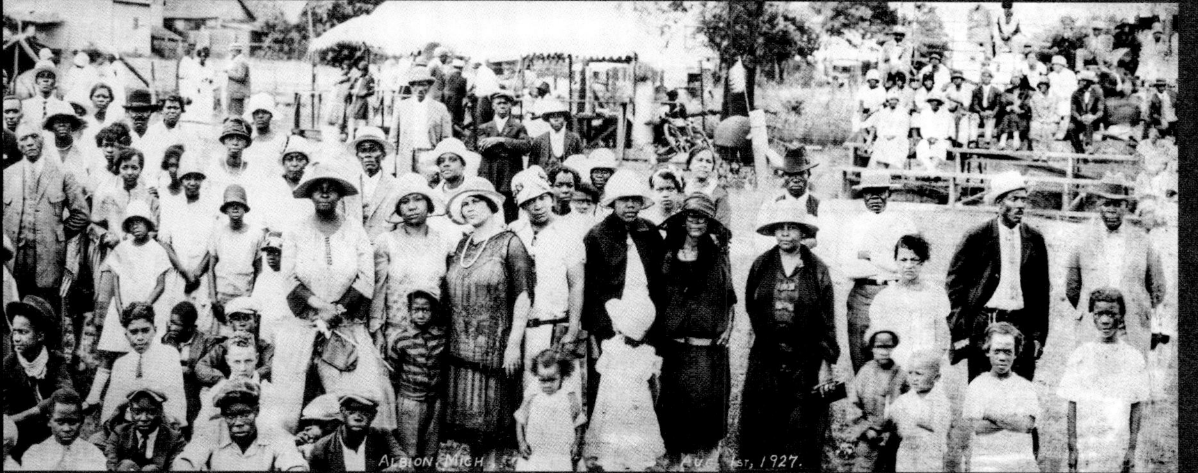

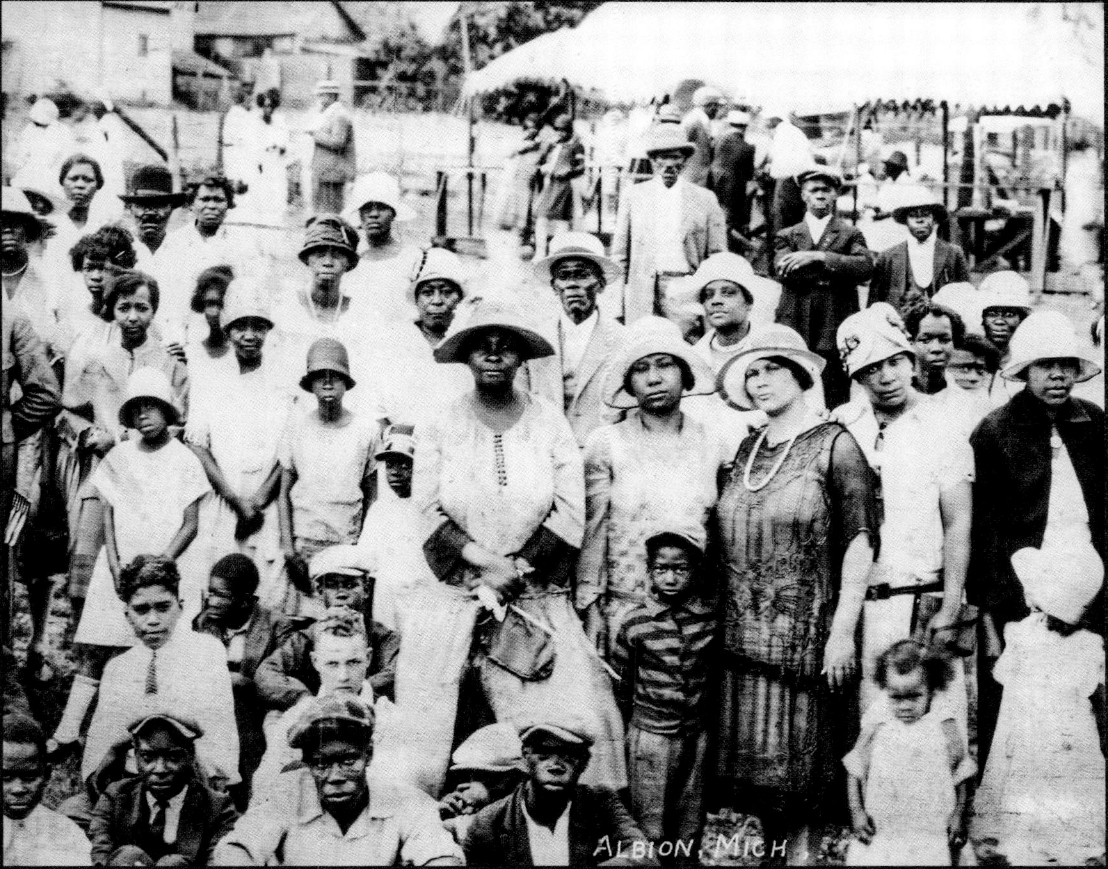

A panoramic photograph of the celebrants at the August 1, 1927, Emancipation Day Celebration at Booker T. Washington Community House in Albion, Michigan. More than a hundred people gathered in proud assembly for the photograph. August 1 was a freedom day first commemorated in communities in the US North prior to the Civil War, marking the emancipation of the enslaved in the British West Indies in 1834. This 1927 gathering is a reminder of the ways that Black communities carried the memory of that first liberation across generations.

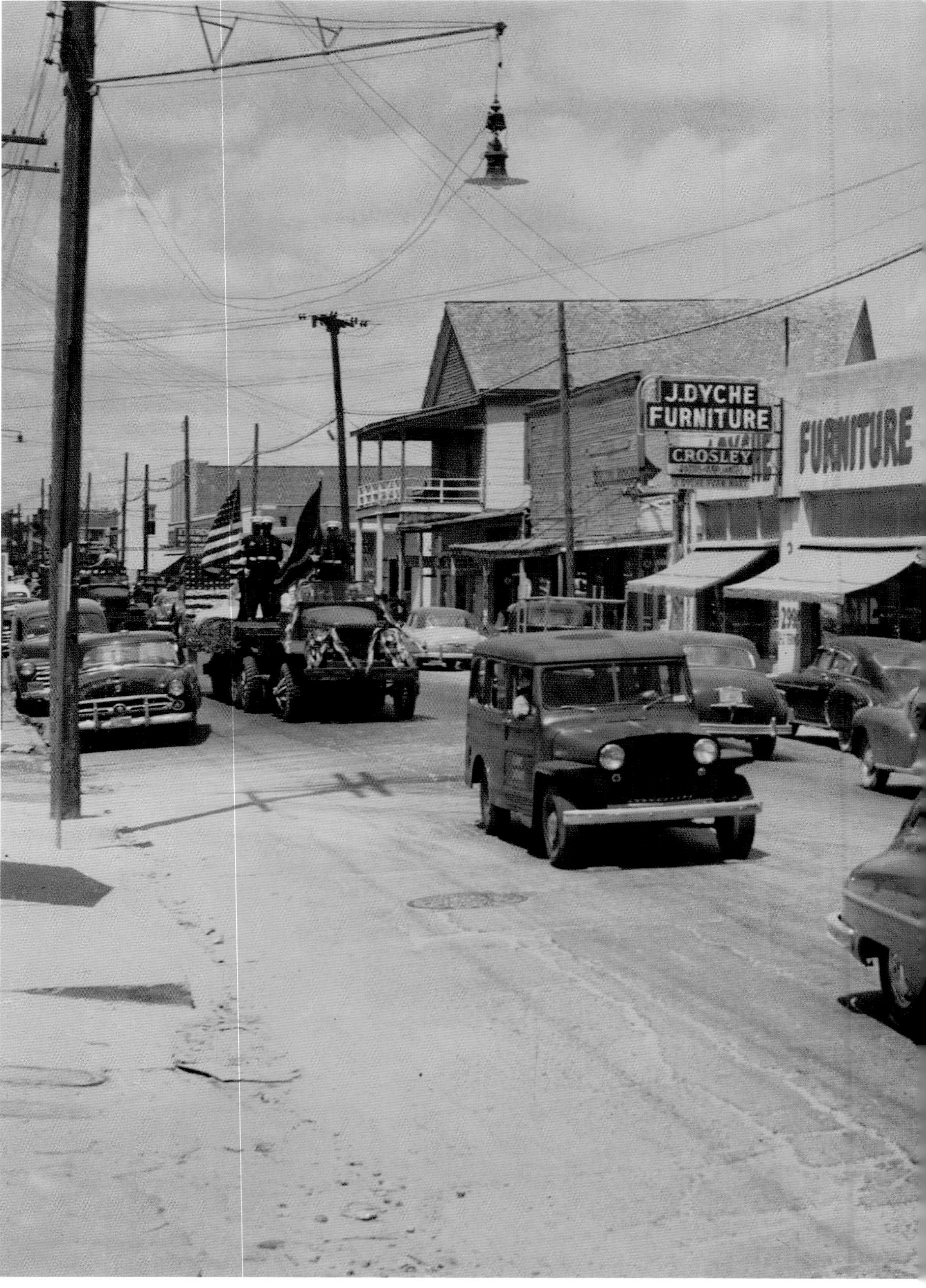
J.DYCHE
FURNITURE
CROSLEY
FURNITURE

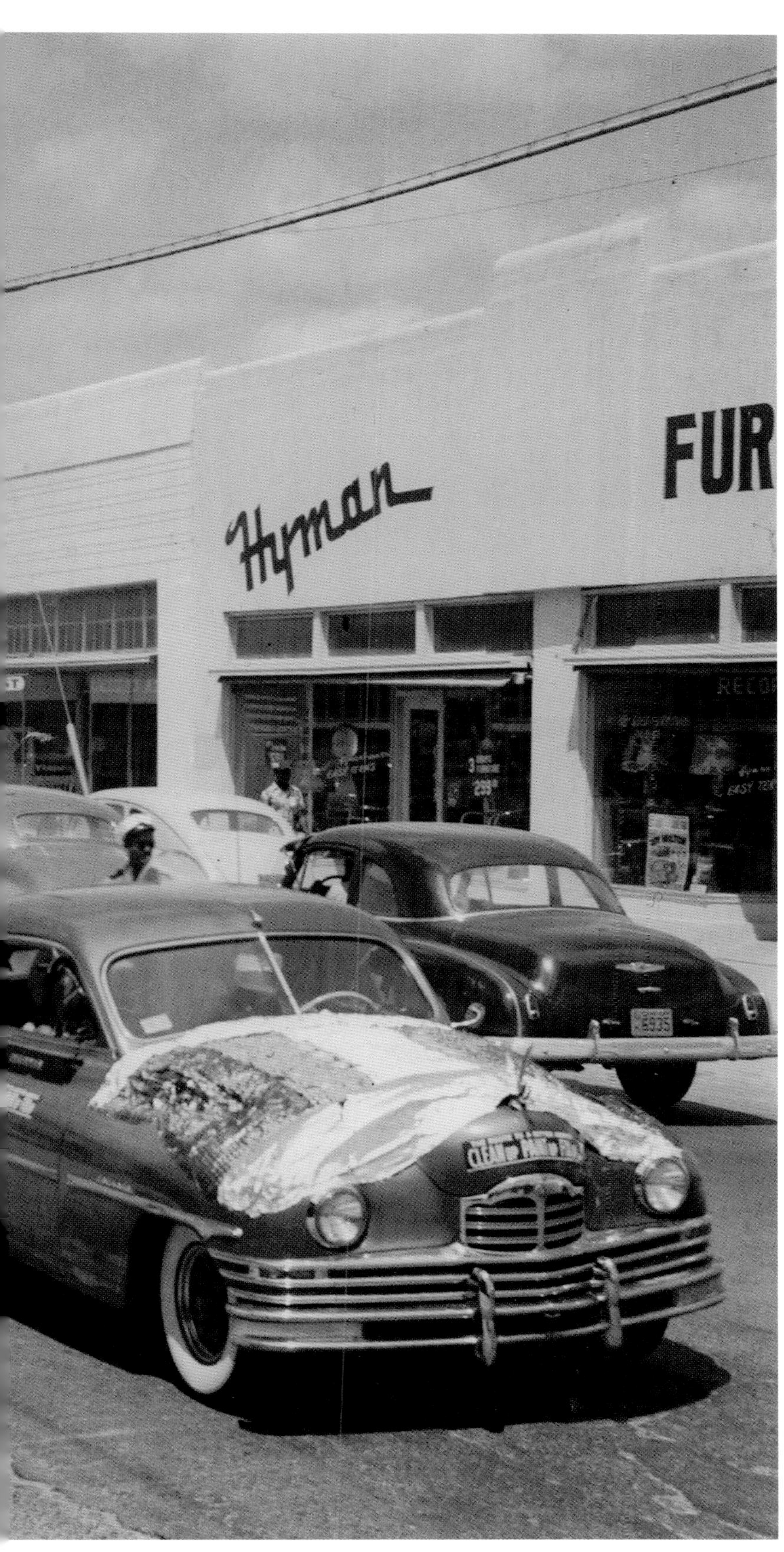

A parade of decorated cars and trucks rolls down Lyons Avenue in Houston, Texas's Fifth Ward in the late 1950s. Decades after emancipation, Juneteenth celebrations remained vibrant in the memory of Texas's Black communities.

Mary Malone, elected San Francisco's Juneteenth Queen by popular vote, poses after being crowned at the St. Francis Hotel. Elected in the 1970s, she reflects the elegance and style of the times, and the spirit that Juneteenth pageants have long celebrated.

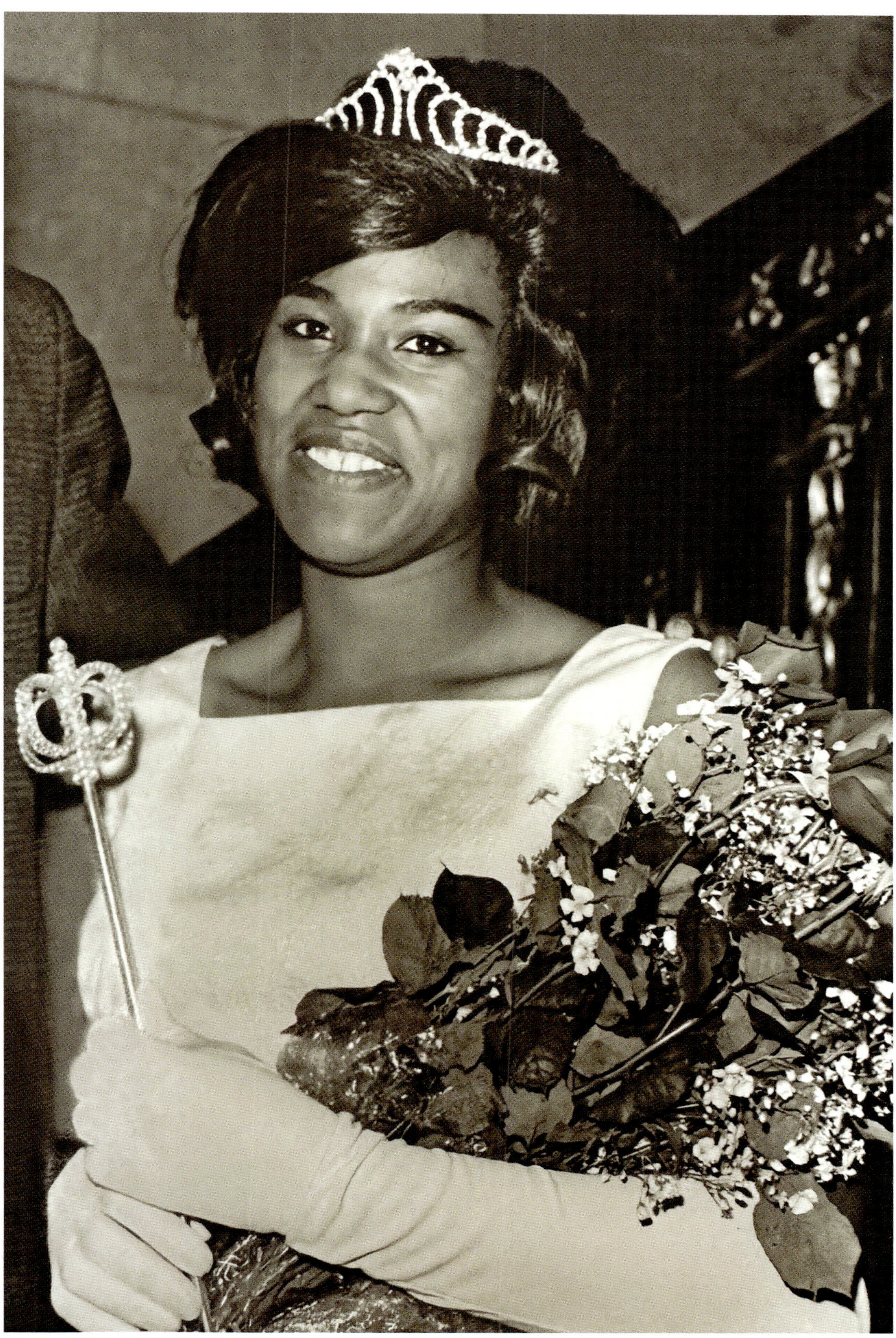

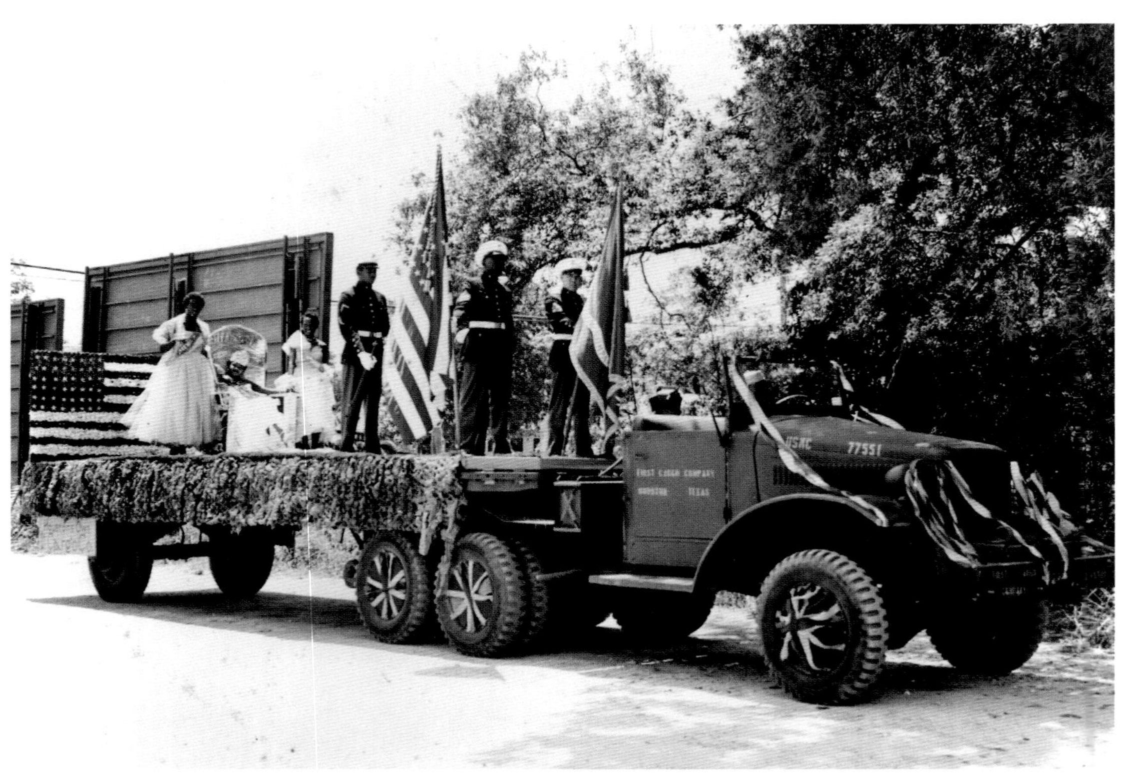

ABOVE: Members of the NAACP Youth Council ride in a late-1950s–era Juneteenth parade. Girls dressed in white with an honor guard of four young men standing at attention with the American flag. The NAACP of the 1950s fought hard to expand the rights of Black Americans, so the presence of these members speaks not only of the celebration of the past, but the fight for freedom in their own generation.

OPPOSITE: Six Black Houstonians lead a 1970s Juneteenth parade, marching behind a banner that reads, "Juneteenth festival, unity of purpose." Two carry the Texas flag and the American flag, symbols of the history of their fight for their rightful place in the state and the nation. More than one hundred years later, the meaning of Juneteenth was still celebrated in the heart of the Houston community.

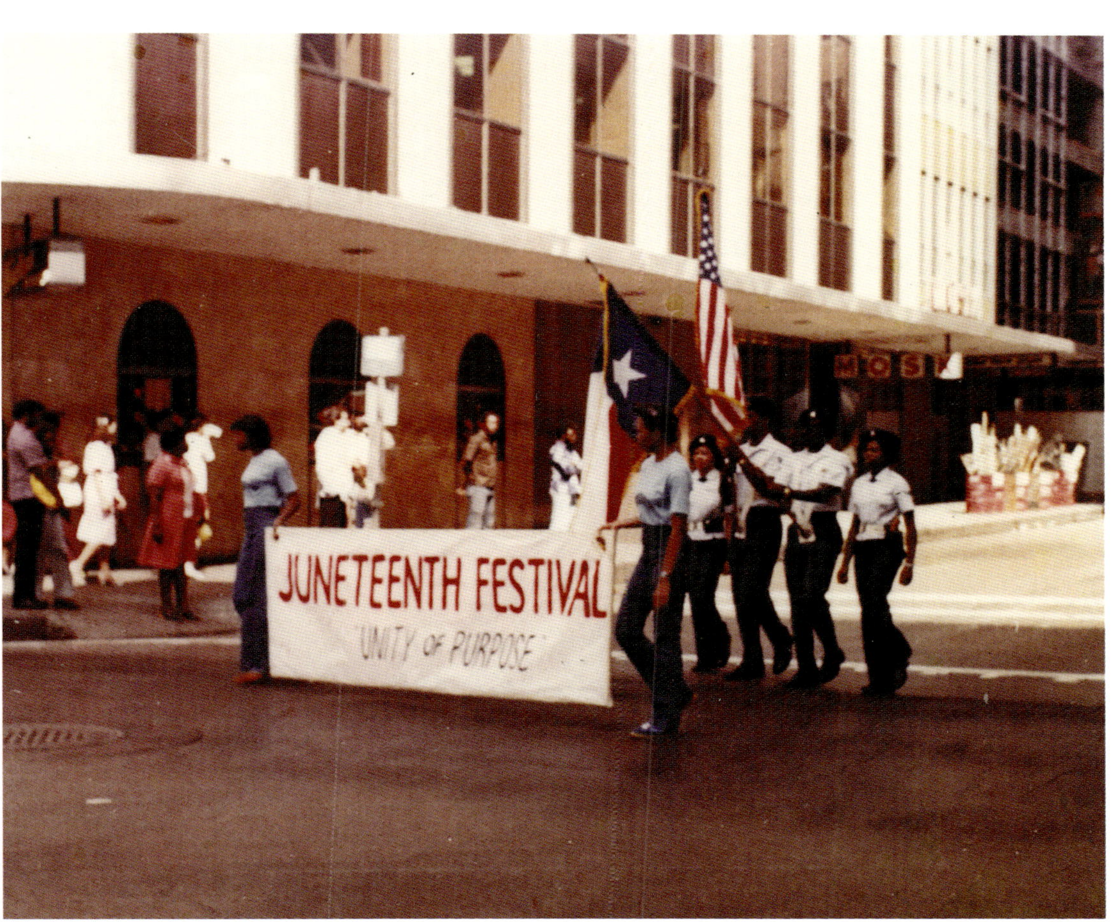
JUNETEENTH FESTIVAL
"UNITY OF PURPOSE"

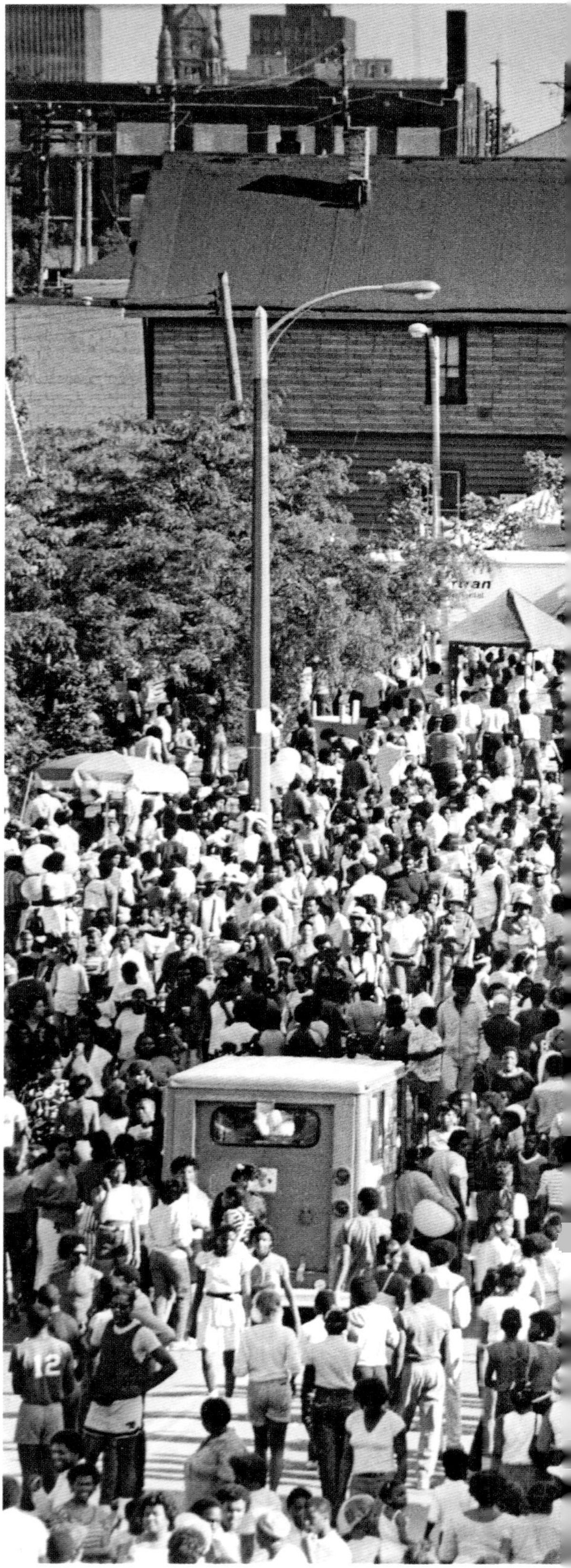

RIGHT: A joyful crowd fills Third Street in Milwaukee, Wisconsin, for Juneteenth in 1984, a testament to how far the annual freedom celebration had traveled from its Texas roots. Carried to cities in the north and Midwest, Juneteenth took root across the United States, becoming a beloved tradition of remembrance and community long before it was recognized as a national holiday.

FOLLOWING: Double image: Milton Larkin on trombone and Clayton Dyess on guitar as part of the Milt Larkin Allstars at the Juneteenth Blues Festival at Miller Outdoor Theater, Houston, Texas, June 19, 1984. Texas native Milton Larkin was a longtime jazzman and Texas native who played Houston's Juneteenth Jazz and Blues Festivals. Music of all kinds are a vibrant part of Juneteenth celebrations.

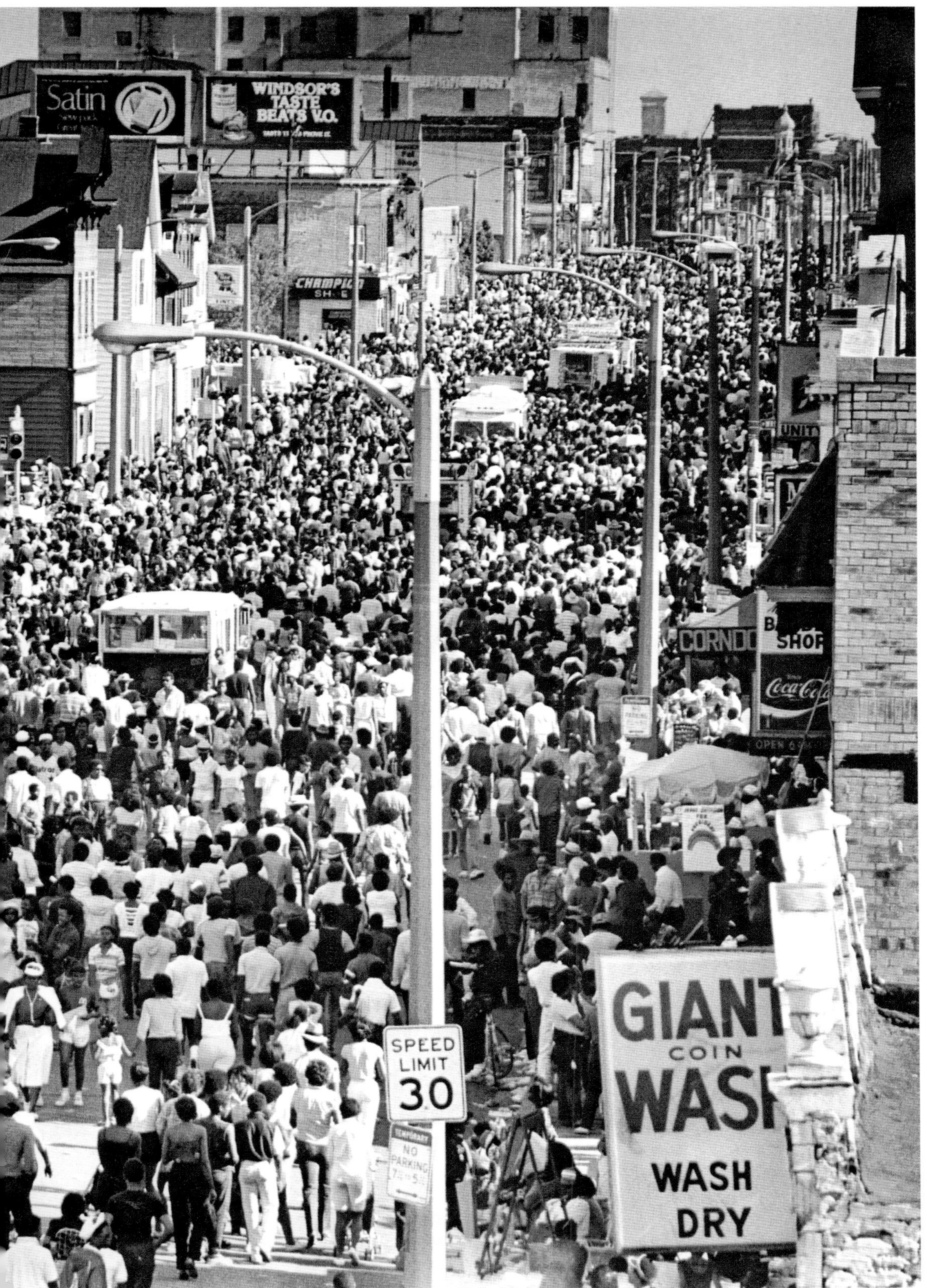
Satin
WINDSOR'S
TASTE
BEATS V.O.
CHAMPION
SHOE
UNITY
CORNDO
SHOP
Coca-Cola
SPEED
LIMIT
30
NO
PARKING
COIN
WASH
DRY

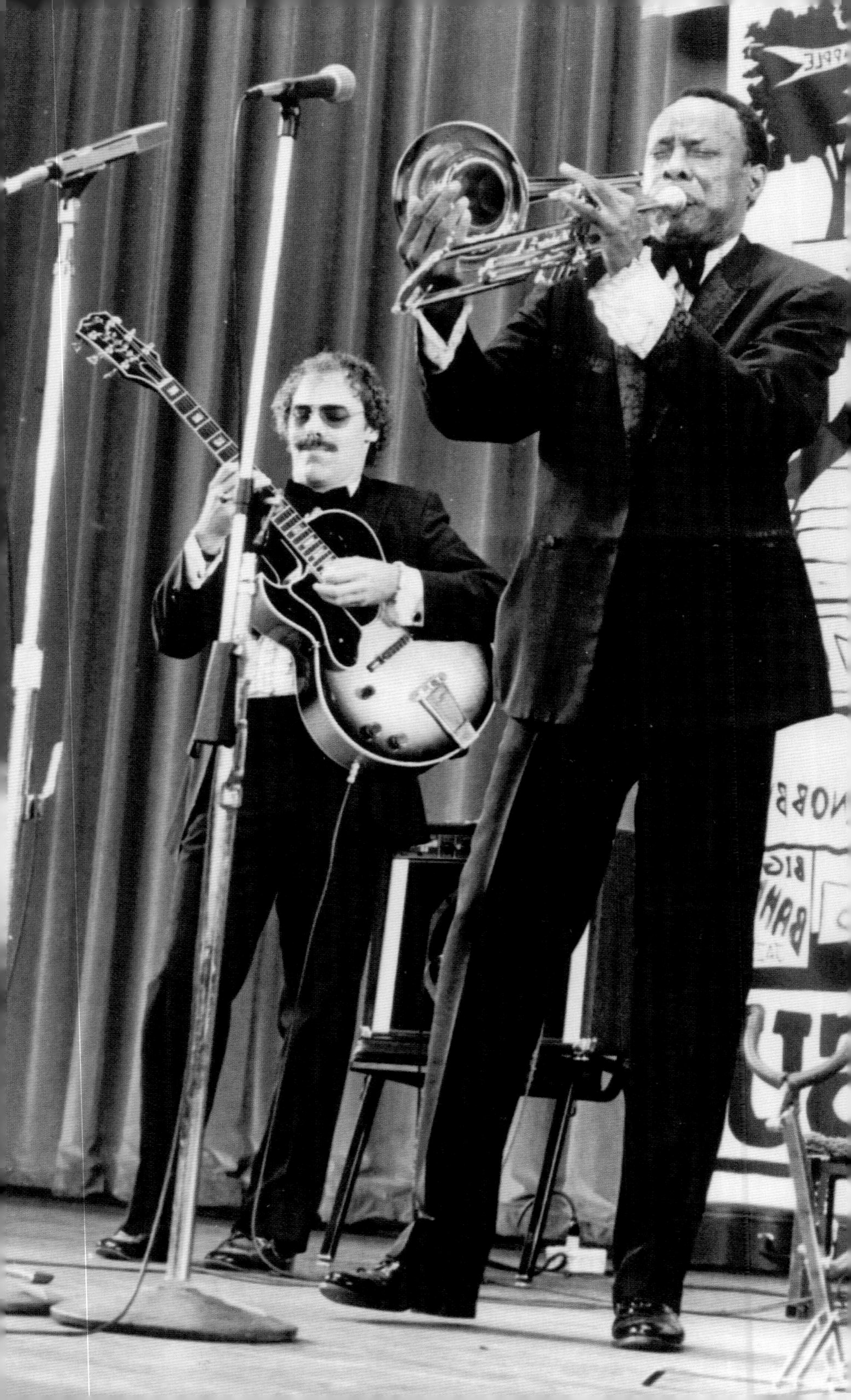

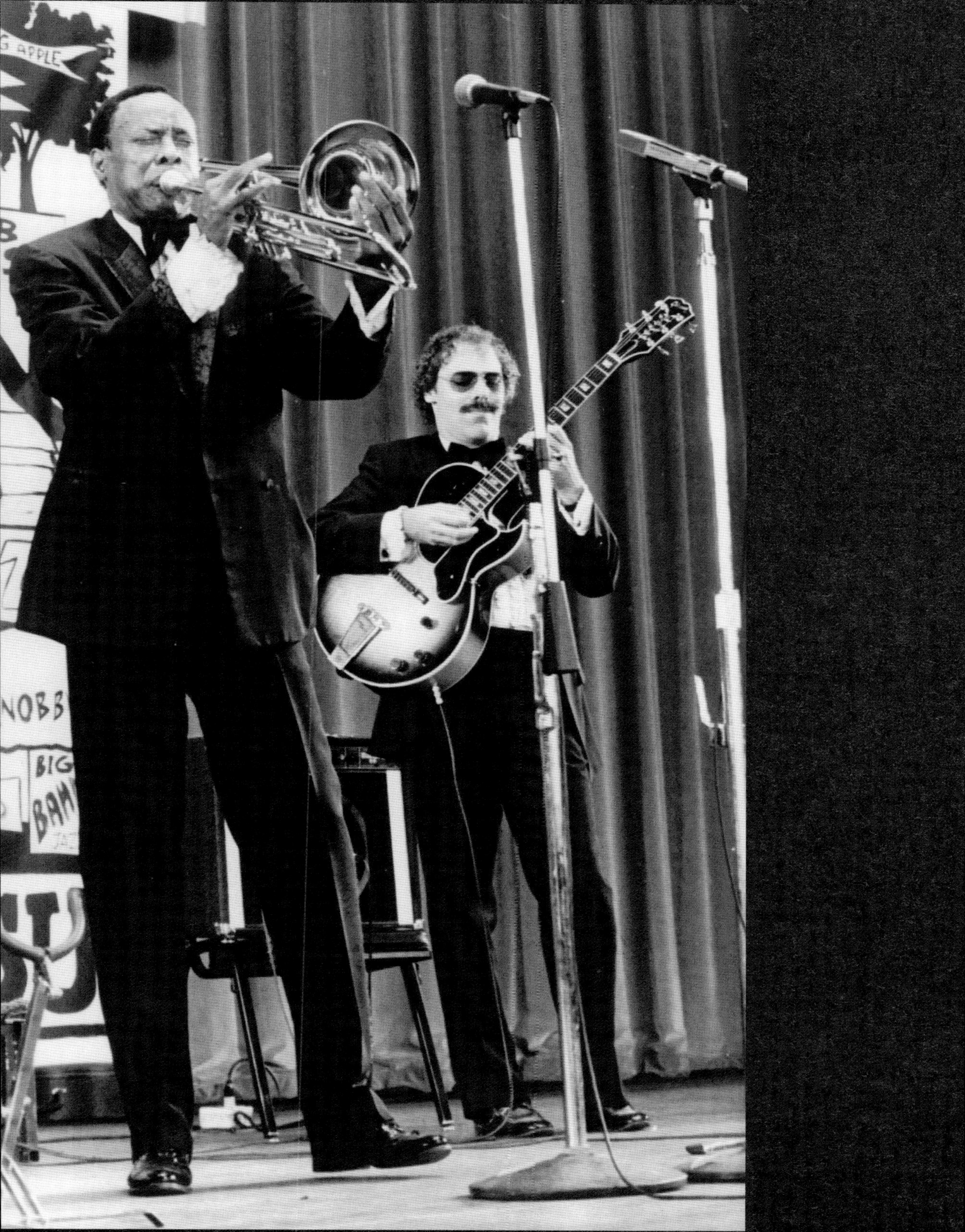
APPLE
BIG

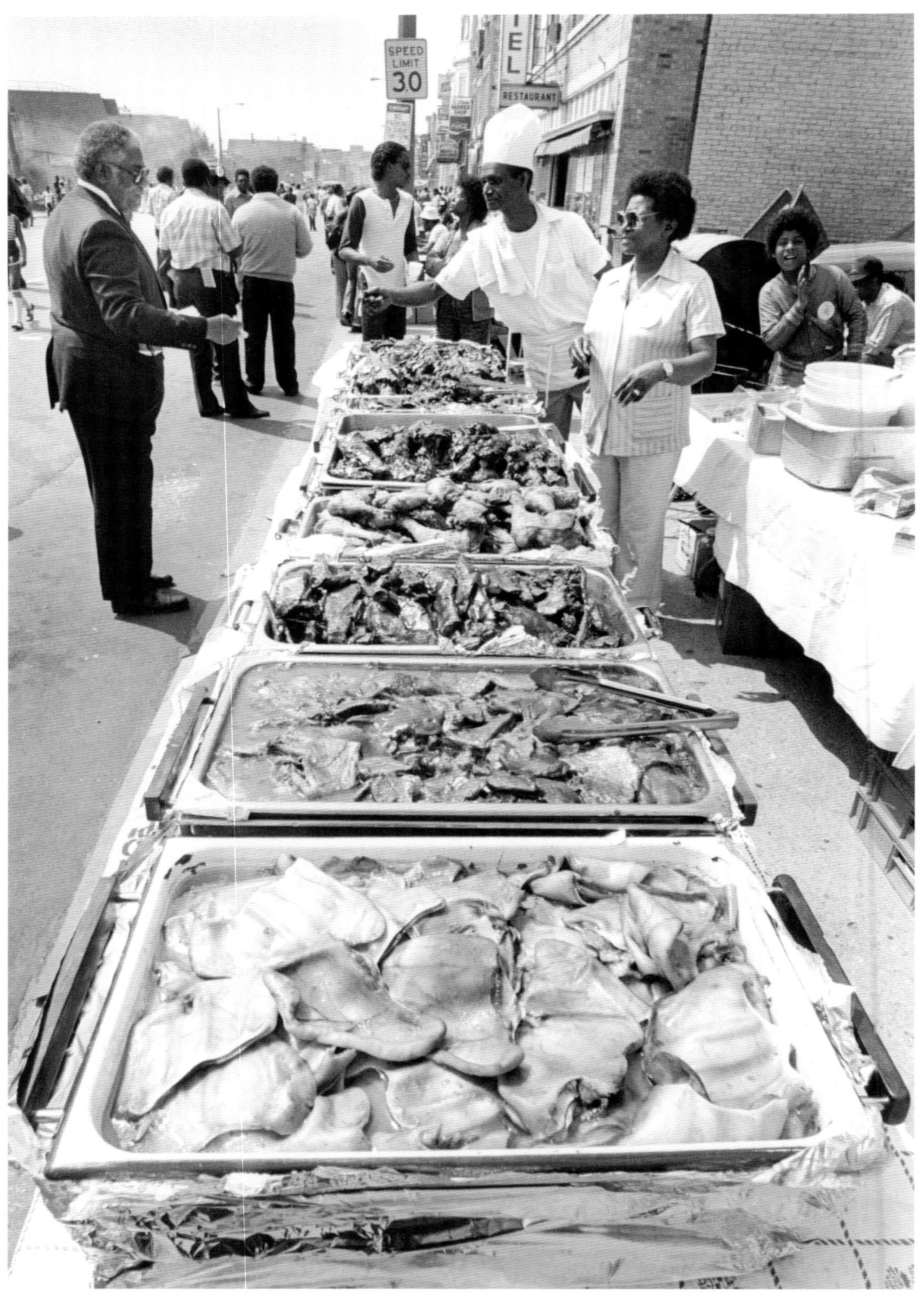
SPEED
LIMIT
30
IEL
RESTAURANT

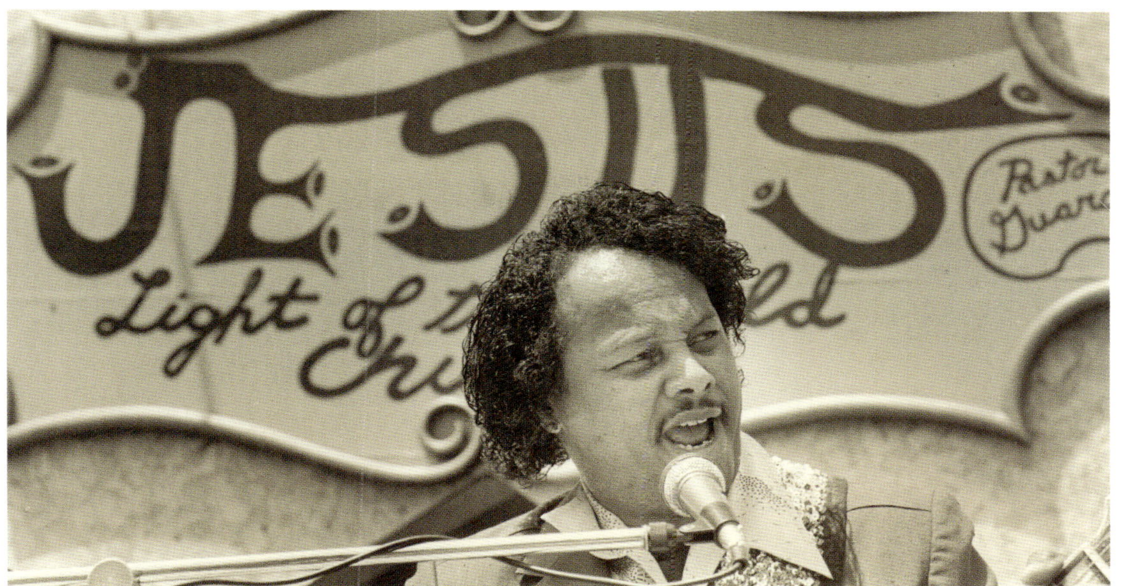

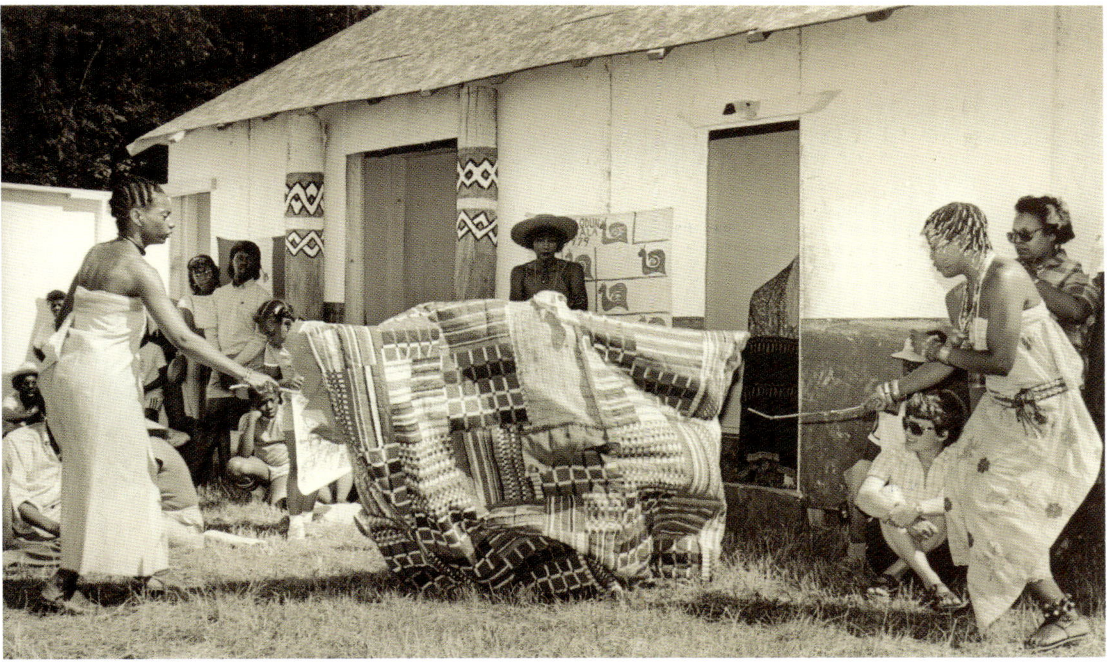

OPPOSITE: Food has always been at the heart of Juneteenth, providing nourishment, memory, and fellowship. Here a couple serves dishes inspired by African cuisine at the 1984 Milwaukee, Wisconsin, Juneteenth celebration.

TOP: Celebration, faith, and songs are always a part of Juneteenth gatherings. Here a gospel singer performs at the 1983 Juneteenth Day celebration in Milwaukee, Wisconsin.

ABOVE: At Milwaukee's 1984 festival, young performers take part in the Egungun ritual "Messenger of the Ancestors" as part of an African Village installation. This revival of West African dance reflected a growing connection between Black American traditions and a diasporic lineage.

This 1988 flyer for San Francisco, California's Juneteenth celebration reflects the legacy first launched by Texas-born Wesley Johnson in 1945. After migrating to San Francisco from Galveston, Texas, Johnson led elaborate, multiday Juneteenth celebrations in his adopted city, riding a white horse through the streets while wearing a white Stetson hat. San Francisco's long-running celebrations blend the traditions of Black Texas with those of the West Coast.

A REPO
PRESENTS
A CULTURAL JUNETEENTH

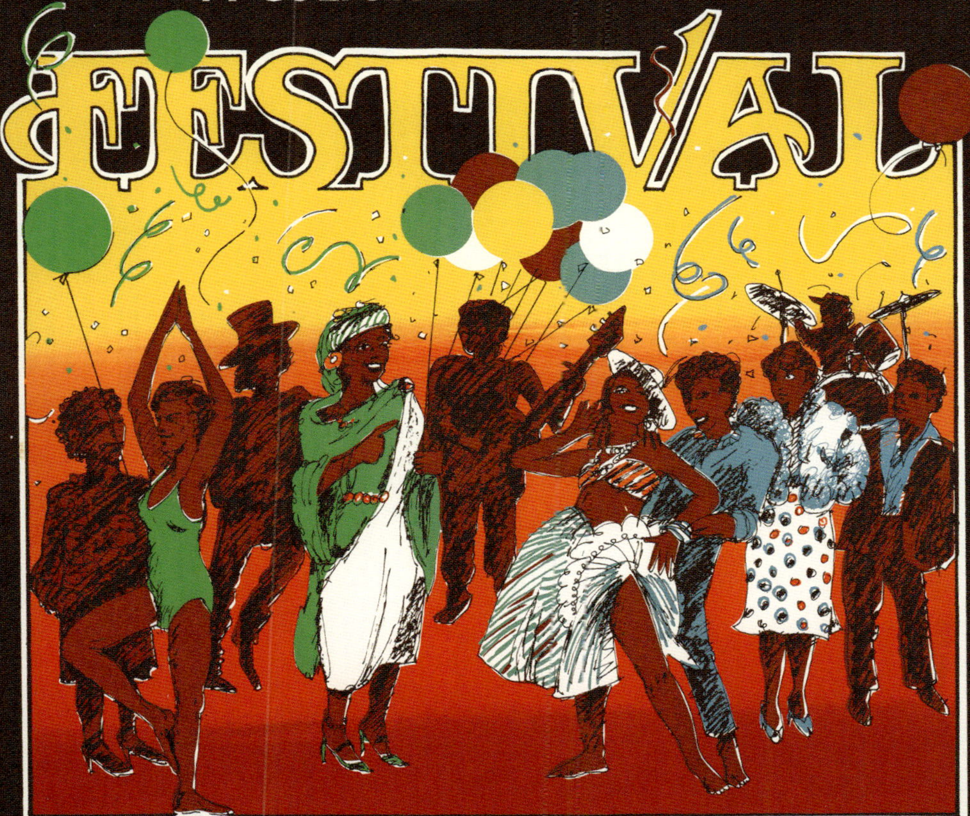

SAT JUNE 16 — 11 AM-10 PM
Bayview Opera House
4705-3rd Street
San Francisco
Parade starts 10:00 AM McKinnon & Lans
For more info: 824-0386

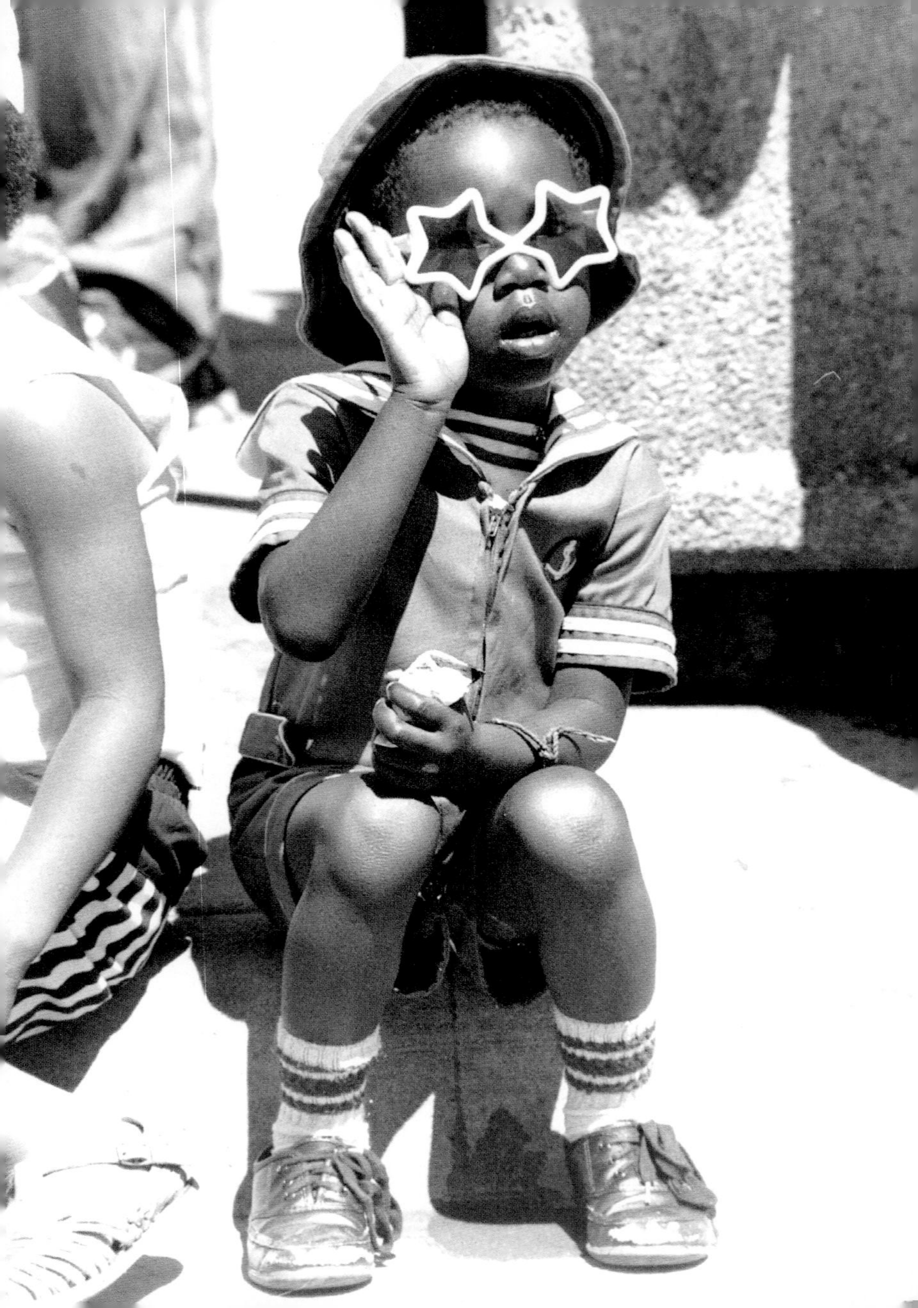

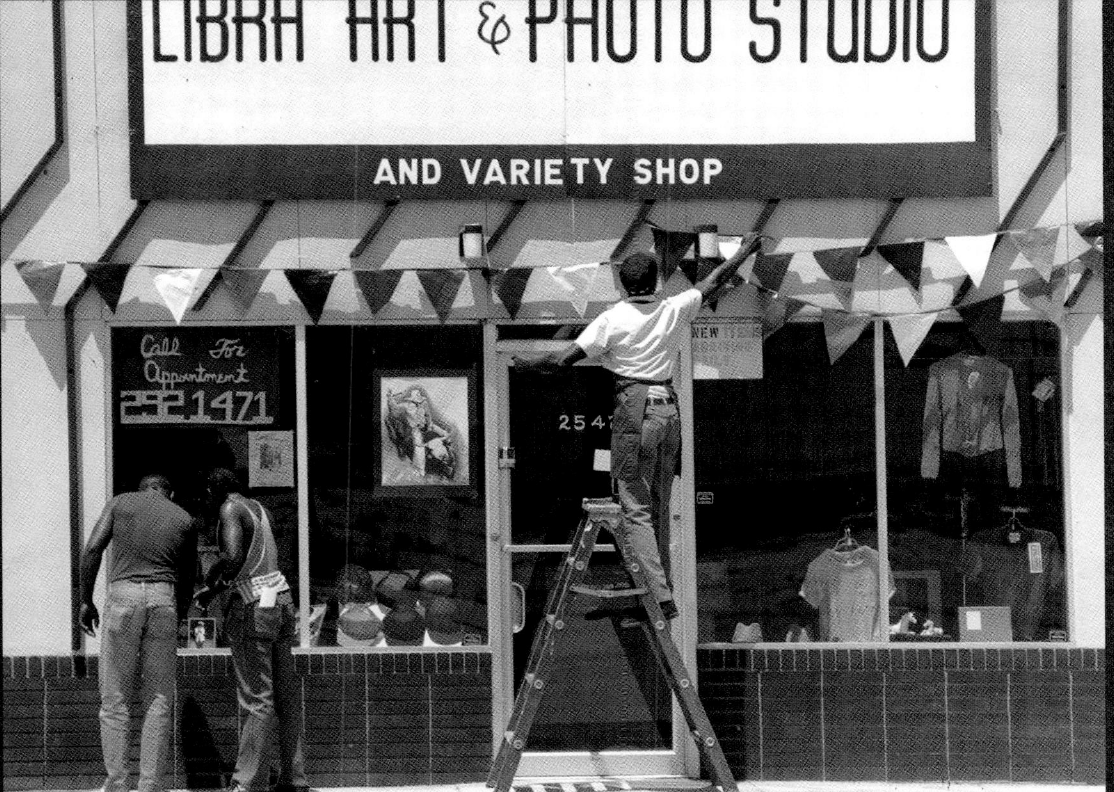

OPPOSITE: Three-year-old Javhon Walker waves in awe at Denver, Colorado's Juneteenth Parade in 1989. He stands in a long linage of Black children whose earliest memories of Juneteenth are filled with joy, community, and the traditions of celebration. Denver's celebrations, led by Black Texan and Denver businessowner Otha Rice, began in the mid-1950s. By the 1980s, Denver's Five Points neighborhood had become the heart of the city's annual Juneteenth celebrations, connecting new generations to the legacy of emancipation far beyond Texas.

ABOVE: Photographer and studio owner Willie Robinson decorating his storefront in Denver in preparation for Juneteenth in 1989. Like many Black business owners, Robinson helped anchor celebrations in the community, linking Black commerce with culture in the ongoing celebration of Black freedom.

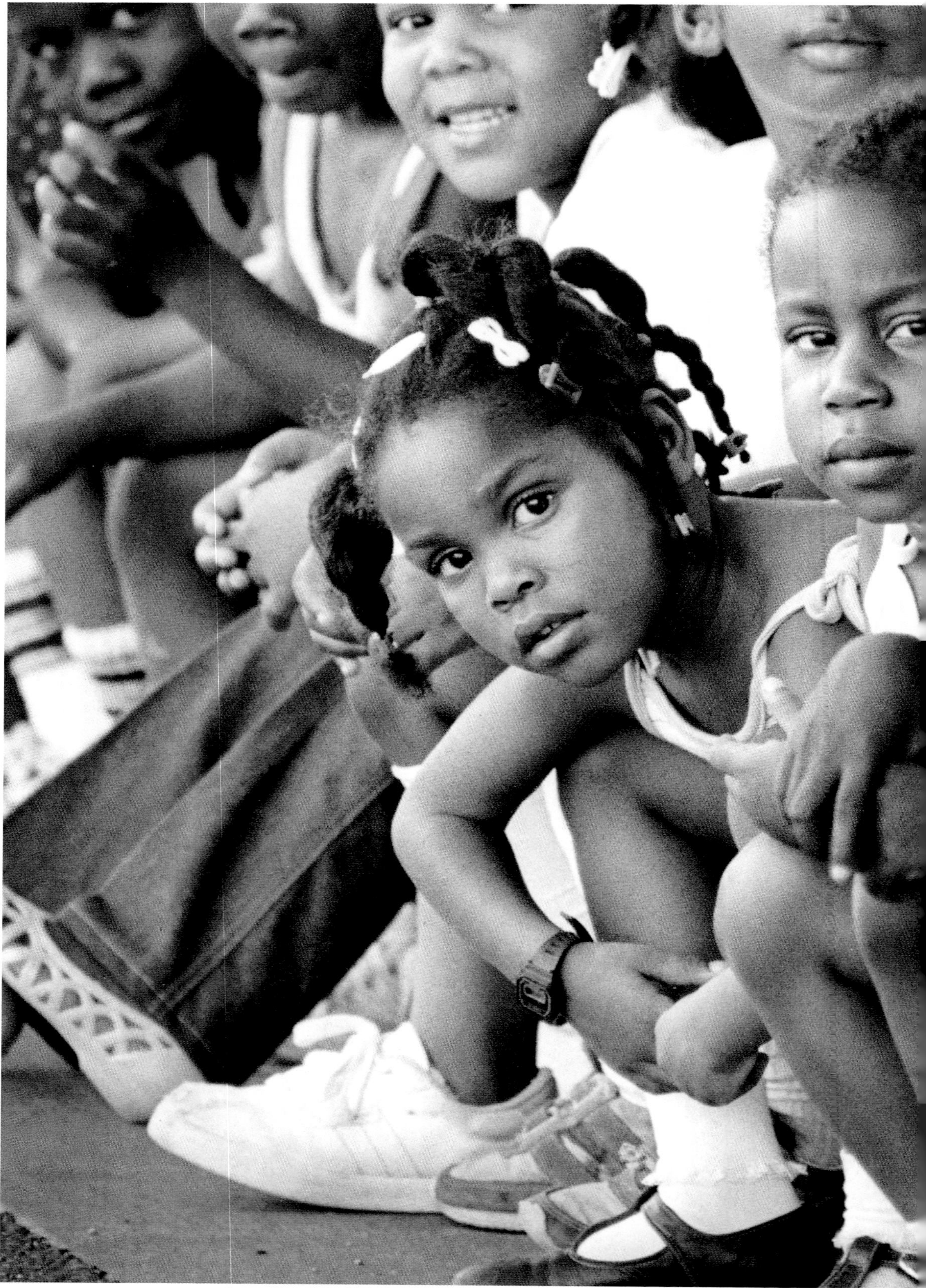

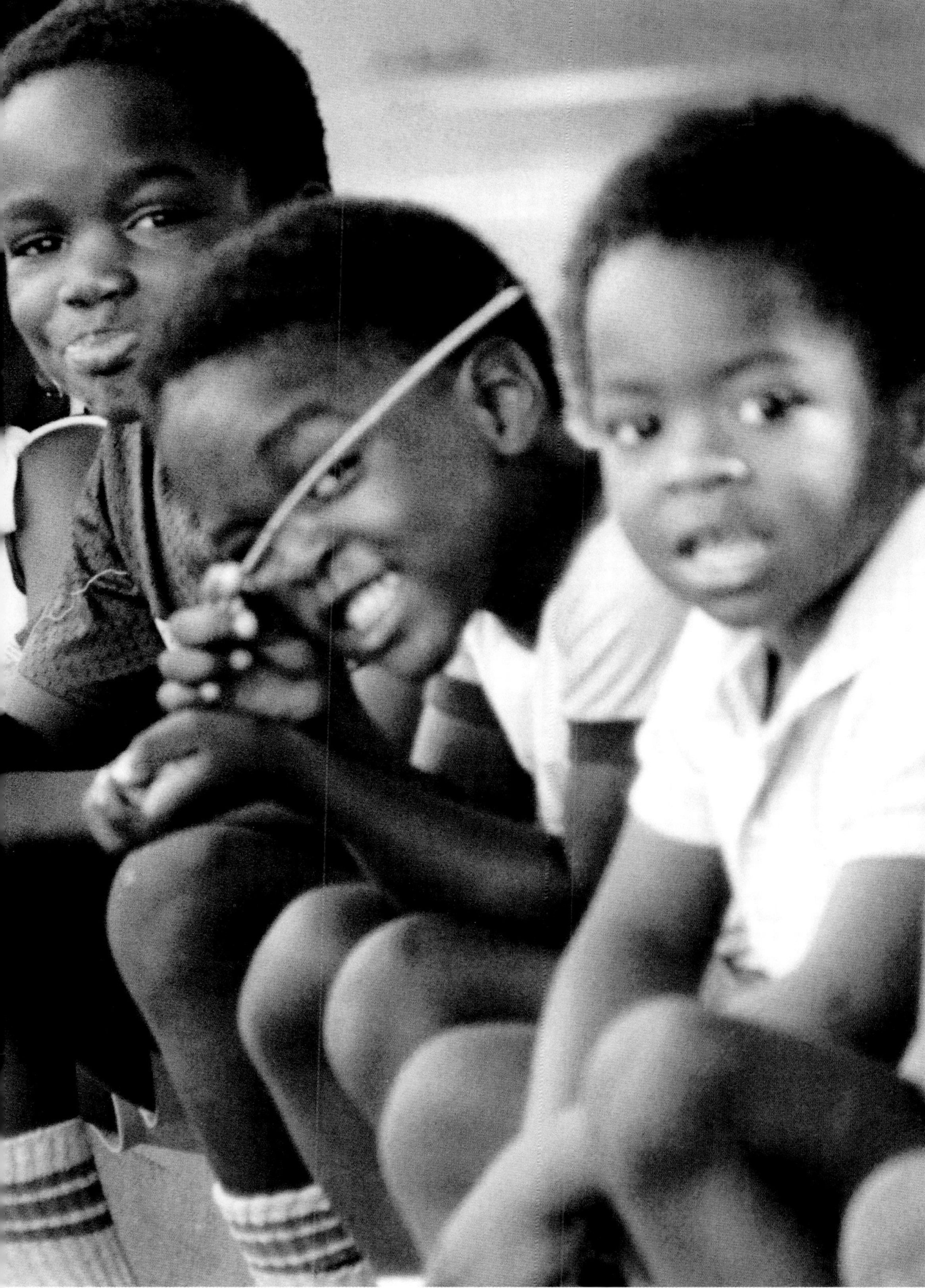

PREVIOUS: Young children watch the Juneteenth parade near downtown Austin, Texas, in 1989. In the city where some of the first Juneteenth celebrations took place, they are heirs to a rich tradition of celebration.

OPPOSITE: Grandfather and grandson ride together on horseback, carrying the American flag in Austin's 1993 Juneteenth parade. For generations, Black riders have taken to the streets on Juneteenth, honoring the legacy of Black cowboys, and staking their rightful place in a state and nation their ancestors helped build.

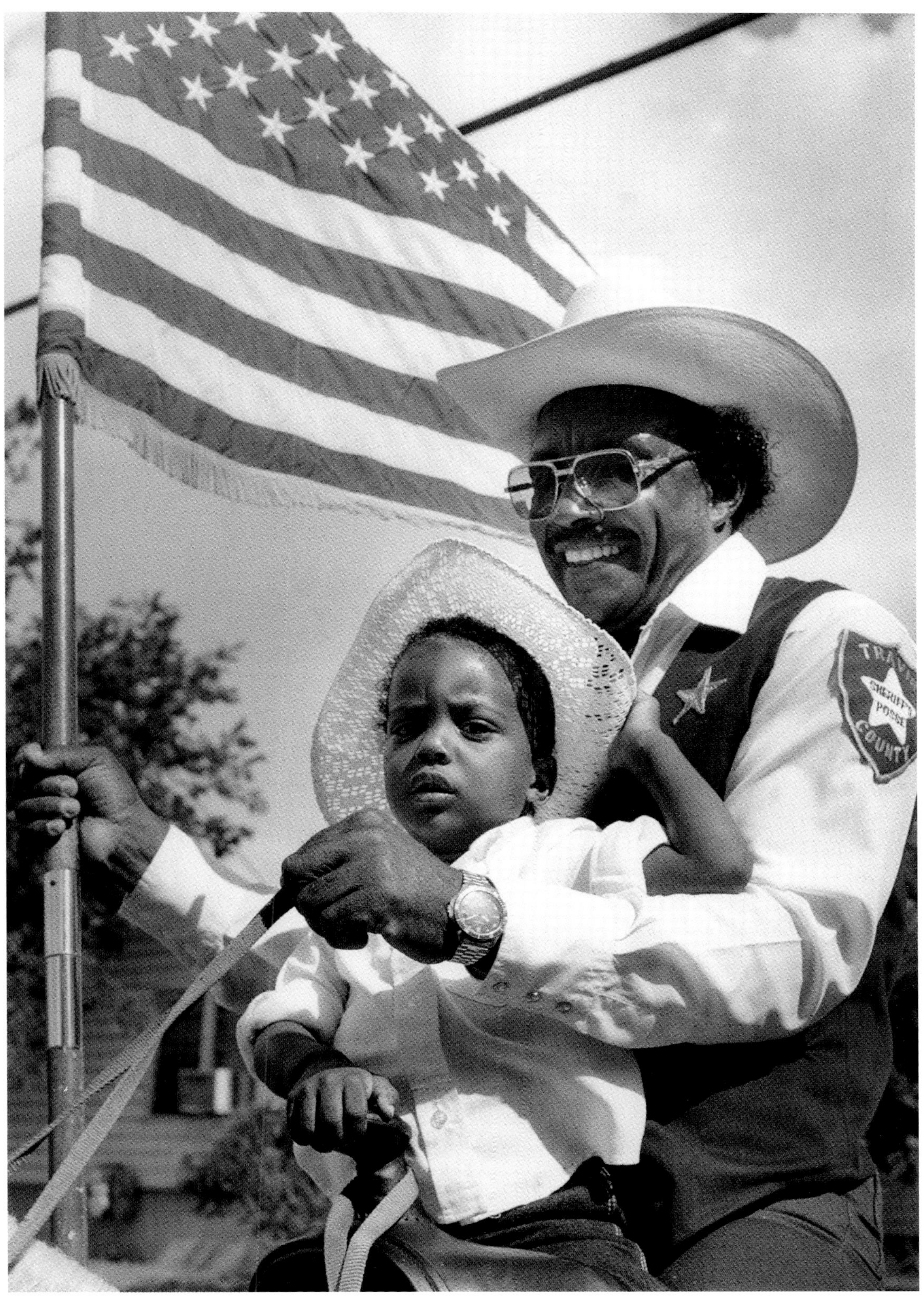
SHERIFF'S
POSSE
COUNTY

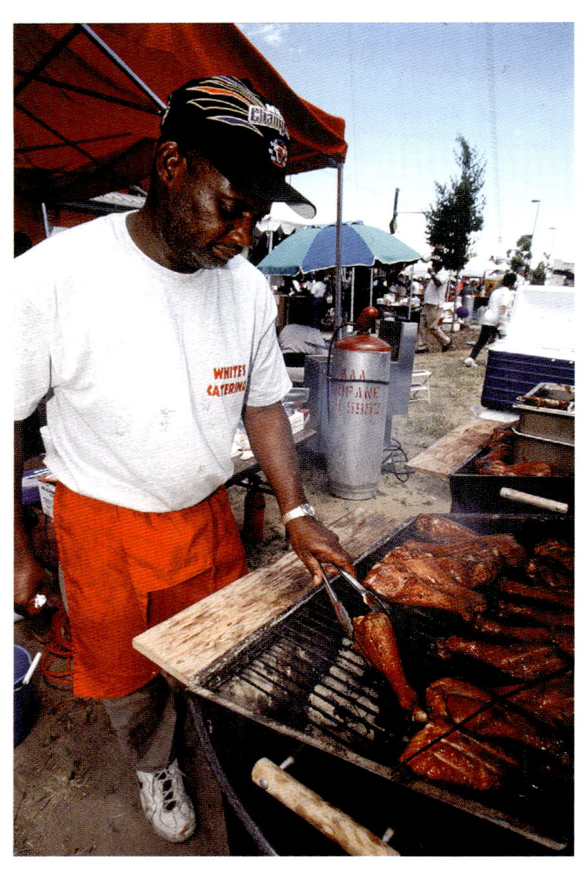
WHITE'S
CATERING

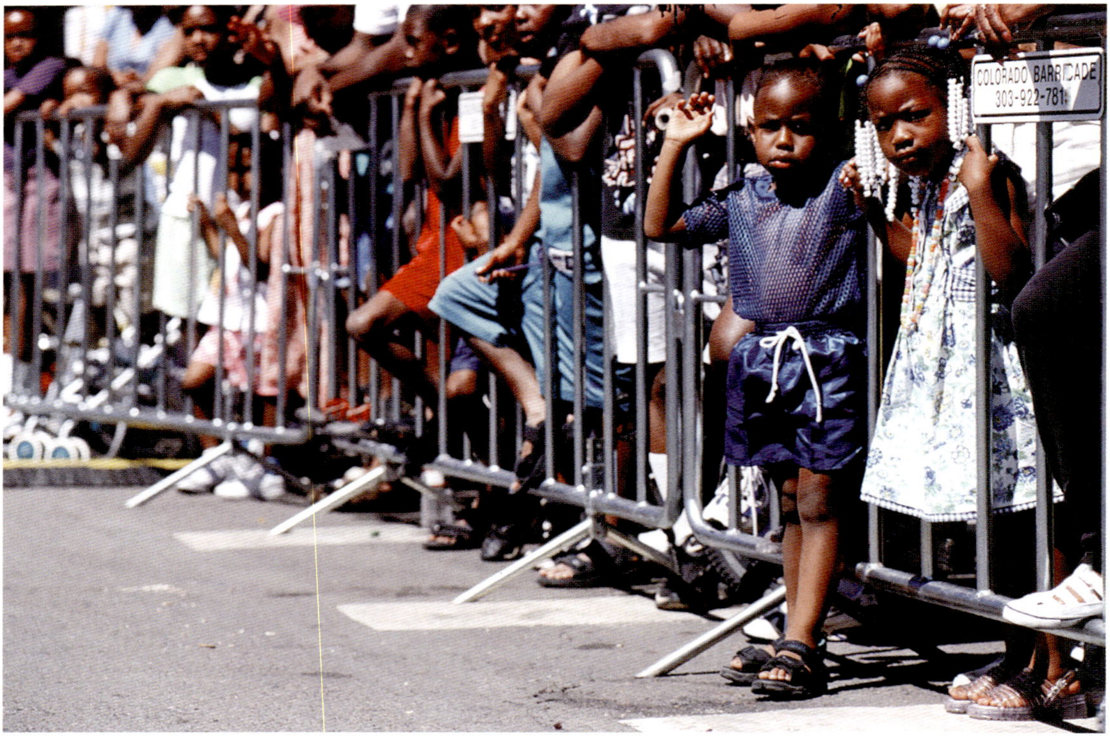

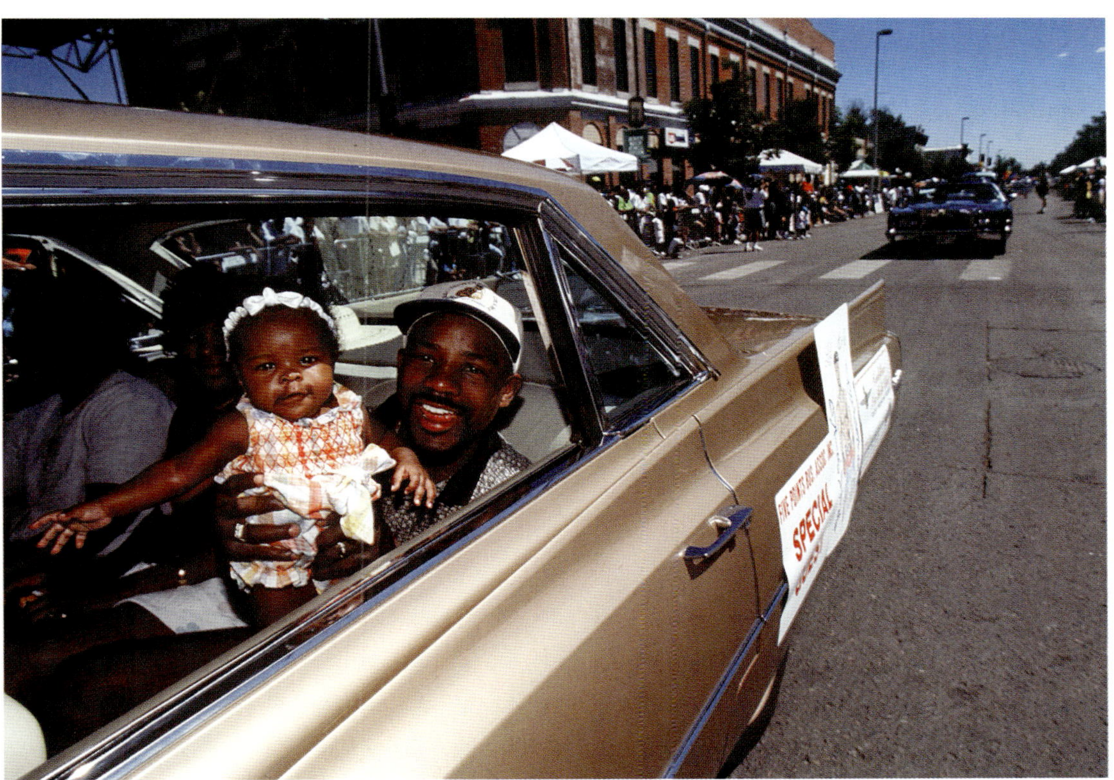

OPPOSITE TOP: Robert White of White's Catering smokes turkey legs at Denver, Colorado's Juneteenth celebration in Five Points in 1998, keeping food traditions at the heart of the holiday.

OPPOSITE BOTTOM: Reggie, 4, and Amber Penney, 5, take in the Juneteenth parade in Denver in 1998, a reminder of the joy and wonder that make these celebrations a cherished part of childhood.

ABOVE: Four-month-old Vivica smiles as her father, local boxing star Stevie Johnston, lifts her to see the crowd during Denver's 1998 Juneteenth parade.

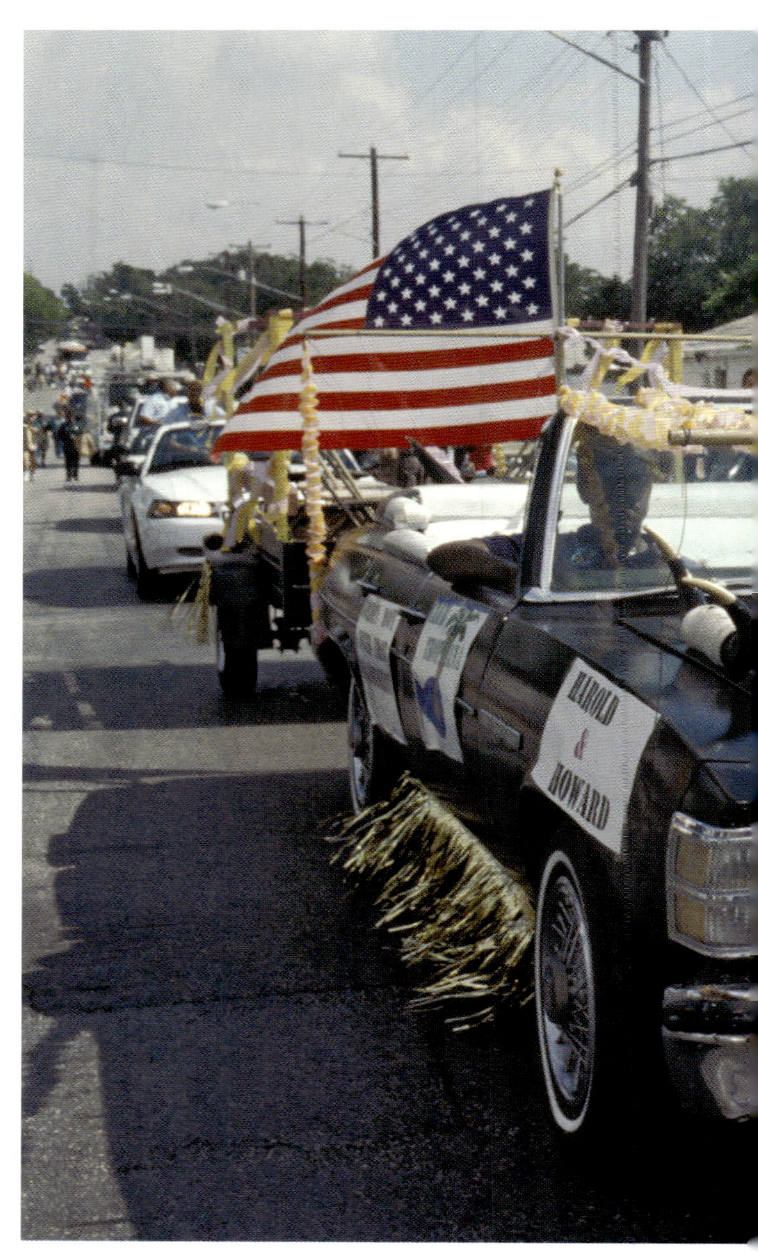
HAROLD
&
HOWARD

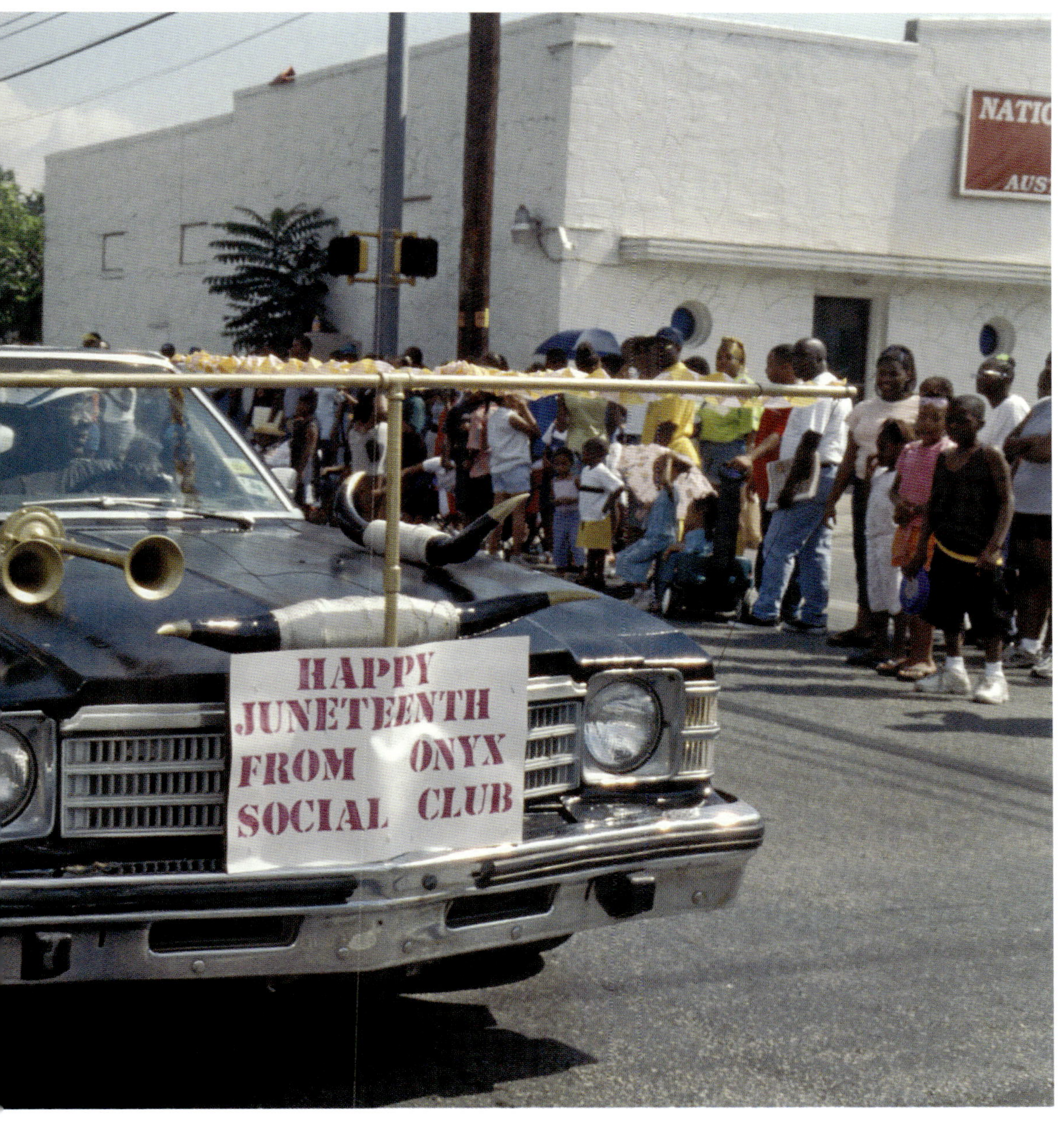

In Austin, Texas's 1988 Juneteenth parade, the Onyx Social Club car was adorned with horns, streamers, and an American flag, just as wagons were decorated for early Juneteenth parades.

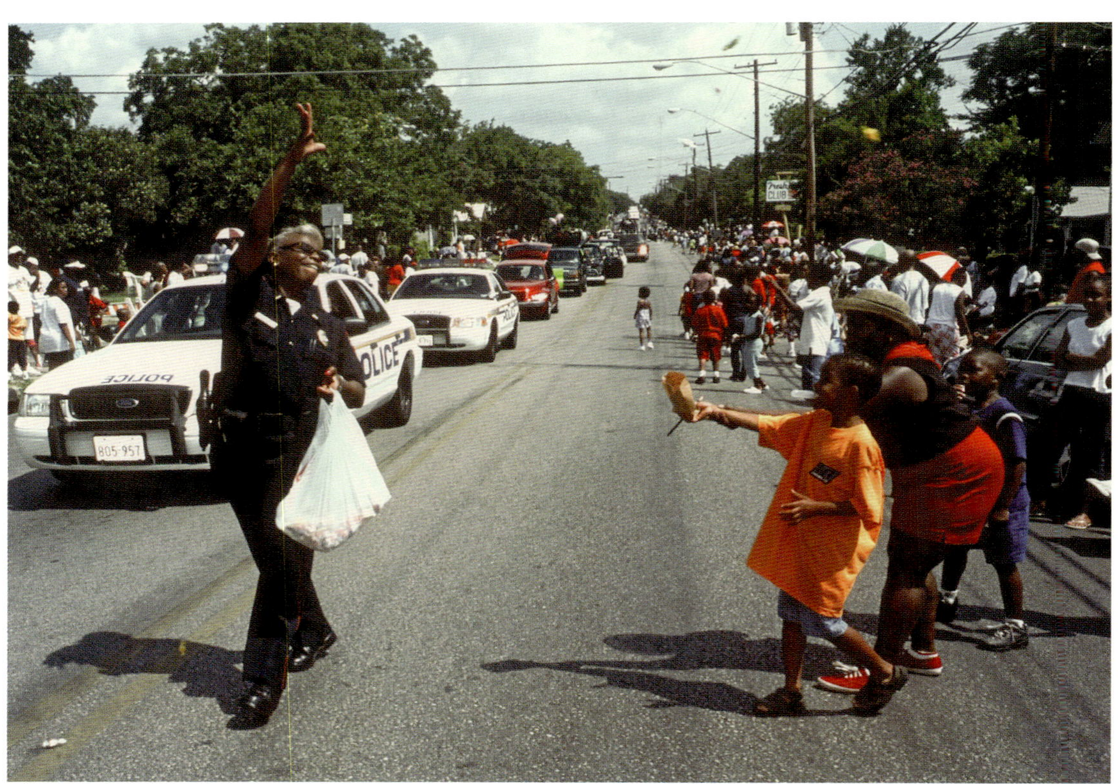

ABOVE: In a moment of anticipation and delight, children catch candy thrown by an Austin, Texas, police officer participating in Austin's 2002 Juneteenth parade.

OPPOSITE: Members of Houston, Texas's Jack Yates High School marching band perform at Austin, Texas's 2002 Juneteenth celebration. Named for the formerly enslaved minister and businessman who helped organize early Juneteenth gatherings in Texas, the students carry forward his rich legacy of freedom.

FOLLOWING: Yereima Layne, of the Houston Association of Panamanians, waves to the crowd during the 2008 Houston, Texas, Juneteenth parade, reflecting the shared legacy of Black freedom among African American and Afro-Panamanian communities in Houston.

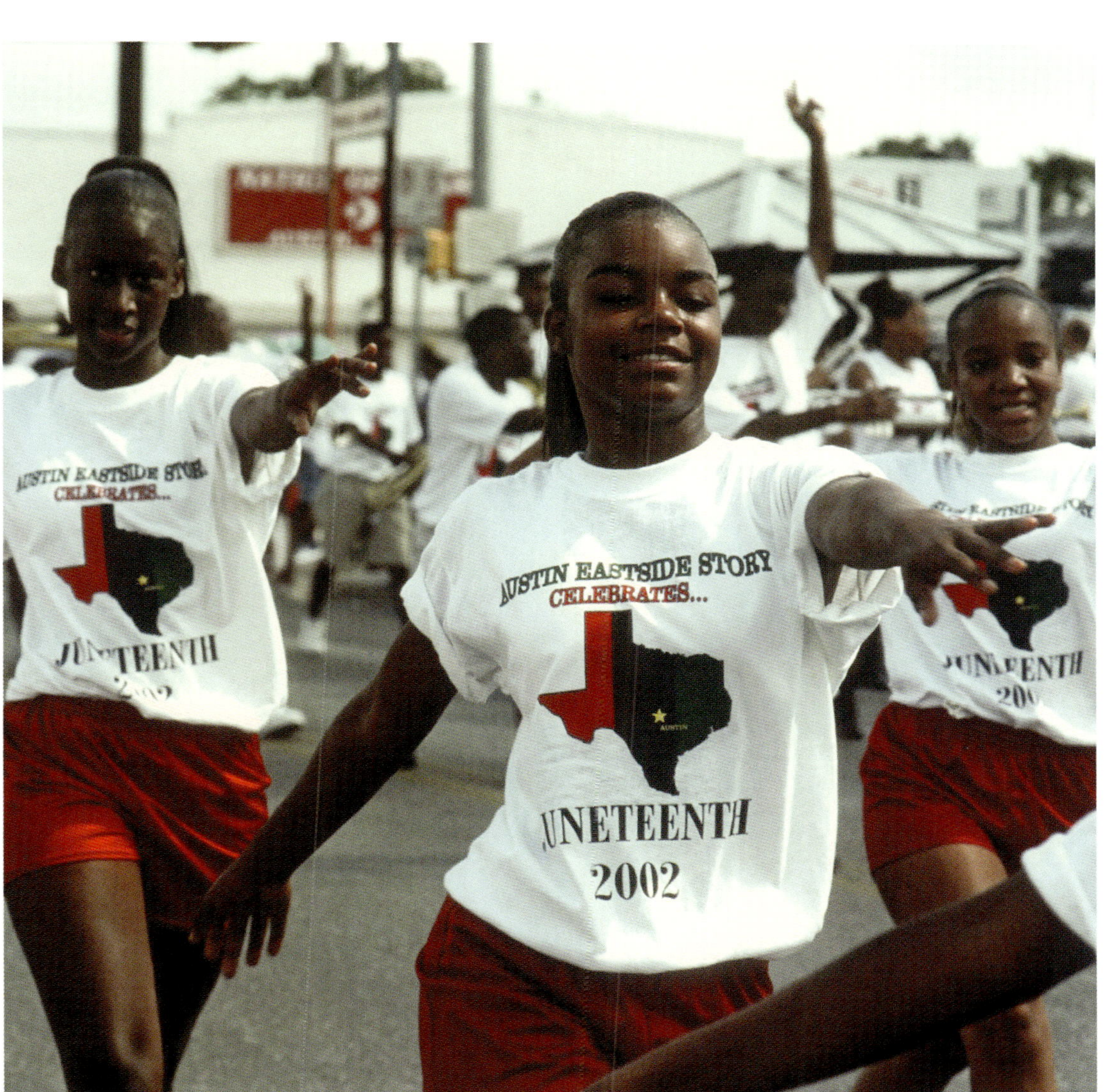
AUSTIN EASTSIDE STORY
CELEBRATES...
AUSTIN
JUNETEENTH
2002

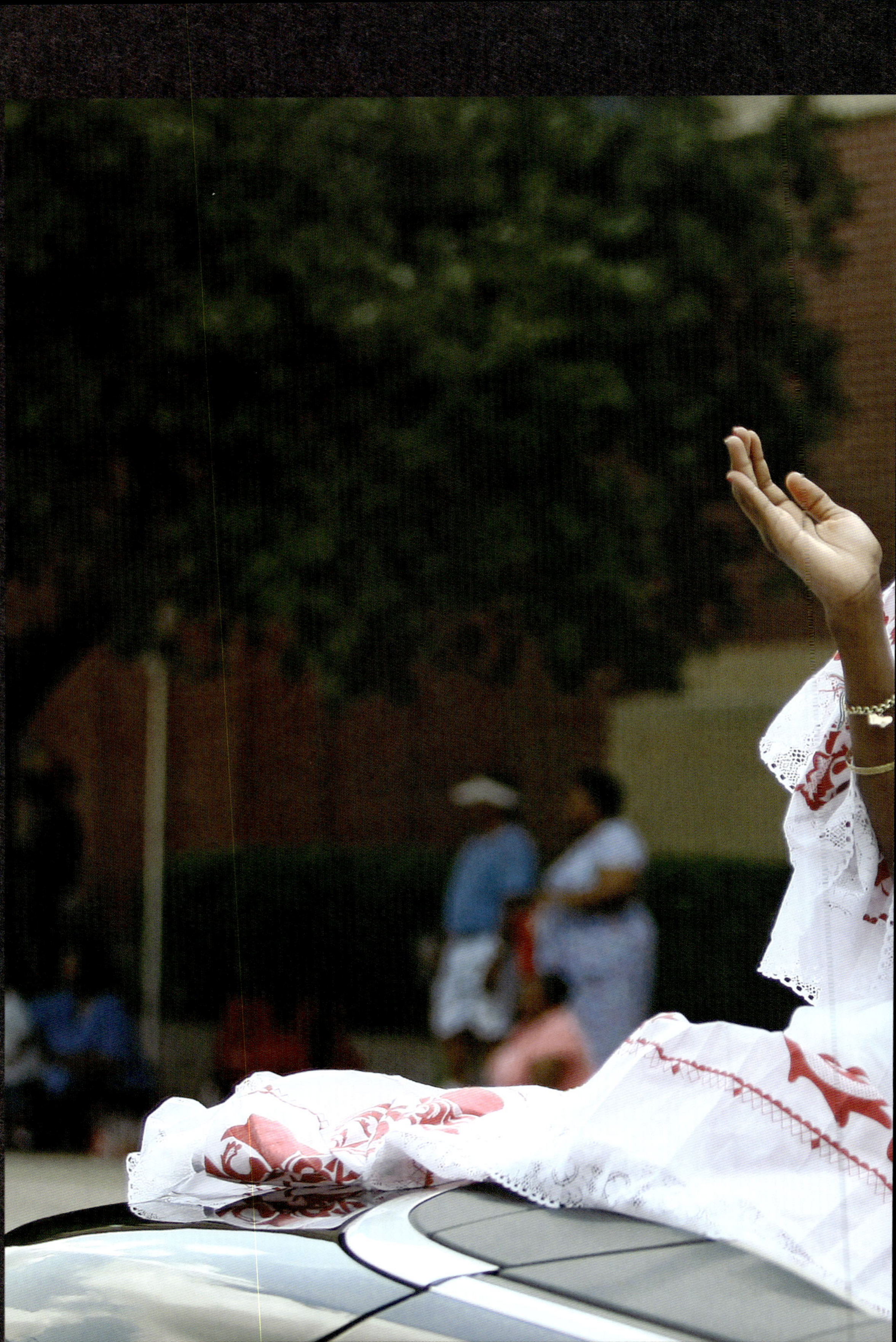

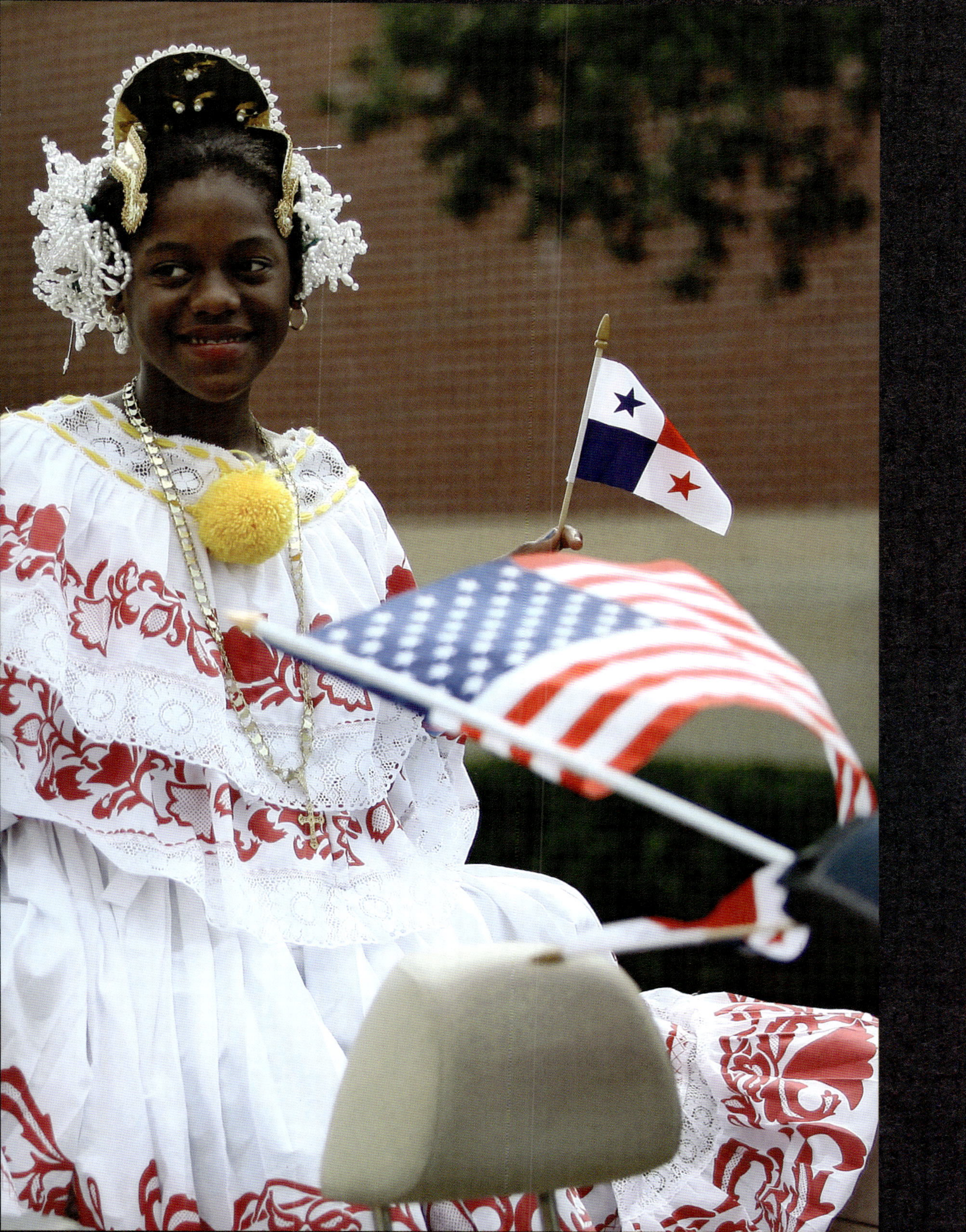

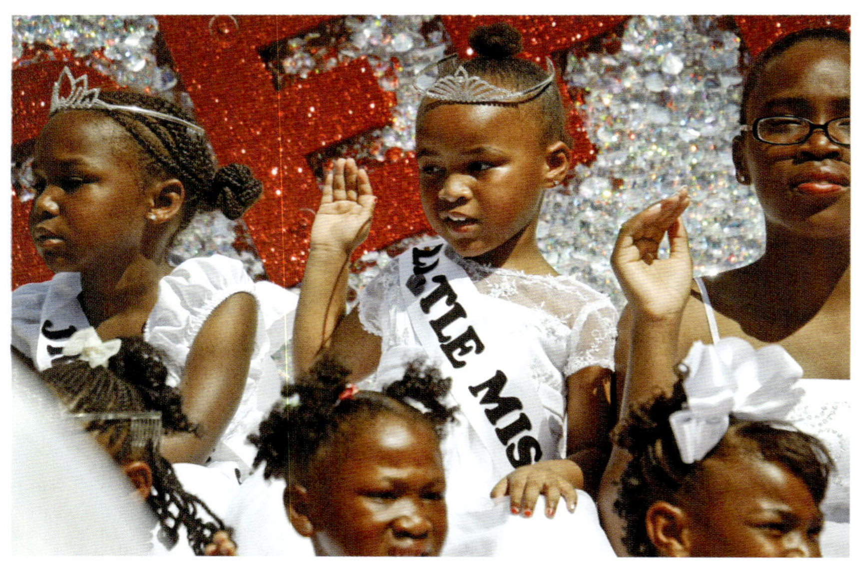
TLE MIS

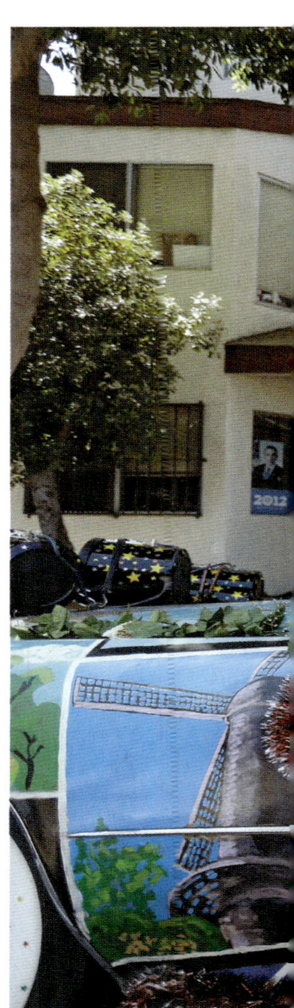
2012

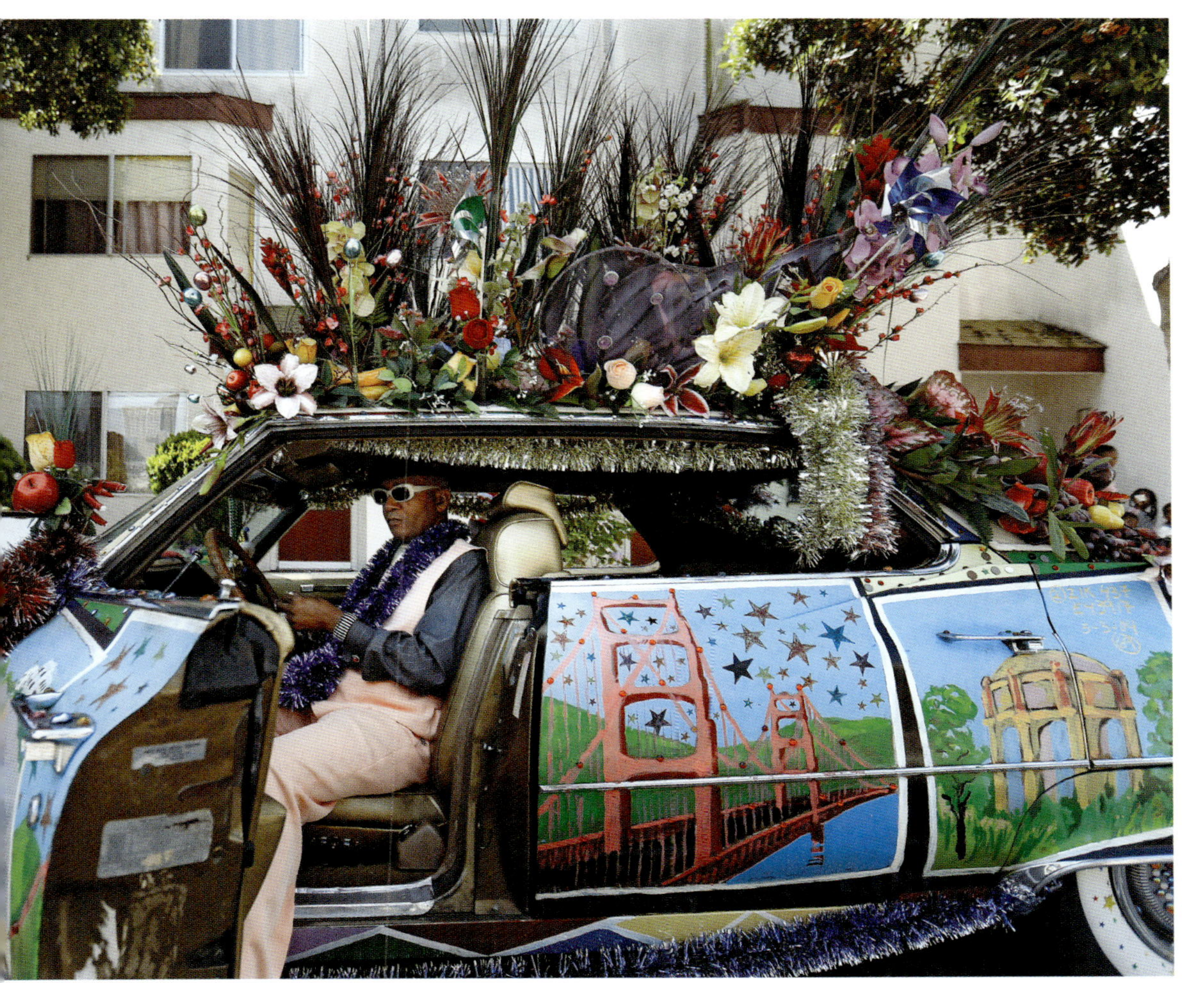

OPPOSITE: Leah Morale, 3, waves proudly along with her fellow Miss Juneteenth pageant winners during Houston, Texas's 38th Juneteenth Freedom Parade in 2011.

ABOVE: Wardell Walters drives "Star 1" through San Francisco, California's Fillmore District during the 2014 Juneteenth parade. Decorated in tribute to the city, his car echoes the tradition of the adorned wagons first used in Texas Juneteenth celebrations, harkening back to long traditions of pride, artistry, and adding local flair.

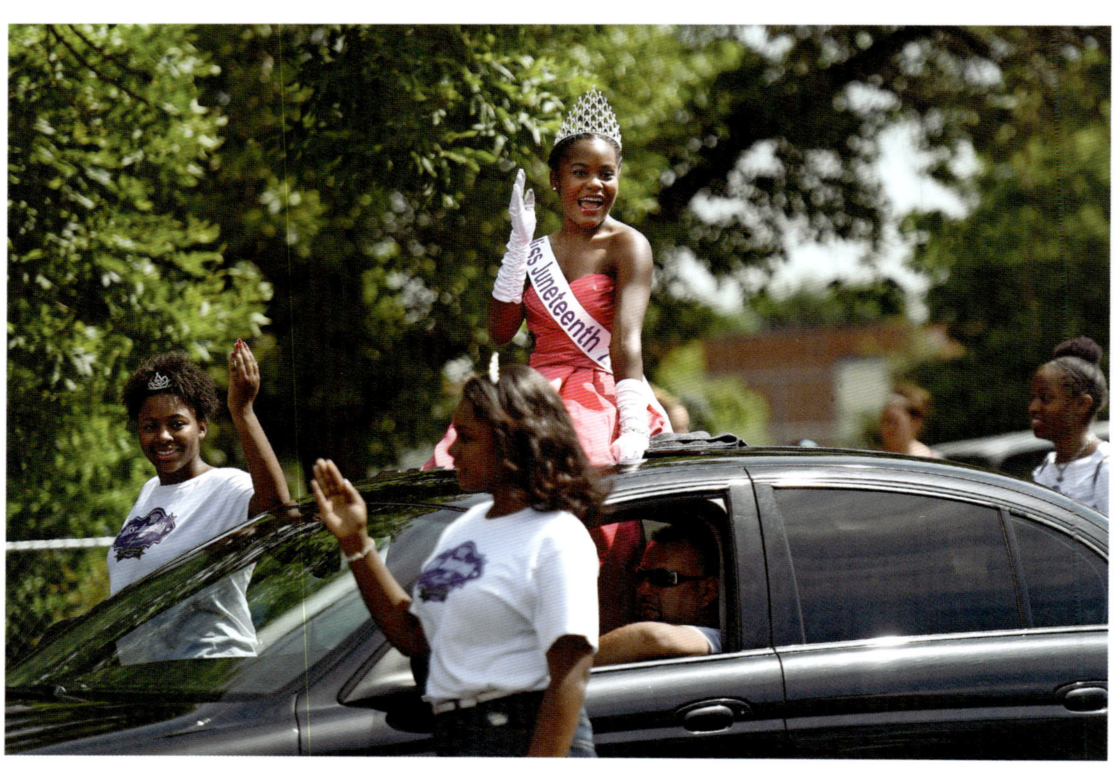

ABOVE: Denver, Colorado's Miss Juneteenth 2015 Sean-Maree Swinger-Otey waves to the crowds along the parade route.

OPPOSITE: Rihonna Davis channeling Black royalty at Flint, Michigan's 2018 Juneteenth celebration. She wanted to dress like royalty, but also in her favorite color for the Juneteenth parade and celebration at University Park.

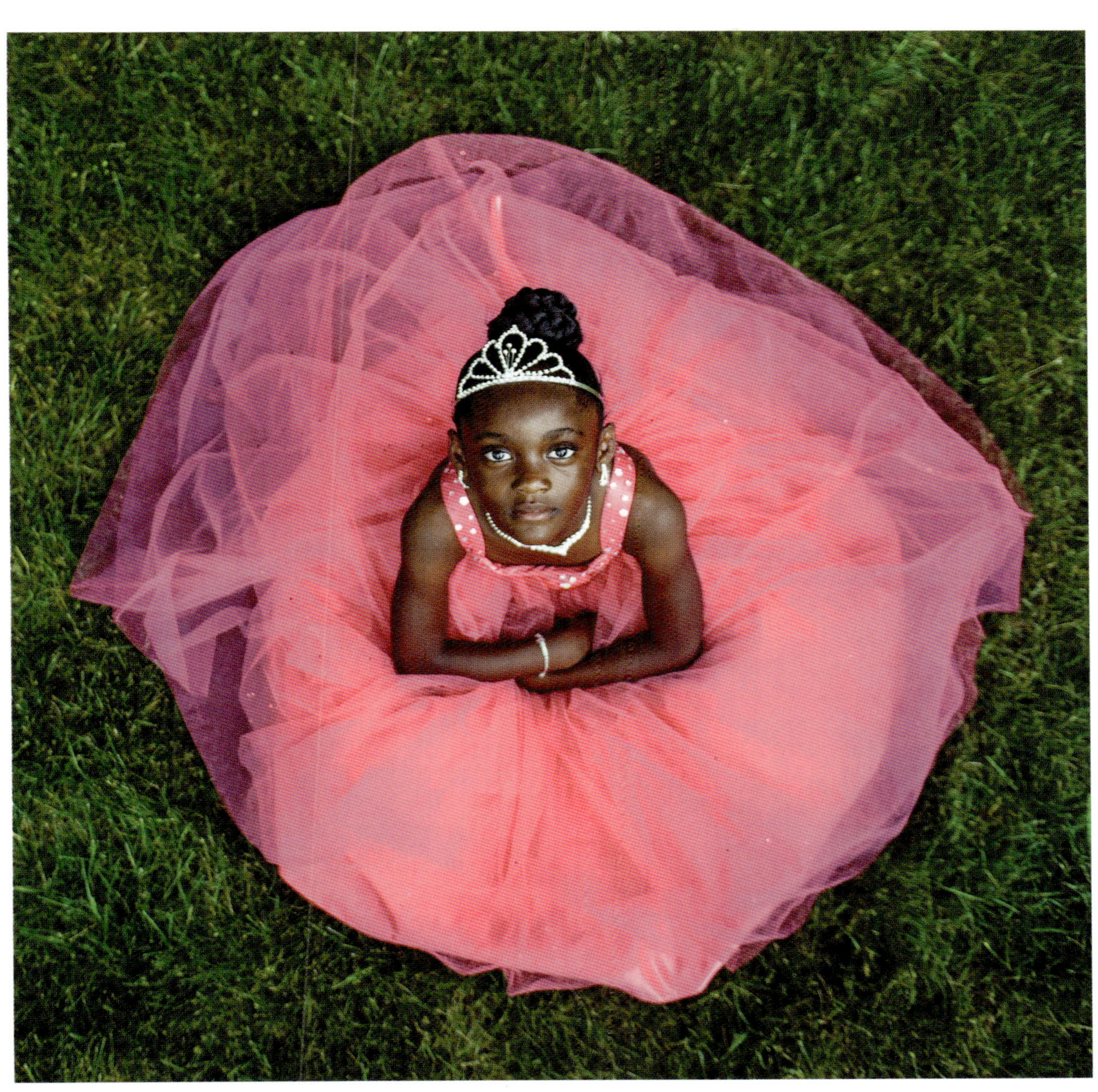

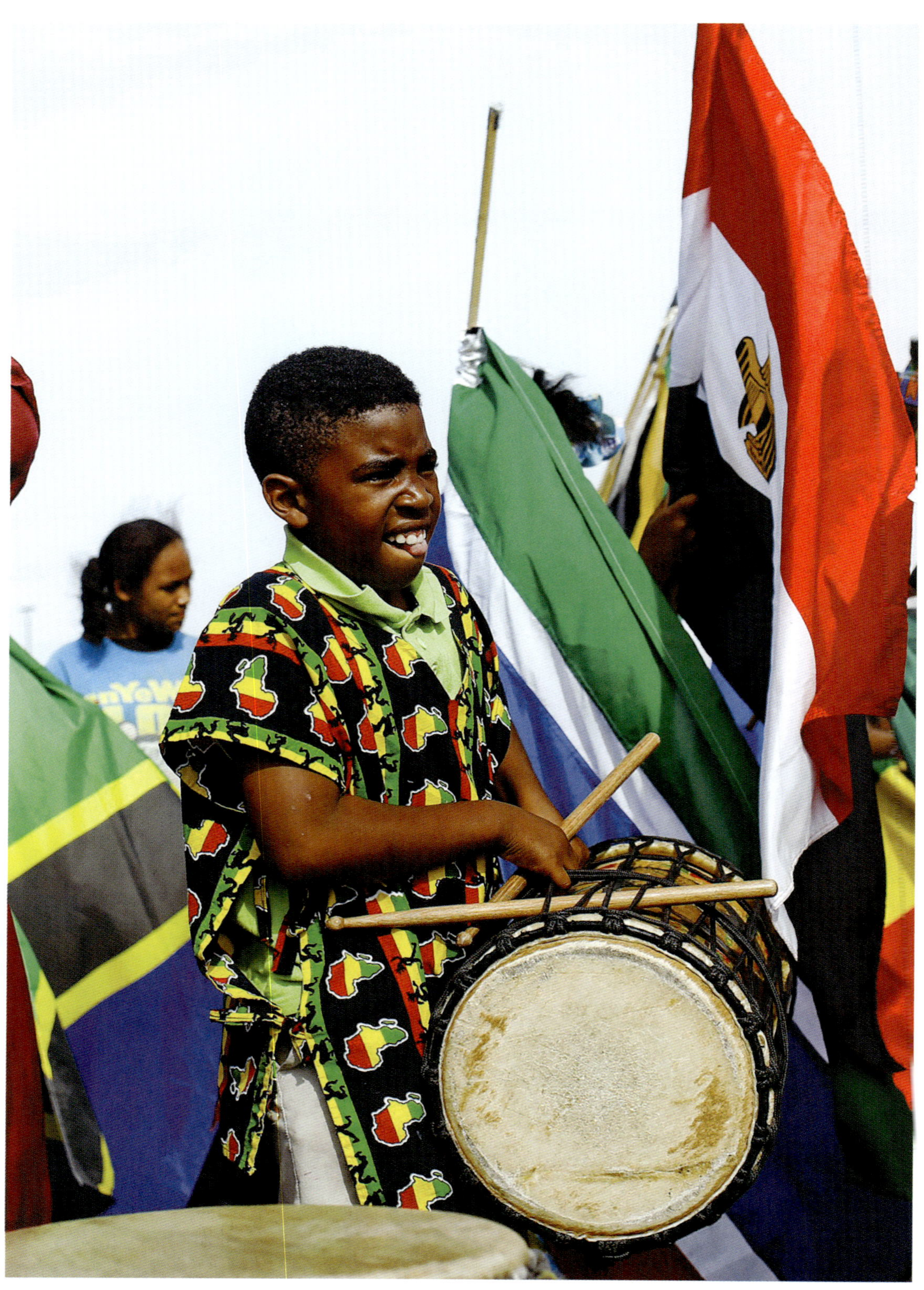

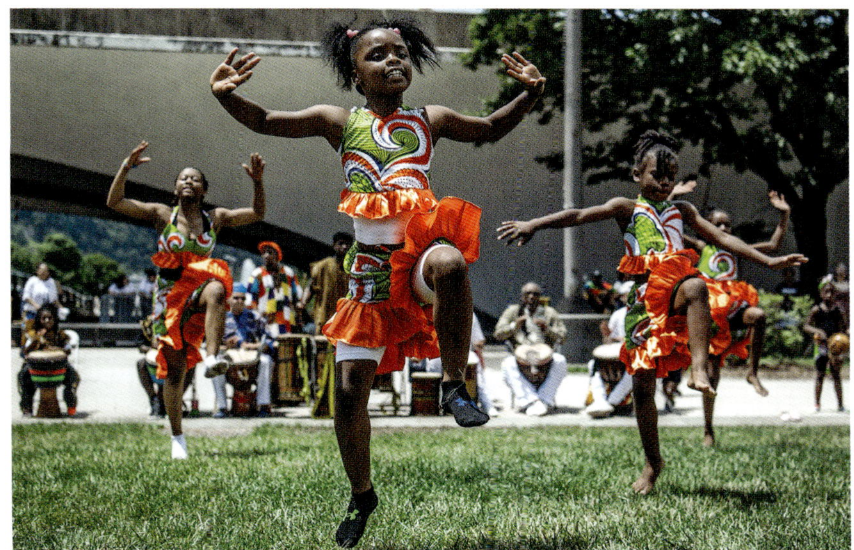

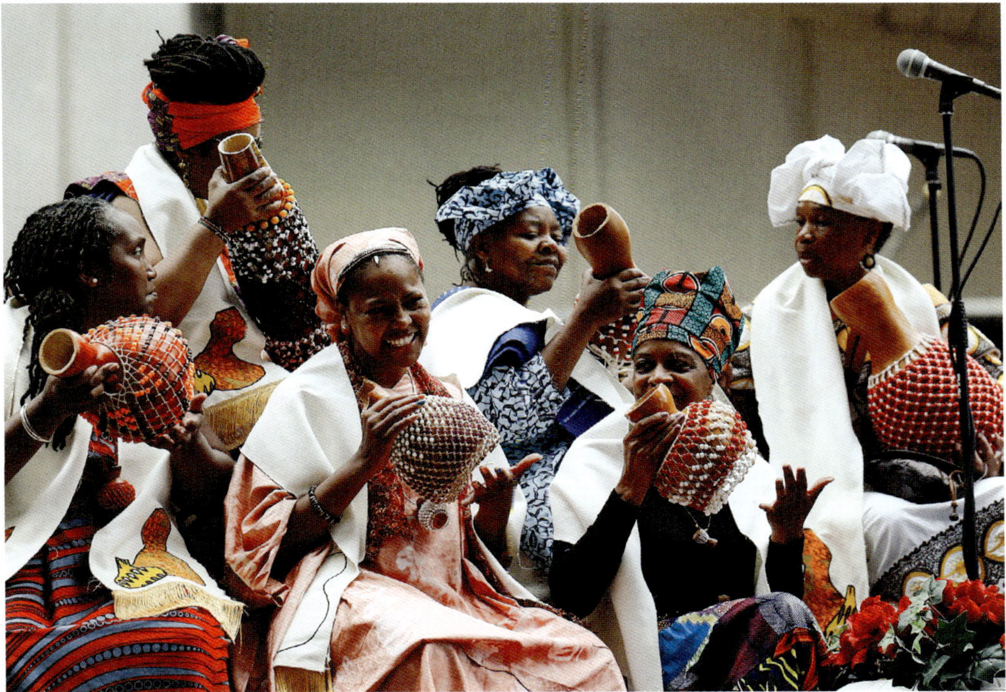

OPPOSITE: A young African-style drummer, Michael Seolton, center, prepares to join the procession at the 25th annual Juneteenth celebration in Flint, Michigan, June 19, 2015.

TOP: Young dancers from Sankofa Village for the Arts perform a vibrant African dance during Pittsburgh, Pennsylvania's 2019 Jubilee of Freemen Parade at Point State Park, honoring Juneteenth through movement and ancestral tradition.

ABOVE: Performers play the shekere during a Juneteenth parade in 2018, bringing African rhythms and traditions to the celebration of Black freedom on Philadelphia, Pennsylvania's East Market Street.

OPPOSITE TOP: Donning traditional African attire, a dancer participates in the annual Juneteenth parade in Center City Philadelphia, Pennsylvania, on June 23, 2018. In the city where American liberty was first declared, the celebration of Black emancipation is particularly poignant, tying back to the long struggle for Black freedom on American soil.

OPPOSITE BOTTOM: Leighdy Morris, Queen of the RBG Brigade—named for Justice Ruth Bader Ginsburg—marched in Philadelphia, Pennsylvania's annual Juneteenth parade in Center City in 2018. "It should be a national holiday," Morris declared, a few years before that vision became reality.

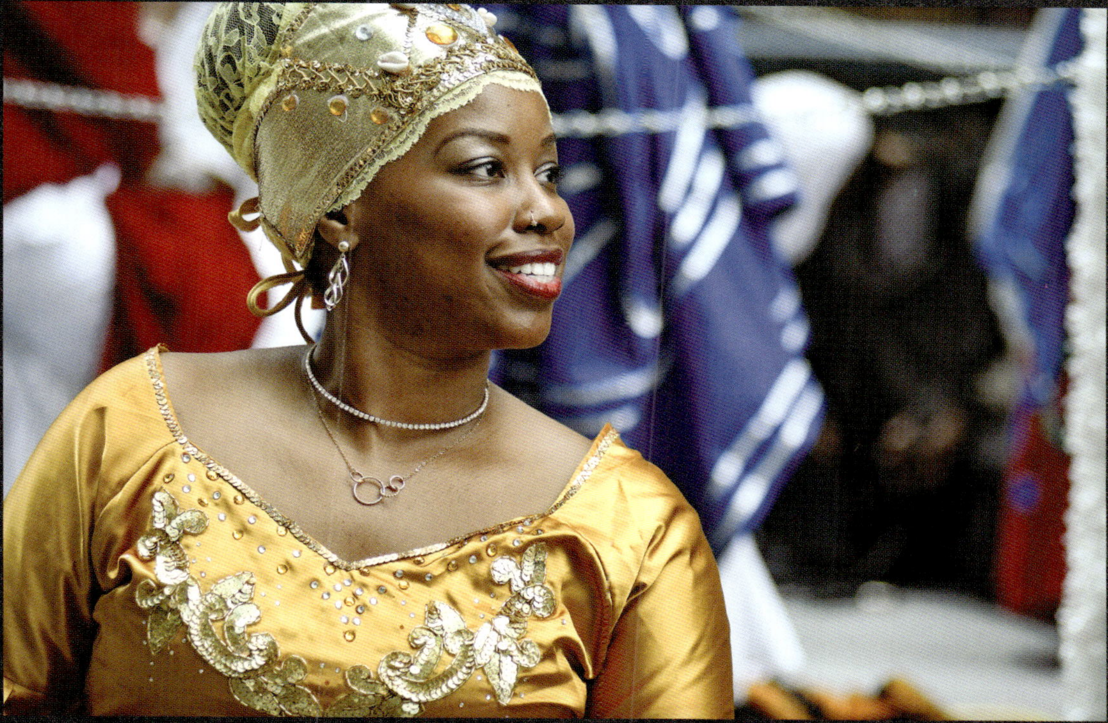

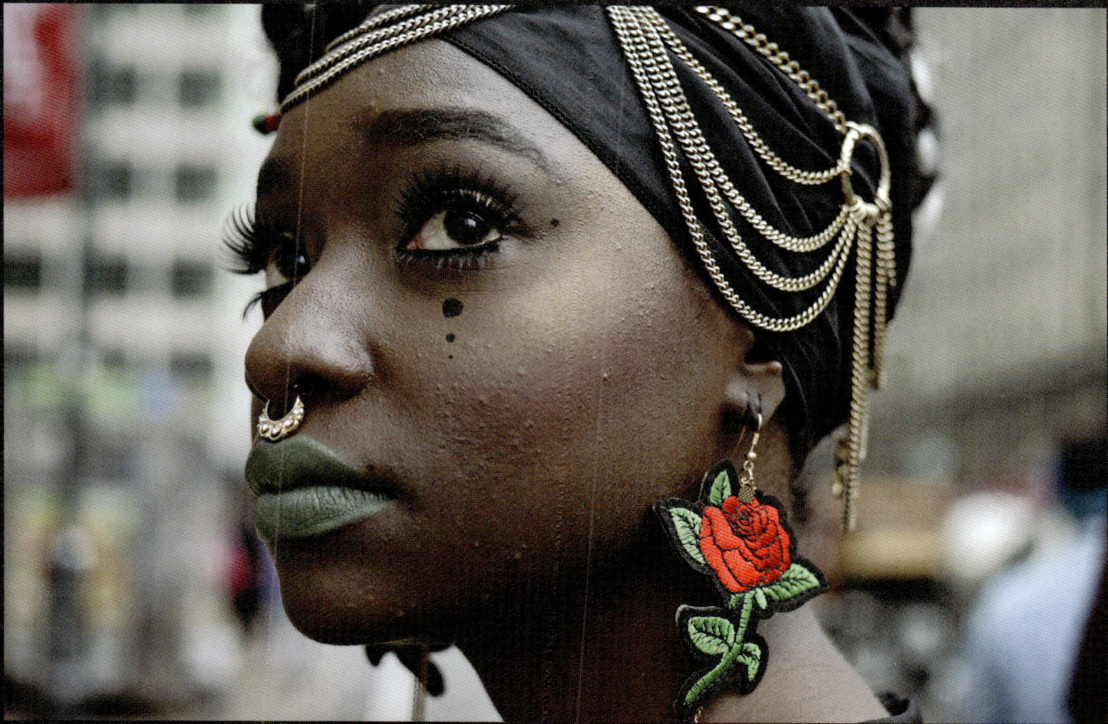

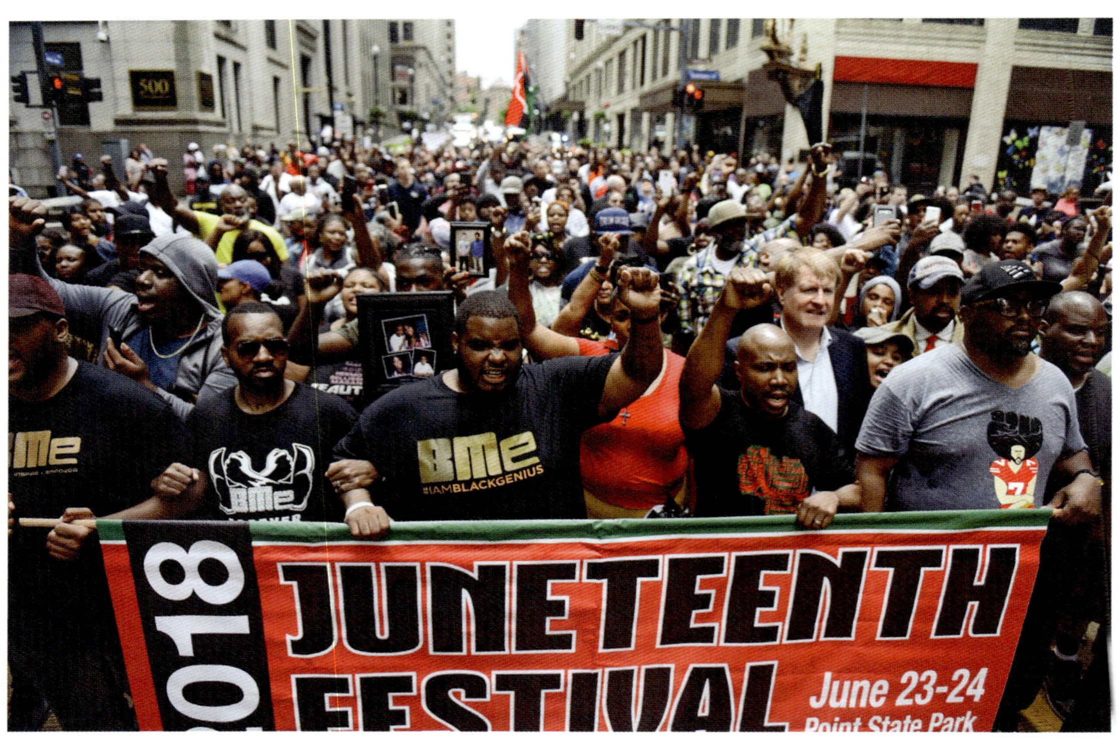

Demands for justice in the wake of the killing of Antwon Rose Jr. rang out during Pittsburgh, Pennsylvania's 2018 Juneteenth Parade. The march not only commemorated emancipation but also voiced outrage over the fatal shooting of 17-year-old Antwon Rose by Pittsburgh police officer Michael Rosfeld. The case sparked local activism and legal battles, which resulted in the acquittal of Rosfeld in March 2019 and a settlement for Rose's family in October of 2019. The ongoing fight for racial justice remains an important part of the broader struggle for freedom that Juneteenth represents.

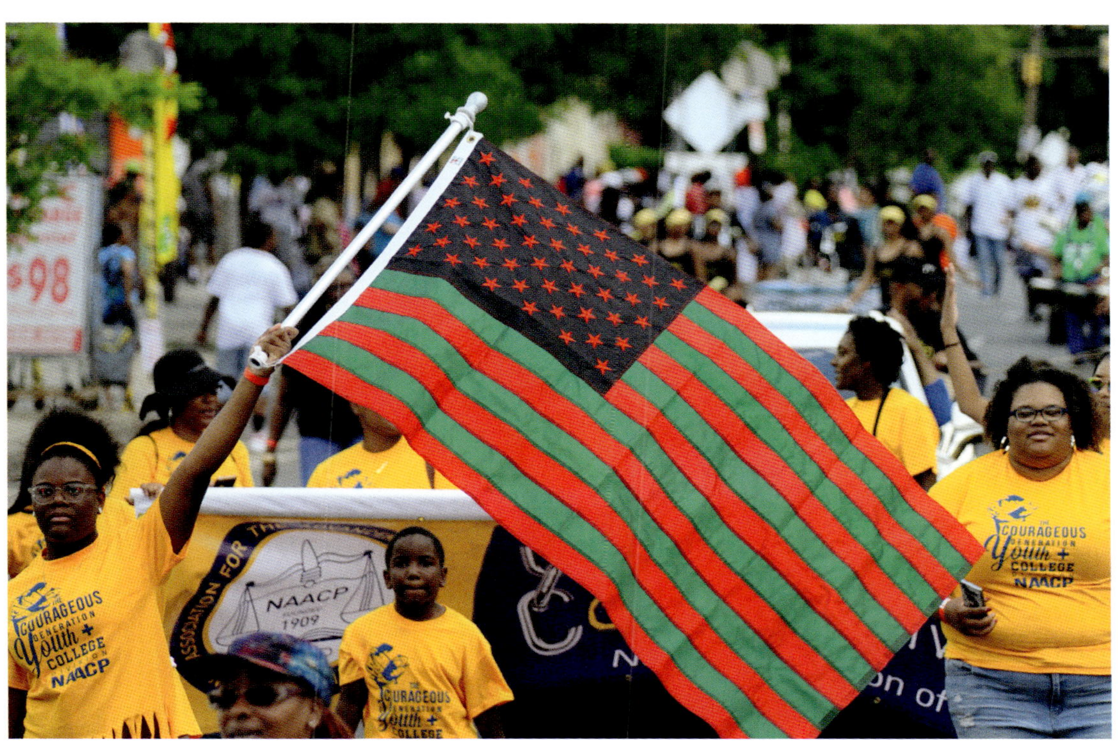

Waving a red, black, and green American flag—colors of the Pan-African flag first created by Marcus Garvey's Universal Negro Improvement Association (UNIA) in 1920 to symbolize Black unity and liberation—marchers filled the streets for Philadelphia's 2019 Juneteenth parade. NAACP members and youth and community leaders joined together just days after Pennsylvania officially recognized Juneteenth as a state holiday.

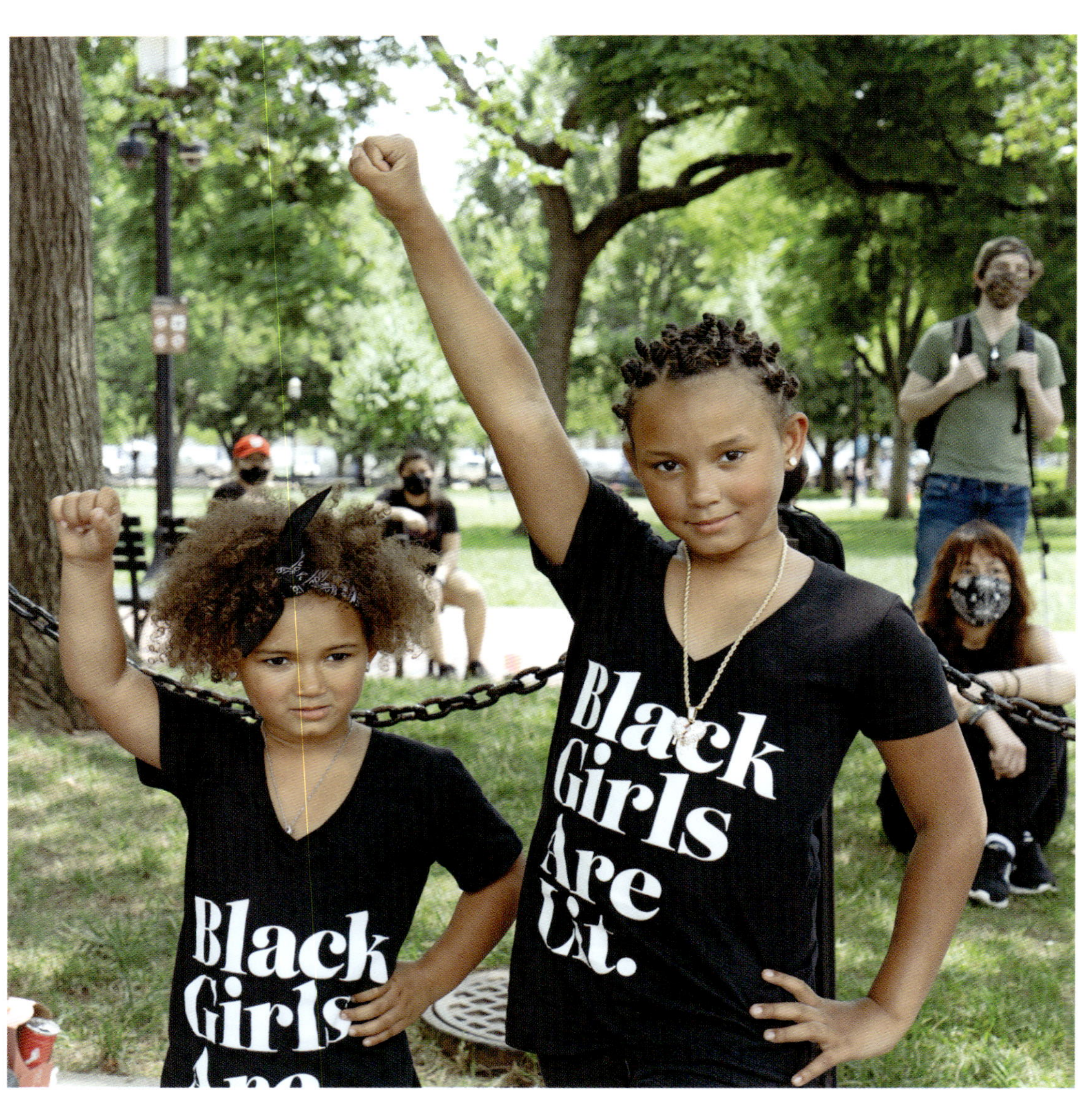
Black
Girls
Black
Girls
Are
Lit.

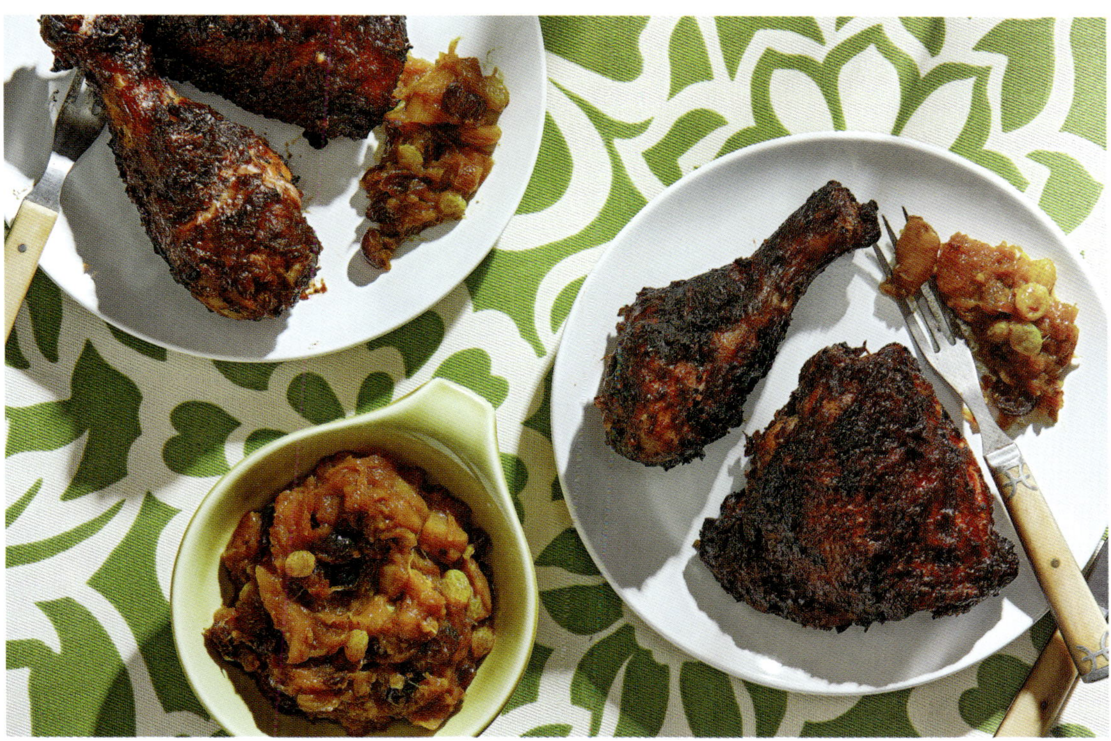

OPPOSITE: Young sisters Kaylee Harrison, 5, and Kamoni Harrison, 8, pose with raised fists in front of the White House during the 2020 Juneteenth celebration in Washington, DC. The gesture became iconic after Tommie Smith and John Carlos raised their fists in support of Black Power during the 1968 Olympics. The sisters' stance echoes generations who fought for the full expression of Black freedom and the fight for justice.

ABOVE: Featured in 2020 in "Eat Voraciously," *The Washington Post*'s cooking guide, this jerk chicken honors the bold flavors of the African diaspora. Rooted in Jamaican Maroon traditions, the spicy, smoky chicken is reminiscent of the smoky, sweet barbecue flavors beloved by Black Americans. Eating is a central part of any Juneteenth celebration.

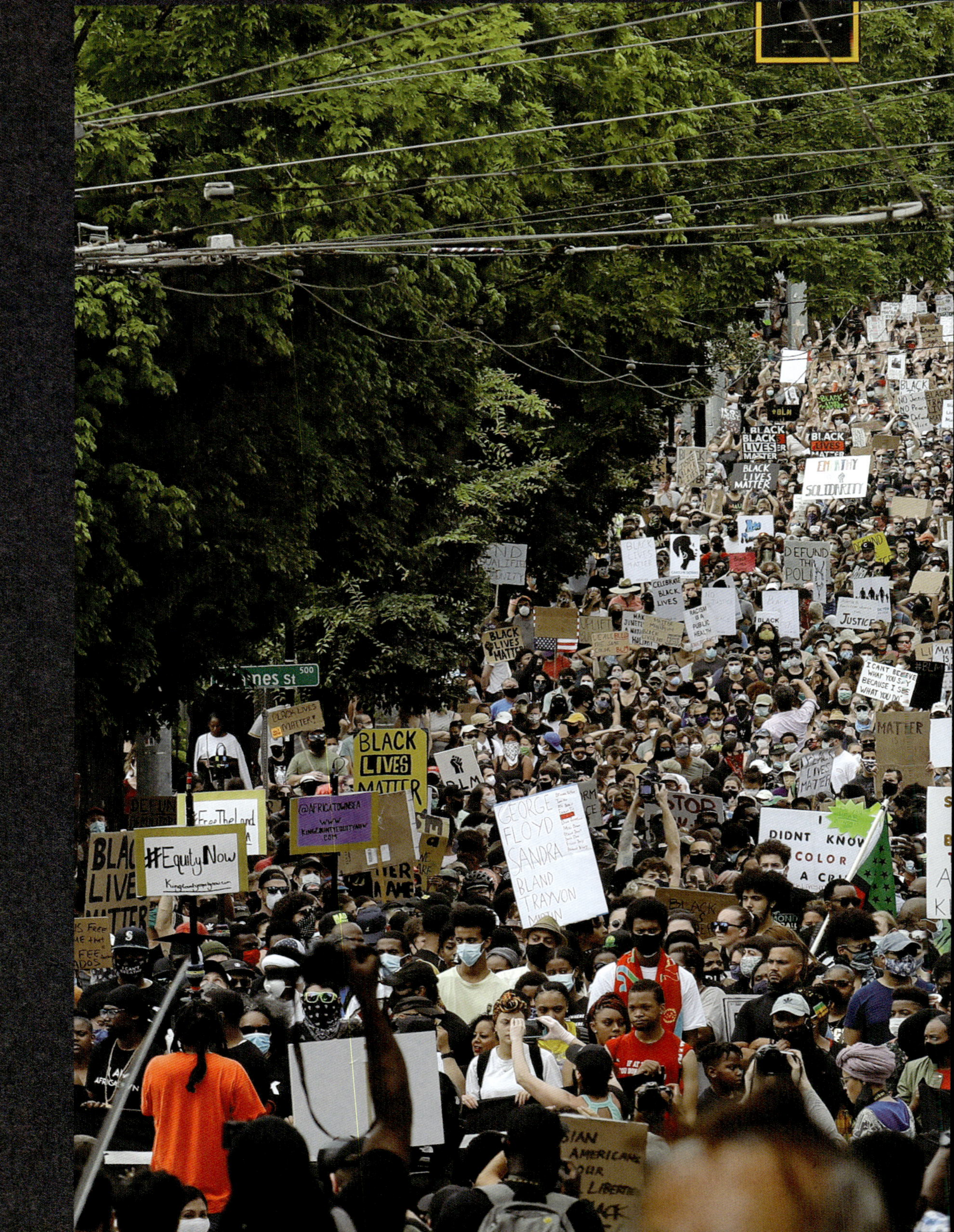

BLACK LIVES MATTER
#Equity Now
GEORGE FLOYD
SANDRA BLAND
TRAYVON
DEFUND THE POLICE
BLACK LIVES MATTER
SOLIDARITY
I CANT BELIEVE WHAT YOU SAY BECAUSE I SEE WHAT YOU DO
DIDNT KNOW
COLOR

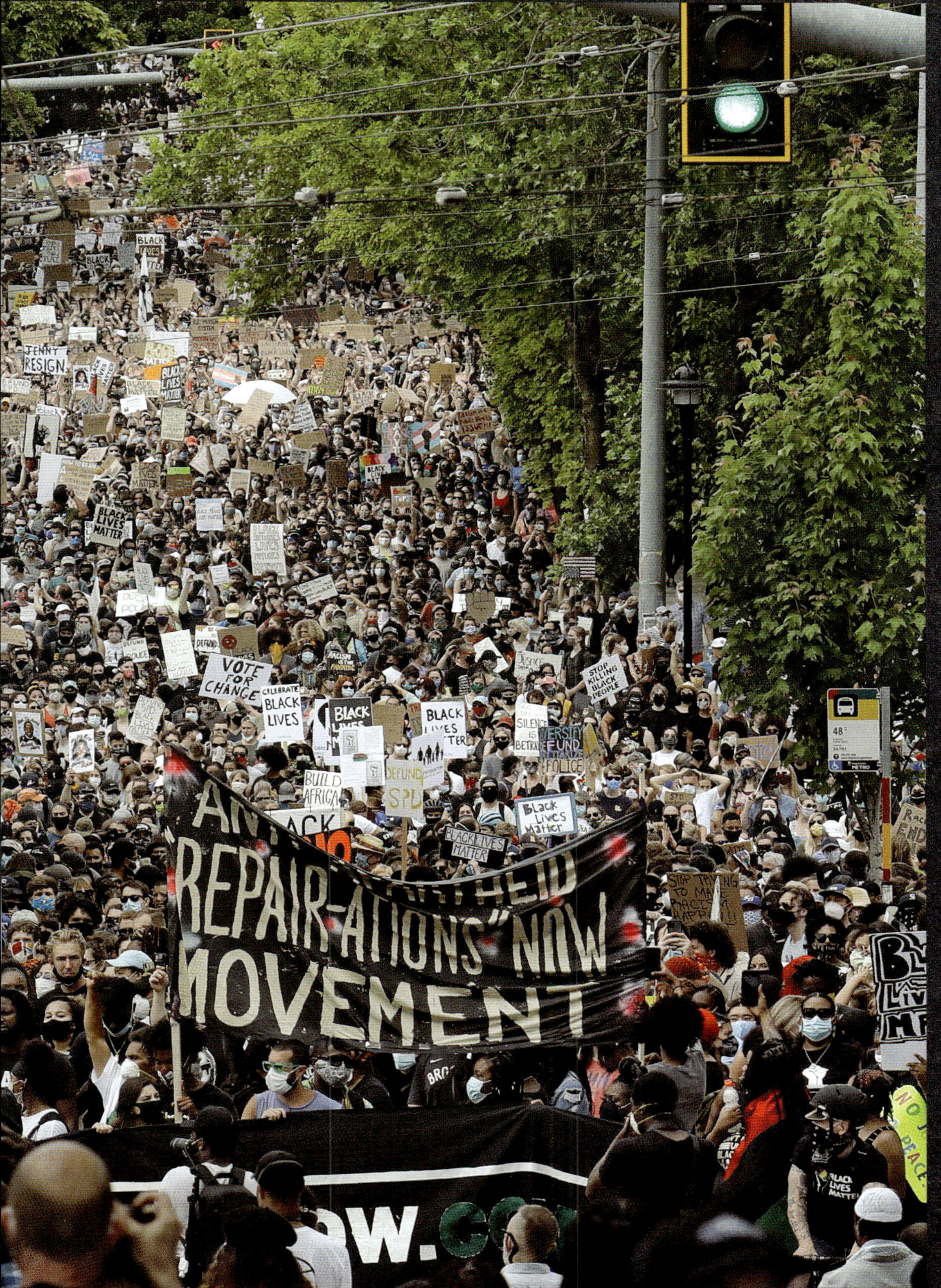

JENNY RESIGN
BLACK LIVES MATTER
VOTE FOR CHANCE
CELEBRATE BLACK LIVES
STOP KILLING BLACK PEOPLE
BUILD AFRICA
DEFUND SPD
Black Lives Matter
BLACK LIVES MATTER
REPAIR-ATIONS" NOW
MOVEMENT

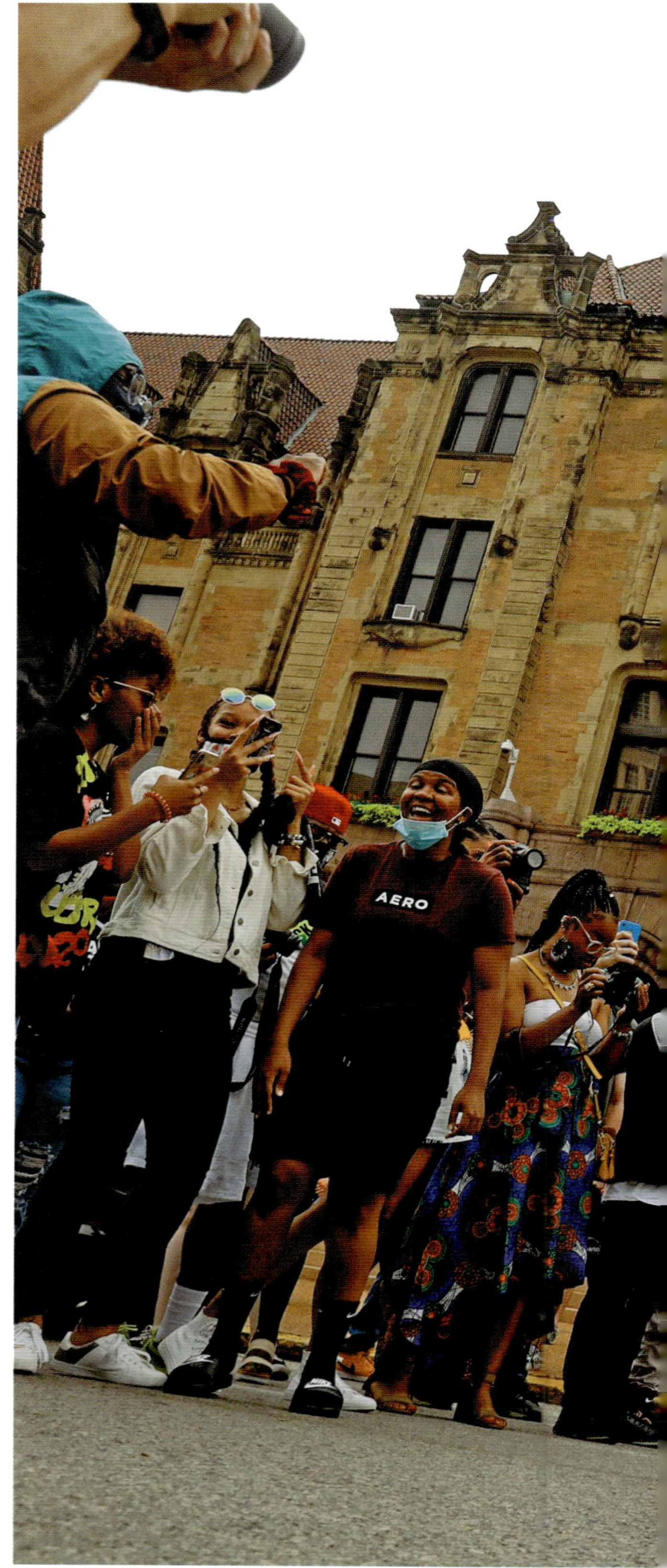

PREVIOUS: Thousands of marchers fill 23rd Avenue in Seattle, Washington, on June 19, 2020. That year, the call to honor the Juneteenth holiday intersected with nationwide protests against police violence and racism.

RIGHT: Andre Mason of Alpha Phi Alpha, Alpha Eta chapter steps in front of Missouri's St. Louis City Hall during a 2020 Juneteenth celebration organized by ExpectUs, a police reform organization. 2020 was the year that contemporary protests merged with the long history of Juneteenth in the wake of the murder of George Floyd.

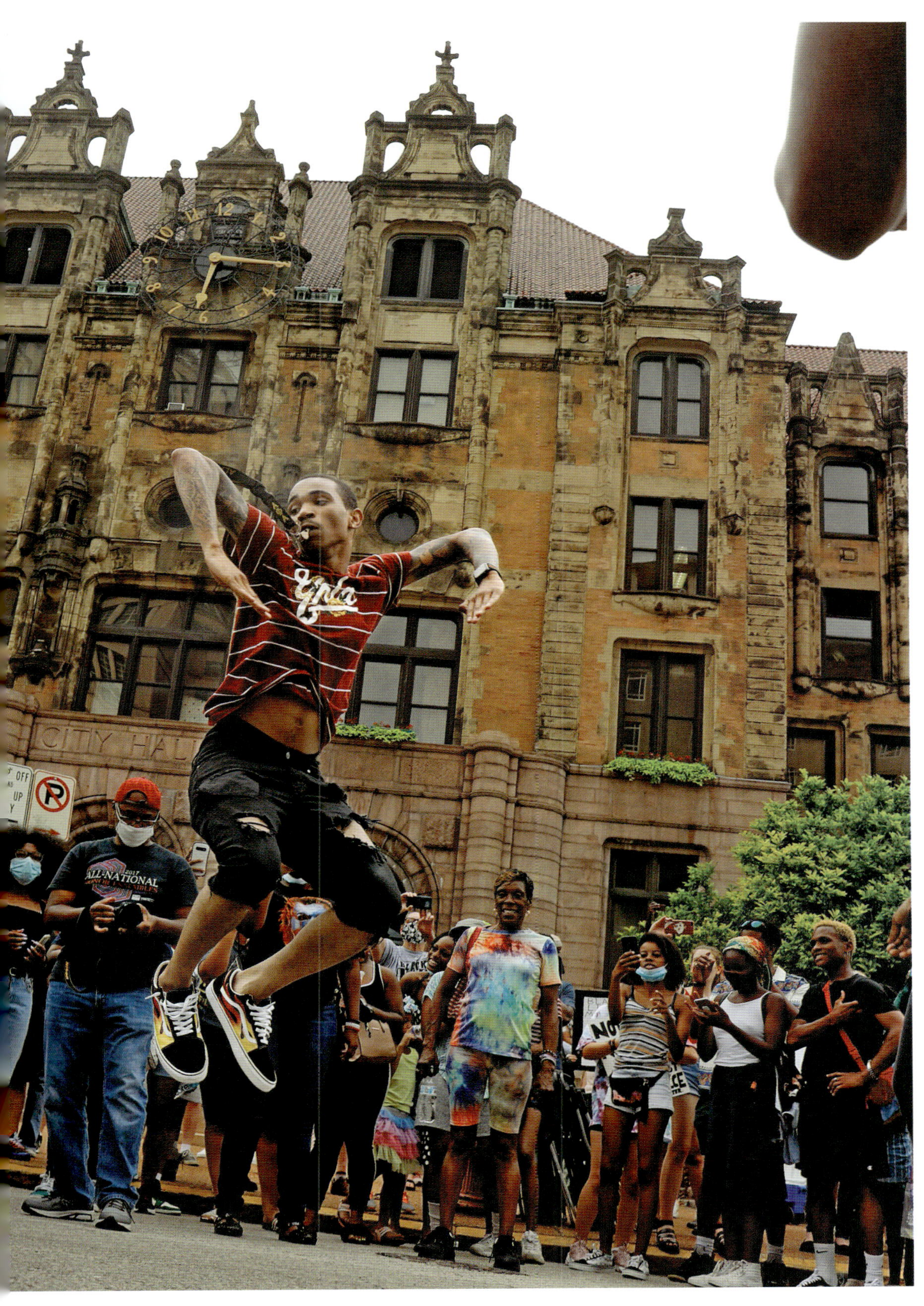
CITY HAL
2017
ALL-NATIONAL

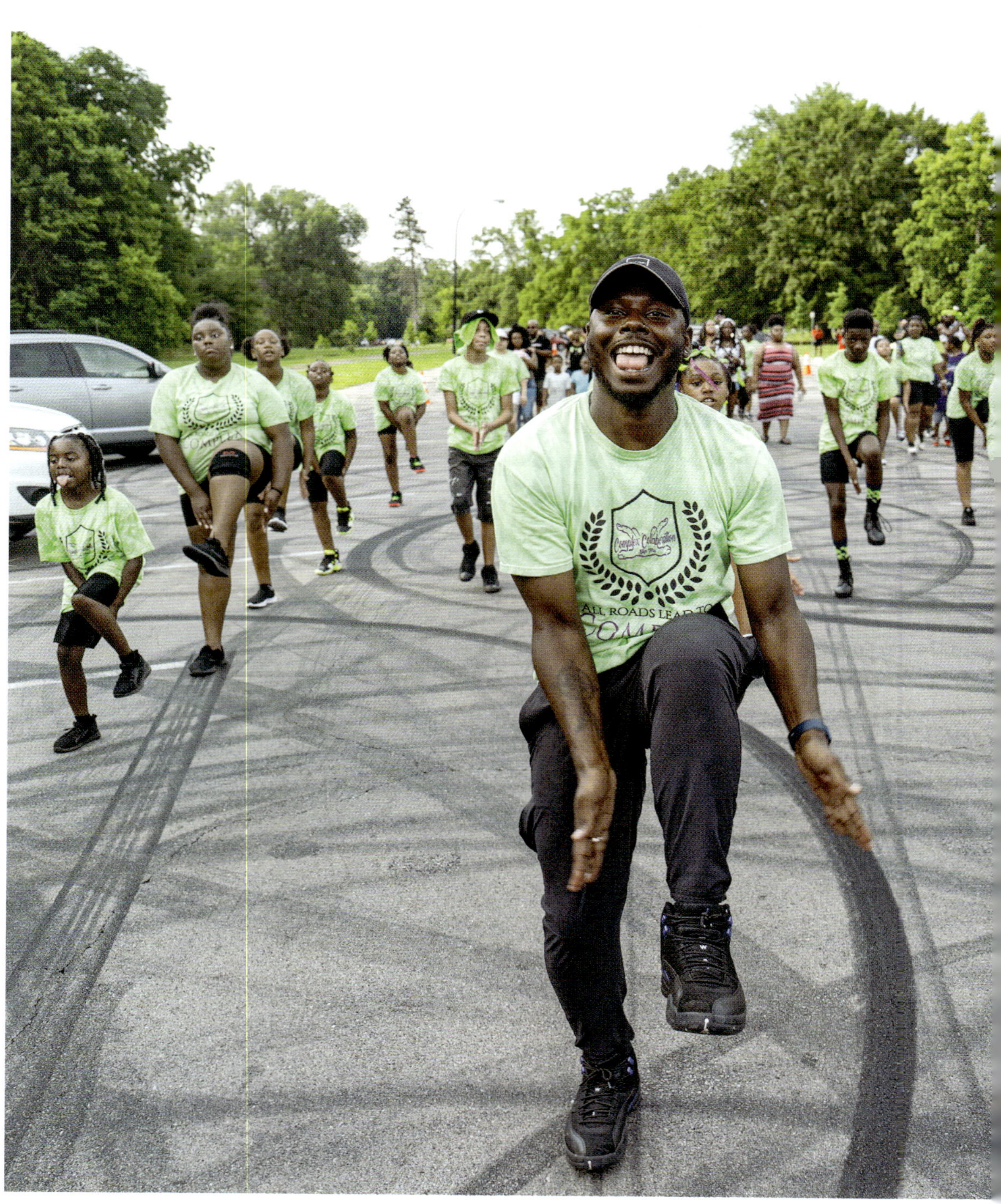
ALL ROADS LEAD TO

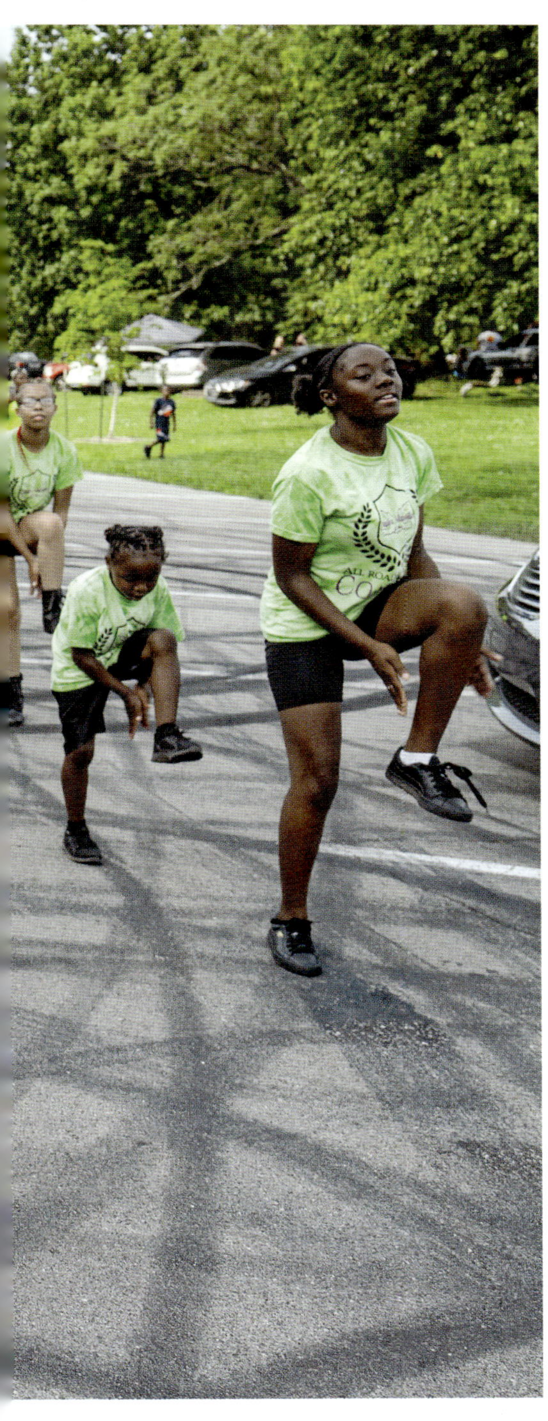

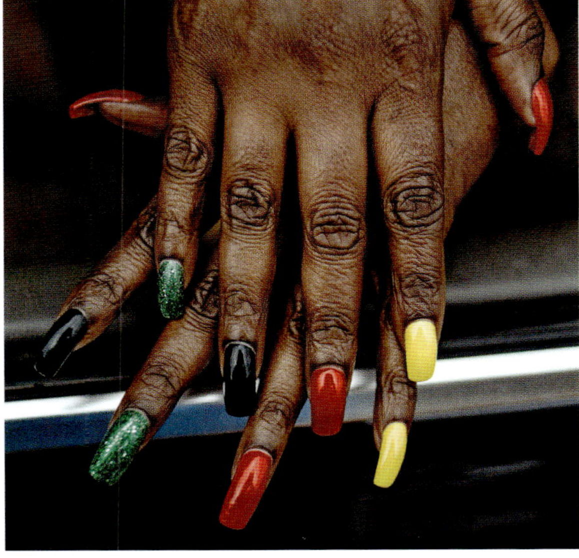

LEFT: Just days after Juneteenth was recognized as a federal holiday, the Complex Collaboration Step Team performed at Louisville, Kentucky's 2021 Juneteenth Unity Parade.

ABOVE: Tracy Palmer shows off her red, black, green, and yellow nails painted in Pan-Africanist colors in honor of Flint, Michigan's 2021 Juneteenth parade.

FOLLOWING: Dancing in unison at the 2022 Juneteenth celebration in Prospect Park, Brooklyn, New York.

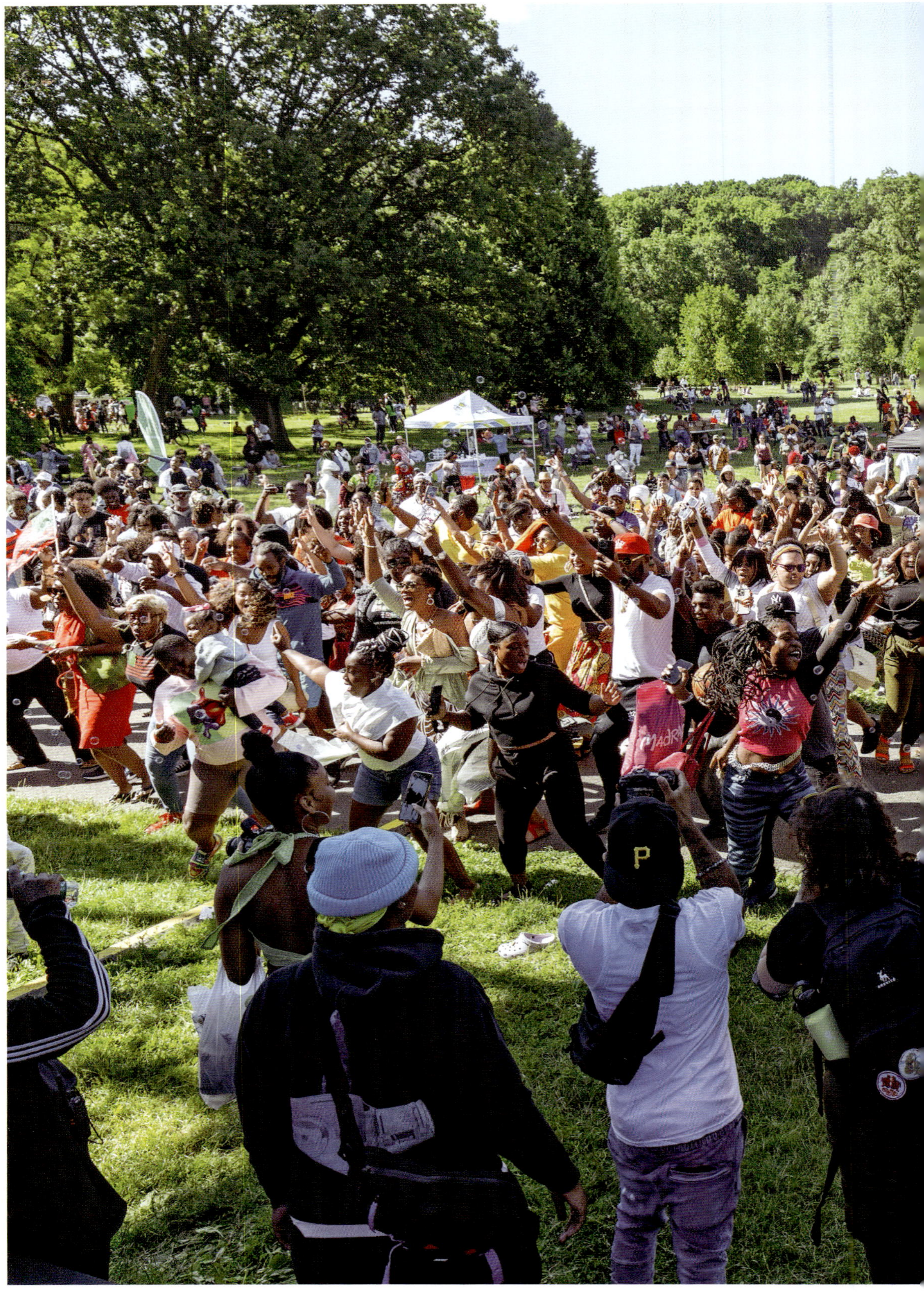

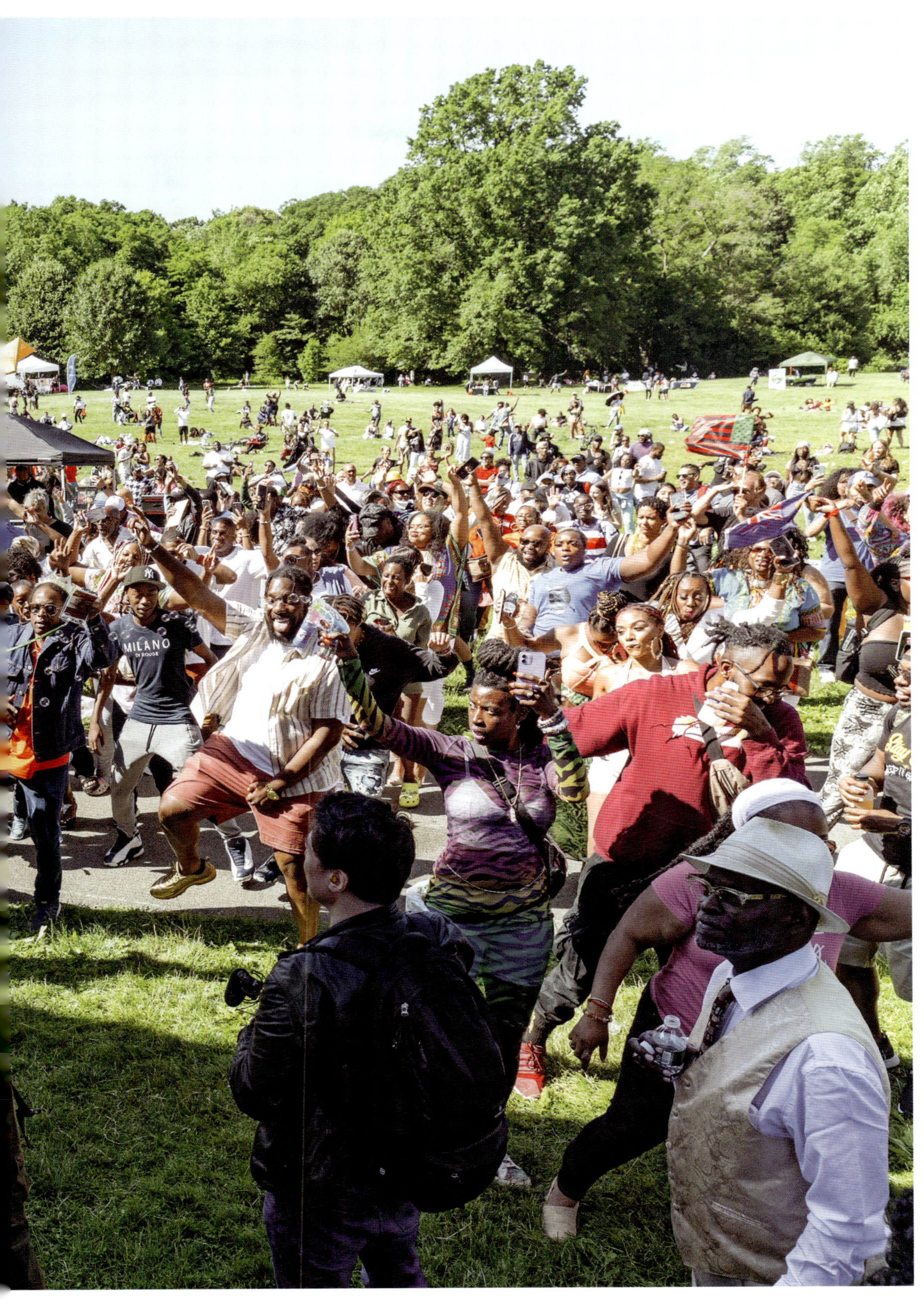
MILANO

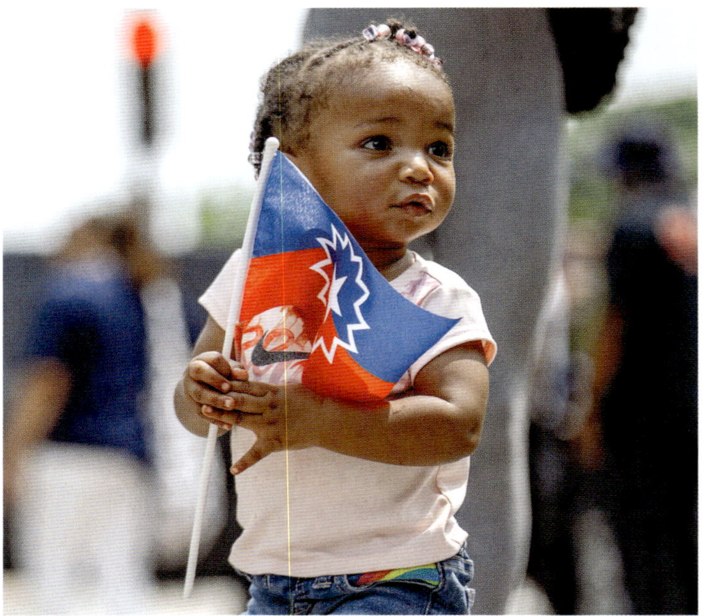

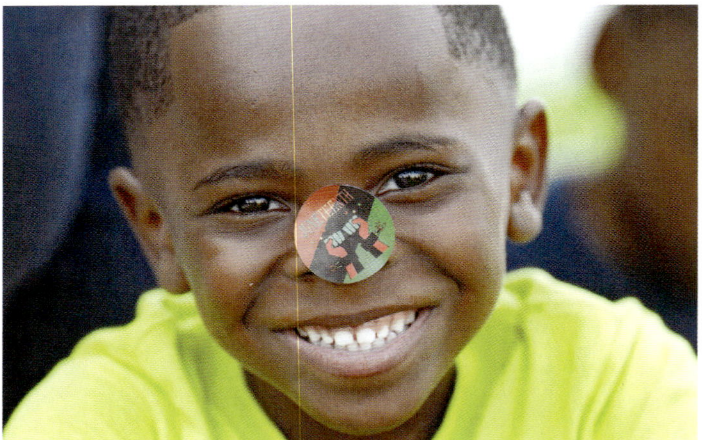

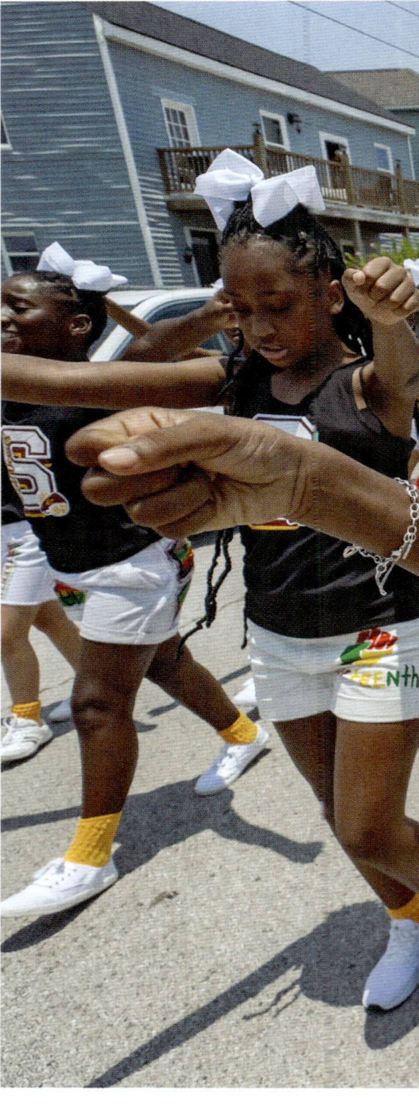

TOP: One-year-old Rose St. John holds the Juneteenth flag during Washington, DC's 2023 celebration. First created in 1997, the flag features a central star representing the "Lone Star state" of Texas, a red field symbolizing the blood of the enslaved, and a rising blue arc evoking the ongoing journey toward true freedom.

ABOVE: Five-year-old Laven Jackson laughs after sticking a Juneteenth sticker on his nose during a 2023 Juneteenth celebration in Galveston, Texas. The city unveiled new highway signage honoring its role as the birthplace of Juneteenth.

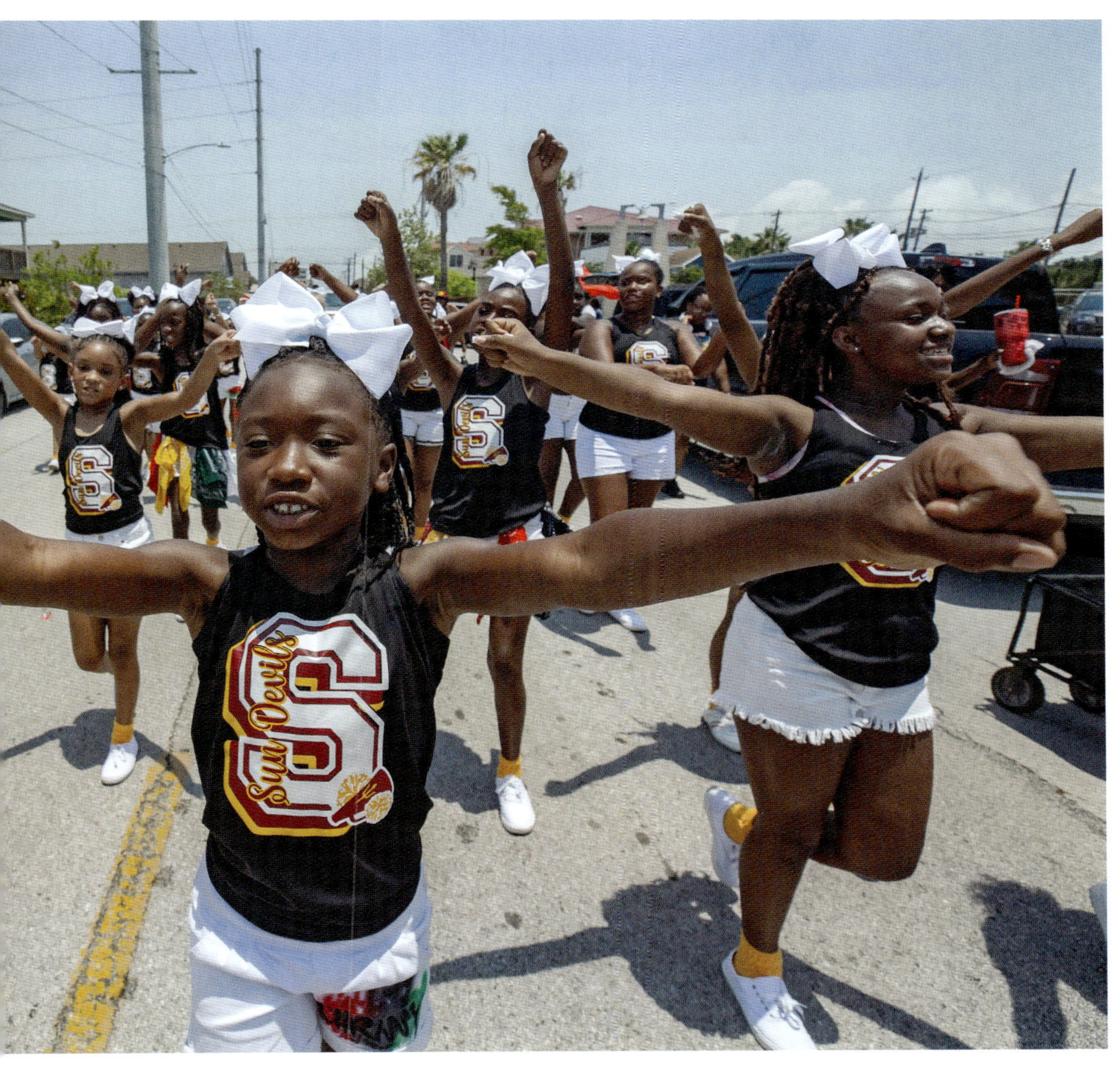

Celebrating liberty where it all began, Chrisyah Riddeaux, center, hypes the crowd along with the rest of her cheer squad during Galveston, Texas's annual Juneteenth Parade in 2023.

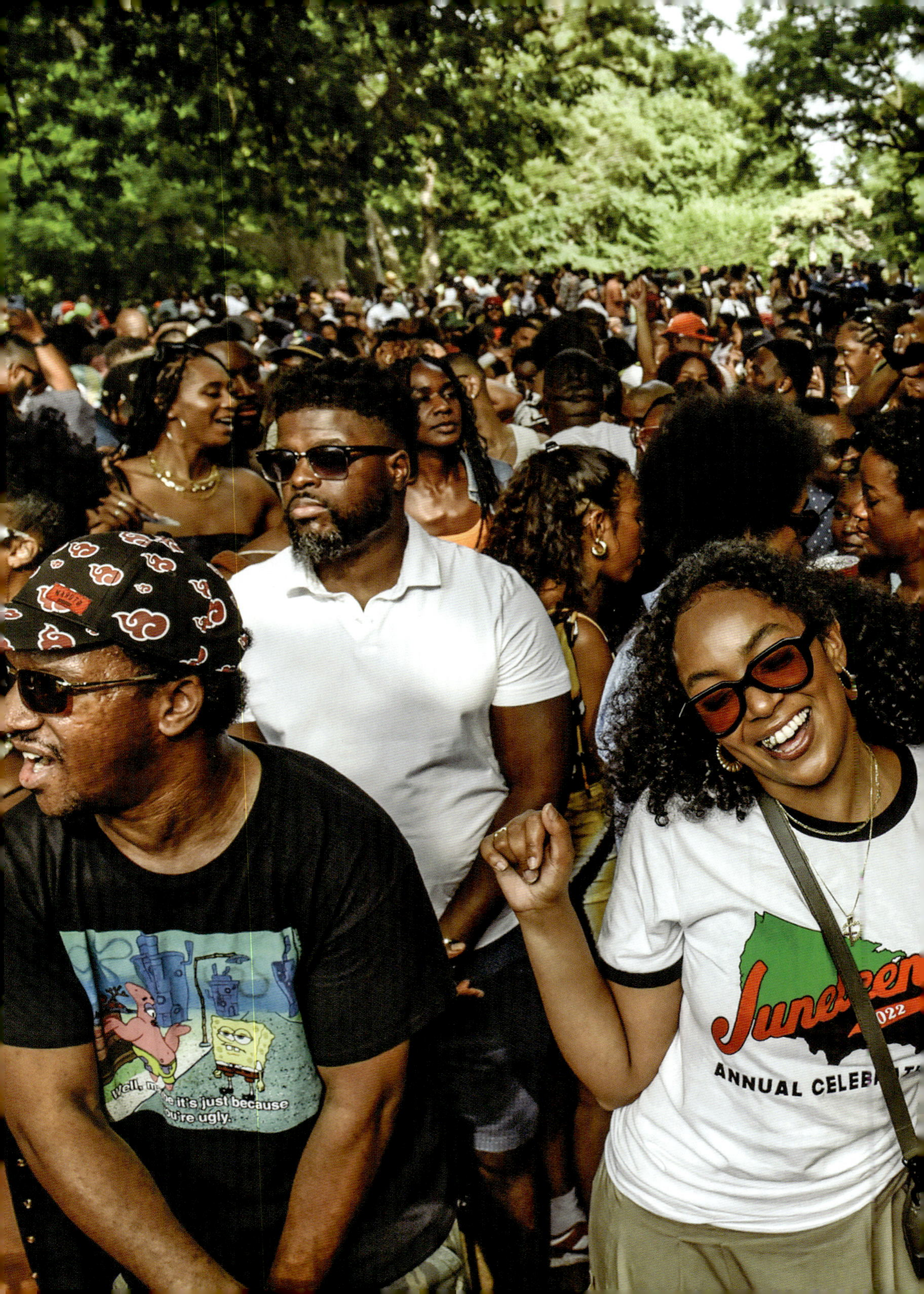

it's just because
ugly.
2022
ANNUAL

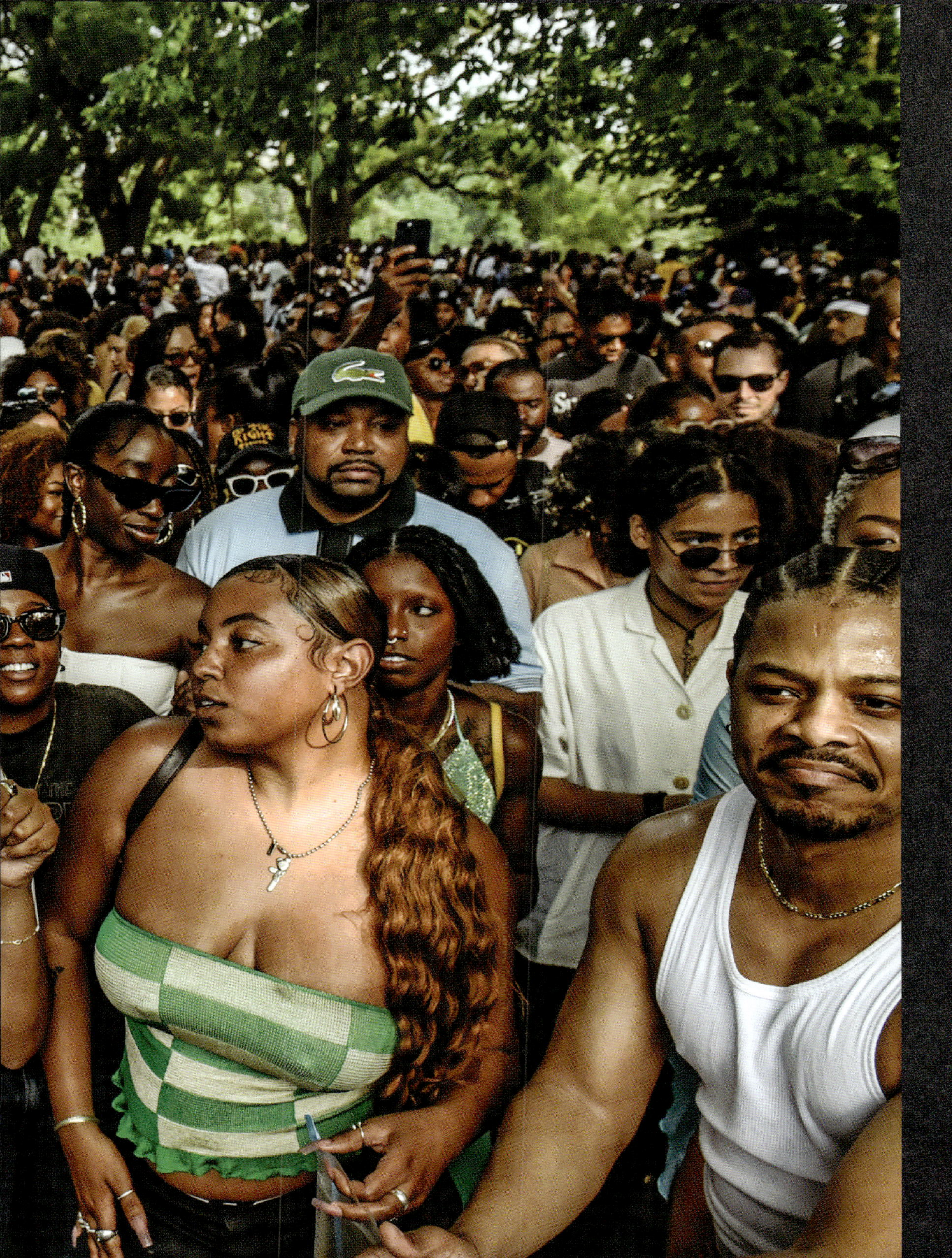

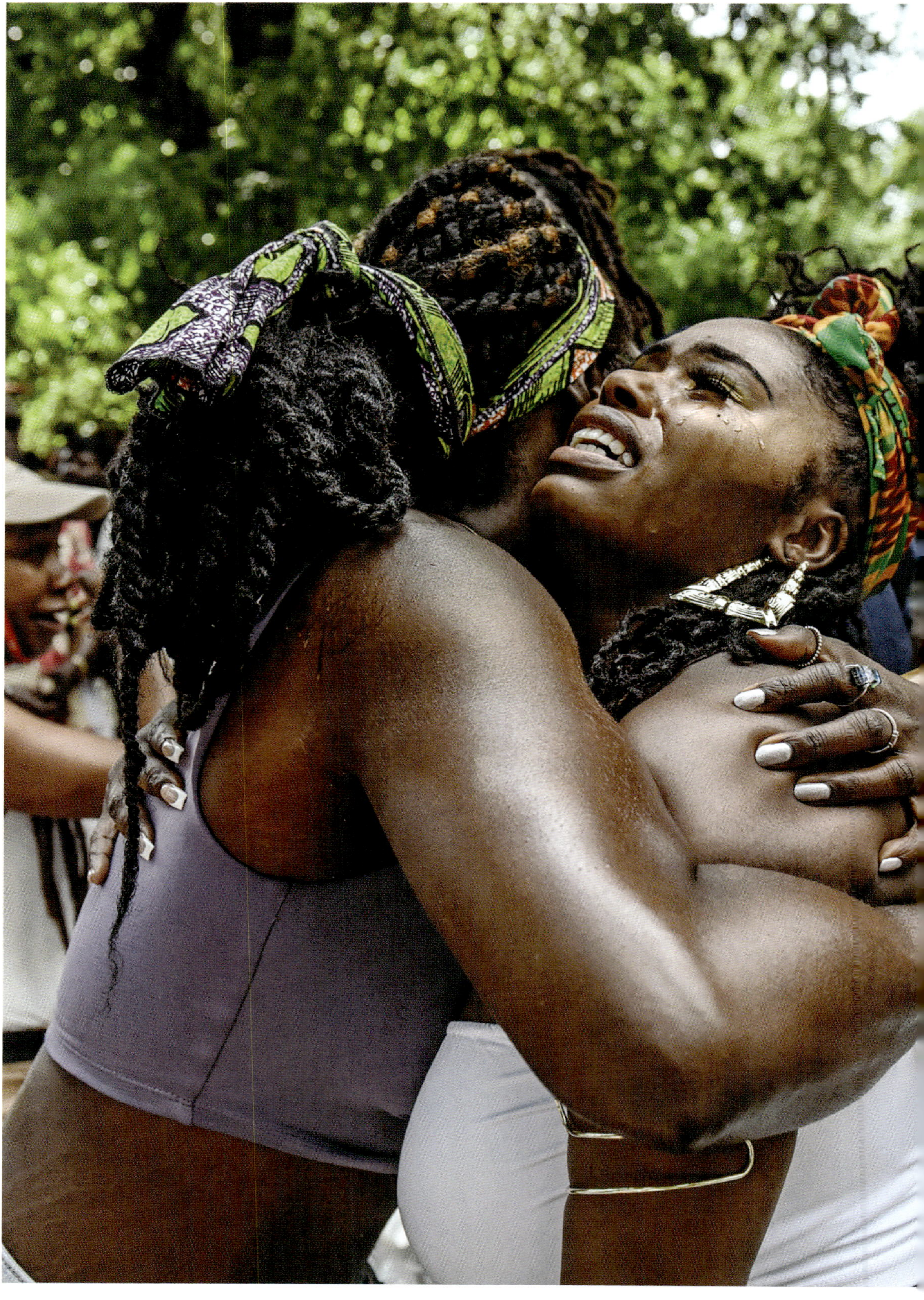

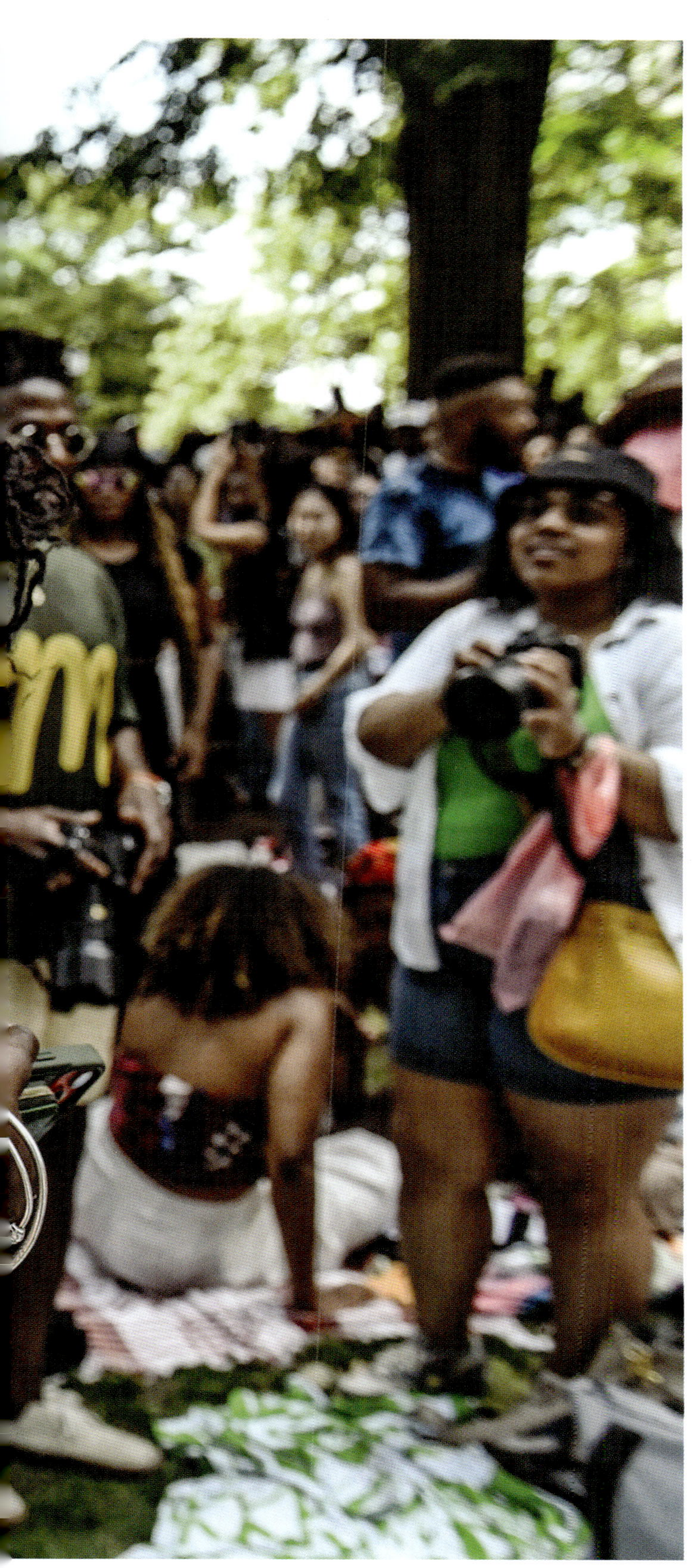

PREVIOUS: Dancers fill Fort Greene Park with energy during Brooklyn, New York's 2023 Juneteenth celebration, honoring freedom by celebrating in motion and as a tight knit community.

LEFT: Two women embrace in a moment of overwhelming emotion during Brooklyn's 2023 Juneteenth celebration.

FOLLOWING: Living history reenactors portraying US Colored Troops and Buffalo Soldiers march past the Lincoln Memorial during the Juneteenth People's Parade in Washington, DC, on June 19, 2024. Their presence honors the Black soldiers who fought for freedom and the legacy of Juneteenth.

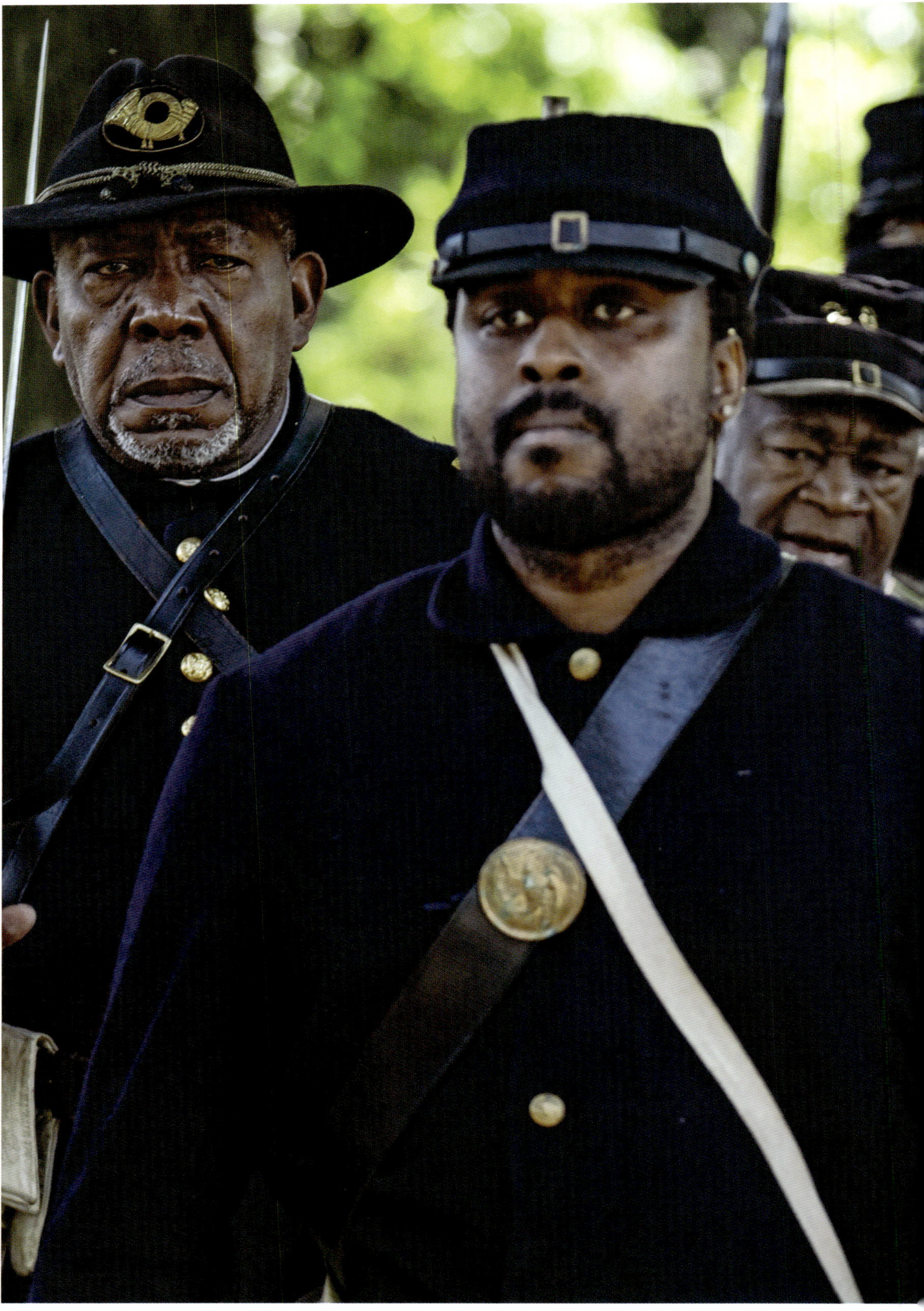

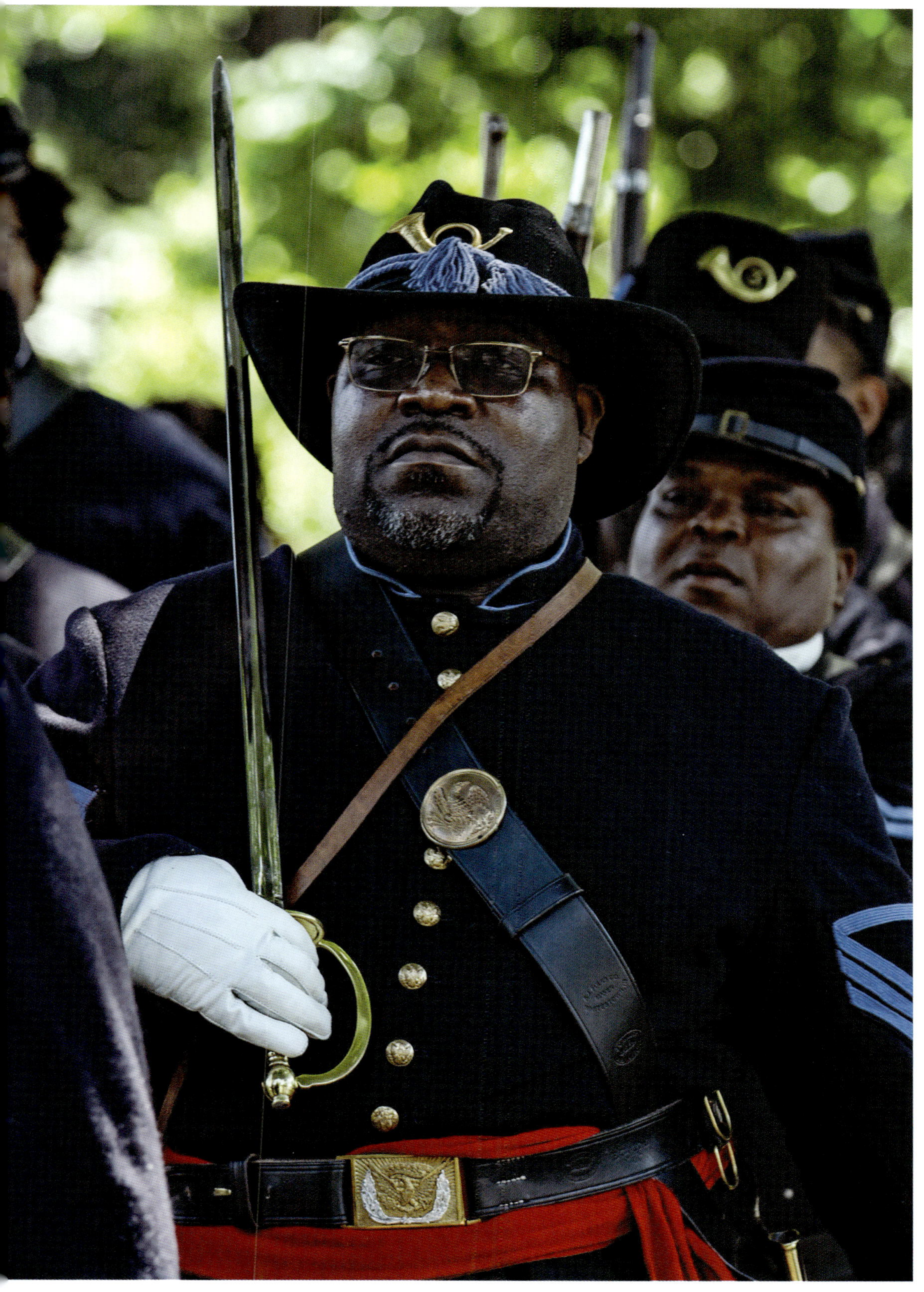

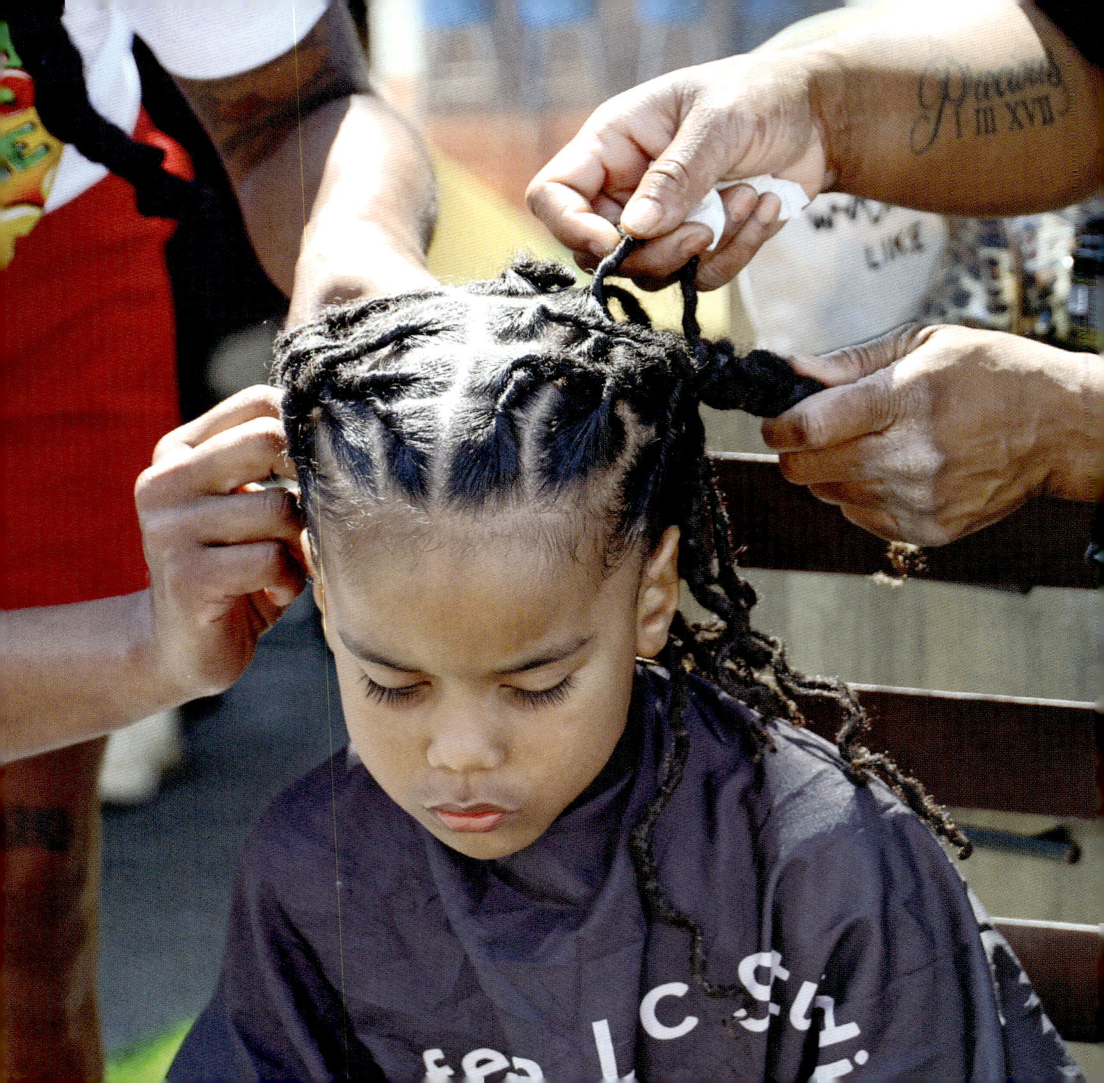
III XVII
LIKE

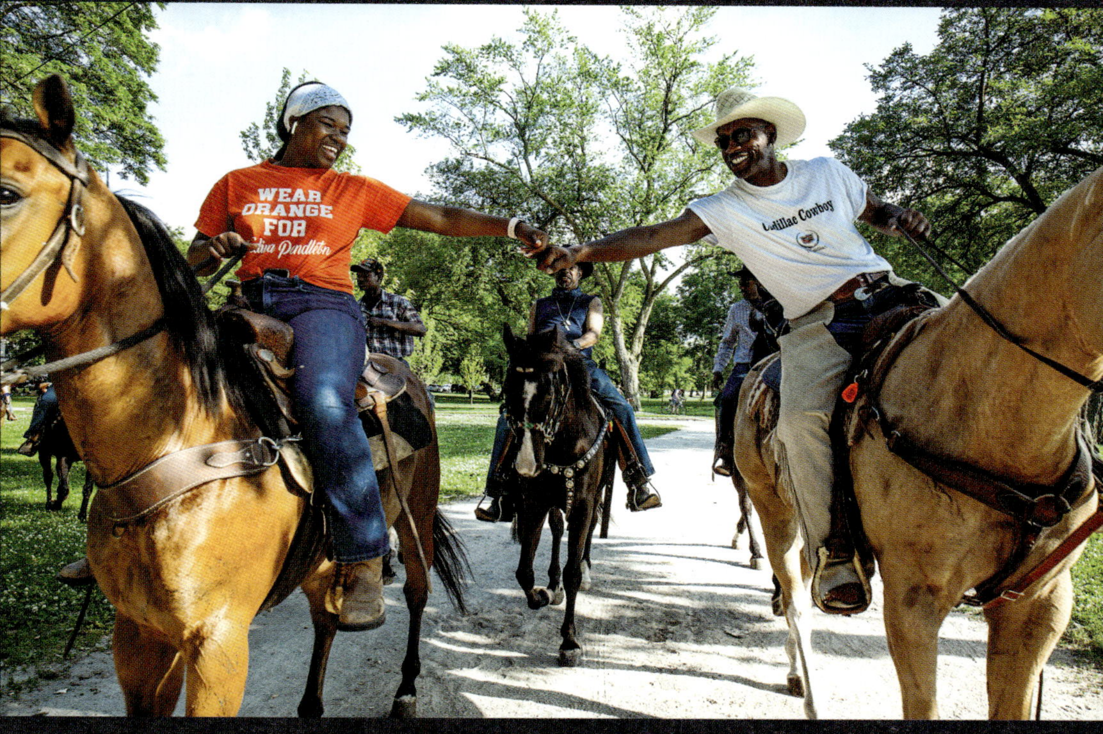

OPPOSITE: A girl has her locs braided at the 4th Annual Black On The Block Juneteenth Festival on June 15, 2025 in Los Angeles.

ABOVE: Black horse riders fist bump each other up during a parade in Chicago, Illinois' Washington Park on June 19, 2020.

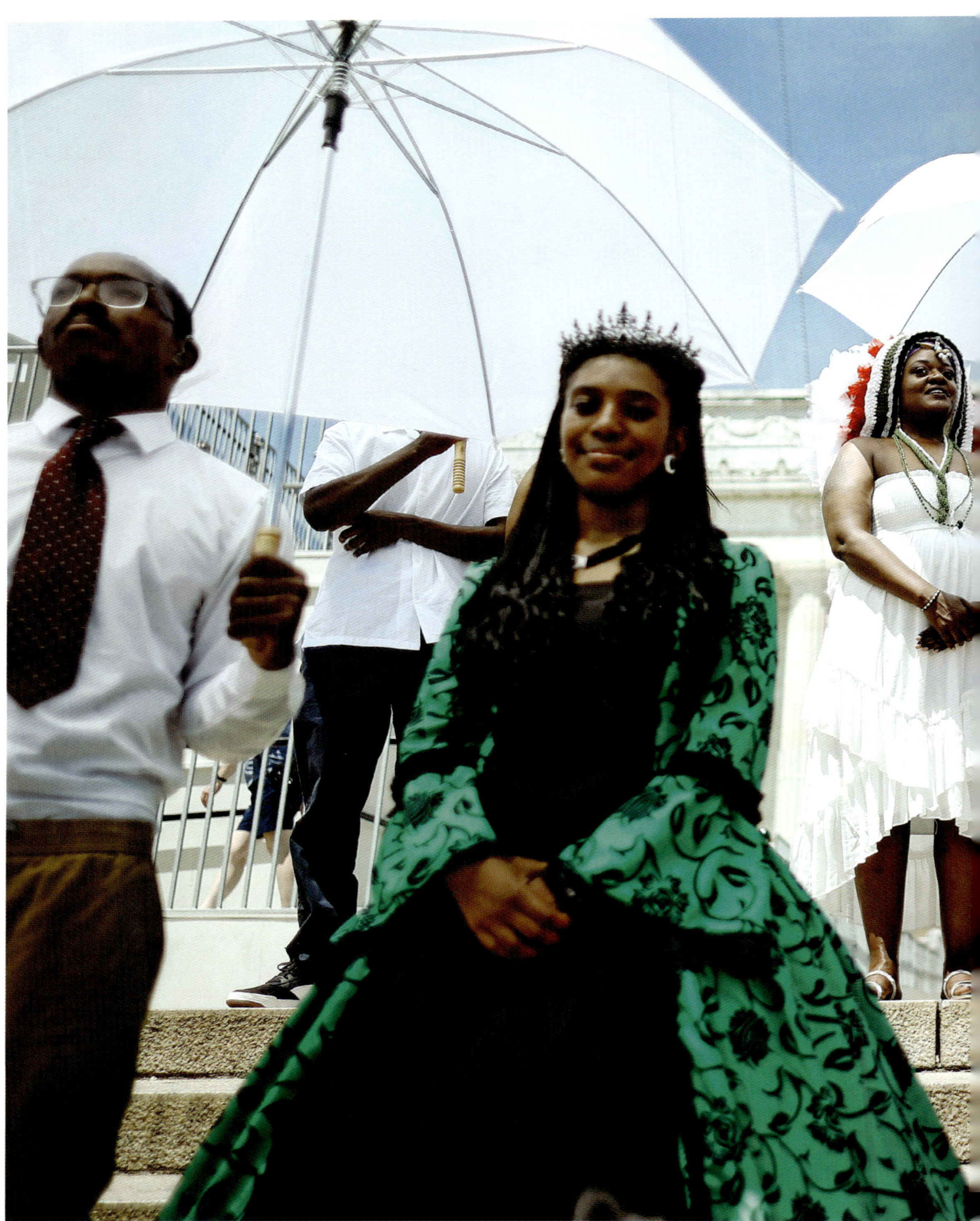

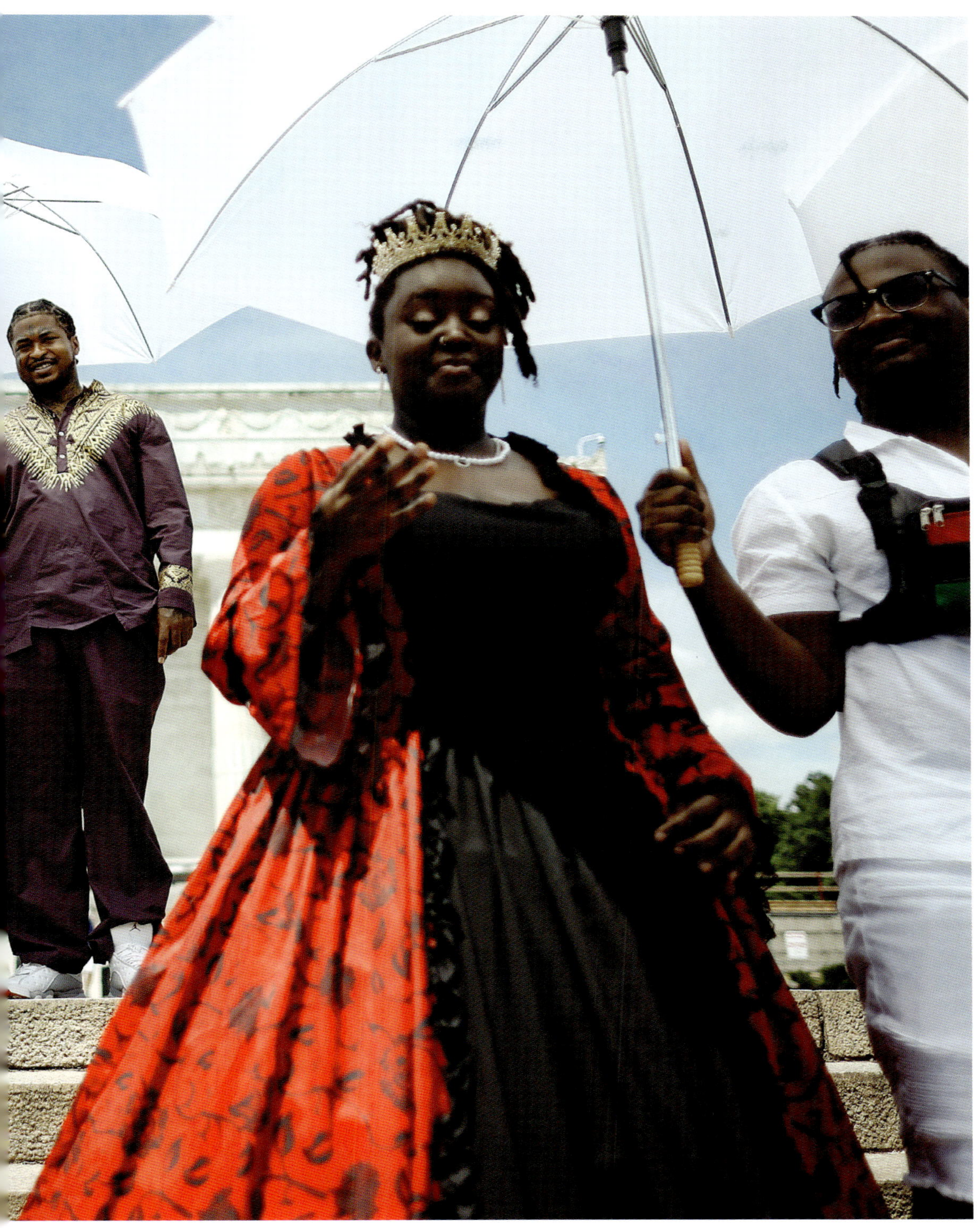

Members of the National Miss Juneteenth Georgia Royal Court pose on the steps of the Lincoln Memorial in Washington, DC, during the 2024 Juneteenth People's Parade.

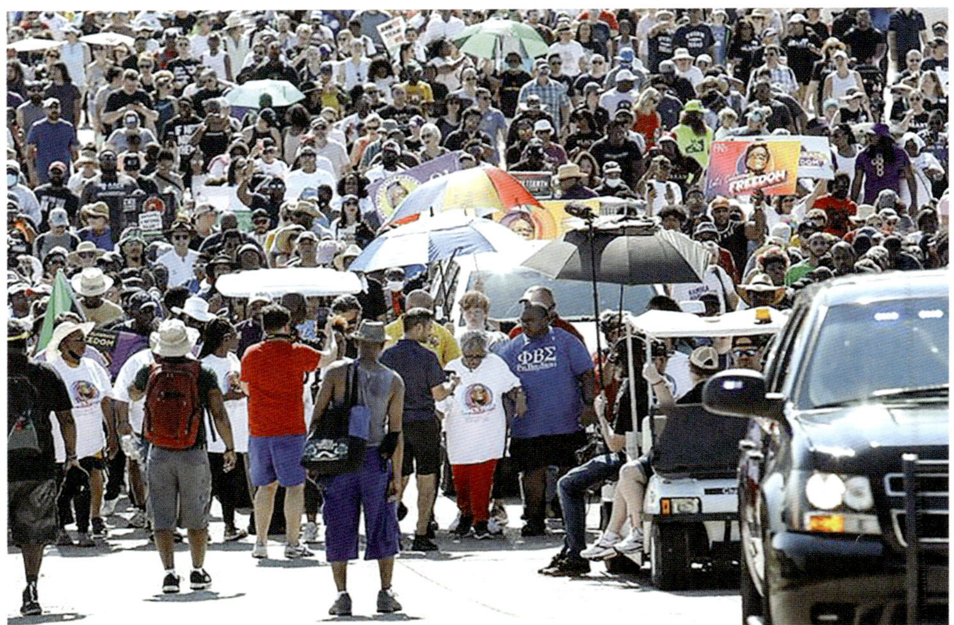

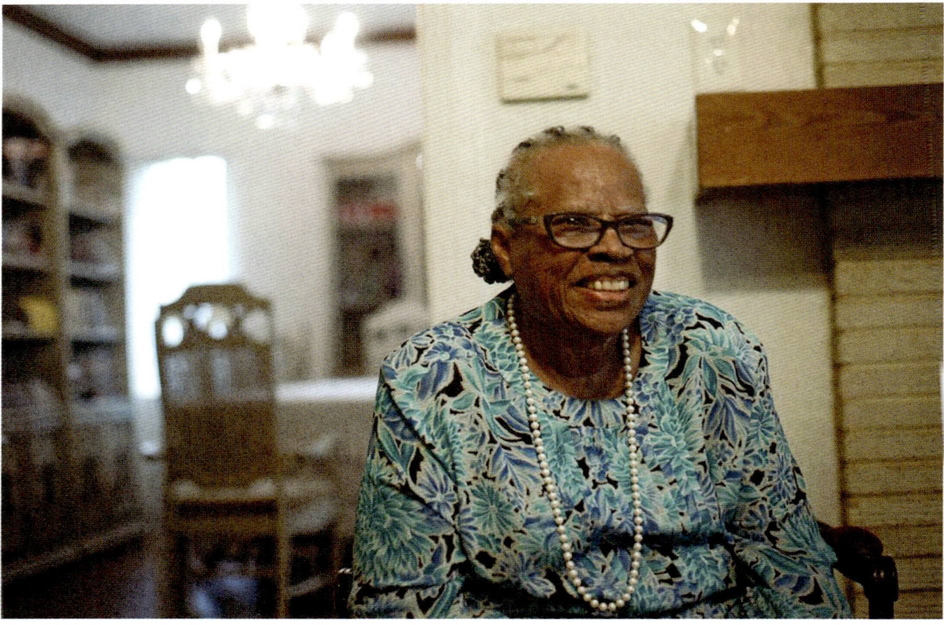

TOP: In Fort Worth, Texas, Opal Lee, the "Grandmother of Juneteenth," walks her annual 2.5-mile Walk for Freedom in 2021, joined by hundreds celebrating the day's official recognition as a national holiday. At 94 years old, Lee saw her decades-long fight come to fruition. Her activism was deeply personal: In 1939, when she was just 12, a white mob burned down her family's home on Juneteenth. That memory fueled her unwavering campaign to ensure the holiday's meaning would be recognized across the nation.

ABOVE: Opal Lee, the "grandmother" of the successful movement to make Juneteenth a national holiday.

OPPOSITE: On May 3, 2024, President Joe Biden awarded Opal Lee, longtime Juneteenth activist, the Presidential Medal of Freedom at the White House. The award is the nation's highest civilian honor, given to recognize those who have made extraordinary contributions to the country and to humanity.

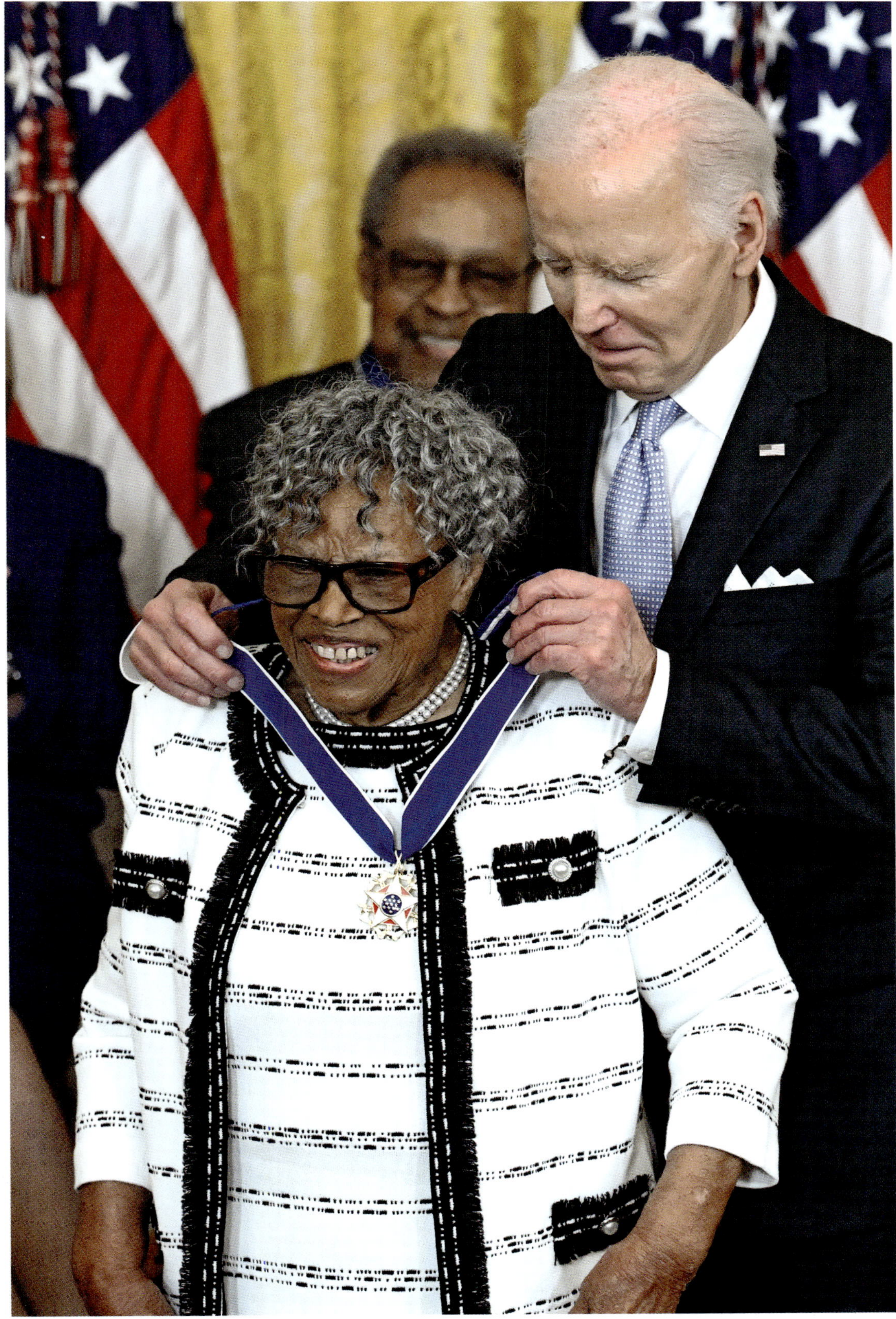

NOTES

INTRODUCTION

But Black Americans refused to let these realities . . . Adrian Miller, "How Red Drink Became the Official Beverage of Juneteenth," *Food & Wine*, June 8, 2024, https://www.foodandwine.com/how-red-drink-became-the-official-beverage-of-juneteenth-7547540.

CHAPTER 1
EMANCIPATION: THE LONG FIGHT FOR FREEDOM

1. *The grand marshals of the parade . . .* "President Hayes Speaks: The Emancipation Celebration: A Brilliant Street Parade," *Richmond Planet*, January 8, 1898, 1.
2. *The celebration of January 1 wasn't the only Emancipation Day . . .* Hilary N. Green, *Unforgettable Sacrifice: How Black Communities Remembered the Civil War* (Fordham University Press, 2025), 130.
3. *One particularly poignant example was the use of an overturned pot . . .* "William M. Adams," *Born in Slavery: Slave Narratives from the Federal Writers' Project , 1936 to 1938.* Library of Congress, Washington, DC. https://www.loc.gov/collections/slave-narratives-from-the-federal-writers-project-1936-to-1938/about-this-collection/
4. *The enslaved community believed he was divinely chosen . . .* Nat Turner. 1831.*The Confessions of Nat Turner, The Leader of the Late Insurrection in Southampton, Va.* Documenting the American South. University Library, The University of North Carolina at Chapel Hill, 1999. https://docsouth.unc.edu/neh/turner/turner.html.
5. *The new laws made it illegal for Black people . . . Acts Passed at a General Assembly of the Commonwealth of Virginia*, 1831, 20. https://babel.hathitrust.org/cgi/pt?id=osu.32437123259463&seq=24.
6. *He saw slavery as an inherently violent institution . . .* David Walker. 1829. *Walker's Appeal, in Four Articles; Together with a Preamble, to the Coloured*

Citizens of the World, 30. Documenting the American South. University Library, The University of North Carolina at Chapel Hill, 1999. https://docsouth.unc.edu/neh/turner/turner.html.

7. *He fiercely rejected the notion that Black people should be colonized . . .* Walker, *Appeal.*
8. *In his writings, president and slaveholder Thomas Jefferson called for freed Black people . . .* Thomas Jefferson. 1788. *Notes on the State of Virginia*, 147. Documenting the American South. University Library, The University of North Carolina at Chapel Hill, 2006. https://docsouth.unc.edu/southlit/jefferson/jefferson.html#p138.
9. *In a debate about a law preventing slaveholders from manumitting their slaves . . .* "House of Delegates, January 15, 1806," *Virginia Argus*, January 17, 1806, 2.
10. *Black people who were freed faced rampant discrimination . . .* Randolph B. Campbell, *An Empire for Slavery* (Louisiana State University Press, 1989).
11. *In the pages of the pro-Union newspaper . . . The Daily Ohio Statesman*, October 10, 1861, 2.
12. *In his famous letter to* New-York Tribune *editor Horace Greeley . . .* Letter from Abraham Lincoln to Horace Greeley, August 23, 1862 (clipping from the August 23, 1862, *Daily National Intelligencer*, Washington, DC). From the Abraham Lincoln Papers archives at the US Library of Congress, Series 2, General Correspondence, 1858–1864, https://www.loc.gov/resource/mal.4233400/.
13. *Union Major General Benjamin Franklin Butler, commander of Fort Monroe on the Chesapeake Bay . . .* Bennett Parten, *Somewhere Toward Freedom: Sherman's March and the Story of America's Largest Emancipation* (Simon & Schuster, 2025), 19–20.
14. *As one historian of Sherman's March noted . . .* Parten, *Somewhere Toward Freedom*, 7–8.
15. *But rather than complying, many enslaved people led Sherman's troops . . .* Parten, *Somewhere Toward Freedom*, 50–67.
16. *As the army neared the Georgia coast, soldiers encountered a formidable obstacle . . .* Parten, *Somewhere Toward Freedom*, 100–103.
17. *A delegation of twenty Black pastors led by Garrison Frazier . . .* Parten, *Somewhere Toward Freedom*, 153.

18. *It was during that service that the first Black man would speak from the church's pulpit . . .* "Richmond," *The Press,* April 11, 1865, 1, https://panewsarchive.psu.edu/lccn/sn84026296/1865-04-11/ed-1/seq-1/.

CHAPTER 2
TEXAS AND THE MEANING OF JUNETEENTH

1. *The three main settlements of Spanish Texas—San Antonio, Nacogdoches, and La Bahía . . .* Campbell, *An Empire for Slavery,* 10–12.
2 *American businessman Moses Austin had lost his fortune in lead mining . . .* Campbell, *An Empire for Slavery,* 14–31.
3. *In 1833, he made his position unmistakably clear . . .* Campbell, *An Empire for Slavery,* 30.
4. *Haywood shared his memory of the first moments of freedom in Bexar County, Texas . . .* Felix Haywood interview in *Born in Slavery: Slave Narratives from the Federal Writers' Project, 1936–1938,* Library of Congress, Washington, DC. https://www.loc.gov/collections/slave-narratives-from-the-federal-writers-project-1936-to-1938/about-this-collection/
5. *She recalled that "George cried out in a powerful voice . . .* Lu Lee in *The American Slave: A Composite Autobiography,* Supplement, Series 2, *Texas Narratives,* vol. 6, part 5, edited by George P. Rawick (Greenwood Press, 1979), 2292–93.
6. *Former slave Andy M. Adams recalled . . .* Andy M. Adams in *The American Slave: A Composite Autobiography,* Supplement, Series 2, *Texas Narratives,* vol. 10, part 7, edited by George P. Rawick (Greenwood Press, 1979), 2453–54.
7. *Former Texas slave Dave L. Byrd recounted the fear . . .* Dave L. Byrd in *The American Slave: A Composite Autobiography,* Supplement, *Texas Narratives,* vol. 2, part 3, edited by George P. Rawick (Greenwood Press, 1979), 566.
8. *One poignant record of part of an early celebration comes from June 12, 1867 . . .* Letter from Enon M. Harris, S. A. Comr., to Lieut. J. T. Kirkman, June 12, 1867, in *Records of the Superintendent of Education for the State of Texas Bureau of Refugees, Freedmen, and Abandoned*

Lands, 1865–1870. Courtesy of the US National Archives and Records Administration, FamilySearch International, and the Smithsonian National Museum of African American History and Culture. Held in the Smithsonian Online Virtual Archives as part of the Freedman's Bureau's Digital Collection in *Texas Education, Letters Received, Unregistered Letters Received, 1866–1867 and 1869–1870*, part 4, 153.

9. *Faced with the prospect of losing his family, Yates was forced . . .* Melanie Lawson, "Exploring the life of Jack Yates: The true story of a Houston hero," ABC13 Eyewitness News, June 18, 2021, https://abc13.com/jack-yates-who-is-houston-history/10807667/, accessed May 11, 2025.
10. *The Yates family and others like them recognized that freedom . . .* "A Family Story: Juneteenth and the Founding of Emancipation Park," Voices of the Civil Rights Movement platform of Comcast NBCUniversal, https://voicesofthecivilrightsmovement.com/articles/juneteenth-2023, accessed March 21, 2025; Rutherford B. H. Yates Sr. and Paul L. Yates, *The Life and Effort of Jack Yates* (Texas Southern University Press, 1985).
11. *For example, in 1883, almost twenty years after the end of the Civil War, Texas newspapers chronicled . . . The Austin Weekly Statesman*, June 21, 1883, 3.
12. *In San Antonio the emancipation festivities included a thirty-eight-gun salute . . . Galveston Daily News*, vol. 42, no. 90, June 20, 1883, 1.
13. *That same year, eight thousand gathered just outside of Brenham, Texas . . . The Austin Weekly Statesman*, June 21, 1883, 3; *Galveston Daily News*, vol. 42, no. 90, June 20, 1883, 1.
14. *In the town of Palestine, the 1883 Emancipation Day celebration . . . The Austin Weekly Statesman*, June 21, 1883, 3; *Galveston Daily News*, vol. 42, no. 90, June 20, 1883, 1.
15. *Even as an uptick in lynching and racial violence swept the South . . .* "Emancipation: The Twenty-Third Anniversary of Emancipation Day Observed by the Colored People," *Fort Worth Daily Gazette*, June 20, 1888, 4; "Emancipation Day," *Galveston Daily News*, vol. 55, no. 88, June 20, 1896, 3.
16. *They did, however, leave room for watermelon jokes and reprint letters . . .* "Emancipation Day: Colored Citizen Points Out Some Mockeries of Celebration," *The Houston Post*, June 23, 1904, 7.

17. *The* Fort Worth Daily Gazette *complained about Black workers in Austin . . .* "Emancipation Day: The Colored People Discard the Day's Cares and Devote It to Fun and Frolic," *Forth Worth Daily Gazette*, June 20, 1891, 6; "Negroes Celebrate Emancipation Day at Douglass Park," *Fort Worth Record-Telegram*, June 20, 1914, 3.
18. *Indeed, in 1915, Black celebrants in Waco, Texas, used Juneteenth . . .* "Negroes Plan a Way to Secure Ballot," *The Waco News-Tribune*, June 20, 1915, 6; "Possible Results of an Amendment," *The Houston Post*, July 9, 1915, 7.
19. *On one particular occasion, segregationist violence and Juneteenth intersected . . .* Otis Flake, Fort Worth, Tarrant, Texas, as recorded in the Sixteenth Census of the United States, 1940; roll: m-t0627-04185; page: 15A; Enumeration District: 257-32. Records held by the US National Archives and Records Administration.
20. *One of their neighbors, J. C. Moore, even hired an attorney who appealed to the Fort Worth . . .* "Annie Street Zoning Is Sought," *Fort Worth Star-Telegram*, June 19, 1939, 2; "Fort Worth Mob Storms Residence, Runs Negro Out," *Times Record News* (Wichita Falls, Texas), June 20, 1939, 1; "Mob Destroys Home to Keep Residential District 'Pure,'" *New Pittsburgh Courier*, July 1, 1939, 1, 4; "'Grandmother of Juneteenth' Taking Back Land Where Childhood Home Was Burned by Racist Mob in 1939," ABC News, March 23, 2024, https://abcnews.go.com/US/grandmother-juneteenth-taking-back-land-childhood-home-burned/story?id=108287076.

CHAPTER 3
CELEBRATIONS OF BLACK FREEDOM

1. *In* A Voice from the South, *Raleigh-born educator and intellectual Anna Julia Cooper . . .* Anna Julia Cooper. 1892. *A Voice from the South.* Documenting the American South. University Library, The University of North Carolina at Chapel Hill, 2000. https://docsouth.unc.edu/church/cooper/menu.html; Karen A. Johnson, *Uplifting the Women and the Race: The Lives, Educational Philosophies and Social Activism of Anna Julia Cooper and Nannie Helen Burroughs (Studies in African American History and Culture)* (Garland, New York, 2000), 37.

2. *As Frederick Douglass so famously stated in 1852 . . .* Frederick Douglass. 1852. "The Meaning of July Fourth for the Negro," *Africans in America: Part Four, Judgment Day, 1831–1865*. PBS Resource Bank, https://www.pbs.org/wgbh/aia/part4/4h2927t.html
3. *In the decades before emancipation came to the American South, free Black communities in the North . . .* Mitch Kachun, *Festivals of Freedom: Memory and Meaning in African American Emancipation Celebrations, 1808–1915* (University of Massachusetts Press, 2003), 54–56.
4. *As historians James Oliver Horton and Lois E. Horton noted . . .* James Oliver Horton and Lois E. Horton, eds., *Slavery and Public History: The Tough Stuff of American Memory* (University of North Carolina Press, 2006), 155.
5. *A local white newspaper,* The Daily Progress, *chronicled Raleigh's first Fourth of July–turned–Emancipation Day . . . The Daily Progress*, vol. 6, no. 199, July 6, 1865, 1–2. All of the following details and quotations about the July 4, 1865, celebration in Raleigh derive from this issue of *The Daily Progress.*
6. *The parade that day led to the grounds of the Peace Institute . . .* Elizabeth Reid Murray, *Wake: Capital County of North Carolina*, vol. 1, *Prehistory through Centennial* (Capital County Publishing Co., 1983), 552.
7. *Anna Julia Cooper, born in bondage in the midst of the Civil War . . .* Cooper, personal note, n.d., Moorland Spingarn Research Center, Anna Julia Cooper Papers, Howard University, Washington, DC.
8. *In addition to the military companies, ten civic and mutual aid organizations planned to participate . . .* "Emancipation Day," *The Savannah Tribune*, December 31, 1887, 3.
9. *The grand parade, with thousands of Black participants proudly marching through the streets of Savannah . . .* "Freedom's Celebration!," *The Savannah Tribune*, January 7, 1888, 2.
10. *At the ceremony that year, the Reverend E. K. Love . . .* "Freedom's Celebration!," *The Savannah Tribune*, January 7, 1888, 2.
11. *His speech captured both the hope and the heartache of Black life in the post-Reconstruction South . . .* Thavolia Glymph, "Liberty Dearly Bought: The Making of Civil War Memory in Afro-American Communities in

the South," in *Time Longer Than Rope: A Century of African American Activism, 1850–1950*, eds. Charles M. Payne and Adam Greene (New York University Press, 2003), 120.

12. *Even as he called for mutual respect and cooperation between Black and white Southerners . . .* "Freedom's Celebration," *The Savannah Tribune*, January 7, 1888, 2–3.
13. *As Black rights increasingly came under attack, the speeches given by Black leaders . . .* Blair LM Kelley, *Right to Ride: Streetcar Boycotts and African American Citizenship in the Era of* Plessy v. Ferguson. (University of North Carolina Press, 2010), 165–66.
14. *The unit's absence was deeply felt by the Black population in the city . . .* "Savannah Negroes Riotous," *The New York Times*, January 2, 1906, 6.
15. *In 1906, as Jim Crow legislation was becoming more ubiquitous throughout the South . . .* "Savannah Negroes Riotous," *The New York Times*, January 2, 1906, 6.

CHAPTER 4
JUNETEENTH TODAY

1. *By 1866, Black Washingtonians began commemorating this landmark in history . . .* Emancipation Day celebrations ended in Washington, DC, at the turn of the century but were revived by historian Loretta Carter-Hines in the 1990s, and the day became an official holiday in the district in 2005. See Alexandra Lane, "Emancipation Day in Washington, D.C.," The White House Historical Association, https://www.whitehousehistory.org/emancipation-day, accessed April 1, 2025.
2. *As the NAACP made clear, the Emancipation Proclamation was simply the first mile of a long . . .* "A National Holiday Commemorating Emancipation of the Slaves," NAACP Resolutions Library, 2014, https://naacp.org/resources/national-holiday-commemorating-emancipation-slaves.

BIBLIOGRAPHY

MANUSCRIPT SOURCES

Abraham Lincoln Papers. US Library of Congress, Washington, DC.

Anna Julia Cooper Papers. Moorland Spingarn Research Center, Howard University, Washington, DC.

Charles N. Hunter Papers. David M. Rubenstein Rare Book & Manuscript Library, Duke University, Durham, North Carolina.

CIVIL WAR PHOTOGRAPHS

Born in Slavery: Slave Narratives from the Federal Writers' Project , 1936 to 1938. Library of Congress, Washington, DC. https://www.loc.gov/collections/slave-narratives-from-the-federal-writers-project-1936-to-1938/about-this-collection/

Collection of the National Museum of African American History and Culture, Smithsonian Institution, Washington, DC.

Collection of the National Museum of American History, Smithsonian Institution, Washington, DC.

George Grantham Bain Collection. Library of Congress, Washington, DC. https://www.loc.gov/pictures/collection/ggbain/

George and Huestis Cook Photographic Collection. The Valentine Museum, Richmond, Virginia.

Liljenquist Family Collection of Civil War Photographs. Library of Congress, Washington, DC. https://www.loc.gov/pictures/collection/lilj/

Prints & Photographs Division. Library of Congress, Washington, DC. https://www.loc.gov/pictures/

BLACK PHOTOGRAPHIC COLLECTIONS

Olee Yates McCullough Papers. Houston Public Library, Houston, Texas.

Reverend Jack Yates Family and Antioch Baptist Church Collection 1872–1986. Houston Public Library, Houston, Texas.

Willie Lee Gay and Carter G. Woodson Junior Historians Collection. African American History Research Center, Houston Public Library, Houston, Texas.

Rhonda White-Warner papers. African American Museum & Library, Oakland Public Library, Oakland, California.

Manuscripts and Archives Division. The New York Public Library, New York, New York.

Texas Photographs, Manuscripts, and Imprints. DeGolyer Library, Southern Methodist University, Dallas, Texas.

NEWSPAPERS AND PERIODICALS

Austin Weekly Statesman

Daily National Intelligencer (Washington, DC)

Daily Ohio Statesman

Daily Progress (Charlottesville, Virginia)

Fort Worth Daily Gazette

Fort Worth Record-Telegram

Fort Worth Star-Telegram

Galveston Daily News

Houston Post

New Pittsburgh Courier

New York Times

Press (Philadelphia, Pennsylvania)

Richmond Planet

Savannah Tribune

Times Record News (Wichita Falls, Texas)

Virginia Argus

Waco News-Tribune

GOVERNMENT DOCUMENTS

Acts Passed at a General Assembly of the Commonwealth of Virginia (1831).

Sixteenth Census of the United States, 1940, NAID 139237090, Records of the Bureau of the Census, RG 29, National Archives, Washington, DC.

SECONDARY SOURCES

ARTICLES

"A Family Story: Juneteenth and the Founding of Emancipation Park." Voices of the Civil Rights Movement. Comcast NBCUniversal. https://voicesofthecivilrightsmovement.com/articles/juneteenth-2023

"A National Holiday Commemorating Emancipation of the Slaves." NAACP Resolutions Library, 2014. https://naacp.org/resources/national-holiday-commemorating-emancipation-slaves

Douglass, Frederick. "The Meaning of July Fourth for the Negro," 1852. *Africans in America: Part Four, Judgment Day, 1831–1865*. PBS Resource Bank. https://www.pbs.org/wgbh/aia/part4/4h2927t.html

Lane, Alexandra. "Emancipation Day in Washington, DC," part of the Slavery in the President's Neighborhood initiative, the White House Historical Association. https://www.whitehousehistory.org/emancipation-day

Lawson, Melanie. "Exploring the life of Jack Yates: The true story of a Houston hero." ABC13 Eyewitness News, June 18, 2021. https://abc13.com/post/jack-yates-who-is-houston-history/10807667/

Miller, Adrian. "How Red Drink Became the Official Beverage of Juneteenth." *Food and Wine,* June 8, 2024. https://www.foodandwine.com/how-red-drink-became-the-official-beverage-of-juneteenth-7547540

Zaru, Deena. "'Grandmother of Juneteenth' Taking Back Land Where Childhood Home Was Burned by Racist Mob in 1939." ABC News, March 23, 2024. https://abcnews.go.com/US/grandmother-juneteenth-taking-back-land-childhood-home-burned/story?id=108287076

BOOKS

Berlin, Ira, Marc Favreau, and Steven F. Miller, eds. *Remembering Slavery: African Americans Talk About Their Personal Experiences of Slavery and Emancipation*. The New Press, 2022.

Blight, David W. *Race and Reunion: The Civil War in American Memory*. Harvard University Press, 2022.

Brundage, W. Fitzhugh, ed. *Where These Memories Grow: History, Memory, and Southern Identity*. The University of North Carolina Press, 2015.

Campbell, Randolph B. *An Empire for Slavery.* Louisiana State University Press, 1989.

Clark, Kathleen Ann. *Defining Moments: African American Commemoration & Political Culture in the South, 1863–1913*. The University of North Carolina Press, 2005.

Cooper, Anna Julia. 1892. *A Voice from the South*. Documenting the American South. University Library, The University of North Carolina, Chapel Hill, 2000. https://docsouth.unc.edu/church/cooper/cooper.html

Dunbar, Erica Armstrong. *A Fragile Freedom: African American Women and Emancipation in the Antebellum City*. Yale University Press, 2008.

Edwards, Justene Hill. *The Rise and Betrayal of the Freedman's Bank Savings and Trust.* W. W. Norton & Company, 2024.

Gannon, Barbara A. *The Won Cause: Black and White Comradeship in the Grand Army of the Republic*. UNC Press, 2014.

Glymph, Thavolia. "Liberty Dearly Bought: The Making of Civil War Memory in Afro-American Communities in the South." In *Time Longer Than Rope: A Century of African American Activism, 1850–1950*, edited by Charles M. Payne and Adam Greene. New York University Press, 2003.

Gordon-Reed, Annette. *On Juneteenth*. Liveright Publishing, 2021.

Green, Hilary N. *Unforgettable Sacrifice: How Black Communities Remembered the Civil War*. Fordham University Press, 2025.

Horton, James Oliver and Lois E. Horton, eds. *Slavery and Public History: The Tough Stuff of American Memory*. University of North Carolina Press, 2006.

Jefferson, Thomas. 1788. *Notes on the State of Virginia*. Documenting the American South. University Library, The University of North Carolina at Chapel Hill, 2006. https://docsouth.unc.edu/southlit/jefferson/jefferson.html

Johnson, Karen A. *Uplifting the Women and the Race: The Lives, Educational Philosophies and Social Activism of Anna Julia Cooper and Nannie Helen Burroughs*. Routledge Publishing, Inc. New York, 2000.

Kachun, Mitch. *Festivals of Freedom: Memory and Meaning in African American Emancipation Celebrations, 1808–1915.* University of Massachusetts Press, 2003.

Kelley, Blair LM. *Black Folk: The Roots of the Black Working Class.* Liveright Publishing, 2023.

Kelley, Blair LM. *Right to Ride: Streetcar Boycotts and African American Citizenship in the Era of* Plessy v. Ferguson. University of North Carolina Press, 2010.

Lorini, Alessandra. *Rituals of Race: American Public Culture and the Search for Racial Democracy*. University Press of Virginia, 1999.

Murray, Elizabeth Reid. *Wake, Capital County of North Carolina: Volume I, Prehistory Through Centennial.* Capital County Pub. Co., 1983.

Parten, Bennett. *Somewhere Toward Freedom: Sherman's March and the Story of America's Largest Emancipation*. Simon & Schuster, 2025.

Rawick, George P., ed. *The American Slave: A Composite Autobiography*. Greenwood Press, 1979.

Schwalm, Leslie A. *Emancipation's Diaspora: Race and Reconstruction in the Upper Midwest*. University of North Carolina Press, 2009.

Taylor, Amy Murrell. *Embattled Freedom: Journeys Through the Civil War's Slave Refugee Camps*. University of North Carolina Press, 2020.

Turner, Nat. 1831. *The Confessions of Nat Turner, The Leader of the Late Insurrection in Southampton, Va.* Documenting the American South. University Library, The University of North Carolina at Chapel Hill, 1999. https://docsouth.unc.edu/neh/turner/turner.html

Walker, David. 1829. *Walker's Appeal, in Four Articles; Together with a Preamble, to the Coloured Citizens of the World*. Documenting the American South. University Library, The University of North Carolina at Chapel Hill, 2001. https://docsouth.unc.edu/nc/walker/walker.html

Willis, Deborah, and Barbara Krauthamer. *Envisioning Emancipation: Black Americans and the End of Slavery*. Temple University Press, 2017.

Yates, Rutherford B. H., Sr. and Paul L. Yates. *The Life and Effort of Jack Yates*. Texas Southern University Press, 1985.

PHOTO CREDITS

28–29: Library of Congress Prints and Photographs Division, Washington, DC; **31**, **32–33**: Collection of the Smithsonian National Museum of African American History and Culture; **34–41**: Library of Congress Prints and Photographs Division, Washington, DC; **42–43**: Corbis via Getty Images; **45**: National Museum of American History, Smithsonian Institution; **46–61**: Library of Congress Prints and Photographs Division, Washington, DC; **62–63**: Manuscripts and Archives Division, The New York Public Library. "Company of colored troops / Alexander Gardner," New York Public Library Digital Collections. Accessed September 11, 2025. https://digitalcollections.nypl.org /items/cc5df6b0-5af3-013c-531d-0242ac110003; **64**: National Archives (182778372); **65**: Library of Congress Prints and Photographs Division, Washington, DC; **66–67**: Hulton Archive, Getty Images; **89**: E. Hergesheimer (cartographer), 1860; **90–91**: National Archives (182778372); **93**: African American History Research Center, Houston Public Library, MSS0281-PH053, MSS 0281; **94**: Austin History Center, Austin Public Library [PICA-20864]; **95**: Austin History Center, Austin Public Library, photo by Grace Murray Stephenson, [PICA-05479]; **97**: Austin History Center, Austin Public Library, photo by Grace Murray Stephenson, [PICA-05478]; **98**: Austin History Center, Austin Public Library, photo by Grace Murray Stephenson, [PICA-05476]; **99**: Austin History Center, Austin Public Library, photo by Grace Murray Stephenson, [PICA-05477]; **100**: Austin History Center, Austin Public Library, photo by Grace Murray Stephenson, [PICA-05484]; **101**: Austin History Center, Austin Public Library, photo by Grace Murray Stephenson, [PICA-05482]; **102–103**: Austin History Center, Austin Public Library, photo by Grace Murray Stephenson, [PICA-05481]; **104–105**: Austin History Center, Austin Public Library, photo by Grace Murray Stephenson, [PICA-05480]; **106**: African American History Research Center, Houston Public Library, MSS0137-PH020, MSS 0137, Black Photographic Collection; **107**: African American History Research Center, Houston Public Library, MSS0281-PH037, MSS 0281, Reverend Jack Yates Family and Antioch Baptist Church Collection; **108–111**: DeGolyer Library, Southern Methodist University; **134–135**: Charles N. Hunter Papers, 1850s–1932 and Undated, David M. Rubenstein Rare Book & Manuscript Library, Duke University; **136–137**: Detroit Publishing Co., Copyright Claimant, and Publisher Detroit Publishing Co. Emancipation Day, Richmond, Va. Richmond Virginia United States, ca. 1905. Photograph, https://www.loc.gov/item/2016804723; **138**: Charles N. Hunter Papers, 1850s–1932 and Undated, David M. Rubenstein Rare Book & Manuscript Library, Duke University; **139**: H. Furlong Baldwin Library, Maryland Center for History and Culture, Resource ID 1023; **141**: Collection of the Smithsonian National Museum of African American

History and Culture, Gift of Dr. Todd E. Robinson; **142**: Gladstone Collection of African American Photographs, Library of Congress; **143**: Charles N. Hunter Papers, 1850s–1932 and Undated, David M. Rubenstein Rare Book & Manuscript Library, Duke University; **144**: North Carolina Newspapers, North Carolina Digital Heritage Center, https://newspapers.digitalnc.org/lccn/sn92072942/1872-01-18/ed-1/seq-4; **145**: C.M. Bell Studio Collection, Library of Congress; **146–147**: State Archives of North Carolina, Barden Collection; **148–149**: Library and Archives Canada, C-012600; **150–153**: Cook Photograph Collection, The Valentine, Richmond, Virginia; **154**: Cook, Will Marion Composer, and Paul Laurence Dunbar. On Emancipation Day. New York, NY: Harry Von Tilzer Music Publishing Co, 1902. Notated Music; **155**: Hampton, Va. Normal And Agricultural Institute. Emancipation Day at Hampton Institute. Hampton, 1911. https://www.loc.gov/item/unk82008943; **156–157**: Schwendemann Manuscripts and Research Collection, Gerth Archives and Special Collections, California State University, Dominguez Hills; **159**: African American History Research Center, Houston Public Library, Juneteenth Parade Attendees, MSS0155-PH005, MSS 0155, Olee Yates McCullough Papers; **168–169**: Library of Congress Prints and Photographs Division, Washington, DC; **170–171**: African American Museum & Library at Oakland, Oakland Public Library, Oakland, California, MS189_1234; **172**: Collection of the Smithsonian National Museum of African American History and Culture, gift of Jennifer Cain Bohrnsted; **173**: The Jenkins, Kentucky Photographic Collection; **174–175**: Albion District Library, Albion, Michigan. Original photographer has not been identified; **176–177**: African American History Research Center, Houston Public Library; MSS0151-PH017, MSS 0151; Willie Lee Gay and Carter G. Woodson Junior Historians #244 Collection; **179**: African American Museum & Library at Oakland, Oakland Public Library, Oakland, California, MS169; **180**: African American History Research Center, Houston Public Library, MSS0151-PH021, MSS 0151; **181**: Olee Yates McCullough Papers, Houston History Research Center, Houston Public Library, MSS0195-0331, MSS 0155; **182–183**: Historic Photo Collection / Milwaukee Public Library; **184–185**: Houston History Research Center, Houston Public Library, RG E 0071 Texas Jazz Archive; **186–167**: Historic Photo Collection / Milwaukee Public Library; **189**: Library of Congress Prints and Photographs Division, © Jos Sances, [LC-DIG-ppmsca-75964]; **190–191**: *The Denver Post* via Getty Images; **192–193, 195**: Bob Daemmrich / Alamy Stock Photo; **196–197**: John Leyba / *The Denver Post* via Getty Images; **198–201**: Bob Daemmrich / Alamy Stock Photo; **202–203**: Mayra Beltran / *Houston Chronicle* via Getty Images; **204**: Michael Paulsen / *Houston Chronicle* via Getty Images; **205**: Michael Macor / *San Francisco Chronicle* via Associated Press; **206**: Joe Amon / *The Denver Post* via Getty Images; **207**: Jake May / *The Flint Journal* via Associated Press; **208**: Christian Randolph / The Flint Journal-MLive.com via Associated Press; **209 (top)**: Alexandra Wimley / *Pittsburgh Post-Gazette* via Associated Press; **209 (bottom)**: Yong Kim / *The Philadelphia Inquirer* via Associated Press; **211 (top and bottom)**: Bastiaan Slabbers / Getty Images; **212**: Andrew Russell / *Pittsburgh Tribune-Review* via Associated Press; **213**:

Bastiaan Slabbers / NurPhoto via Getty Images; **214**: Carol M. Highsmith's America Project in the Carol M. Highsmith Archive; **215**: Tom McCorkle for *The Washington Post* via Getty Images; food styling by Lisa Cherkasky for *The Washington Post* via Getty Images; **216–217**: Ted S. Warren / Associated Press Images; **218–219**: Christian Gooden / *St. Louis Post-Dispatch* via Associated Press; **220–221**: Jon Cherry / Getty Images; **221**: Jake May / MLive.com / *The Flint Journal* via Associated Press; **222–223**: Wirestock, Inc. / Alamy Stock Photo; **224 (top)**: Andrew Harnik / Associated Images; **224 (bottom)**: Elizabeth Conley / *Houston Chronicle* via Associated Press; **224–225**: Stuart Villanueva / *The Galveston County Daily News* via Associated Press; **226–227, 228–229**: Stephanie Keith / Getty Images; **230–231**: Samuel Corum / Sipa USA; **232**: Kayla Oaddams / Getty Images; **233**: Natasha Moustache / Getty Images; **234–235**: Chip Somodevilla / Getty Images; **236 (top)**: Amanda McCoy / *Fort Worth Star-Telegram* / Tribune News Service via Getty; **236 (bottom)**: Rodger Mallison / *Fort Worth Star-Telegram* / Tribune News Service via Getty **237**: Andrew Caballero-Reynolds / AFP via Getty Images

INDEX

Page numbers in **bold** refer to illustrations or their captions.

R

S

ACKNOWLEDGMENTS

The work of creating an illustrated volume might seem deceptively simple—gathering images, creating captions, writing essays to accompany the photography—but in reality, it's work that takes incredible care and thoughtfulness. I am thankful to those who took the journey of crafting *Black Freedom* with me.

I have benefited greatly from the phenomenal students and scholars who worked with me to search for photos, articles, and illustrations for this volume. Thanks go to Melody Hunter Pillion, Jasmine Cannon, Ari Green, and Brittany Hutchinson for their research support. Extraordinary thanks go to Philip McDonald whose skill as an archivist, folklorist, and photo editor has enriched this collection at every turn.

Profound thanks go to my editor Lisa Tenaglia. Your vision and patience made this work better at every turn. Thank you for all you did to keep this complicated undertaking in excellent order.

Thanks to my agent and dear friend, Tanya McKinnon who always has a vision for what might be possible for me and my work as a historian. I am always grateful for advocacy and vision. You are truly the best.

The research and writing of this book could not have been completed without the support of the University of North Carolina at Chapel Hill, including the Department of American Studies and the wonderful team at the Center for the Study of the American South. I am grateful to my colleagues there for nurturing my work during an extremely difficult time. Thanks also to my colleagues at the National Humanities Center for their support and encouragement.

As always none of my work would mean anything without my family. Thanks to my children, Demi and Brooks, for their patience, love, and constant feedback. Thanks, as always to my husband, Patrick Kelley. Your belief in us makes everything possible.